Microsoft Power Platf
Functional Consultant.
PL-200 Exam Guide

Learn how to customize and configure Microsoft Power
Platform and prepare for the PL-200 exam

Julian Sharp

BIRMINGHAM - MUMBAI

Microsoft Power Platform Functional Consultant: PL-200 Exam Guide

Commissioning Editor: Kunal Chaudhari
Acquisition Editor: Karan Gupta
Content Development Editor: Kinnari Chohan
Senior Editor: Rohit Singh
Technical Editor: Pradeep Sahu
Copy Editor: Safis Editing
Project Coordinator: Deeksha Thakkar
Proofreader: Safis Editing
Indexer: Tejal Daruwale Soni
Production Designer: Aparna Bhagat

First published: December 2020

Production reference: 1031220

Published by Packt Publishing Ltd.
Livery Place
35 Livery Street
Birmingham
B3 2PB, UK.

ISBN 978-1-83898-568-4

www.packt.com

To my wife, Clare Sharp, for her constant support and demonstrating that learning never stops.

– Julian Sharp

Packt.com

Subscribe to our online digital library for full access to over 7,000 books and videos, as well as industry leading tools to help you plan your personal development and advance your career. For more information, please visit our website.

Why subscribe?

- Spend less time learning and more time coding with practical eBooks and Videos from over 4,000 industry professionals

- Improve your learning with Skill Plans built especially for you

- Get a free eBook or video every month

- Fully searchable for easy access to vital information

- Copy and paste, print, and bookmark content

Did you know that Packt offers eBook versions of every book published, with PDF and ePub files available? You can upgrade to the eBook version at www.packt.com and as a print book customer, you are entitled to a discount on the eBook copy. Get in touch with us at customercare@packtpub.com for more details.

At www.packt.com, you can also read a collection of free technical articles, sign up for a range of free newsletters, and receive exclusive discounts and offers on Packt books and eBooks.

Contributors

About the author

Julian Sharp is a Dynamics 365 solutions architect, trainer, and Microsoft Business Applications MVP. He completed his MA at the University of Cambridge. He worked for Vigence for 20 years, with the last 16 years focused on Dynamics CRM/365, before founding Ready 365 to focus on training. Prior to Dynamics, he worked with both the Siebel CRM and on systems for contact centers.

He has spoken at Microsoft Ignite and many other events. For the past 13 years, he has been an MCT delivering certification training around Dynamics 365, Azure, and the Power Platform. He has developed courseware for Dynamics 365 certification training and taught thousands of students with a high pass rate.

I want to thank the Power Platform community worldwide, who have freely given their time, expertise, and encouragement to others.

About the reviewers

Robert Rybaric is a Microsoft Power Platform and Microsoft Dynamics 365 architect and certified trainer. He also holds several other certifications in Microsoft 365, Microsoft Azure, Microsoft SQL Server, and Microsoft BizTalk Server, along with TOGAF 9, ITIL 2011, IBM, and Oracle.

Robert has worked as an architect for the Microsoft Corporation on numerous Microsoft Dynamics 365 presale and project implementation activities for enterprise customers across Europe. He is now a freelance architect and trainer, implementing Microsoft Dynamics 365 solutions for global customers, and leads many Microsoft Power Platform training sessions.

EY Kalman, as a seasoned Dynamics 365 and Power Platform solutions architect, combines his understanding of business processes together with technical software delivery. With experience dating from Microsoft CRM 3.0, he's worked in a number of different companies over the years, ranging from general IT support to CRM end users, and more recently has moved into the consulting space.

Engaging regularly with Microsoft community events and gatherings under his brand of *The CRM Ninja*, EY blogs regularly around technical topics, hosts a weekly interview series called *The Oops Factor*, and enjoys speaking at events. He's also a recipient of the Microsoft MVP award for Business Applications.

James Novak is a Microsoft Business Applications MVP out of Virginia and has been a software engineer for 20 years. Starting with Microsoft CRM 4, his focus for the last 10 years has been on the Power Platform. He runs his own independent consultancy, Futurez Consulting, where Jim provides architectural guidance and hands-on development for building enterprise Power Platform solutions.

Packt is searching for authors like you

If you're interested in becoming an author for Packt, please visit `authors.packtpub.com` and apply today. We have worked with thousands of developers and tech professionals, just like you, to help them share their insight with the global tech community. You can make a general application, apply for a specific hot topic that we are recruiting an author for, or submit your own idea.

Table of Contents

Section 3: Power Apps

Preface

Welcome to this guide to the Microsoft Power Platform Functional Consultant Exam, PL-200.

This guide will help you understand and prepare for the PL-200 exam; probably the most important exam for those involved in implementing solutions in the Power Platform and Dynamics 365 solutions. By reading this book, you will become familiar with the most important elements of the low-code aspects of the Power Platform and you will be well placed to take—and pass—this exam.

Passing the exam demonstrates that you have the skills required to customize solutions based on Dynamics 365 Customer Engagement and the Power Platform.

As I have been writing this book, the Power Platform has seen many changes, reflecting the investment Microsoft is making in business applications and the importance of the Power Platform to Microsoft. The impact of the Power Platform is making itself felt across the whole of the Microsoft product portfolio, with Power Apps now embedded in Microsoft Teams.

 At the time of publishing, Microsoft Dataverse (formerly known as the Common Data Service) was undergoing a branding change. This branding change has not been completed and some screenshots in this book may reflect the former branding. Along with the name change, there are several changes to terminology such as tables (formerly entities), columns (formerly fields), rows (formerly records), choices (formerly option sets), and yes/no (formerly two options). These terminology changes will be applied to the user interface, documentation, and exam over time. You should be aware that the terms used in the book may not match the tools and documentation.

The book starts off with Dataverse (formerly known as the Common Data Service), where you create the data model that you will build your apps on. You will learn about business logic, security, automation, and other features that make Dataverse a great platform for building apps. Next, you will learn about creating and deploying apps, how to automate flows, and to build your own chatbots. The book then looks at using the Power Platform with other tools such as Power BI and Microsoft 365 services.

Each chapter concludes with a *Further reading* section, which is a very important part of the book because it will give you extra and sometimes crucial information for passing the PL-200 exam. As the questions of the exam will change slightly over time and this book will eventually become outdated, the *Further reading* sections will be the place that provides access to all the updates.

Who this book is for

This book targets functional consultants involved in the implementation of solutions based on the Power Platform or Dynamics 365. Functional consultants create and customize apps to translate business requirements into workable systems. They should have awareness of the Power Platform and have access to a Power Platform environment.

This book also targets people experienced in Dynamics 365, who want to learn about the Power Platform and bring their skills right up to date.

What this book covers

Chapter 1, *PL-200 Exam*, introduces the exam contents, the purpose of the exam, the skills measured, and who the exam is aimed at. This chapter will also look at how the PL-200 exam fits with the Dynamics 365 and Power Platform role-based certifications.

Chapter 2, *Power Platform*, provides a high-level overview of the Power Platform and its components, examines the different Power Platform environments, and explains how to configure and administer environments.

Chapter 3, *Data Modeling*, covers modifying the data model to meet business requirements, extending the schema for Dataverse with entities, relationships, and fields, and how to use solutions to manage your changes.

Chapter 4, *Business Rules*, explains how to validate data, perform calculations, and manipulate fields on forms, all without the need to write JavaScript.

Chapter 5, *Classic Workflows*, covers using classic workflow processes to automate data changes and communications using triggers, conditions, and action steps.

Chapter 6, *Managing Data*, discusses the features for importing data into, and exporting data from, the Dataverse.

Chapter 7, *Dataverse Settings*, covers the features for managing data once it is in Dataverse, including finding duplicates, cleansing data, how to remove stale data, and how to monitor and control data volumes.

Chapter 8, *Security*, provides an overview of the available security features in the Power Platform and then examines the security features used most frequently in Power Platform solutions.

Chapter 9, *Model-Driven Apps*, explains the components in model-driven apps and looks at how to configure forms, views, charts, and dashboards, before bringing the components together to create an app for business users.

Chapter 10, *Canvas Apps*, explains how to create canvas apps for web and mobile users, add controls to apps, use multiple data sources, and deploy apps.

Chapter 11, *Portal Apps*, covers the building of Portal apps to expose data in Dataverse to external users, customize the pages and layout, and add content.

Chapter 12, *Power Automate Flows*, covers automating steps within the Power Platform and across cloud systems including Office 365, Azure, and third-party services, creating flows, using connectors, adding steps, using expressions, and using logic to control the actions a flow performs.

Chapter 13, *Business Process Flows*, explains how to create business process flows to guide users through an end-to-end business process by adding stages, steps, and conditions, using branching, applying security, and using business process flows with other components of the Power Platform.

Chapter 14, *UI Flows*, explains how you can automate user activities on legacy applications when there isn't an API available, by creating and running UI Flows.

Chapter 15, *Creating Chatbots*, describes how to create, publish, and monitor Power Virtual Agents bots, and explains the key concepts involved in building chatbots.

Chapter 16, *Configuring Chatbots*, describes how to configure and author your own chatbots using topics, entities, and variables, along with adding questions and responses to tailor your chatbot to your business scenario.

Chapter 17, *Power BI*, describes how to create powerful visualizations, reports, and dashboards using the data captured in the Common Data Service (Dataverse).

Chapter 18, *AI Builder*, explains to add **Artificial Intelligence (AI)** to your apps and flows with no code, explains the AI model types, shows how to build your own AI models, and demonstrates how to use prebuilt and custom models in Power Apps and Power Automate.

Chapter 19, *Microsoft 365 Integration*, explains how to configure and use the integration with Microsoft 365, Word, and Excel, along with how to create templates and how to use the Power Platform with Microsoft Teams.

Chapter 20, *Application Life Cycle Management*, describes the tools and processes around moving changes from development through testing to production environments using solutions.

Chapter 21, *Tips and Tricks* covers tried and tested strategies that will help improve the reader's capabilities to solve and manage the exam questions on D day. These tips and tricks will help readers prepare mentally to have a relatively less stressful exam.

Chapters 22-25 cover practice tests and their answers. It will enhance your understanding of the concepts by testing your knowledge and to help prepare yourself for the certification exam.

To get the most out of this book

A Power Platform environment is required to get the most out of this book. You can start a free 30-day trial at https://www.microsoft.com/evalcenter/evaluate-power-platform, or you can utilize the Power Platform Community Plan at https://powerapps.microsoft.com/communityplan

All you need is a modern browser, except for in Chapter 14, *UI Flows*, where you will need a computer running Windows 10 Pro if you want to explore desktop UI flows.

Download the color images

We also provide a PDF file that has color images of the screenshots/diagrams used in this book. You can download it here: https://static.packt-cdn.com/downloads/9781838985684_ColorImages.pdf.

Conventions used

There are a number of text conventions used throughout this book.

`CodeInText`: Indicates code words in text, database table names, folder names, filenames, file extensions, pathnames, dummy URLs, user input, and Twitter handles. Here is an example: "You should download the app as a `.zip` file."

Bold: Indicates a new term, an important word, or words that you see onscreen. For example, words in menus or dialog boxes appear in the text like this. Here is an example: "This specification is the **Common Data Model (CDM)**."

 Warnings or important notes appear like this.

 Tips and tricks appear like this.

Get in touch

Feedback from our readers is always welcome.

General feedback: If you have questions about any aspect of this book, mention the book title in the subject of your message and email us at `customercare@packtpub.com`.

Errata: Although we have taken every care to ensure the accuracy of our content, mistakes do happen. If you have found a mistake in this book, we would be grateful if you would report this to us. Please visit `www.packtpub.com/support/errata`, selecting your book, clicking on the Errata Submission Form link, and entering the details.

Piracy: If you come across any illegal copies of our works in any form on the Internet, we would be grateful if you would provide us with the location address or website name. Please contact us at `copyright@packt.com` with a link to the material.

If you are interested in becoming an author: If there is a topic that you have expertise in and you are interested in either writing or contributing to a book, please visit `authors.packtpub.com`.

Reviews

Please leave a review. Once you have read and used this book, why not leave a review on the site that you purchased it from? Potential readers can then see and use your unbiased opinion to make purchase decisions, we at Packt can understand what you think about our products, and our authors can see your feedback on their book. Thank you!

For more information about Packt, please visit `packt.com`.

Section 1: Introduction

The objective of *Section 1* is to lay out the scope of the exam for the reader.

This section contains the following chapter:

- Chapter 1, *PL-200 Exam*

PL-200 Exam

The Power Platform is a set of tools, including Power BI, Power Apps, Power Automate, and Power Virtual Agents, for building business solutions without the need to write code. Using the Power Platform, anyone can create an app. The Power Platform is not just for citizen developers; the capabilities of the Power Platform can be used by IT professionals and can be extended by developers.

In this chapter, you will be introduced to the exam contents, the purpose of the exam, the skills measured, and who the exam is aimed at. We will discuss role-based certifications and how the PL-200 exam fits in with the Dynamics 365 and Power Platform role-based certifications.

The topics covered in this chapter are as follows:

- Understanding role-based certifications
- Introducing Dynamics 365 and Power Platform roles
- Exploring the PL-200 exam and objectives
- Reviewing the skills measured
- Related exams

By the end of this chapter, you will understand the scope of the PL-200 exam and its structure. You will also have an idea about who the exam is aimed at and be familiar with the exam paper before you sit the exam.

Understanding role-based certifications

In response to customer expectations and feedback on certification, Microsoft has changed the way candidates for certifications are examined in order to provide candidates and employers with more relevant certifications for their jobs.

Certifications have evolved to focus on the core skills aligned to specific job roles, moving toward teaching you how to use the technology to help you develop the skills you need to fulfill a specific job role.

The value of certifications has been reevaluated at Microsoft, with many Microsoft staff now having to gain certifications themselves. This has led to a greater focus on certifications and an increase in the quality of courses and the relevance of certifications.

The PL-200 exam is a good example of the new type of certification testing for certain job roles. The following sections explain the roles and their impacts on the questions in the certification exams.

Job roles

Previously, questions in Microsoft exams were about the features of the Microsoft product that a given exam covers. This often meant that you had to learn about functionalities or capabilities that you never used, and would never use, just to pass the exam.

Microsoft has changed to certifications that revolve around the day-to-day tasks of certain job roles. Microsoft consulted widely to define several job roles and the certifications around those roles across the following core solutions areas: Cloud, Modern Workplace, Data and AI, and Business Applications.

You can see the full list of job roles at `http://aka.ms/TrainCertPoster`.

There are certifications for each role, with each role certification requiring one or, sometimes, two exams.

Questions in the role-based exams are written to test your day-to-day skills instead of testing your memory.

Exam questions

The migration from product-based to role-based certifications has affected the way exam questions are written. The following diagram represents the levels of complexity in learning. These exams used to concentrate on remembering and understanding. They now focus on evaluating, analyzing, and applying knowledge:

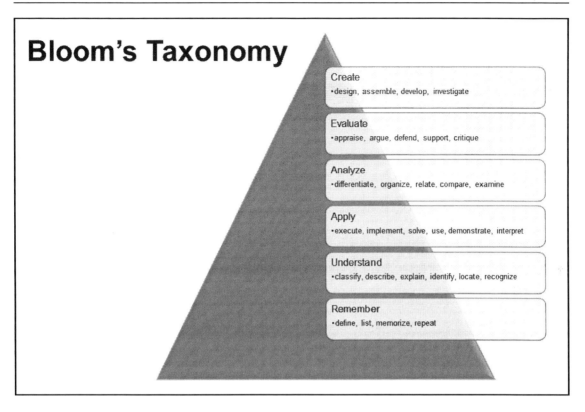

Figure 1.1 – Bloom's taxonomy representing the complexity levels in learning

An effective way to understand these changes is that questions are now about the *why* and the *how*, not the *what*; that is, a question may test you on *how* to implement a feature, and not on *what* needs to be implemented.

You'll find some tips and tricks to help you toward the end of the book, in the `Tips and Tricks` section. This will provide you with tips for taking the exam, as well as two sets of practice test questions to help you prepare.

 To find out more about role-based certification, you can visit `http://aka.ms/rolebasedcerts`.

Question types

Along with the change to role-based certification, the exams themselves have evolved; there are many new question types. If you have taken older Microsoft exams, you may have just experienced multiple-choice questions.

In role-based exams, you can expect to see question types that are more interactive, such as the following, for example:

- Active screen
- Build list
- Case study
- Drag and drop
- Graphic interpretation
- Multi-source reasoning

The introduction of these exam item types has made exams both easier and harder at the same time. Easier, because you no longer need to remember arcane facts, or learn about things you will never use. Harder, because you can't just read and remember; you must be familiar with the Power Platform and have performed the actions that the questions refer to.

Don't worry, we have relevant exercises to help you.

 To learn more about the different question types in use, watch the videos at https://docs.microsoft.com/learn/certifications/certification-exams#exam-formats-and-question-types.

Performance-based testing

Performance-Based Testing (PBT) is being introduced to some exams. In this form of testing, you are presented with a system in a controlled browser lab-type environment and are given a set of tasks to perform.

PBT makes it even more important for you to be familiar with and comfortable using the Power Platform.

I have written more about PBT at `https://community.dynamics.com/365/b/` `dynamicscrmukmct/posts/performance-based-testing`. You can get some more information on PBT there.

Now that we have outlined the changes to role-based certification, we will now look at the roles relevant to the PL-200 exam.

Introducing Power Platform and Dynamics 365 roles

With the emergence of the Power Platform, Microsoft has sought to distinguish between the functionality of the Dynamics 365 apps and the underlying features of the Power Platform.

There are several roles covering both Dynamics 365 and the Power Platform. The PL-200 exam contributes to several of the Dynamics 365 roles.

Dynamics 365 and Power Platform roles

This section will explore the roles for Dynamics 365 model-driven apps that are relevant to the PL-200 exam, and the impact of these roles on candidates.

The Dynamics 365 and Power Platform roles are as follows:

- Power Platform App Maker
- Power Platform Functional Consultant
- Power Platform Developer
- Data Analyst Associate
- Dynamics 365 Functional Consultant
- Dynamics 365 + Power Platform Solutions Architect

For each of these roles, one or more exams have been created.

The PL-200 exam is required for the Power Platform Functional Consultant role and is one of the two exams that is required for the Dynamics 365 Functional Consultant role. The PL-200 exam is required for the Solutions Architect role, but the true focus for the exam is the Functional Consultant role, which we will talk about next. We will cover more on the PL-200 exam later in this chapter, in the *Exploring the PL-200 exam and its objectives* section.

The Functional Consultant role

The **Functional Consultant** role covers many job titles including business analyst, application specialist, and applications consultant. The key denominator here is the gathering of requirements from users and turning those requirements into solutions based on Dynamics 365 or the Power Platform. A functional consultant leverages Microsoft Dynamics 365 and the Power Platform to meet customer needs.

A functional consultant is not a developer; instead, they use the out-of-the-box tools and customization capabilities provided by Microsoft to deliver solutions. Microsoft refers to such capabilities as *low code/no code*.

Let's start with the definition of a functional consultant.

Role definition

A Power Platform Functional Consultant is responsible for capturing and documenting user requirements and turning those requirements into a working system. The Functional Consultant role implements a solution using the out-of-the-box capabilities provided by Microsoft.

The key activities for the Functional Consultant role are listed next.

Key role activities

The role of a Dynamics 365/Power Platform Functional Consultant is to do the following:

- Gather and document requirements from users.
- Identify where and how Dynamics 365 and Power Platform can be used to meet those requirements.
- Design the solution, in collaboration with the solutions architect.
- Implement the design.
- Follow standards.
- Ensure that the solution meets both functional and non-functional requirements.
- Perform testing of any configured artifacts.

- Collaborate with the quality assurance team to ensure that the system operates correctly.
- Package artifacts for deployment.
- Provide training to Dynamics 365/Power Platform administrators.

A functional consultant will have experience in delivering systems based on Dynamics 365 and/or the Power Platform.

Required experience

The experience expectations for a Dynamics 365/Power Platform Functional Consultant are as follows:

- Must have experience of the full life cycle of Dynamics 365/Power Platform systems from requirements, through design and implementation, to ongoing support and upgrades
- Must understand the features and capabilities of each of the Dynamics 365 apps
- Must have a broad knowledge of the Power Platform, understanding its capabilities, boundaries, and constraints
- Must be able to customize and configure Dynamics 365 and the Power Platform
- Must be able to apply their knowledge of customization and configuration to meet customer needs
- Should have a basic understanding of solutions architecture and quality assurance
- Should understand the extensibility capabilities of Dynamics 365 and the Power Platform
- Must have experience in configuring entities, fields, and relationships; customizing forms and views; customizing charts and dashboards; configuring the security model; configuring processes; managing solutions and instances; and configuring for mobile devices
- Must have experience of integrating with other applications and services
- Must effectively communicate with members of the delivery team, stakeholders, and customers

There is not a single functional consultant role, but separate roles for each of the main Dynamics 365 apps, and also for the Power Platform.

Functional Consultant roles

Microsoft has created Functional Consultant job roles for each of the main Dynamics 365 model-driven first-party apps. There are five functional consultant roles:

- Power Platform Functional Consultant Associate
- Dynamics 365 Sales Functional Consultant Associate
- Dynamics 365 Customer Service Functional Consultant Associate
- Dynamics 365 Field Service Functional Consultant Associate
- Dynamics 365 Marketing Functional Consultant Associate

The PL-200 exam is a prerequisite for each of these role certifications, and for other role-based certifications.

Exploring the PL-200 exam and its objectives

PL-200 is the base exam required for any functional consultant, and it demonstrates their ability to configure, customize, and deploy solutions to meet customer requirements. As such, PL-200 is at the core of a functional consultant's day-to-day job.

While PL-200 is aimed at functional consultants, others involved in Dynamics 365 and Power Platform systems, such as testers, support staff, developers, administrators, and solutions architects, should consider taking the PL-200 exam as it covers many of their core day-to-day skills.

For PL-200, although you need to be aware of the first-party apps (Sales, Customer Service, Field Service, and Marketing), you don't need to have detailed knowledge about the features and functionality of each of the apps. The exam is more about the underlying platform for Dynamics 365, that is, the Power Platform and the Common Data Service.

This exam covers the skills around configuring, customizing, and deploying the platform to meet user needs and completing design tasks that relate to implementing new features and functionalities.

The following sections explore these tasks and the skills required.

At the time of publishing, Microsoft Dataverse (formerly known as the Common Data Service) was undergoing a branding change. Along with the name change, there are several changes to terminology such as tables (formerly entities), columns (formerly fields), rows (formerly records), choices (formerly option sets), and yes/no (formerly two options). These changes have not yet been applied to the exam. You should be prepared to see the former terms in the exam.

Skills measured

The exam tests a series of skills. These skills are referred to as the exam's *objective domain*.

Being familiar with the objective domain is important to candidates for the exam. You won't see questions on all the skills listed, as the questions in a given exam are randomized from a pool of questions, and you might see questions that aren't listed as some of the skills are vague and/or could be interpreted in different ways. However, making sure you have covered everything in the objective domain will give you a much better chance of passing the exam.

The objective domain is broad, with a lot of separate topics listed. If you have taken older product-orientated exams, this might seem daunting. But for these role-based exams, you don't need to learn all the facts about each item as you had to do previously.

The way the questions are written for PL-200 provides a good test of your skills. If you use the Power Platform on a day-to-day basis, you should, by following this guide, be much better placed to pass the exam.

There are various skills measured in the objective domain for PL-200. We will discuss them in the following sections.

You should always check the exam page (`https://docs.microsoft.com/learn/certifications/exams/pl-200`) before taking the exam in case Microsoft has made any changes to the objective domain.

Configure the Common Data Service (25–30%)

This part of the exam is all about the Common Data Service, extending the data model, and moving data into and out of the database:

- **Manage an existing data model**: These are the core skills around data modeling, which is the starting point for any Power Platform app; that is, entities, fields, and relationships.
- **Create and manage processes**: Processes are a major part of any system based on model-driven apps and the skills in this section are about understanding, configuring, and applying each of these types of processes: business rules, business process flows, and classic workflows.
- **Configure Common Data Service settings**: Several items must be configured when creating environments, such as using audit and search. This section is about a set of administration topics and you need to know how to enable and configure these settings.
- **Configure security settings**: You must have an understanding of the security features in the Common Data Service and how to configure and apply them.

Create apps by using Power Apps (20–25%)

This part of the exam is all about creating Power Apps on the Common Data Service:

- **Create model-driven apps**: This section of the exam covers customizing the user interface in the Common Data Service and creating model-driven apps.
- **Create canvas apps**: This section of the exam is all about creating and managing canvas apps.
- **Create portal apps**: You need to know about portal apps; specifically, how to deploy and configure portal apps.

Create and manage Power Automate (15–20%)

This part of the exam is focused on the capabilities of Power Automate:

- **Create flows**: You will need to understand the components that make up a flow and how to create flows for the Common Data Service.

- **Create and manage business process flows**: This section of the exam is about creating and editing business process flows and using business process flows with other forms of automation.
- **Build UI flows**: This set of skills involves building web and desktop robotic process automation flows.

Implement Power Virtual Agents chatbots (10–15%)

This part of the exam is about creating chatbots with Power Virtual Agents:

- **Create a chatbot**: This covers the set of skills necessary for creating chatbots and deploying the chatbots to channels.
- **Configure topics**: You need to understand how topics are used in chatbots and how to add greetings and conversation triggers.
- **Configure entities**: You need to understand the built-in entities and how to create custom entities for use in chatbots.

Integrate Power Apps with other apps and services (15–20%)

This part of the exam is about using the apps you build with other components in the Power Platform and with Microsoft Teams:

- **Integrate Power BI with Power Apps**: This covers the skills required to create Power BI reports and dashboards, and then embed Power BI tiles in Power Apps and embed Power Apps in Power BI dashboards.
- **Implement AI Builder**: You need to understand the capabilities of AI Builder and be able to create an AI model that you can use with Power Apps and Power Automate flows.
- **Integrate Power Apps with Microsoft 365**: This set of skills requires understanding the different capabilities of Word, Excel, and Outlook templates, and how to create each of these templates. You need to be able to add a power app to Microsoft Teams.

This last set of skills brings us to the end of this objective domain.

Before we conclude the chapter, let's also have a look at other exams that might interest you.

Related exams

There are several exams for Dynamics 365 and the Power Platform. Let's discuss them briefly:

- **MB-901: Dynamics 365 Fundamentals**: If you are new to Dynamics 365, you should take this exam before you attempt PL-200. This exam introduces you to some of the concepts in Dynamics 365. PL-200 assumes some familiarity with Dynamics 365 model-driven apps.
- **PL-900: Power Platform Fundamentals**: If you are new to the Power Platform, you should take this exam before you attempt PL-200. This is for many reasons—it introduces you to the components of the Power Platform; and PL-200 assumes a certain level of knowledge. This exam gives you vital exam experience so that when you come to take PL-200, you will know how the questions work.
- **PL-100: Power Platform App Maker**: This exam covers many of the same topics as PL-200 but is aimed more at the citizen developer, that is, a person who creates apps for themselves or their colleagues as part of their job. PL-200 is aimed more at the IT professional whose job is to build solutions with the Power Platform. If you have only built a couple of apps, the PL-100 exam is a more appropriate exam.
- **MB-210: Dynamics 365 Sales**: PL-200 and MB-210 complement each other, the former focusing on out-of-the-box application functionality and the other on customizing and deploying the apps.
- **MB-220: Dynamics 365 Marketing**: The Marketing exam focuses on using, configuring, and administering the Marketing application. Marketing is a complex application built for B2B marketing and is often implemented alongside the Sales app.
- **MB-230: Dynamics 365 Customer Service**: The Customer Service exam focuses on using, configuring, and administering the Customer Service application. PL-200 and MB-230 complement each other, with the former focusing on out-of-the-box application functionality and the other on customizing and deploying the app.
- **MB-240: Dynamics 365 Field Service**: The Field Service exam focuses on configuring and administering the Field Service application. Field Service is a complex application that requires significant domain-level knowledge. Field Service can be implemented on its own or along with the Sales or Customer Service apps.

- **PL-400: Power Platform Developer**: The PL-400 exam is aimed at the developer role and is for candidates who are extending the Power Platform. The PL-400 exam is not a prerequisite for the developer certification but there are many areas in PL-200 that a developer needs to know. There are overlaps in the topics covered by these two exams; for example, creating entities, fields, and relationships; security; and processes. I believe a good developer should have many of the skills tested in PL-200 and should attempt PL-200 before taking PL-400.
- **MB-600: Power Apps + Dynamics 365 Solutions Architect**: The MB-600 is aimed at the Solutions Architect role. A solutions architect is responsible for leading implementations, addressing the broader business and technical needs of the organization. The PL-200 exam is a prerequisite for the Solutions Architect Expert certification.

You can find more about each respective exam at the following URLs:

- https://docs.microsoft.com/learn/certifications/exams/mb-901
- https://docs.microsoft.com/learn/certifications/exams/pl-100
- https://docs.microsoft.com/learn/certifications/exams/pl-200
- https://docs.microsoft.com/learn/certifications/exams/mb-210
- https://docs.microsoft.com/learn/certifications/exams/mb-220
- https://docs.microsoft.com/learn/certifications/exams/mb-230
- https://docs.microsoft.com/learn/certifications/exams/mb-240
- https://docs.microsoft.com/learn/certifications/exams/pl-400
- https://docs.microsoft.com/learn/certifications/exams/mb-600

As you can see, each of these exams relates to the PL-200 exam.

Summary

In this chapter, we learned about role-based certifications, the Functional Consultant role, and the purpose and content of the PL-200 exam. The exam is aimed to cover the day-to-day tasks and skills of someone who creates systems based on the Power Platform from the start of a project to its completion.

You now understand the scope of the exam and the knowledge and skills that will be tested in the PL-200 exam.

The next chapter is a high-level overview of the Power Platform. This is a piece of important and fundamental knowledge for the remainder of this book and the exam.

Questions

After reading this chapter, test your knowledge with these questions. You will find the answers to these questions in the Assessments chapter at the end of the book:

1. The role of a Dynamics 365 Functional Consultant is restricted to customizing Dynamics 365 apps. True or false?

   A) True
   B) False

2. The role of a Power Platform Functional Consultant includes extending the Power Platform. True or false?

   A) True
   B) False

3. The PL-200 exam contains only multiple-choice questions. True or false?

   A) True
   B) False

4. The PL-200 exam is required for which of the following roles? (Choose two)

   A) Dynamics 365 Functional Consultant
   B) Power Platform Developer
   C) Power Platform and Dynamics 365 Solutions Architect
   D) Data Analyst
   E) App Maker

5. At what level of complexity are the questions in the MB-200 exam?

   A) Understanding
   B) Remembering
   C) Applying
   D) Creating

Further reading

If you are new to the Power Platform, then you should review some of the learning content on Microsoft Learn:

- Dynamics 365 and Power Platform Consultant Pre-Reading Collection: `https://docs.microsoft.com/users/julians/collections/w2ydudg50jg4j8`

For more information on certifications and exams, see the following:

- PL-200 exam page: `https://docs.microsoft.com/learn/certifications/exams/pl-200`
- Role-based certifications: `https://aka.ms/RoleBasedCerts`

Section 2: Microsoft Dataverse

2

The objective of *Section 2* is to configure Microsoft Dataverse (formerly known as the Common Data Service) to manage data for your apps. By the end, the reader will be able to create a database schema for their business data.

This section contains the following chapters:

- Chapter 2, *Power Platform*
- Chapter 3, *Data Modeling*
- Chapter 4, *Business Rules*
- Chapter 5, *Classic Workflows*
- Chapter 6, *Managing Data*
- Chapter 7, *Dataverse Settings*
- Chapter 8, *Security*

2
Power Platform

The Power Platform is a Software-as-a-Service solution for creating solutions to solve business requirements. In this chapter, we will get a high-level overview of Dynamics 365, as well as the Power Platform and its components. This is fundamental knowledge for the remainder of this book and the exam.

The topics covered in this chapter are as follows:

- Introducing Dynamics 365 and the Dynamics 365 apps
- Exploring the Power Platform and its components
- Understanding Power Platform environments and how to manage them

By the end of this chapter, you will be able to identify components of the Power Platform and administer and configure environments. The topics covered will also help you understand how to manage applications using the administration portals.

Introducing Dynamics 365 and the Dynamics 365 apps

Dynamics 365 is a portfolio of modern modular business apps that work together to support business operations. The Dynamics 365 apps can work on their own, together, or with other business applications.

Although Microsoft, in its marketing, talks of Dynamics 365 as a single suite of products, the **Customer Relationship Management (CRM)** and **Enterprise Resource Planning (ERP)** roots of Dynamics 365 are still apparent with different technologies involved.

Dynamics CRM was always a great platform for developing custom business applications, with the ability to create entities and fields and create a form-based user interface, with a workflow to support business processes. However, customers had to pay for functionality they didn't require, and a lot of effort was expended in hiding that functionality from users.

Over the past few years, Microsoft has worked to separate the Dynamics CRM/365 apps away from their underlying platform, enabling the platform and apps to be updated separately and reduce dependencies between them.

If you have been involved with Dynamics CRM/365 for a while, you may have heard this underlying platform referred to as the Dynamics XRM platform. That XRM platform has evolved into what is now known as **Common Data Service (CDS)**.

The frequent changes in Dynamics 365 and the Power Platform is something you need to be aware of when preparing for the exam. There are two main releases a year, in spring and fall, but in practice, there are new and improved features released every month.

The PL-200 exam, and this book, are primarily concerned with CDS and the Power Platform. However, before we dive into CDS and Power Platform, the PL-200 exam requires that you have an awareness of the various Dynamics 365 apps.

Dynamics 365 apps

There are many apps for Dynamics 365 that you can use individually or together. You need an understanding of these apps and their capabilities so that you can decide whether to use the **out-of-the-box (OOTB)** functionality of the apps, customize the apps, or even build your own custom apps.

You can find out more about the Dynamics 365 apps at `https://docs.` `microsoft.com/dynamics365/`.

Although the focus of the PL-200 exam is the Power Platform, you need an awareness of the Dynamics 365 apps. The main Dynamics 365 model-driven apps built by Microsoft on the Power Platform and that use CDS are as follows:

- Dynamics 365 Sales
- Dynamics 365 Customer Service
- Dynamics 365 Field Service
- Dynamics 365 Project Operations
- Dynamics 365 Marketing

These are known as first-party model apps – in short, the apps provided by Microsoft to differentiate them from the apps that software companies (third parties) supply, or that you create using the Power Platform.

One advantage that has arisen since Microsoft separated the apps from the platform is the ability to add new features independently; features are released when ready without having to wait for the other apps or changes to the platform to be released.

The PL-200 exam is not about the functionality of these apps (there are separate exams for that), but the exam does include customizing these apps using the tools in the Power Platform.

Now that you have learned about the Dynamics 365 apps, we will now look at the Power Platform.

Exploring the Power Platform and its components

The Power Platform is Microsoft's business application development platform. This platform allows organizations to build custom apps quickly, automate workflows across applications, and analyze data to provide insights, all in a low-code/no-code interface.

You can meet your users' requirements by creating new applications, integrating applications with existing systems, or building on top of existing applications, all with the Power Platform.

The Power Platform works with Microsoft's cloud services – that is, Dynamics 365, Microsoft 365, and Azure – but is also able to connect with many other cloud services and on-premises systems.

The Power Platform is a platform for easily building and running business applications. It is important to Microsoft and has been created from a set of innovative technologies by Microsoft. We will now look at the components that make up the Power Platform.

Power Platform components

Microsoft has created several low-code development technologies that are merged into the Power Platform:

- Power Apps
- Power Automate
- Power BI
- Power Virtual Agents

The exam is focused on CDS, but there are questions on parts of the Power Platform – for example, Power Automate.

 Learn more about the Power Platform at `https://powerplatform.microsoft.com`.

In the following sections, we will see a concise description of each of the Power Platform components.

Power Apps

Power Apps is a suite of web and mobile low-code apps that you can build from within a browser. Power Apps can connect to many different data sources, displaying and creating data.

There are three types of Power Apps:

- Canvas
- Model-driven
- Portal

Canvas apps are made up of screens, forms, and controls, as shown in the following screenshot:

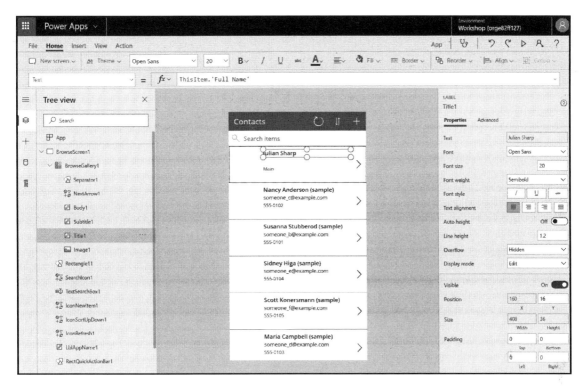

Figure 2.1 – Power Apps canvas studio

You have full control over all the visual elements of your app via the **Properties** pane shown in the preceding screenshot. There, you can set values and properties, control navigation, and save data using Excel-like functions and expressions. Canvas apps are explained in Chapter 10, *Canvas Apps*.

Model-driven apps are apps built upon the data model you create in CDS. Model-driven apps are constructed from separate components, such as forms, views, charts, and dashboards. Each component type has its own editor and to build an app, you assemble the separate components. Model-driven apps are explained in Chapter 9, *Model-Driven Apps*.

The following screenshot shows a custom model-driven app:

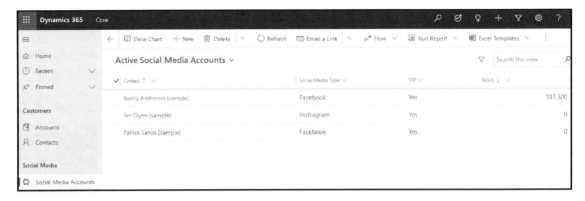

Figure 2.2 – Model-driven app

Portal apps are customer-facing websites built on top of CDS. With a portal app, you can expose your data to customers and allow customers to create and update records:

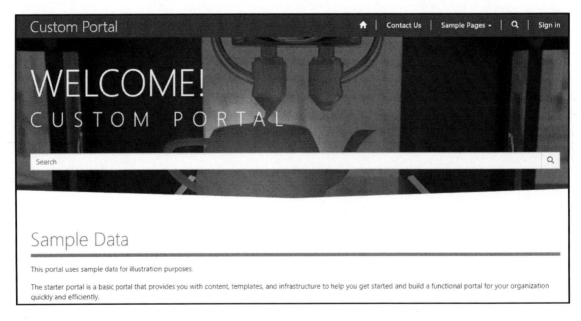

Figure 2.3 – Portal app

You can find a detailed explanation of portal apps in Chapter 11, *Portal Apps*.

Power Automate

Power Automate is a cloud service for creating and executing workflows within and across cloud services. Like Power Apps, Power Automate can connect to multiple data sources and services.

You can use Power Automate to send notifications, synchronize data and files, perform integrations between systems, and many other workflows. Here's what the Power Automate interface looks like:

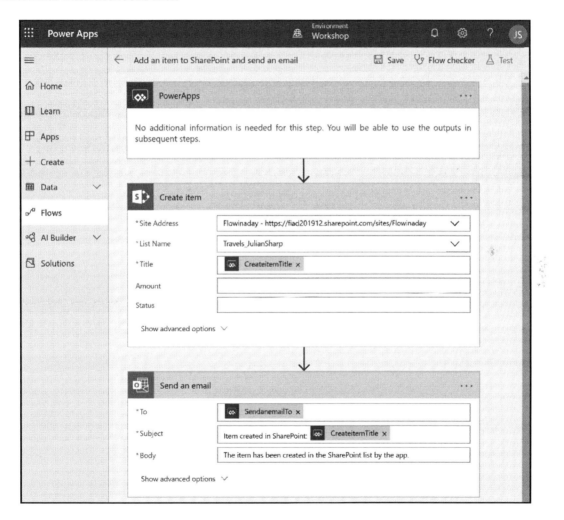

Figure 2.4 – Power Automate designer

We will discuss Power Automate further in `Chapter 12`, *Power Automate Flows*, later in this book.

Power BI

Power BI is a self-service analytics service that allows users to gain insights into their data. It allows you to merge data from various sources and create models, visualizations, reports, and dashboards.

The Power BI user interface is designed to be familiar to users of Office:

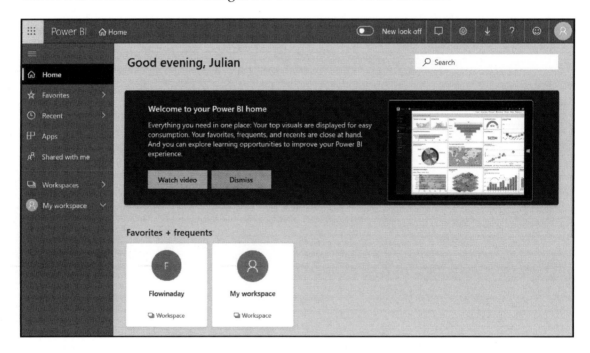

Figure 2.5 – Power BI

We will learn about creating Power BI reports and dashboards in `Chapter 17`, *Power BI*.

Power Virtual Agents

Power Virtual Agents allows you to create chatbots without writing code from within a browser interface.

The following screenshot shows editing and running a chatbot in Power Virtual Agents:

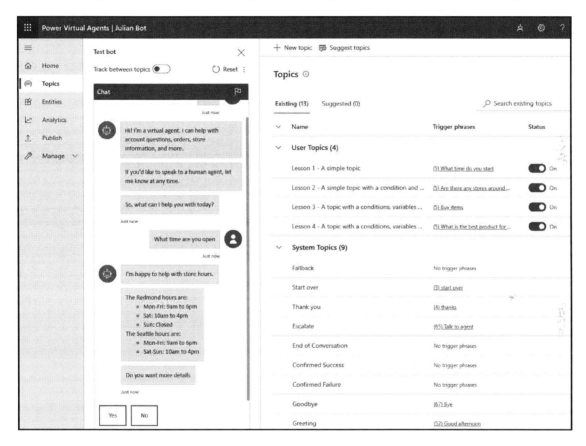

Figure 2.6 – Power Virtual Agents

We will learn how to create chatbots using Power Virtual Agents in `Chapter 15`, *Creating Chatbots*.

The Power Platform tools do not work on their own, but rather use and depend on related features, which we will discuss next.

Related components

There are several related features that are used with the components of the Power Platform:

- Connectors
- Dataverse (formerly the Common Data Service)
- Common Data Model
- AI Builder

These features are outlined in the following sections.

Connectors

Connectors define the services and data sources that the Power Platform tools can access. There are connectors for Office 365 services, such as email and SharePoint, Azure services, such as Azure SQL, as well as many non-Microsoft sources. Popular connectors are Twitter, SendGrid, Dropbox, and Mailchimp.

Each connector defines its set of triggers and actions; triggers are used with Power Automate to initiate a flow, and actions perform operations such as the reading and writing of data. You can connect to on-premises data sources using the on-premises data gateway. You can build your own custom connectors for situations where there isn't an existing connector.

 For more information on connectors, you can visit `https://docs.microsoft.com/connectors/`.

CDS has a connector. Although the Power Platform tools work with many Microsoft products and services, they are particularly suited to work with CDS.

Dataverse (formerly) Common Data Service

CDS, previously known as the Common Data Service for Apps, is the name given to the data and services on which Dynamics 365 model-driven apps run.

At the time of publishing, Microsoft Dataverse (formerly known as the Common Data Service) was undergoing a branding change. This name change has not yet been applied to all the tools, connectors, and user interfaces in the Power Platform. You will see the use of Common Data Service and the abbreviation CDS throughout this book.

You can customize Dynamics 365 model-driven apps and build your own apps on top of CDS using the tools of the Power Platform.

You can also create a CDS environment without first-party apps and create custom business applications at a lower cost in terms of both time and licensing.

You can later install a Dynamics 365 app on your environment if you find that you need the functionality of that app.

CDS uses a mixture of Azure services to store data: Azure SQL, Azure Data Lake, and Azure Blob storage.

To find out more about CDS, read `https://docs.microsoft.com/ powerapps/maker/common-data-service/data-platform-intro`.

As stated earlier, CDS has evolved from the Dynamics CRM/365 platform. Microsoft is building new interfaces for the Power Platform and CDS tools.

The schemas used when creating Dynamics 365 and CDS environments are defined in the Common Data Model.

Common Data Model

The Common Data Model is an open-source data model on GitHub (see `https://github.com/Microsoft/CDM`) with a set of standardized schemas that can be used by systems to ensure consistency and interoperability of data across systems.

To find out more about the Common Data Model, read `https://docs. microsoft.com/common-data-model/`.

Microsoft is expanding the schemas in the Common Data Model to include industry accelerators such as healthcare and manufacturing.

Microsoft is enabling AI within Dynamics 365 first-party apps and is now making AI available to the Power Platform for you to include AI in your own apps and processes.

AI Builder

AI Builder is a set of AI model types that can use data in CDS to create, tailor, and train AI models that can be used by the Power Platform.

There are five AI model types:

- Prediction
- Category classification
- Form processing
- Object detection
- Entity extraction

The following screenshot shows the model types for AI Builder:

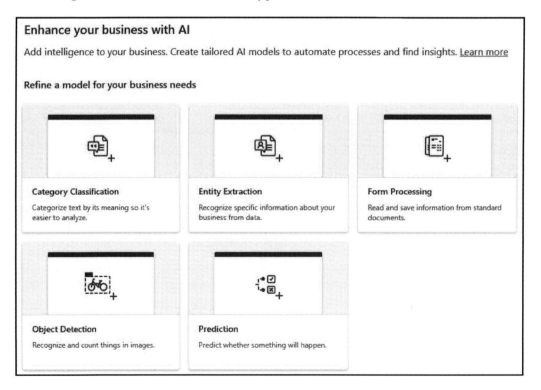

Figure 2.7 – AI Builder

Several pre-built models are available to speed up your use of AI within Power Apps and Power Automate. You will learn how to create and use AI Builder models in `Chapter 18,` *AI Builder.*

To enable you to manage and separate your apps and data, Microsoft provides environments.

Understanding Power Platform environments

An environment is a container for your data, apps, and flows. An environment is created when you install Dynamics 365, and you can create additional environments as needed.

With multiple environments, you need to manage access to their apps and data through security. Microsoft provides different types of environments that are used for different purposes.

Multiple environments

You can create environments to handle different user communities or security requirements, or for application life cycle management purposes.

You should have, as a minimum, separate environments for development and production purposes.

Environments have databases and properties and are controlled by security.

Environments and databases

Each environment can optionally have a single CDS database; if you need another CDS database, then you need to create another environment.

You have storage capacity in your tenant based on the number and type of license purchased. You can only create an environment if you have 1 GB of storage available.

Environment security

Each environment is controlled by security to control who can manage and access the environment. The security access is different depending on whether there is a CDS database in the environment or not.

Without a CDS database, access is controlled by users being given any one of the following roles in the environment:

- Environment maker
- Environment admin

> These roles are not Microsoft 365 administration roles; they are roles within the CDS environment.

> For more details on security in environments, refer to `https://docs.microsoft.com/power-platform/admin/environments-overview#environment-permissions`.

Users do not need a role to run an app; instead, apps are shared with users.

Once a CDS database has been added to an environment, access is controlled by *security roles* within CDS. Users must have a security role to be able to access data in the CDS database.

Environments can be linked to an Office 365 security group. Once linked, only users in that security group will be able to access the environment.

Environment types

Each environment has a type that defines its purpose and what can be done with it. There are six types of environment:

- **Production**: For permanent work.
- **Sandbox**: For non-production environments, such as development and testing.
- **Default**: Each Microsoft 365 tenant has a default environment created automatically.

- **Trial**: For short-term testing needs; automatically deleted after 30 days.
- **Support**: Created by Microsoft Support as a copy of another environment. Support environments do not affect your storage capacity.
- **Developer**: Created by users signing up for the Community Plan. Developer environments are restricted to the user.

Depending on the type of environment, you can perform operations on environments, as discussed next.

Environment operations

There are many operations that can be performed on environments:

- **Create**: New environments can be created. You can specify that the environment is a trial, production, or sandbox. You can optionally create a CDS database.
- **Switch**: You can edit an environment and switch environment type but only switch between sandbox and production and vice versa.
- **Delete**: Sandbox, trial, and support environments can be deleted. You cannot delete a production environment, but you can change it to a sandbox and then delete it. You cannot delete the default environment.
- **Convert**: You can convert a trial environment to production.
- **Reset**: Sandbox environments can be reset, which will delete all customizations, data, apps, and flows from the environment.
- **Copy**: You can copy a production or sandbox environment to a sandbox environment. There are two options when copying: copy over everything or copy over customizations and schemas only. After the copy, the environment will be in administration mode.

Sandbox environments can be placed in administration mode. In this mode, only users with the system administrator or system customizer roles will be able to sign in to the environment; all other users will be shown a message that an administrator can change. Optionally, all background processing can be suspended in administration mode.

 For more information on the operations available for an environment, refer to `https://docs.microsoft.com/power-platform/admin/ environments-overview`.

Accessing environments and actioning these operations is performed through several web portals.

Administration and maker portals

Microsoft provides several web portals for creating apps and managing environments.

 Some administration tasks are not possible in the Power Platform; you still need to occasionally switch back to "classic" mode – for instance, for the Dynamics 365 customization tools.

The URLs for each portal and its capabilities are listed as follows.

The Power Apps maker portal

The maker portal (`https://make.powerapps.com`) is the main site for building apps. You can do the following:

- Manage CDS (entities, fields, relationships, forms, views, and rules).
- Create apps.
- Import data.
- Export data.

You cannot create environments in the maker portal.

The Power Platform administration center

The Power Platform admin center (`https://admin.powerplatform.microsoft.com`) is the main site for managing environments. You can do the following:

- Create environments.
- Open environments.
- Access environment settings.
- Perform environment operations (copy, switch, delete, reset, admin mode, security group, convert trial).
- Manage data loss prevention policies.
- Integrate data.
- Install/update applications and solutions.

The following screenshot shows the list of environments in the Power Platform admin center:

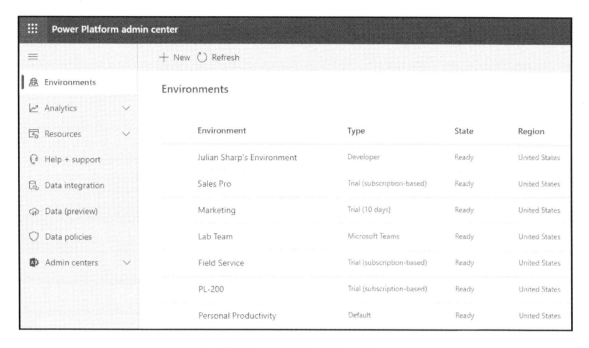

Figure 2.8 – Environments in the Power Platform admin center

Microsoft 365 administration center

The Microsoft 365 admin center (`https://admin.microsoft.com/Adminportal/Home`) is the portal used to manage the following Microsoft 365 features:

- Users
- Subscriptions
- Allocation of licenses to users
- Security groups and membership

Microsoft AppSource

AppSource (https://appsource.microsoft.com) is where you can find authorized third-party apps and install them onto your environment.

You will use the various portals when creating, installing, and updating apps in your environments. You should be clear about which portal to use and the steps required for these operations.

Summary

In this chapter, we learned about the components of the Power Platform. We also discussed the different types of environments and the operations you can perform on them.

You will now be able to configure environments and applications.

The next chapter is about modifying the data model to meet business requirements. The chapter will explain how the schema for CDS can be extended with entities, relationships, and fields. The different field types will be explained too. You will also learn how to use solutions to manage your changes.

Questions

After reading this chapter, test your knowledge with these questions. You will find the answers to these questions under Assessments at the end of the book:

1. True or false: you can reset a production environment.

   A) True
   B) False

2. True or false: after copying an environment, users can access the environment.

   A) True
   B) False

3. True or false: AI Builder requires a CDS database.

   A) True
   B) False

4. You need to select an application to manage the delivery of work at customer locations. Which application should you choose?

   A) Dynamics 365 Sales
   B) Dynamics 365 Customer Service
   C) Dynamics 365 Field Service
   D) Dynamics 365 Project Operations

5. You need to provision an environment to support testing. Which three environment types can you create?

   A) Default
   B) Developer
   C) Production
   D) Sandbox
   E) Support
   F) Trial

Further reading

For more details on the topics covered in this chapter, reference the following resources:

- The Dynamics 365 documentation: `https://docs.microsoft.com/dynamics365/`
- The Power Platform documentation: `https://docs.microsoft.com/power-platform/`

3
Data Modeling

The **Common Data Service** is the underlying data platform for the Power Platform and for some of the Dynamics 365 apps. Creating your data model is one of the most important steps when creating a business application.

In this chapter, we will look at modifying the data model to meet business requirements. The chapter will explain how the schema for the common data service can be extended with entities, relationships, and fields. The different field types will be explained, and you will learn how to use solutions to manage your changes.

We will cover the following topics in this chapter:

- Understanding the Common Data Model
- Introducing the Common Data Service
- Introducing solutions
- Changing the data model

By the end of this chapter, you will be able to create and modify entities, relationships, and fields. You will also have learned about using solutions to manage your work.

Understanding the Common Data Model

A major problem when building systems is migration, and the integration of data. To address the problems of incompatible data types, unknown data value ranges, and terminology differences, Microsoft has created a shared data language and specification for use by a wide range of business applications and processes. This specification is the **Common Data Model (CDM)**.

The CDM is supported in the Common Data Service, Dynamics 365, Power Apps, Power BI, and Azure data services.

It is not simply a series of data types or a list of attributes, but is a set of schemas in standardized notation. In this section, we will look at the components of the CDM, the importance of metadata, and the Open Data Initiative.

Data definitions in the CDM

The CDM is not a database; it is a set of schemas that define entities, attributes, and relationships, as well as their properties.

The CDM has a core schema consisting of about 20 business entities, for example, **Account**, **Contact**, **Currency**, and **Task**. The core schema is extended by other schemas for use in apps and services, for example, the CRM Foundation, and the Sales schemas are added to the core schema to define the schema for Dynamics 365 Sales.

As well as schemas for the Dynamics 365 apps, there are schemas for a growing number of accelerators, including non-profit, healthcare, and automotive. A representation of some of these schemas follows:

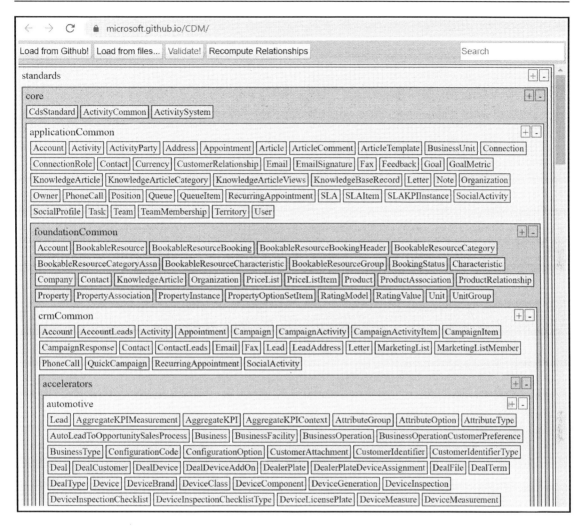

Figure 3.1 – CDM schemas

The previous diagram shows the CDM with the core, application, CRM, and automotive accelerator schemas and their entities. The schemas do not just define the entities, relationships, and attributes, but also properties relating to these elements, that is, their metadata (data about data).

The importance of metadata

CDM defines various properties of entities, attributes, and relationships. The properties are more than just the name or data type; they are the range of values, their display names, and traits such as whether they are editable, mandatory, or can be set to a null value.

This metadata can be leveraged by apps to affect how the user interacts with data. Dynamics 365 and Power Platform apps make use of this metadata to control and improve the user experience.

Microsoft realized that others have valuable contributions to make when it comes to creating a shared data language and has opened the CDM to others via the **Open Data Initiative**.

Open Data Initiative

Microsoft has made the CDM extendable. This means that other interested parties can contribute their data definitions to the CDM. For example, the accelerator schemas have been created in consultation with industry and implementation partners.

Anyone can contribute to the CDM as it is open sourced in GitHub. For example, ISVs can, and are, adding their own data models to the CDM.

Adobe and SAP have joined with Microsoft in the Open Data Initiative, using the CDM to make the integration of data between applications and platforms far simpler in the future.

 You can view the CDM in its GitHub repository at https://github.com/Microsoft/CDM.

One example of an implementation of the CDM is the Common Data Service.

Introducing the Common Data Service

The **Common Data Service (CDS)** is the data and services platform for Dynamics 365 and the Power Platform. At the time of publishing, Microsoft Dataverse (formerly known as the Common Data Service) was undergoing a branding change. You will see the use of Common Data Service and the abbreviation CDS throughout this chapter. There are several changes to terminology such as tables (formerly entities), columns (formerly fields), rows (formerly records), choices (formerly option sets), and yes/no (formerly two options). These terminology changes will be applied to the user interface, documentation, and exam over time. You should be aware that the terms used in this chapter may not match the tools and documentation.

A CDS database contains the standard entities, fields, and relationships as defined by the schema definitions in the CDM.

However, the CDS is more than just a data store. It is a secure platform that provides services to applications such as security, automation, integration, and business logic.

More importantly, the CDS is extensible; you can easily add to the data model to match your business needs and processes. The CDS has many other benefits that make it a compelling platform to build your business apps and processes.

Benefits of the CDS

The CDS removes the need to manage the database. You do not need to be a **database administrator (DBA)**; Microsoft automatically handles activities such as backup and optimization. You can focus on creating and using the data model rather than administering the database.

Using the CDS as the data store for your apps, or to build your apps on, has many benefits:

- **Managed data in the cloud**: You do not need to perform backups or configure the database as this is done for you by Microsoft.
- **Storage**: You don't need to worry about how the data is stored as Microsoft takes care of this for you.
- **Secure**: All data is encrypted at rest and in transit.
- **Metadata**: Properties you define on your data model are used by Dynamics 365 and Power Apps, speeding the building of apps.

- **Data access**: You can control who can access which entities, records, and fields.
- **Audit**: You can track who accesses and changes data.
- **User interface elements**: Components for model-driven apps such as forms, views, charts, and dashboards are created and stored in the CDS.
- **Logic**: Calculations, rules, and validation can be added to fields and applied automatically.
- **Processes**: Your business processes can be added to ensure data quality and perform automation.
- **Import and export**: There are various tools to manage your data, including Excel and Word.
- **Scalable**: Dynamics 365 apps are built using the CDS and support tens of thousands of users.
- **Skills**: You do not need to be a DBA to manage the CDS.

We will look at how to import data into, and export data from, the CDS in `Chapter 6`, *Managing Data*.

Applications built on the CDS, such as Dynamics 365 apps, benefit from all these capabilities.

Dynamics 365 apps and the CDS

When you install a Dynamics 365 app for the first time, a new environment and database are created. The database schema is created using the schemas in the CDM.

What's important as far as the rest of this book is concerned is that customizing Dynamics 365 apps is performed by customizing the CDS that the Dynamics 365 app runs on.

For the purpose of customization, you can think of a Dynamics 365 app, such as Dynamics 365 Sales, as just a model-driven app. It has the same customization and extensibility capabilities as any custom model-driven app that you create. You can build new apps against the Dynamics 365 entities or add entities to the Dynamics 365 apps.

> This book is about customizing the Power Platform. The skills you gain in Power Platform are transferable to Dynamics 365, and vice versa.

There are some technical details as to how the CDS is implemented that you need to be familiar with.

Understanding the technologies used in the CDS

Power Platform environments in your Microsoft 365 tenant can optionally have a CDS database. You can add a database when creating an environment, or you can add a database later.

We will look at the security aspects for managing environments in `Chapter 8`, *Security*.

 Each environment can only have one CDS database.

The CDS is a cloud data store based on Azure SQL, Azure Data Lake, and Azure Blob storage. You interact with CDS via the Power Apps Maker portal (`https://make.powerapps.com`).

 You cannot currently connect to the CDS using SQL Server Data Manager or other similar data tools. There is a **Tabular Data Stream** (**TDS**) endpoint in preview that will allow SQL queries to be used with the CDS.

The CDS provides data and services to apps, as shown in the following diagram:

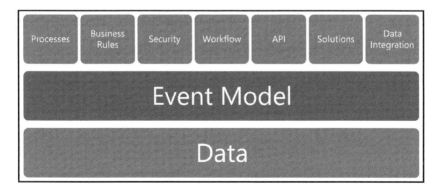

Figure 3.2 – Services provided by the CDS

The rest of this book addresses many of these application services.

Before we start customizing the CDS, you need to be able to manage your changes. To manage work and control changes, we employ solutions.

Introducing solutions

Solutions are a set of components that provide the functionality that meets a set of business requirements.

When an environment is created, a solution named the **Default** solution is created that contains all the components in the system, and an empty solution named the **Common Data Services Default** solution is created.

You can modify the components of the system directly in the **Default** solution, add customized components to the **Common Data Services Default** solution, or create new solutions to package your customizations.

Default solution

The Default solution contains all the components in your CDS environment.

Performing customizations within the Default solution will become more and more difficult as you create more components and apps. You will need to navigate through the hundreds of components in the environment.

The Default solution cannot be exported from the environment and then imported into another environment.

 Performing customization work in the Default solution is not recommended.

Common Data Services Default solution

The Common Data Services Default solution is used if you create apps or customize the data model outside of a solution in the Maker portal, as shown in *Figure 3.3*:

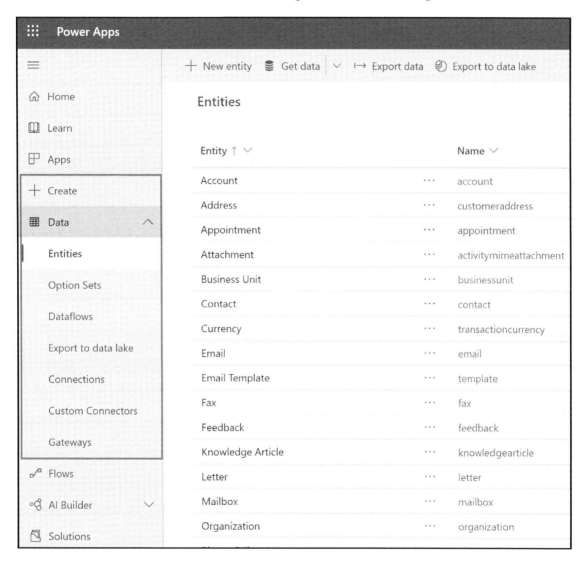

Figure 3.3 – Customizing outside of a solution

The Common Data Services Default solution exists so that makers who are not aware of solutions can easily transfer their changes from one environment to another.

The best practice is to create your own custom solutions to manage the components you plan to customize.

Using custom solutions

Solutions are a method for grouping together a set of components so that you can customize them, and then transfer these components from one environment to another.

Solutions also allow for **Independent Solution Vendors** (**ISVs**) to package up their products and control what their customers can do with the components contained in the solution, offering some protection for their intellectual property.

Solutions have several benefits to help you manage your changes and deployment process:

- You operate on a subset of components, reducing the need to scroll through all components.
- Solutions can be exported and then imported into another environment for testing, or for deployment into a production environment.
- Exported solution packages only contain the components in the solution; the package file will be smaller and will import much more quickly.
- Exported solution package files can be stored in your change control system.
- Imported solutions can be rolled back to a previous version (with some limitations).

To differentiate between solutions from different providers, each solution must have a publisher.

Publishers and prefixes

The purpose of the publisher record is to show who created the solution, and for ISVs, it is linked to their company in Microsoft AppSource.

The publisher has a name and a prefix, and a text field between 2 and 8 characters in length. This prefix is used when creating new components within a solution and is added to the schema name of the component.

The purpose of the prefix is to prevent clashes between different vendors and between your customizations and any new components added in later versions of the Power Platform.

 It is strongly recommended to create your own publisher with a unique prefix. The prefix will uniquely identify your customizations as this will prevent clashes between different suppliers.

Once you have a publisher record, you can create your own solution.

Creating solutions

Before you start customizing the CDS, you should create a solution. The solution will act as a container for all your customization changes.

Solutions are created in the Power Apps Maker portal. You create a solution by clicking on **Solutions** at the bottom of the left-hand navigation pane and then clicking on **+ New solution**, as shown in *Figure 3.4*:

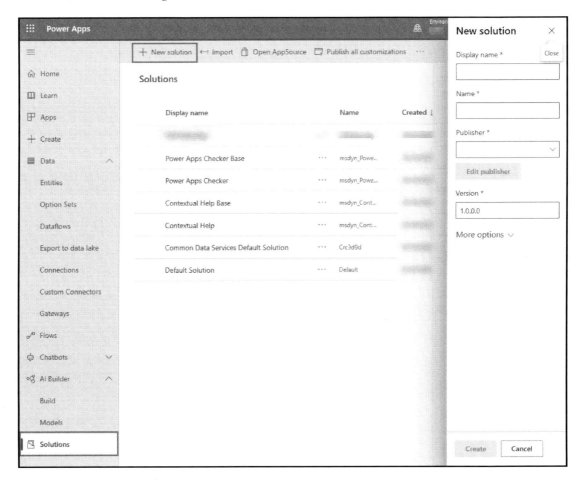

Figure 3.4 – Creating a solution

A pane will open on the right-hand side as shown in the previous screenshot. When creating solutions, start by specifying the following fields:

- **Display name**
- **Name**
- **Publisher**
- **Version**

Name defaults to **Display name**, with all spaces and special characters removed. The name cannot be changed once the solution has been created.

The **Version** number helps you track where your changes have been deployed to each of your environments. This is especially useful if you have separate environments for development, staging, test, training, and production.

The version number is four parts separated by decimal points: `major.minor.build.revision`. When you export a solution, the version number is appended to the filename. The version number is incremented automatically when you export or clone a solution.

We will cover a lot more about using solutions in `Chapter 20`, *Application Life Cycle Management*.

Once you have created a solution, you can add the various components of the CDS and apps to this solution that you want to customize. There are over 30 types of components that can be included in a solution.

Components

Components are the names collectively given to the individual items that you can customize in the CDS. You can add existing components to your solution and edit them, or you can create new components from within your solution.

Some of the more common components that you include in a solution are as follows:

- Apps
- Entities
- Dashboards
- Option sets
- Site map

- Security roles
- Web resources
- .NET assemblies
- Email templates

An entity contains its properties, fields, relationships, forms, business rules, charts, and alternate keys. These are known as entity assets. You can include an entity in a solution with all its assets, or you can select a subset of the assets to add to the solution.

 You should only include components and assets in your solution that you have changed or plan to change. Keeping solutions small helps to reduce errors, accelerates customization, and improves export and import performance.

 Solutions cannot contain data records; a solution can only hold customized components.

After you have created a solution, there are several operations that you can perform on the solution and its components.

Solution operations

Within a solution, there are various operations that can be performed on components and the solution itself.

The following is a list of the operations available within a solution:

Operation	Description
New	Creates a new component of the type selected. The new component will inherit the prefix of the associated publisher.
Add existing	Adds an existing component to the solution.
Edit	Edits an existing component in the solution.
Add subcomponents	Selects assets of the selected entity (fields, forms, and views) and include them in the solution.
Remove	Removes the component from your solution but does not delete it from the environment.

Delete	Removes the component from your solution and deletes it from the environment. Note that system components cannot be deleted. A component that another component is dependent upon cannot be deleted.
Export	Exports the solution. A `ZIP` file is created containing a set of `XML` files.
Import	Imports a solution into your environment. Allows you to select to solution `ZIP` file.
Add the required components	Adds all components that the selected component is dependent upon.
Publish	Publishes the selected component(s).
Publish all customizations	Publishes all components in the solution.
Clone a patch	Creates a patch solution. This will be explained in `Chapter 20`, *Application Lifecycle Management*.
Clone solution	Creates a new version of the solution. This will be explained in `Chapter 20`, *Application Lifecycle Management*.
Export translations	Creates a `ZIP` file containing all the text for display names, messages, and option set labels to be translated.
Import translations	Imports a `ZIP` file containing the translated text for display names, messages, and option set labels.
Managed properties	This action lists the managed properties settings for the component.
Show dependencies	Displays a list of all components that are dependent upon the selected component. If you try and delete a component that has dependencies, this list will be displayed.

Now that you understand how to create solutions, create, and edit components, we can now examine one of the main components – the entities in the data model.

Changing the data model

The CDS data store in your environment will contain a standard set of entities. Which, and how many, entities will depend on whether you included any Dynamics 365 apps.

It will be rare that the entities provided will meet your business requirements, and you will need to add to the data model provided.

In this section, we will look at creating entities, relationships, and fields to create the data model to support your app. We will look at the options for creating these and how to create and edit these components.

The first step is to decide on the entities, relationships, and fields you require. This is known as **data modeling**.

Data modeling

Data modeling is the process of identifying entities, fields, and relationships. The solution architect is responsible for defining the data model. A functional consultant may assist in the data modeling process. Data modeling is a skill and is something you get a lot better at with experience.

One of the key activities in the initial stages of your project is to create a high-level **Entity Relationship Diagram** (**ERD**) showing the entities and their relationships. An ERD helps the project team and business stakeholders understand the data in your system and how it relates to the other data.

Data modeling sounds simple, but it is anything but simple. At a base level, it involves identifying the reuse of existing entities, identifying new entities, determining the ordinality and cardinality of relationships between entities, and choosing fields and their data types. You will use techniques such as data normalization to help guide you in building your ERD.

You need to verify that your ERD supports all your reporting requirements, that your end-to-end processing of data can be handled by the data model, and that the system will not be overly complex because of your data model. You will get better at data modeling, and find it easier, with experience.

The following diagram is an example of an ERD for a simple requirement for an organization that manages the rental of floors within buildings and needs to track how much space is occupied in their buildings:

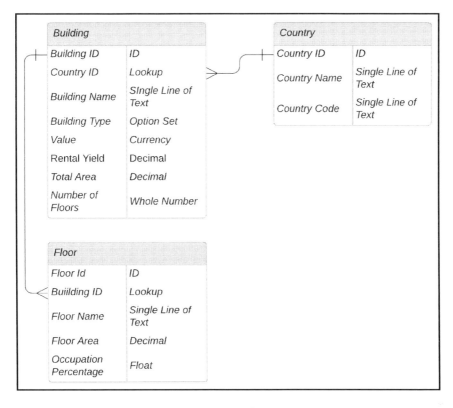

Figure 3.5 – Example of an ERD

The ERD in *Figure 3.5* shows three entities – **Building, Country**, and **Floor**, as rectangles. For each entity, its fields are listed with their data type. There is a one-to-many relationship between Country and Building, and another one-to-many relationship between Building and Floor.

 Microsoft Visio is an appropriate tool in which to build the ERD for your entity-relationship model.

There are several key decisions to be made when data modeling:

- Should you use a CDM entity or create a custom entity?
- Determine the cardinality of each relationship: one-to-many, many-to-one, or many-many.

- Should many-to-many relationships be resolved by creating a custom intersect entity?
- Should reference data be held in option sets or in entities?
- Should a custom entity be an activity entity?
- Should external data be integrated, or can you use virtual entities?

Understanding the data model is important for a functional consultant. The tools in the Power Platform do not allow you to visualize the data model. A functional consultant should be able to draw the ERD. You should use whatever you have available to create an ERD:

- Paper and pen
- A whiteboard
- Microsoft Visio
- Third-party tools, such as Lucidchart
- XrmToolBox

XrmToolBox (https://www.xrmtoolbox.com) is a set of tools for the Power Platform created and managed by the community. There are two tools in XrmToolBox for generating an ERD, one tool that generates a Visio diagram, and another tool that creates an image like this:

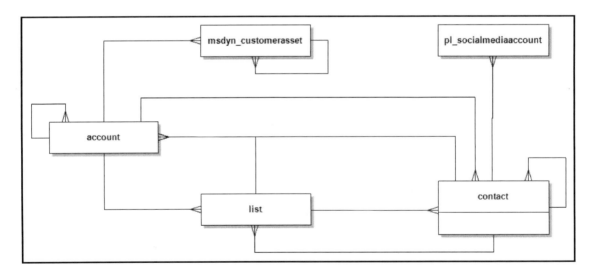

Figure 3.6 – ERD generated by XRMToolBox

Once you have identified your new entities, you can create them.

Entities

Entities represent objects or things of interest. These can be physical things such as buildings and products, or more abstract things, such as orders and projects. Entities have the following properties:

- A general type or class, such as `building` or `country`
- Instances of that type; `France` and `India` are instances of `country`
- Attributes, such as name and ISO country code
- Relationships – describes links to other entities, such as *this building is located in this country*; *this country has these buildings*

Entities are used to model and manage business data. Conceptually, an entity is like a database table, and the entity attributes correspond to the table columns. Creating an entity record is like adding a row to a database table.

Entities are the key building blocks of the CDS. In the CDS, an entity is more than just a database table with columns and relationships. An entity contains other components to support applications. The components of an entity are as follows:

- Fields
- Relationships
- Forms
- Views
- Keys
- Charts
- Business rules

Plus, there are properties for entities that affect both functionality and the user interface.

With other platforms, a developer will first create the database tables and attributes, add the foreign key attributes and constraints, develop the data access layer, then create the business object layer, and finally build the user interface layer.

In the CDS, it is vastly different; you create an entity and the Power Platform creates the database table and attributes, adds the entity to the data access layer, adds the entity to the business object layer, and creates a basic user interface for the entity, all automatically.

Entities are created from solutions in the Power Apps Maker portal.

Creating entities

To create a new entity, you edit your solution, click on **+ New**, and, from the drop-down list, select **Entity**, as shown in the following screenshot:

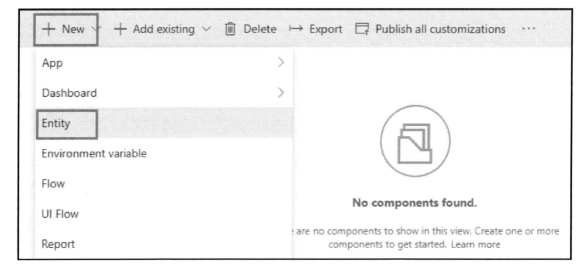

Figure 3.7 – Creating an entity

A pane will open on the right-hand side, as shown in the following screenshot:

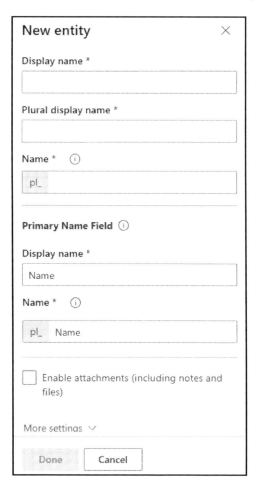

Figure 3.8 – Entity properties

When creating an entity, start by specifying the following fields:

- **Display name**: The name of the entity.
- **Plural display name**: This is used in the user interface in navigation and views.
- **Name**: This is the internal name used for the entity. It will have the publisher's prefix.
- **Primary Name Field**: The name of a text field used to represent records for the entity in the app user interface.

To create the entity, click on **Done**.

Name defaults to **Display name** with all spaces and special characters removed. The name cannot be changed once the entity has been created.

The entity will be provisioned in the background and can take several minutes. When complete, you will see several fields, relationships, views, and forms created, as shown in the following screenshot:

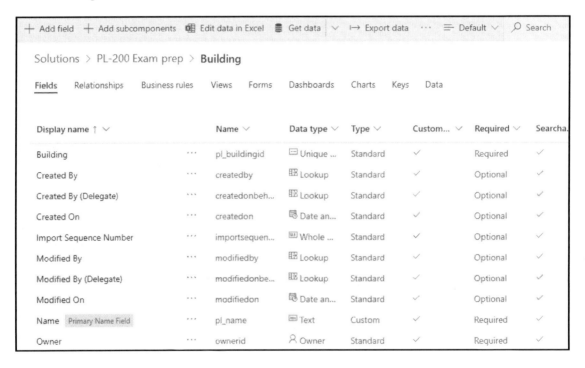

Figure 3.9 – Newly created entity

An entity has many properties. One that cannot be changed after the entity has been created is the type of entity.

Entity types

When creating an entity, you can specify the type of entity, as shown in the following screenshot:

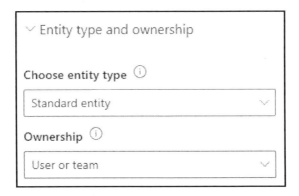

Figure 3.10 – Entity type and ownership

There are three types of entity that you can select when creating an entity:

- **Standard entity**
- **Activity entity**
- **Virtual entity**

Standard entities are custom entities where you can store data and add to the navigation in model-drivel apps. Most entities you create will be standard entities.

 You cannot change the entity type after creating the entity.

Activity entities

Activity entities are used to store interactions such as phone calls, tasks, and appointments. There is a set of activity entities in a CDS database. These entities share the same set of fields and share the same security privileges. Activity entities appear in the timeline on model-driven app forms.

You should create an activity entity if no standard activity entity for your required community type is available.

Virtual entities

Virtual entities allow you to create the entity and fields in the CDS, but then use an external data source to store the data. To the user, the data appears in their apps like any other data. The alternative is to create an integration, which can be difficult, time-consuming, and expensive.

There are several limitations associated with using virtual entities, the most important being that virtual entities are read-only and users will not be able to create or update records for a virtual entity.

Entity ownership

When creating an entity, you can specify the ownership type for the entity. There are two types of ownership that you can select when creating an entity:

- **User or team**
- **Organization**

If an entity is a **User or team** owned, then records will have an **Owner lookup** field. This means that the record can be assigned to a user or a team. A **User or team** owned entity means that you can employ the security model described in *Chapter 8, Security*, to control access to subsets of the records in the entity.

If an entity is **Organization** owned, then there is no owner field and security can only control access to all the records in the entity. You cannot change the ownership type after creating the entity.

If you are unsure as to which ownership type to use, choose **User or team** as you can hide the owner field and configure security so that the entity operates like an **Organization** owned entity.

Other entity properties

There are other properties for the entity that you can configure. These properties can affect the user interface in model-driven apps, such as controlling a button on the action bar or adding functionality. Throughout the rest of this book, we will enable some of these properties when investigating the functionality of the Power Platform. For example, in the next chapter, the **Duplicate detection property** will be *enabled*.

In the Maker portal, the entity properties are grouped into four sections:

- **Entity type and ownership**: These two properties were discussed previously in this chapter.
- **Collaboration**: This section includes many options, including connections and queues.
- **Create and update settings**: This section includes duplicate detection, quick create forms, and change tracking.
- **Offline**: This section is for offline access with mobile devices and the Outlook client.

 Some properties have a dagger symbol, †, next to them. The dagger symbol signifies that once enabled, the property cannot be disabled. This typically indicates that enabling the property adds fields or creates relationships for the entity.

There are some entity properties that are not available in the Maker portal. You need to switch to classic to set the following properties:

- Auditing
- Color for the entity
- Icons for the entity
- Entity level controls for editable grids and calendar layout

Entities on their own are not especially useful. The real power of entities comes when they are related to other entities. In your ERD, you defined the relationships between entities.

Relationships

When working with the CDS, you need to try to keep information about different types of data in separate entities. This is known as **data normalization**. Relationships define how records are related to one another in the CDS.

Each entity has a primary key to provide a unique reference to the records in the entity. In the CDS, the primary key is a **Global Unique Identifier** (**GUID**) that is generated automatically by the CDS when a record is created. Relationships are created by adding a reference to the primary key. This is known as a **foreign key**. In the CDS, relationships are created by using a field on one entity to hold the foreign key value. This foreign key is a pointer to the primary key on the other entity.

Two types of relationship are supported in the CDS:

- **One-to-many (1:N)**: A building has many floors, but each floor is for one building.
- **Many-to-many (N:N)**: Each contact attends several events, and each event is attended by several contacts.

One-to-one relationships are not supported in the CDS.

Microsoft uses the terms *Primary entity* and *Related entity*, in preference to *Parent* and *Child* or *Master* and *Detail*, terms you may be more familiar with.

A many-to-one (N:1) relationship is a one-to-many relationship when viewed from the other entity in the relationship. You can either create a one-to-many relationship from the primary entity (the *one* end of the relationship) or create a many-to-one relationship from the related entity (the *many* end of the relationship).

In other systems, a developer will create the foreign key fields and relationships in the database and then add in data and business logic. In the CDS, relationships are created and edited using the Maker portal and the Power Platform creates the foreign key and relationship for you.

In the CDS, foreign keys appear as lookup fields. In fact, creating a lookup field for an entity creates a new many-to-one relationship between the two entities.

It is recommended that you create relationships rather than create lookup fields as you will need to edit the resulting relationship to configure its properties to the defaults that apply when creating lookup fields. You are not able to set relationship properties when creating a lookup field.

We will now look at how to create a one-to-many relationship.

Creating a one-to-many relationship

To create a new one-to-many relationship, you edit your solution, select the entity, click on the **Relationships** tab, click on **+ New relationship**, and, from the drop-down list, select **One-to-many**, as shown in the following screenshot:

Figure 3.11 – Add relationship

A pane will open on the right-hand side, as shown in the following screenshot:

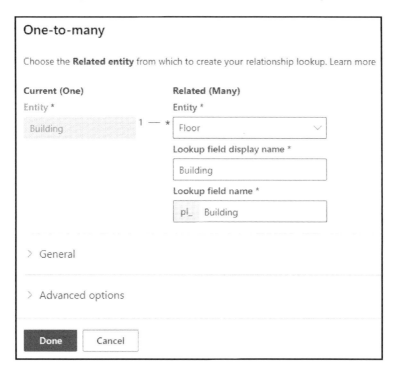

Figure 3.12 – Select related entity

The current entity is shown as the **One** end of the relationship. When creating a relationship, specify the following fields:

- **Related (Many)**: The entity you wish to create the relationship to.
- **Lookup field display name**: This will default to the name of the current entity.
- **Lookup field name**: This is the internal name used for the lookup field. It will have the publisher's prefix.

To create the relationship, click on **Done**.

After creating the relationship, navigate to the entity you selected as **Related** and verify that a lookup field has been created. You should consider setting the requirement level for the lookup field.

The lookup field is not automatically added to the related entity form. You must remember to add the lookup field to forms and views.

Behaviors and cascading rules

In a one-to-many relationship, you can control how the relationship behavior cascades to records in the related entity when records in the primary entity have actions such as assign, share, and delete performed on them.

When creating and editing a relationship, you can configure the type of behavior, as shown in the following screenshot:

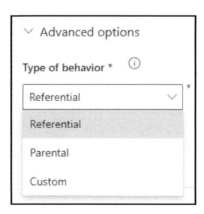

Figure 3.13 – Relationship options

The type of behavior can be set to one of the following:

- **Parental**: Using this option means that for operations performed on a record in the parent entity, the same operations are performed on the child records in the related entity. For example, if the parent record is deleted, all the child records are also deleted.
- **Referential**: Using this option means that any operations performed on a record in the parent entity do not affect the child records in the related entity. This can lead to orphaned related records with no parent. If you choose the **Referential** option, a separate dropdown for **Delete** is shown with the options **Remove Link** and **Restrict**. The **Restrict** option prevents a parental record from being deleted if there are any related records.
- **Custom**: You can configure the cascade options for each operation, including **Assign**, **Share**, and **Delete**.

If you are unsure as to what behavior to choose, the **Referential** with **Restrict** option is the safest. These options maintain the referential integrity of your data.

Mappings

Mappings streamline data entry when you create new records that are associated with another record. When two entities are in a one-to-many relationship, you can create new related entity records from the primary entity form.

Mappings let you set default values for a record that is created within the context of another record. This can save a lot of time when you are entering data and helps to reduce errors.

When the user creates a new related record from within the context of a primary record, mapped data from the primary entity record is copied to the form for the new related entity record. You control what data is copied by adding new mappings in the relationship between the two entities.

Mapping only applies if a record is created within the context of the primary entity form. Mappings are not used if you create a record from the main application navigation and then select the parent record in a lookup field.

Users can make changes to the mapped fields before saving the record. Subsequent changes to the data in the primary record are not synchronized to the related record. This is a once-only copy to aid data entry.

Editing the mappings is not yet supported in the Maker portal and you will need to switch to the classic setting to be able to add or remove the mappings.

Creating a many-to-many relationship

To create a new many-to-many relationship, you edit your solution, select the entity, click on the **Relationships** tab, click on **+ New relationship**, and, from the drop-down list, select **Many-to-many**, as shown in *Figure 3.11*. A pane will open where you can select the other entity for the relationship.

When you create a many-to-many relationship, a hidden intersect entity is created to hold the data for the relationship.

Many-to-many relationships suffer from some important limitations:

- You cannot describe the relationship by adding fields.
- Classic workflow and Power Automate flows cannot be triggered when records are associated.

Instead of creating a many-to-many relationship, you should consider either of the following options:

- Creating a custom entity with two many-to-one relationships
- Using connections

Connections

Connections are an alternative to creating relationships between entities. Connections are a special type of many-to-many relationship. To use connections, an entity must be enabled for connections, as shown in the following screenshot:

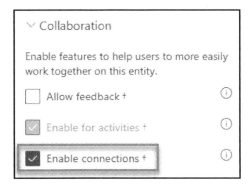

Figure 3.14 – Enabling an entity for connections

Once enabled, a user can connect a record in the entity to a record in another entity that is also enabled for connections using the **Connect** button in the action bar of a model-driven app form, as shown here:

Figure 3.15 – The Connect button in a model-driven app form

Clicking on **To Another** opens the connection from where a user can select the other record. The following screenshot shows connecting to a custom entity for a social media account:

Figure 3.16 – Connection form

When a record is selected, a user can optionally select a connection role. Connection roles describe the relationship. In *Figure 3.16*, you may have roles for the administrator of the social media account, followers of the social media account, or which other accounts the social media account follows.

Configuring connection roles

Connection roles need to be configured before they can be used. Clicking on **Connection roles** in the **Power Platform admin center** opens a window, showing the list of connection roles in the environment, as shown in the following screenshot:

Figure 3.17 – Connection roles

There is a set of connection roles that are created when the environment is created or when a Dynamics 365 app is installed. You can use these roles or create roles to meet your requirements.

Consider deactivating the existing roles and creating your own connection roles that suit your requirements.

To create a new role, click on the **New** button and the following screen will appear:

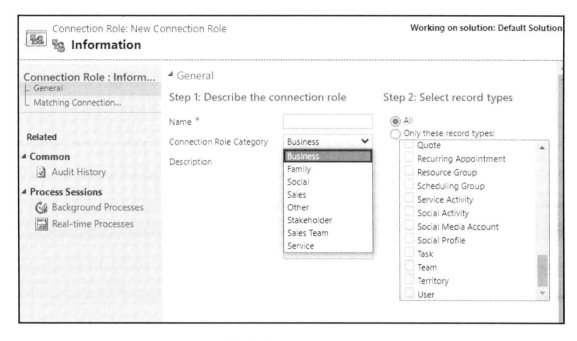

Figure 13.18 – New connection role form

The form has the following fields that should be completed:

- **Name**: This is the name the user will see when selecting connection roles.
- **Connection Role Category**: This is used to group connection roles.
- **Select record types**: Choose which entities the role can be used with. You should select only those entities that are relevant to the role.

Connection role category is a global option set that you can edit and add items to.

Each connection role can have one or more matching connection roles. The matching connection role describes the relationship when looking from the perspective of the other record in the relationship.

In the following example screenshot, the **Followed by** connection role for the social media account has matching roles for **Follower** and **Administrator**:

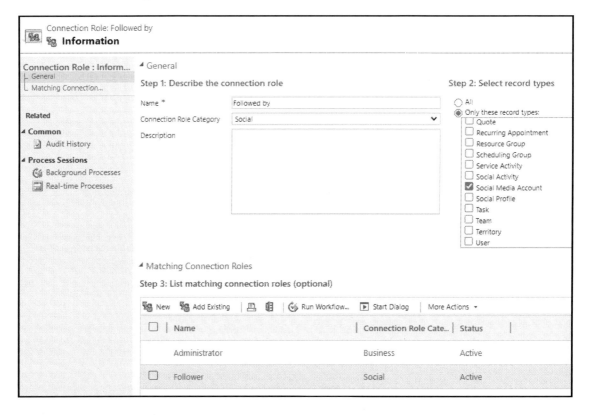

Figure 3.19 – Connection role with matching connection roles

It is best practice for each role to have at least one matching connection role. This makes it easier for users to select the correct roles.

 Connection roles can be created in, or added to, a solution.

There are privileges for connections and connection roles in security roles. A user needs both the **Append** and **Append To** privileges to create connections, as shown in the following screenshot:

Figure 3.20 – Privileges required to create a connection

A manager or administrator will need to **Create**, **Write**, **Append**, and **Append To** privileges on **Connection Role** to manage the list of roles, create new roles, and add matching connection roles.

An entity needs fields to hold individual items of data. Fields are created from solutions in the Power Apps Maker portal.

Fields

In the CDS, fields define individual data items that can be used to store data in an entity.

You can use the Maker portal to edit system fields and to create, edit, or delete custom fields.

With other systems, a developer will first create a column in the database table, then add the attribute to the data access layer, then add the attribute to the business object layer, and then to the user interface layer. In the CDS, it is different; you create a field, and the Power Platform adds a column in the database table, the attribute into the data access layer, and the field into the business object layer, all automatically. When added to a form, a field becomes a control. When added to a view, a field is a column.

This power makes it very quick to build applications on the CDS. But with this power comes a compromise; with the CDS, your data layer is your business layer, and your business layer is your user interface layer. You cannot create new data types. You cannot combine fields from multiple entities into a single user interface component through the tools provided. You will see later in the book how the user interface and process capabilities of the Power Platform have been enhanced to reduce clicks and hide the complexity of the data model from users.

Data types

Fields can only store specific types of data. The CDS supports a wide variety of data types, including numeric values, text, dates, images, and files.

> Review the list of data types at `https://docs.microsoft.com/powerapps/` `maker/common-data-service/types-of-fields`.

You select the data type when creating a field. You cannot change the data type once you have created the field, so you should make sure that you are consistent with your choice of data types across your fields and entities. You will not be able to perform operations such as calculations or comparisons on two fields if they are of different data types.

Creating a field

To create a new field relationship, you edit your solution, select the entity, click on the **Fields** tab, and then click on **+ Add field**, as shown in the following screenshot:

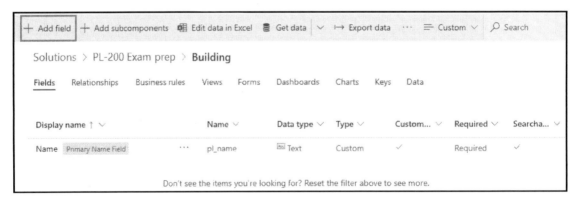

Figure 3.21 – Add field

A pane will open on the right-hand side, as shown in the following screenshot:

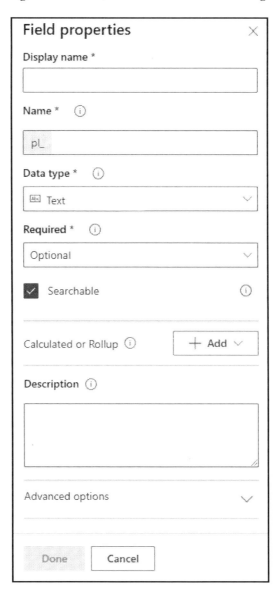

Figure 3.22 – Field properties

When creating a field, start by specifying the following properties:

- **Display name**: The name of the field.
- **Name**: This is the internal name used for the field. It will have the publisher's prefix.
- **Data type**: Choose from the list of data types.
- **Required**: Whether the field must be entered when a record is created.

 Depending on the **Data type** selected, other properties are displayed; for example, text fields have a maximum length and numeric fields have minimum and maximum values.

To create the field, click on **Done**.

Option sets

Option sets are one of the data types available. An option set defines a list of options. When an **Option Set** is displayed on a form, it uses a drop-down list control.

An option in an **Option Set** is a key-value pair, a text label, and an integer value. The integer value is stored in the field on the record and the label is stored in metadata.

There are two types of option sets: **Global** and **Local**. **Global** option sets are separate components in your solution that you can reuse on multiple entities and fields. **Local** option sets are defined for one field. The Maker Portal defaults to creating global option sets.

Calculated fields

You may need to perform a calculation using one or more fields on your entity. You can create a calculated field that contains a calculation using fields from the entity and fields from entities where there is a many-to-one relationship.

When you create a field, it is a simple field. This means you can enter data into it. You can create a calculated field by clicking on **+ Add | + Calculation** in *Figure 3.22*. A new window will appear, as shown in the following screenshot:

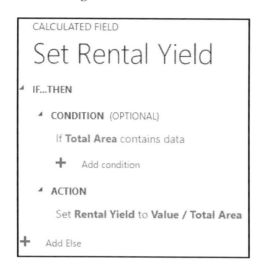

Figure 3.23 – CALCULATED FIELD

In this window, you can optionally add a condition to control whether the calculation is performed, and then add an action to perform the calculation. This example is mathematical. You can also concatenate strings or perform calculations on dates. There are a series of date functions that you can use.

 Calculated fields are recalculated when the record is saved.

Rollup fields

Rollup fields contain aggregate values calculated from related records in a one-to-many relationship.

You can create a rollup field by clicking on **+ Add** | **+ Rollup** in *Figure 3.22*. A new window will appear, as shown in the following screenshot:

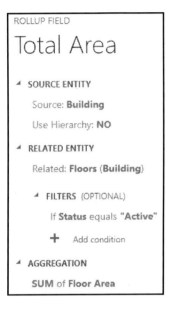

Figure 3.24 – ROLLUP FIELD

In this window, you select the related entity from a list of entities that have a one-to-many relationship with the source entity, specify which records you want to aggregate by using the filter, choose the aggregation (SUM, MIN, MAX, COUNT, and AVG), and choose the field for the aggregate.

 Rollup fields are only updated every hour.

Alternate keys

The primary key for records in the CDS is a GUID. This GUID is set when the record is created, either by a developer setting it explicitly or by the Power Platform generating it.

The CDS allows for alternate keys to be defined. An alternate key allows external systems that need to read and write records to efficiently access the records without having to first run a query to find the GUID. For example, accounting systems often have an alphanumeric account number that uniquely identifies the account. You can set the account number field in the CDS entity to be an alternate key so that the accounting system can read and write the account using the data it holds in its own system.

Alternate keys are defined in the Maker portal in the **Keys** tab on the entity. You simply choose which fields you want to act as the alternate key.

Summary

In this chapter, we learned about the CDM, the CDS, and how to extend the data model in the CDS with entities, relationships, and fields. We also introduced solutions to manage change.

This chapter is the foundation for all further customization work. The skills you have learned will enable you to modify the data model in the CDS to meet your specific business requirements.

The contents of this chapter are foundational knowledge for the remainder of the book, and creating a data model is a key step in building your solution. The next chapter is about canvas apps. This chapter will explain the purpose of canvas apps, and how to create canvas apps using your data model.

Questions

After reading this chapter, test your knowledge with these questions. You will find the answers to these questions under `Assessments` at the end of the book:

1. How many Common Data Service databases can a Power Platform environment have?

   A) One
   B) Two
   C) Five
   D) No limit

2. What is the Common Data Model?

   A) A data store for common data
   B) A set of data definitions to aid collaboration between systems
   C) Your master data that other systems can reference
   D) An entity relationship diagram

3. You can delete any entity in the Common Data Service.

   A) True
   B) False

4. A calculated field is updated when a field it references is updated.

   A) True
   B) False

5. You can change the time schedule for the recalculation of rollup fields.

   A) True
   B) False

6. You can change the plural name of an entity after it has been created.

   A) True
   B) False

7. You are a Power Platform functional consultant. You need to document the data model. What should you create?

   A) A solution
   B) An entity relationship diagram
   C) A snapshot of the entities in the Maker portal
   D) A FetchXML builder query in XRMToolBox

Further reading

For more details on the topics covered in this chapter, please refer to the following resources:

- **Common Data Model:** `https://docs.microsoft.com/common-data-model/`
- **Common Data Service:** `https://docs.microsoft.com/powerapps/maker/common-data-service/data-platform-intro`
- **Solutions:** `https://docs.microsoft.com/powerapps/maker/common-data-service/solutions-overview`
- **Types of entity:** `https://docs.microsoft.com/powerapps/maker/common-data-service/types-of-entities`
- **Creating and editing virtual entities that contain data from an external data source:** `https://docs.microsoft.com/powerapps/maker/common-data-service/create-edit-virtual-entities`
- **Entity relationships:** `https://docs.microsoft.com/powerapps/maker/common-data-service/create-edit-entity-relationships`
- **Types of field:** `https://docs.microsoft.com/powerapps/maker/common-data-service/types-of-fields`
- **Calculated fields:** `https://docs.microsoft.com/powerapps/maker/common-data-service/define-calculated-fields`
- **Rollup fields:** `https://docs.microsoft.com/powerapps/maker/common-data-service/define-rollup-fields`
- **Alternate keys:** `https://docs.microsoft.com/powerapps/maker/common-data-service/define-alternate-keys-portal`

4
Business Rules

This chapter will explain how you can use **business rules** to validate data, perform calculations, and manipulate fields on forms, all without the need to write JavaScript code.

We will begin with an introduction to business rules, then we will look at the various actions and conditions that make up a business rule. We will then look at how to create business rules. We will look at how and when business rules are executed and how business rules work with other components of the Power Platform.

Business rules enable a non-developer to create calculated values, validate that data is correct, and change the appearance of forms at runtime in a simple click-and-point user interface.

In this chapter, we will cover the following topics:

- Introducing business rules
- Using actions in business rules
- Using conditions in business rules
- Creating and editing business rules with the visual rule designer
- Using business rules

By the end of this chapter, you will be able to create business rules, use actions and conditions, and understand when business rules are applied and how to use business rules to perform validation.

Introducing business rules

Business rules are a component of **Common Data Service** and have two purposes. The first way that business rules are used is within model-driven app forms, to change how fields are displayed. The second way that business rules are employed is at the data layer to validate data and calculate values.

There are many occasions when minor changes need to be made to the form at runtime – for example, setting a field value or hiding a field. You can control form fields in JavaScript, but this requires specialist skills. Business rules were introduced to make simple form manipulation achievable without the need for such developer skills.

Business rules have been extended further to allow you to apply business logic, both in the client app and on the data platform, without the need to write code.

The client-side logic is immediate because the rules are executed when a user opens or updates a form, while the server-side logic applies when a user, or any process, saves a record.

Business rules are created and edited from within the Power Apps maker portal and are a sub-component of an entity.

The business rules visual designer has a simple user interface, similar to the other component editors for Common Data Service. The following figure shows how the business rules visual designer looks:

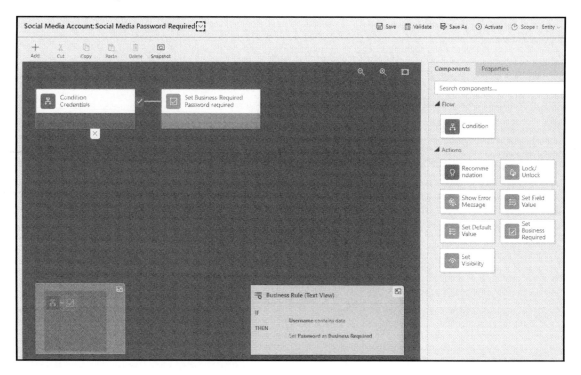

Figure 4.1 – Business rules visual designer

A business rule consists of conditions and actions. In the preceding figure, you can see the canvas, where the conditions and actions are displayed as tiles, and the right-hand pane, where you can add conditions and actions and set their properties.

Before you start creating business rules, you need to understand what you can do in a business process flow with actions.

Using actions in business rules

Business rules can perform a limited set of actions. They are as follows:

- Set the **visibility** of the field.
- Set a field to be **business required**.
- Set a field to be **read-only**.
- Set the **value** of a field.
- Set the **default value** of a field.
- Show an **error message**.
- Prompt the user with a **recommendation**.

The following screenshot shows these actions in the right-hand pane of the business rules designer:

Figure 4.2 – Actions in business rules

Each tile represents an action that you can use. You drag an action tile onto the canvas to add the action to the rule.

 Actions can only be performed on fields. You cannot use actions with any other form component, such as sections or tabs.

To use business rules effectively, you need to know what each of these actions is capable of.

Types of action

There are seven actions available in business rules. These can be grouped into three types of actions:

- **Managing the value of the field: Show Error Message, Set Field Value, and Set Default Value**
- **Controlling how a field appears on the form: Set Visibility, Lock/Unlock, and Set Business Required**
- **Prompting the user with a recommendation for a field: Recommendation**

We will examine each of these actions, in turn, starting with the validation of data with a **Show Error Message** action.

Show Error Message

You should use the **Show Error Message** action if the data within a field is not valid. The text you specify will be displayed with an error icon near the field and will also be displayed next to the save icon at the bottom of the form. The following screenshot shows how to set an error message in the **Properties** tab of the **Show Error Message** action:

Figure 4.3 – Show error message for a field

This message prevents the record from being saved. The user will need to change the data that caused the condition in the business rule to call the **Show Error Message** action.

Set Field Value

You should use the **Set Field Value** action to calculate and set the value of the field.

You choose the field to set the value for and then choose the type of calculation. There are four methods for performing a calculation:

- **Value**: Sets the value of the field to a value you enter in the business rule designer.
- **Field**: Replaces the value of the field with the value of another field.

- **Formula**: Sets the value to the result of a simple calculation. The calculation can use either a value of another field or a value you enter in the business rule designer.
- **Clear**: Removes the value from the field; it sets the value to null.

The following screenshot shows how to use a formula to calculate the **Klout** field from the product of the **Followers** and **Posts** fields:

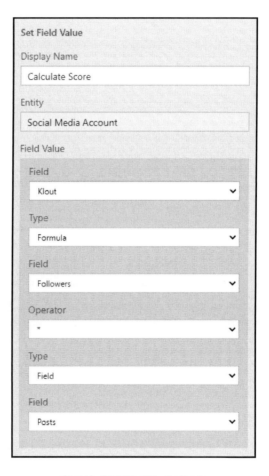

Figure 4.4 – Calculating a field with a formula

Formulas are only available for numerical and date data types. The **Formula** option is not shown for text fields.

Set Default Value

You should use **Set Default Value** to define the starting value for the field when creating a new record. The following screenshot shows how to use **Set Default Value** on a field:

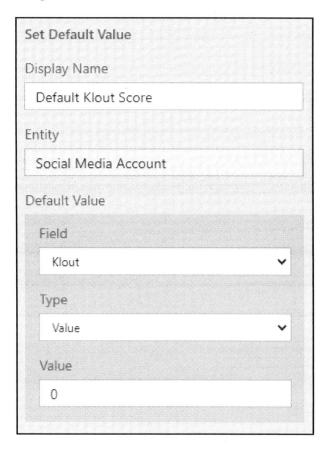

Figure 4.5 – Setting a default value on a field

The preceding screenshot shows setting a default value for the **Klout** field. If a user does not enter a value into the **Klout** field, the business rule will set its value to 0.

We will now look at the actions that change how a field appears on forms, starting with making a field required.

Set Business Required

You should use **Set Business Required** to change the requirement level for a field. As shown in the following figure, the options to change the requirement level are **Not Business Required** and **Business Required**:

Figure 4.6 – Setting a field as business required

The preceding screenshot shows how to set the password field to be mandatory. Making a field business required makes the field mandatory. This means that if the field does not have a value, the form cannot be saved.

 When editing a field, you can set the field as **Required**, **Recommended**, or **Optional**. **Not Business Required** is the same as the **Optional** setting. There is no equivalent to **Recommended** in business rules.

If a field is changed to business required, you should also ensure that the field is not hidden using the **Set Visibility** action.

Set Visibility

You should use **Set Visibility** to change whether a field is displayed in the form or not. As shown in the following figure, the options to change visibility are **Yes** and **No**:

Figure 4.7 – Hiding a field

The preceding screenshot shows how to hide a field. Setting the field to **No** will hide the field on the form.

Locking or unlocking a field

You should use **Lock/Unlock** to change whether the field is enabled in the form. *Enabled* means that a user can change the value in the field. If you disable a field, it is read-only, and the user cannot click into the field or change its value.

As shown in the following figure, the options to change visibility are **Lock** and **Unlock**:

Figure 4.8 – Setting a field as read-only

The preceding screenshot shows how you can set a field as read-only. The final action, **Recommendation**, provides a suggestion to the user when entering data in forms.

Recommendation

Recommendations are a little bit different than the other actions. A recommendation prompts the user to enter a value in a field. You would use the **Recommendation** action to guide users when they fill out a form. It displays a suggestion bubble with text next to the field with an **Apply** button.

The following screenshot shows a recommendation as it appears to the user:

Figure 4.9 – A recommendation on a form

The following screenshot shows how to set up the recommendation:

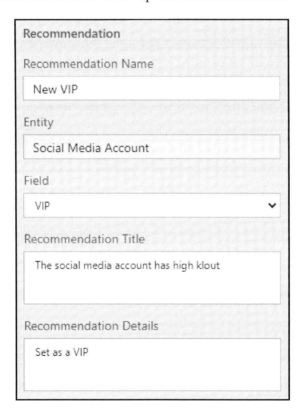

Figure 4.10 – Recommendation properties

Along with the recommendation is an action that will be performed if the user accepts the recommendation. In the following screenshot, a set value is used to set the **VIP** field to **Yes**:

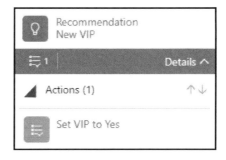

Figure 4.11 – A set value action for a recommendation

 When you add a recommendation action, a single set value action is added automatically.

Now that you are aware of all the actions, we can combine these actions together to form a business rule.

Combining actions in a business rule

You are not limited to single actions; you can perform multiple actions to achieve your goal:

Figure 4.12 – Multiple actions

The preceding figure shows three actions performed together.

It is common for you to perform the same set of actions on a field, for example, as follows:

- Set Business Required
- Show field
- Unlock field

Actions performed by a business rule on a field in the form will also perform the same action on the corresponding data step in a business process flow.

Now that you are aware of all the actions, we will look at the conditions that you will use to determine when to apply your actions.

Using conditions in business rules

In business rules, conditions are if-then-else statements. If the statement is true, the business rule branches to the tile to the right of the condition, as shown in the following screenshot. If false, the business rule branches to the tile under the condition, as shown in the following screenshot:

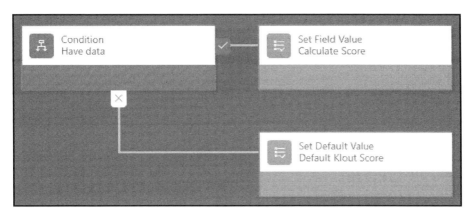

Figure 4.13 – Condition in a business rule

Conditions control the logic of the business rule and determine which actions are applied. Conditions are checked when the form loads and whenever any field referenced within the condition changes. You can choose three different types of conditions:

- **Field**: Compares the value of a field with another.
- **Value**: Compares the value of a field with a value you enter in the business rule designer.
- **Formula**: Compares the result of a simple calculation. The calculation may use either a value in another field or a value you enter in the business rule designer.

The following screenshot shows how to compare a field with a value:

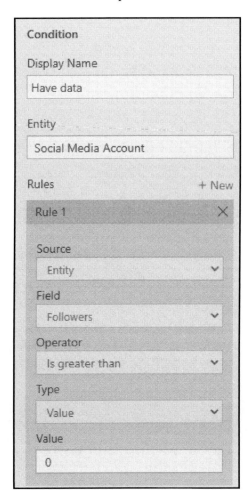

Figure 4.14 – Properties for a condition in a business rule

You can add more than one rule to a condition by clicking on the **+ New** button, shown at the top right of the following figure:

Figure 4.15 – Multiple rules in a condition

The rule logic can be either AND or OR. You cannot combine AND and OR in the same condition.

Now that you understand the components involved in business rules, we will see how to create a business rule.

Using the visual rule designer to create and edit business rules

Business rules are created and edited from the **Business rules** tab for an entity in the Power Apps maker portal. The following screenshot shows the **Business rules** tab for an entity in the maker portal:

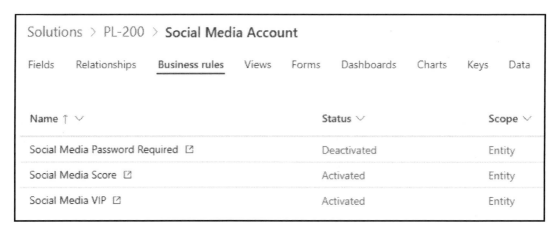

Figure 4.16 – Business rules in the maker portal

The preceding screenshot shows the business rules that have been created for the social media account entity, whether the rules have been enabled or not, and the scope of the rules.

You can also use the solution explorer in the classic portal to create and edit business rules.

Finding business rules in the classic portal

In the classic solution explorer, there are four ways that you can view, create, or edit business rules:

- **Entity**: From the business rules node
- **Field**: From the business rules node
- **Form Editor**: From the Business Rules Explorer
- **Field Property in Form Editor**: From the **Business rules** tab

The following screenshot shows the business rules node for an entity:

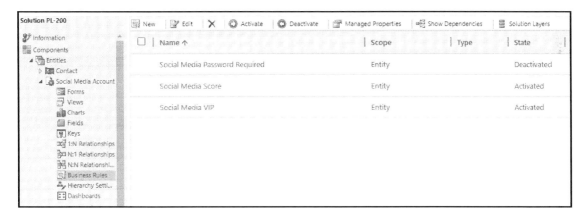

Figure 4.17 – Business rules in the solution explorer

The preceding screenshot shows the business rules that have been created for the social media account entity, whether the rules have been enabled or not, and the scope of the rules. All business rules are shown for the entity.

The following screenshot shows the business rules node for a field:

Figure 4.18 – Business rules in the field editor

The preceding figure shows the business rules that have been created for the **Klout** field, whether the rules have been enabled or not, and the scope of the rules. For fields, only the business rules that reference the field are listed.

Creating a business rule is straightforward and we will look at this next.

Creating a business rule

Business rules are created without using code. You can either drag and drop conditions and actions or use point and click using the business rule visual designer tool. You use this tool to create and edit business rules.

Business rules are created and edited using a browser. Although you can still use the classic portal, the exam and this book use the Power Apps maker portal: `https://make.powerapps.com`.

To create a business rule, you should navigate to the **Business rules** tab for an entity, and click on **Add business rule** in the action bar. The following figure shows how the business rule visual designer looks:

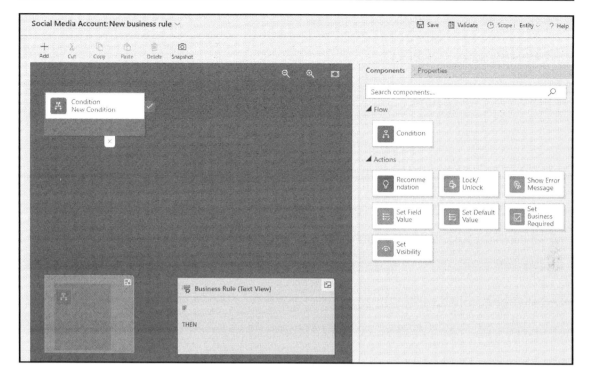

Figure 4.19 – Business rule visual designer

After you click on **Create**, the business rule designer is opened. The designer has the following:

- A toolbar on the left to add components to, and remove components from, the business rule
- A toolbar at the top to perform actions on the business rule as a whole, such as save
- A **Components** pane to add components to the business rule
- A **Properties** pane to set names and other properties for components
- A central canvas where you place components
- A mini-map at the bottom left to allow you to see the entire business rule
- A text or code view of the business rule logic and actions
- An empty condition called **New Condition**

You can use both the toolbar and the **Components** pane to add components to the business process flow. You click and point with the toolbar, and drag and drop with the **Components** pane.

A business rule must have a condition as it's the first tile. That condition is created for you. But before you start, you should name your business rule.

Setting the name of the rule

The name of the rule is set by clicking on the down chevron at the top of the screen. This exposes the business rule name as description fields, as shown in the following figure:

Figure 4.20 – Business rule name

You should enter a name for the rule that summarizes its purpose. You can also add a description to explain what the rule does and why.

Adding conditions to a business rule

Every business rule starts with a condition. When you create a new business rule, a condition is added automatically. To add more conditions to your business rule, you drag the **Condition** component from the **Components** tab to any plus sign in the designer canvas, as shown in the following figure:

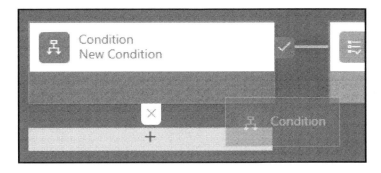

Figure 4.21 – Adding a condition to a plus sign

To set properties for the condition, click the **Condition** component in the designer canvas, and then set the properties in the **Properties** tab on the right side of the screen.

To add an additional clause (an AND or OR) to the condition, click **+ New** in the **Properties** tab to create a new rule, and then set the properties for that rule. In the **Rule Logic** field, you can specify whether to add the new rule as an AND or an OR.

As you set the properties, the designer creates a textual representation of the condition at the bottom of the **Properties** tab. Use this view to check that your logic is correct. The following screenshot shows the text view for a condition:

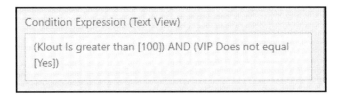

Figure 4.22 – Condition expression as text

When you have completed the properties for the condition, click **Apply**. To remove a condition, select the condition and choose the **Delete** button.

 For a developer to create the same conditions and actions in JavaScript, it would take significantly more time and effort to create, edit, and test.

Once you have added your conditions, you can add your actions.

Adding actions to a business rule

A business rule must have at least one action. No actions are added automatically when a rule is created.

To add actions to your rule, drag one of the actions from the **Components** tab to a plus sign in the designer canvas. Drag the action to a plus sign next to a checkmark if you want the business rule to take that action when the condition is met, or to a plus sign next to an **x** if you want the business rule to take that action if the condition is not met.

You can add an action in two ways. The first method is to drag the action tile from the **Components** pane and drop it over the indicated area to a plus sign, as shown in the following figure:

Figure 4.23 – Adding an action by drag and drop

The other method is to click on the **+ Add** button in the action bar, select the action, and then click the plus sign in the canvas where you want to add the action. To set properties for the action, click the **Action** component in the designer canvas, and then set the properties in the **Properties** tab. When you have completed the properties for the action, click **Apply**.

If you do not click **Apply** in **Properties**, your setting will not be saved. No warning is provided.

Saving the business rule

Click on the **Save** button in the toolbar to save your changes. If there are any errors in your rule – for example, you have not completed the **Properties** pane for a condition or an action – you will not be able to save. The following screenshot shows an example of an error message:

Figure 4.24 – Validation errors

The previous screenshot shows that the rule has two errors. The errors will also be indicated on the canvas with the tiles in error highlighted.

You need to correct the errors first before saving.

Validating the business rule

You can click on **Validate** in the toolbar to check for errors and to see whether you have corrected them:

Figure 4.25 – No validation errors

The previous screenshot shows that there are no errors in the rule and that you can now save the rule.

 Clicking on **Save** performs a validation prior to saving, so clicking on **Validate** is not necessary.

Setting the scope of the business rule

You must ensure that you have set the scope of your business rule. Scope controls under what circumstances the business rule is executed.

The following screenshot shows how to set the scope:

Figure 4.26 – Business rule scope

The previous screenshot shows the scope set to **Entity**. This is the default option if creating in the maker portal. If you use the classic portal to create your business rule, then it may default to a different option depending on where you create the rule.

 Always check that you have set the scope. If you do not set the scope correctly, then your rule may not be applied. If in doubt, set the scope to **Entity**; the rule will then be applied in all circumstances.

We will examine the options for scope later in this chapter.

Copying business rules

You will often need to create similar rules for different fields. It can be quicker to copy a rule and make changes than to create a new rule from scratch.

There is no copy rule option. Instead, you edit an existing rule and use the **Save As** button.

 The **Save As** function creates a copy of the business name with **Copy of** prefixing the name of the new rule. You should first rename the copied rule.

Business rules are linked to an entity. You cannot copy business rules from one entity to another.

Documenting the business rule

The snapshot button in the action bar creates an image file in **Portable Network Graphic (PNG)** format. The image created shows the condition and action tiles from the canvas. The following figure shows how to take a snapshot:

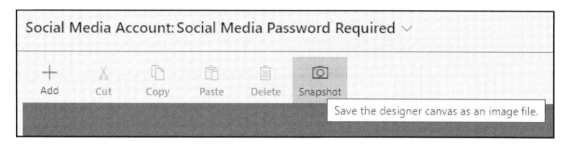

Figure 4.27 – Taking a snapshot

The next screenshot is an example image generated by clicking on the **Snapshot** button:

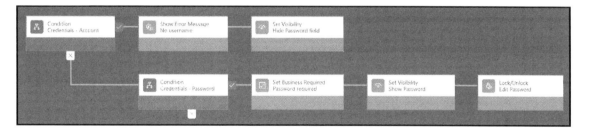

Figure 4.28 – An example snapshot

Snapshots such as the one in the preceding figure are useful for documenting business rules or for discussing the business rule with others in a workshop as they show the logic and actions in a visual representation that everyone can understand.

Snapshots show the entire canvas, but when you are editing a business rule, you only see a small part of the rule. The mini-map can help you see the entire process.

Navigating complex rules with the mini-map

You can use the mini-map at the bottom left of the canvas to navigate quickly to different parts of the process. This is useful when you have a complex process with many conditions and actions, which requires you to scroll the canvas.

The next figure shows a mini-map for a business rule:

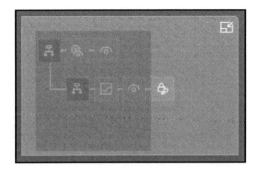

Figure 4.29 – Mini-map

In the previous screenshot, the area that is darker is the part of the process shown in the canvas. You can drag that area to the right to see the action that is not currently shown. You will commonly have business rules with many more actions, and the mini-map is invaluable when editing such rules.

Viewing the structure and logic of a business rule with code view

As you add conditions and actions, the designer creates a textual representation of the conditions and actions at the bottom of the canvas. This provides a readable view of the logic. You should use this view to check that your rule is correct.

The screenshot here shows an example text view for a business rule:

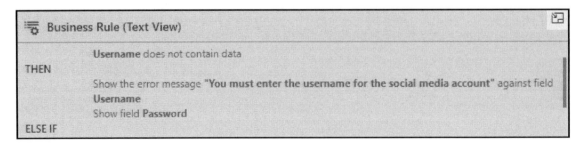

Figure 4.30 – Text view of a business rule

You can see in the previous screenshot the **THEN** and **ELSE IF** conditions and the multiple actions that will be applied. In this example, if the username has not been entered, an error message is displayed for the username field and the password field is made visible.

Activating business rules

Once you have finished editing your business rule, you should validate and save the business rule.

You must then activate the business rule. Until the rule has been activated, it will not be applied.

Click on the **Activate** button in the toolbar to activate your business rule. A dialog will be displayed for you to confirm that you want to activate the business rule, as shown in the following screenshot:

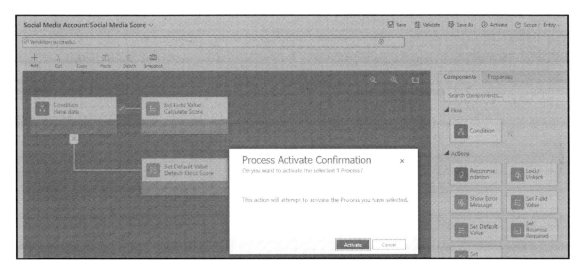

Figure 4.31 – Activating a business rule

If you want to change an activated business rule, you must deactivate it before you can edit it.

You have now completed your business rule. We will now look at when business rules are applied.

Using business rules

Business rules are evaluated, and any actions performed are in the following situations:

- After the form has finished loading
- After any value in a field referenced within a condition in the rule is changed

 Business rules are run automatically in the order that they were activated. You cannot run a business rule manually.

How scope controls the running of business rules

Business rules have an option called scope that you set in the action bar in the business rule designer. The scope defines under which circumstances a business rule is applied.

The scope is set in the designer using the action bar, as shown in the following figure:

Figure 4.32 – Business rule scope

The previous screenshot shows the scope set to **Entity**. This is the default when using the maker portal.

The scope defines the situations in which a rule is applied. The options are as follows:

- An individual named form
- All forms
- An entity

An entity can have multiple forms with different users accessing different named forms. If you choose a named form for the scope, then the business rule will only be applied when users are in that form. The business rule will not be applied to the other forms.

A restriction of the scope selection is that Microsoft only lists **Main** forms. You cannot have a business rule that just targets a **Quick Create** form. If you want to apply the business rule to a **Quick Create** form, you must select one of the other scope options.

The drop-down list is a single-select option set. This means you cannot select multiple forms. If you have three main forms and want your rule to apply to only two out of the three forms, then you will need to have two separate business rules.

 If you create a business rule from within the classic form editor, the scope will default to that form.

If you choose **All Forms** for the scope, the business rule will be applied for all the **Main** forms and the **Quick Create** form.

 If you create a business rule from the business rules node in the classic solution explorer, the scope will default to **All Forms**.

If you choose **Entity** for the scope, the business rule will be evaluated for all the **Main** forms and the **Quick Create** form, and the business rule is applied again on the **Common Data Service** platform when the record is saved.

When the scope is set to **Entity**, the business rule is applied whenever the record is created or updated through whatever method. So, any actions will be performed if a user creates the record, the record is created by a Power Automate flow, or if the record is created via the APIs or with the portal.

If the **Show Error Message** action is used on a business rule with the scope set to **Entity**, this will throw an exception and the record will not be saved. The text used in **Show Error Message** will appear as an error to the user similar to the following screenshot:

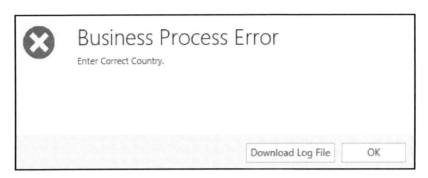

Figure 4.33 – Show Error Message with the scope set to Entity

The previous screenshot shows the text **Enter Correct Country** from the **Show Error Message** action as it appears to the user.

So far, we have looked at using business rules with model-driven apps. The named form and all form scopes of business rules are solely related to model-driven app forms. Let's look at how business rules work with canvas apps.

Business rule scope and canvas apps

If you choose a named form or **All Forms** as the scope for your business rule, then the business rule will not apply to any canvas app.

If you chose **Entity** for the scope of your business rule, the business rule affects any app or service that uses Common Data Service. If you have a canvas app that uses Common Data Service for its data, then when the canvas app creates or updates a record in Common Data Service, the business rule actions will be applied. However, only the group of actions that affect data will be performed, as follows:

- Set Field Value
- Set Default Value
- Show Error Message

The following actions are not available in canvas apps:

- Set Business Required
- Set Visibility
- Lock/Unlock
- Recommendation

> If you want to control visibility, read-only, or mandatory fields in a canvas app, you need to add formulas to your canvas apps.

As well as the limitations of business rules with canvas apps, there are some other considerations for using business rules.

Understanding the limitations of business rules

Business rules are intended to address simple common requirements. Compared to what a developer can do using JavaScript in a form, business rules have limitations.

Here are a few limitations when using business rules:

- Business rules run only when the form loads and when the value of the field referenced in the rule is changed. Rules do not run again when a record is saved unless the scope for the rule is set at an entity level.
- If a business rule references a field that is not present on a form, the rule will not be applied. There will be no error message to inform you that the rule hasn't been applied.
- When the scope is set to **Entity**, the rule will run twice – once on the form and once on the platform.
- Business rules work only with fields. If you need to manipulate other form elements, such as tabs or sections, you must use JavaScript.
- You can't have more than 10 if-else conditions in a rule.
- Nested if-else statements are not supported.
- Grouping of expressions in a condition is not supported.
- Rules in conditions can be combined either using AND or using OR, but not both.
- When you set a field value using a business rule, OnChange JavaScript event handlers for that field will not be triggered.

However, business rules can meet a lot of requirements and you should balance the effort of creating rules against development.

Best practices

Business rules can be very effective. The following is some guidance on using business rules:

- Only use business rules to manipulate a small number of fields.
- Keep business rules simple by having multiple rules, especially where there is a clear separation of conditions and actions. Do not try to fit everything into one rule.
- Always have the opposite actions through conditions; that is, if you are hiding a field based on a condition, make sure there is an opposite else condition to show the field.
- If you need to reference fields in the business rule that are not on the form, add these fields to a hidden tab or section on the form.
- If you are hiding and showing fields, it creates a better user experience for the fields to be set as hidden on the form and then use business rules to show them, rather than having the fields disappear after the form has loaded.
- If the business rule is not going to be simple, convert it into JavaScript as it will be quicker to develop and test.
- Do not mix and match JavaScript and business rules on the same form.
- Change the name of your forms from **Information** so that it makes it easier to set the scope.

Summary

In this chapter, you were introduced to business rules, the actions that can be performed, how business rules are created, how the designer is used, and how to add actions and conditions. You should now understand how to create business rules, define scope, and understand how business rules work with other components of the Power Platform.

You will be able to create business rules, understand when business rules are applied, and understand how to use business rules to perform validation.

In the next chapter, we will learn how to configure classic workflows and actions.

Questions

After reading this chapter, test your knowledge with these questions. You will find the answers to these questions under Assessments at the end of the book:

1. You are creating a new business rule to calculate the value of the field. Users report that the field is not calculated when they create a record. What two actions should you do?

    A) Share the business rule with the user.
    B) Verify all fields in the business rule are on the form.
    C) Update security roles for the business rule.
    D) Set the scope of the business rule.

2. A field is hidden on the form. You need a business rule to force the user to enter a value in the field. What three actions should you use?

    A) **Show Error Message**
    B) **Unlock Field**
    C) **Set Business Required**
    D) **Set Default Value**
    E) **Set Visibility**

3. You create a canvas app and need to calculate a field value with a business rule. What should you set the scope of your business rule to?

    A) Set scope to **All Forms**.
    B) Set scope to **Entity**.
    C) Set scope to the name of your canvas app screen.
    D) Change the name of your canvas app screen to **Main**.

4. You create a new business rule. You need to set a field as mandatory. Arrange four of these steps into the correct order:

    A) Validate.
    B) Snapshot.
    C) Add a **Set Visibility** action.
    D) Add a **Set Business Required** action.
    E) Save.
    F) Activate.
    G) Publish.
    H) Set a rule in a condition.
    I) Add a condition.

5. You create a business rule to prompt the user to set a field value. What action should you use?

A) **Show Error Message**
B) **Recommendation**
C) **Set Business Required**
D) **Set Default Value**
E) **Set Visibility**

Further reading

For more details on the topics in this chapter, reference these resources:

- Applying business logic in Common Data Service: `https://docs.microsoft.com/powerapps/maker/common-data-service/cds-processes`
- Creating a business rule for an entity: `https://docs.microsoft.com/powerapps/maker/common-data-service/data-platform-create-business-rule`

Classic Workflows 5

All organizations have business processes that the organization uses to meet customer needs and to deliver products and services. **Classic workflows and actions** consist of a set of activity steps that are performed to achieve the desired outcome. Classic workflows are a capability of the **Common Data Service (CDS)** that help users perform repeatable tasks, keep other users and customers informed of progress, and reduce the need for users to check work.

This chapter will explain how to create classic workflow processes to automate data changes and communications within the CDS. We will begin with an introduction to processes and their capabilities, and then where and how to create them by adding triggers, conditions, and action steps.

In this chapter, we will cover the following topics:

- Introducing processes
- Creating a classic workflow
- Creating and using action processes
- Monitoring classic workflows

By the end of this chapter, you will be able to create classic workflows, understand how the workflow is triggered, and use real-time workflows.

Introducing processes

CDS processes can be used to remove the need for users to manually perform complex tasks in sequence and control the activities required to deliver business processes consistently and repetitively. Processes are one of the major reasons for using Dynamics 365 apps and CDS.

A CDS process defines the following:

- The entity the process will execute against
- The type of process
- The name of the process
- How and when the process is initiated
- Conditions evaluated
- Actions taken

CDS has several different types of process:

- Classic workflow
- Dialog
- Action

Classic workflows, dialogs, and action processes are based on the **Windows Workflow Foundation (WWF)** technology. WWF is integrated into the CDS platform. WWF provides a runtime engine and a base set of activities. The CDS provides basic create, read, update, and delete operations. The WWF runtime engine manages process execution. WWF supports long-running processes without adversely affecting performance, and it persists the state of process execution during computer outages.

WWF is old technology. Nowadays, however, Power Automate is the preferred tool for creating automation for apps using the CDS. Dynamics 365 workflows are referred to as classic workflows, to differentiate them from Power Automate flows.

Power Automate provides the following advantages:

- Access to services outside of the CDS to create more complex and powerful automation.
- The ability to run queries and process a set of records, for example, to retrieve a list of related records in a one-to-many relationship and loop through them.
- It can integrate with other systems without code.
- The ability to handle more than just data records, for example, files.

Microsoft recommends using Power Automate in place of a classic workflow. You will see the message in the following screenshot when you go to create a classic workflow:

We recommend using Microsoft Flow instead of background workflows. Click here to start building Flows!

Figure 5.1 – Microsoft recommends using Power Automate

Classic workflows have one advantage over Power Automate flows: they can be run in real time, that is, synchronously.

You should always consider using a Power Automate flow instead of a classic workflow. At a future date, Microsoft will deprecate classic workflows. Power Automate is more powerful and flexible.

In this section, we will look at each of these process types.

Classic workflows

Classic workflows are processes used for automated business processes that don't require user input. The following screenshot shows a classic workflow in the workflow editor:

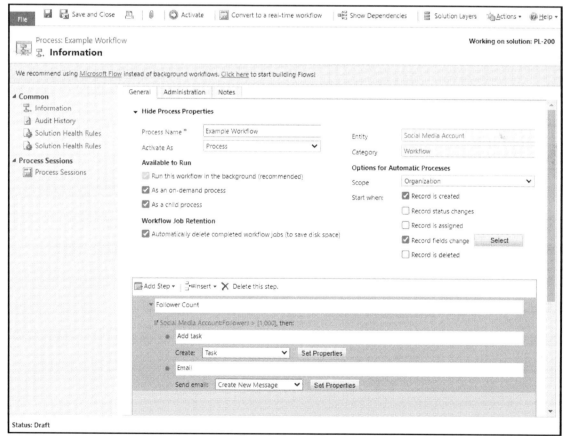

Figure 5.2 – Classic workflow

With classic workflows, you can perform the following tasks:

- Use branching and nesting logic
- Create and update records
- Send emails
- Create activities
- Append information to existing records
- Wait for a specific date, length of time, or field value before continuing
- Assign the ownership of records
- Change the status of a record
- Call child workflows

Classic workflows are normally initiated by system events and run on the platform. A classic workflow executes steps and can be run either in the background or in real time.

Dialogs

Dialogs are interactive processes used to automate step-by-step business processes that capture user input using a wizard-style interface.

With dialogs, you can perform the following tasks:

- Prompt users for data input
- Use branching to show different pages
- Create and update records
- Send emails
- Create activities

Dialogs are initiated manually by users. A typical use for dialogs is as **agent scripts**.

 Dialogs have been deprecated and will not be discussed further.

Action processes

Actions are automated processes that create a new **operation** that is not available as standard in the CDS or to combine multiple operations into a single operation. For example, in the case of a help desk, you could combine create, assign, and change status operations into a single new **escalate** operation.

Action processes can be initiated from code, by Power Automate flows, and by classic workflows.

Let's now look at what makes up a process, how they are initiated, and the activities that they can perform.

How processes are triggered

A classic workflow can be triggered by the following events on records in the CDS:

- Creating a record
- Updating a record
- Deleting a record
- Changing the status of a record
- Change of ownership (assigning) of a record

The following screenshot shows the triggers for a classic workflow:

Figure 5.3 – Triggers

On the update trigger, you can define the fields that will trigger the workflow if they are changed.

Only specify the fields required for the update trigger. Do not select all fields.

The CDS does not differentiate an update when a field is updated with the same value. Updating a field to the same value will trigger the workflow.

A classic workflow can also be run manually. This is called on-demand. Classic workflows can also be called from other workflows. This is known as a child process.

The following screenshot shows where a classic workflow can be run:

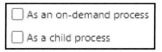

Figure 5.4 – Available to be run

The triggers for a classic workflow are powerful but simple, that is, they will trigger on a field being updated but you cannot restrict the trigger to a field being updated to a specific value. For this, you need to use a check condition.

How processes perform work

Processes can check conditions, apply branching logic, and perform actions. Processes perform the actions as a series of steps.

There are two types of conditions for processes:

- Check conditions
- Wait conditions

A process can use fields from the entity or any field from an entity in a many-to-one relationship in a condition.

Check conditions

Check conditions are how you implement if-then-else logic in a workflow process.

The following screenshot shows an example of a check condition:

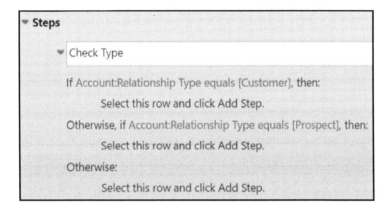

Figure 5.5 – Check condition

Microsoft has used **Otherwise if**, in place of **else if,** and **Otherwise** in place of **else**. Also, check conditions can have ANDs and ORs to create complex conditions.

Check conditions can be nested, but be careful as the process editor cannot handle more than five levels of nesting.

Wait conditions

Wait conditions pause the process until one of the conditions in the wait list is met.

A wait condition can wait for the following:

- For a field to contain any value, in other words, not null
- For a field to be a specific value
- Until a period of time before or after the value in a **Date** and **Time** field
- For a specific period of time

The following screenshot shows an example of each of these wait conditions:

Wait until Account:Relationship Type contains data, then:
Select this row and click Add Step.
Otherwise, wait until Account:Status does not equal [Active], then:
Select this row and click Add Step.
Timeout until 1 Month then
Select this row and click Add Step.
Or Timeout until 7 Days After Account:Last Date Included in Campaign then
Select this row and click Add Step.

Figure 5.6 – Wait condition

In the preceding example, the processing will continue only when any one of the four conditions is met.

 Wait conditions can only be used in background workflows.

 A wait condition should always have a parallel wait condition to prevent the process from running forever.

Moreover, conditions control the logic. Conditions are steps that you add, but there are many more steps you can use.

Steps

Steps are the activities within a process. There are several different types of steps as listed in the following table:

Step	Process type	Description
Stage	Classic workflow, Action	Stages make the logic easier to read. Stages do not affect the logic or behavior of workflows. They allow the steps to be collapsed when viewing a process to gain a higher-level view of the process logic.
Check Condition	Classic workflow, Action	Logic with the *if-then* statement. You can check values for the record that the workflow is running on, any of the records linked to that record in a many-to-one relationship, or any records created in earlier steps. If the statement is true, you add steps underneath the check condition.

Conditional Branch	Classic workflow, Action	Branching logic with an *else-if* statement. You can add a conditional branch to an existing check condition to add steps underneath the conditional branch when the check condition is false.
Default Action	Classic workflow, Action	Branching logic with an *else* statement. You can add a default action to an existing check condition to add steps underneath the conditional branch when the check condition and all conditional branches are false.
Wait Condition	Classic background workflow	Pauses a background classic workflow until the criteria defined in the wait condition have been met.
Parallel Wait Branch	Classic background workflow	You can add an alternative wait condition to an existing wait condition. You can use parallel wait branches to create time limits in your process logic. Parallel wait branches help prevent the process from waiting indefinitely when the criteria defined in a wait condition can never be met; for example, when a record has been deactivated.
Assign Value	Action	Sets a variable or output parameter.
Create Record	Classic workflow, Action	Creates a record in the CDS.
Update Record	Classic workflow, Action	Updates the record that the workflow was triggered by. You can also update records in a many-to-one relationship with the workflow record.
Assign Record	Classic workflow, Action	Assigns (changes ownership of) the record that the workflow was triggered by. You can also assign records in a many-to-one relationship with the workflow record.
Send Email	Classic workflow, Action	Sends an email. There are two options. Firstly, you can use an email template. Secondly, you can create a new email message and complete the email using the form assistant.
Start Child Workflow	Classic workflow, Action	Starts a classic workflow process that has been configured as a child workflow. If the child workflow is a background workflow, the child workflow will run independently. If the child workflow is a real-time workflow, the workflow will wait until the child workflow has completed.
Perform Action	Classic workflow, Action	Starts an action process. Actions are always real time. The workflow will wait until the action has completed.
Change Status	Classic workflow, Action	Changes the status and status reason of the record that the workflow is running for, any of the records linked to that record in a many-to-one relationship, or any records created in an earlier step.
Stop	Classic workflow, Action	Stops the process. You can set a status to either `Succeeded` or `Cancelled` and specify a message.

Now that you have seen the conditions and steps for a classic workflow, we will look at how to create processes.

Creating a classic workflow

The creation and editing of classic workflows are not available in the Power Apps maker portal. You need to edit your solution in the solution explorer by using the **Switch to classic** option.

You create and edit classic workflows from within the process node of the solution explorer, as shown in the following screenshot:

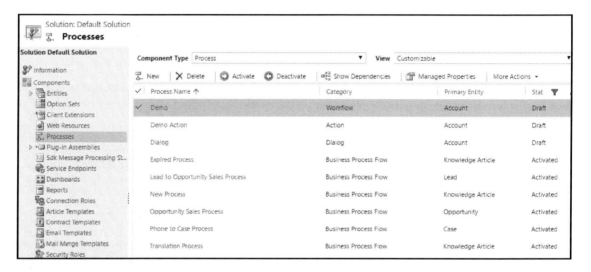

Figure 5.7 – Process node in the solution explorer

To create a classic workflow, click on the **New** button in the toolbar. The following window is opened:

Create Process

Define a new process, or create one from an existing template. You can create four kinds of processes: business process flows, actions, dialogs, and workflows.

Process name: *

Category: *

Entity: *

Type:
- ⦿ New blank process
- ○ New process from an existing template (select from list):

Template Name ↑	Primary Entity	Owner

No process template records are available in this view

Properties

OK   Cancel

Figure 5.8 – Create Process window

You need to go through the following steps:

1. Enter a name for the process that summarizes its purpose.
2. Select the category. This is the process type.
3. Select the entity the process is associated with.

 Once you click on **OK**, you cannot change the process type or the entity.

Once you click on **OK**, the process is created, and the workflow editor opens, and you can set the trigger conditions in the properties of the editor and add your steps.

Process properties

You can find the properties of the process in the top half of the editor.

The following screenshot shows the properties of a classic workflow:

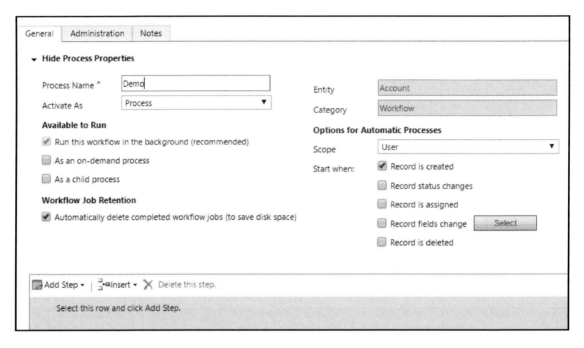

Figure 5.9 – Process properties

Note that **Entity** and **Category** are grayed out and cannot be changed.

There are a few sections in the properties that need to be completed:

- **Options for Automatic Processes**
- **Scope**
- **Available to Run**
- **Workflow Job Retention**

We will now examine these settings, starting with scope.

Setting the scope of the process

You must ensure that you have set the scope of your workflow. New workflows have a default scope of **User**.

The scope settings work in the same way as access levels in security roles. A scope of **User** means the workflow will only be run for the owner of the workflow.

Change the scope to **Organization**. The workflow will then be executed for all users and all records in the entity.

Setting the options for automatic processing

The options for the automatic process define the triggers of the workflow process.

A newly created classic workflow will default to trigger only on the creation of a record. Hence, you should amend the triggers for your process.

Classic workflows can be triggered in the following instances:

- When a record is created
- When a record status changes
- When a record is assigned
- When record fields change
- When a record is deleted

You can have more than one trigger defined in a workflow process.

Settings when the process is available to run

The options under **Available to Run** define how the workflow can be initiated in addition to the triggers defined for the workflow.

When created, classic workflows default to run in the background. The **Run this workflow in the background** setting is grayed out. You cannot change from background to real time by editing the field. You must use the **Convert to a real-time workflow** button in the toolbar.

If the **As an on-demand process** setting is checked, then users can select and run this workflow in a model-driven app form by clicking on the **Run Flow** button in the command bar. The **on-demand** process setting also allows the workflow to be called as a global workflow or a stage transition workflow in a business process flow.

If the **As a child process** setting is checked, then this workflow can be called from another workflow or action.

Once you have set your triggers, you can add your steps to the process.

Adding steps to a process

The options to add steps are in the bottom half of the editor. The following screenshot shows how you can add a step:

Figure 5.10 – Adding steps

Click on **Add Step** and then choose the condition or action you require. As you select a step, it is added to the canvas underneath the currently selected step.

Once added, the steps must be configured. Conditions and actions have different configuration options.

If you have used the **Advanced find** tool, you will be familiar with the condition editor shown in the following screenshot:

Figure 5.11 – Adding a condition

The following screenshot shows the **Set properties** window for creating a record, with **Form Assistant** in the right-hand pane:

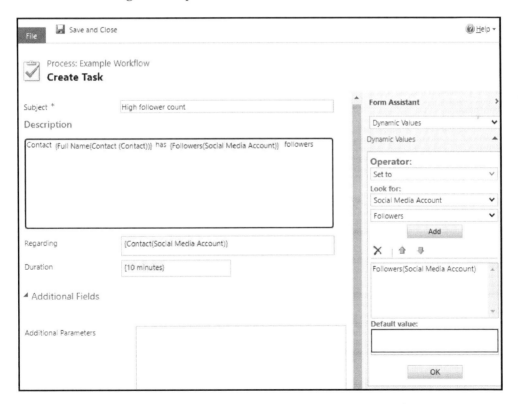

Figure 5.12 – Creating record properties

You can use **Form Assistant** to select and add fields to the form. Shown next is a screenshot of a **simple completed workflow** with a **condition step** and a **create record step** after setting the properties for the steps:

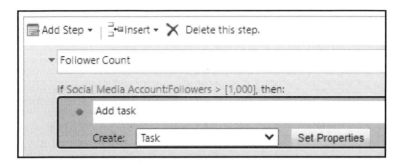

Figure 5.13 – A condition step and a create record step

By default, workflows are run in the background. You need to understand what this means and how it affects users. Let's see how a background workflow runs.

Running a background workflow

A workflow defined as running in the background means the workflow process is executed asynchronously on the CDS platform. Depending on what other background processes are running or the volume of queued processes, a background workflow may be executed within a few seconds, or it could take several minutes.

A background workflow is triggered when a record is newly created, or an updated record is saved, or a record is deleted. The form the user is on refreshes and they can carry on working while the workflow is running. This means that the user will need to refresh their screen to see any results of any steps that the workflow performs.

An example where this causes confusion for users is where a background workflow is run on creation of a record and the workflow creates a phone call record. The user creates a record and does not see the phone call in the timeline until they exit the record and reopen it, or if they press *F5* to refresh their browser. In such circumstances, you should consider changing the workflow to run in real time.

Security for background workflows

The security context for a background workflow can differ depending on how the workflow is initiated.

When a background workflow is initiated manually by a user using the **Run flow** command, the workflow operates in the context of the initiating user and their security privileges. Therefore, a background workflow that is run manually can only perform steps that the user could do themselves.

When a background workflow starts based on an event, the workflow operates in the context of the user who owns the workflow. Usually, this is an administrator. Therefore, a background workflow that is triggered can run with elevated privileges and can perform steps that the user is not able to. It does have the downside that any record created or updated will have the administrator's name stamped on the record and not the name of the user.

There are several reasons for considering switching to a real-time workflow. Let's see how a real-time workflow runs.

Running a real-time workflow

A workflow defined as running in real time means that the workflow process is executed synchronously on the CDS platform.

A real-time workflow is triggered when a record is newly created, or an updated record is saved, or a record is deleted. The form the user is on will wait until the workflow completes. If the workflow takes a long time, the user will see the circular processing image and will be unable to work until the workflow has finished. This means that the user will not need to refresh their screen to see the results of any steps that the workflow performs.

The following screenshot shows the properties for a classic workflow after it has been converted to run in real time:

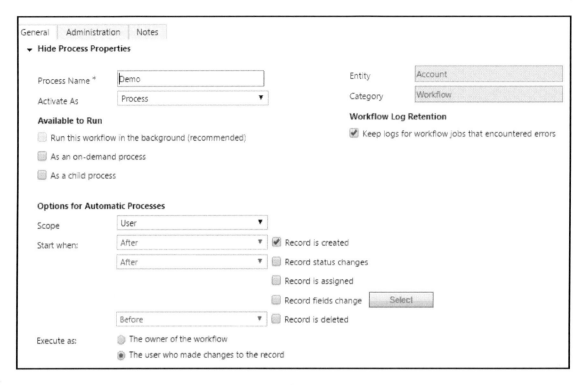

Figure 5.14 – Real-time workflow properties

The trigger options are different for background and real-time workflows. The triggers can be configured so that the workflow is run before or after the record is saved. **Before** should be used to validate the data before it is saved to the database.

Security for real-time workflows

The security context for a real-time workflow can be chosen when editing the workflow. The **Execute as** setting has two options. You can choose whether the workflow should run as the owner of the workflow or run as the user who made the change that triggered the workflow. The workflow will use the security privileges of the selected option.

To run with elevated privileges and perform steps that users are not able to, you should set **Execute as** to run the workflow as the **owner** of the workflow.

Converting between real-time and background workflows

You can change a background workflow into a real-time workflow by choosing **Convert to a real-time workflow** on the toolbar. The following screenshot shows how the icon looks:

Figure 5.15 – Workflow editor toolbar

 If the background workflow you convert uses a **wait** condition, it will become invalid and you won't be able to activate it until you remove the wait condition.

You can change a real-time workflow into a background workflow by choosing **Convert to a background workflow** on the toolbar.

Activating processes

Finally, a process must be activated before it can be used. However, note that you must first deactivate a process before you can edit it. So far, we have looked at classic workflows. We will now look at action processes.

Creating and using action processes

Microsoft uses the word **action** for several different things in processes – for a type of process and for steps within processes. We looked at action steps earlier in this chapter. In this section, we will focus on **action processes**.

Action processes are like workflows in their capabilities in terms of what can be performed with step; in other words, action processes can use conditions, and can create and update records.

Action processes differ from classic workflows in the following ways:

- Action processes cannot be triggered automatically.
- Action processes are invoked from other components.
- Action processes can have input and output arguments.
- Action processes are associated with a single entity or can be set as global (not associated with any entity).
- Action processes always run under the security context of the calling user.
- Action processes always run synchronously, in other words, in real time.

The following screenshot shows the properties that can be set for **action** processes:

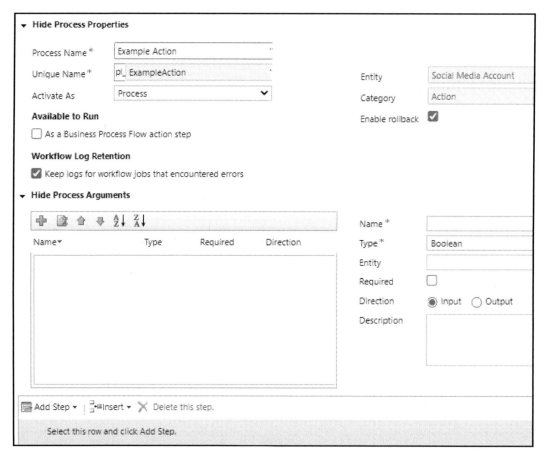

Figure 5.16 – Action process properties

You can invoke action processes in many ways:

- From .NET code
- From JavaScript
- From a classic workflow
- From a Power Automate flow
- As a step in a business process flow

A common use of action processes is to call an action from a JavaScript function with a button you add to the ribbon in order to perform a common set of activities.

 To call an action process in a Power Automate flow, you need to use the Common Data Service (current environment) connector. You should use **Perform a bound action** for action processes associated with an entity, and use **Perform an unbound action** for action processes set as **Global**.

Built-in actions

There are built-in actions in the CDS that you can use, such as the following:

- **Set Word Template**: Creates a Word document from a Word template
- **Add To Queue**: Adds a record to a queue

The Dynamics 365 apps, too, have actions that you can use. For instance, they have actions for leads, opportunities, quotes, orders, and invoices:

- **CloseOpportunity**
- **GetQuoteProductsFromOpportunity**
- **GetSalesOrderProductsFromOpportunity**
- **LockInvoicePricing**
- **LockSalesOrderPricing**
- **QualifyLead**
- **ResolveQuote**
- **ReviseQuote**
- **UnlockInvoicePricing**
- **UnlockSalesOrderPricing**

The following screenshot shows some of the actions available in the Dynamics 365 apps:

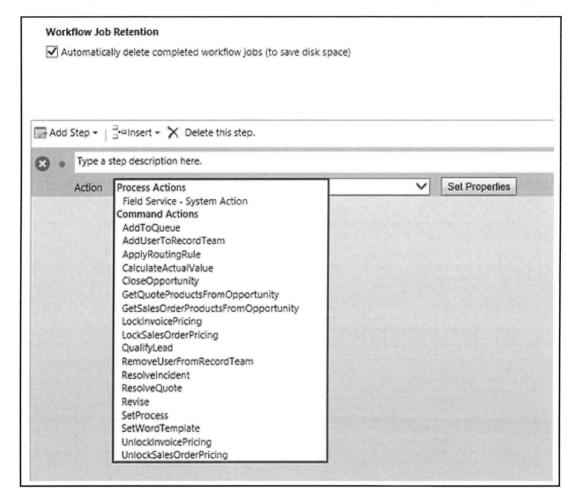

Figure 5.17 – Microsoft-provided actions

Microsoft uses the term **custom actions** for extending the capabilities of processes with .NET assemblies.

Extending processes with custom actions

The steps that classic workflows and action processes can perform are limited; for example, there is no capability to handle many-to-many relationships. You cannot add a contact to a marketing list, or remove a case from a queue using a workflow.

Developers can extend the capabilities of classic workflows and actions by writing custom workflow activities in C# and uploading a .NET assembly to the CDS.

Typical custom workflow actions that you might require are the following:

- Date/time functions; for example, date difference and business day calculations
- String functions; for example, trim
- Regex functions; for example, phone number validation
- List functions; for example, add and remove a contact to/from a marketing list
- Calculations; for example, tax

These functions appear as additional steps in the workflow editor. You add these custom actions as steps like any other step and set their properties.

 Creating custom actions is outside the scope of this exam, but adding custom actions as a step in a classic workflow is in the exam.

An important aspect of using classic workflow processes is the monitoring of the processes for errors.

Monitoring classic workflows

Each time a workflow is executed, a log is created. You can use these log records to monitor how often a process runs and check for errors. There are different logs for background and real-time workflows.

Logs for background workflows

Background workflows generate system job records to track their status. You can access these system jobs from **Settings | System Jobs**.

By default, the system job records are deleted automatically if the workflow process is successful. You can toggle the **Keep logs for workflow jobs** setting in the properties of the workflow editor so that you can analyze the number of workflows executed.

There are multiple views of system jobs and you can create personal views to assist you in your monitoring of errors, for example.

Logs for real-time workflows

Real-time workflows and action processes do not create system job records. Any errors that occur will be displayed to the user in their app with the heading **Business Process Error**.

Moreover, in a real-time workflow, there is no log for successful operations. You can enable **Error logging** by checking the keep logs for workflow jobs that encountered errors during setting. You will find this setting in the **Workflow Log Retention** area in the process editor.

 If you want a view of the errors, use **Advanced Find**, and create a view for the **Process Session** entity.

Summary

In this chapter, you were introduced to classic workflows, how they are created, and how the workflow editor is used. You should now understand processes, their capabilities, and how they are executed and monitored.

You will be able to create classic workflows, using triggers, conditions, and steps, to automate repetitive processes, create and update records, and to send emails.

In the next chapter, we will learn how to import and export data using the features of the Common Data Service.

Questions

After reading this chapter, test your knowledge with these questions. You will find the answers to these questions under Assessments at the end of the book:

1. You create a classic workflow that runs in the background. What should you use to find any errors in your workflow?

    A) Process sessions
    B) Plugin trace logs
    C) System jobs
    D) Workflow logs

2. You have created a workflow, but it is not running when users create records. It works when you create records. What should you do?

    A) Activate the workflow.
    B) Set the scope to **Organization**.
    C) Add a check condition and add a condition on flows created by all users.
    D) Share the workflow.

3. You create an action process for an entity and need to call it from a Power Automate flow. What action should you add?

    A) Perform a bound action.
    B) Perform an unbound action.
    C) Relate records.
    D) Execute a changeset request.

4. You convert a background workflow to real time. You cannot activate the workflow. What should you do?

    A) Change **Execute As** to your user.
    B) Assign the workflow to your user.
    C) Delete the wait condition.
    D) Set it as an on-demand process.

5. You are creating a workflow process, but are unable to add it as a stage workflow to a business process flow. What should you do?

    A) Convert it to a real-time process.
    B) Assign the workflow to your user.
    C) Change the entity for the process.
    D) Set it as an on-demand process.

Further reading

- Best practices for workflow processes: `https://docs.microsoft.com/dynamics365/customerengagement/on-premises/customize/best-practices-workflow-processes`
- Workflow extensions: `https://docs.microsoft.com/powerapps/developer/common-data-service/workflow/workflow-extensions`
- Actions overview: `https://docs.microsoft.com/dynamics365/customerengagement/on-premises/customize/actions`

6
Managing Data

An application is nothing without its data. In earlier chapters, we discussed creating data models. Once you have a data model, you must be able to get data into and out of your environment.

In this chapter, we will discuss the features for importing and exporting data into and from Common Data Service.

The topics covered in this chapter are the following:

- Importing data
- Exporting data

By the end of this chapter, you will be able to import data from different file types and locations and export data to files and other locations. Knowing how to use these features is a key skill for a functional consultant who wants to get a Power Platform solution ready for use.

Importing data from different sources

You can manually enter data through the user interface, but there will normally be a need to import data. The import could be a one-off migration from a legacy system at go-live, or it could be the regular upload of records extracted from other systems.

Common Data Service provides several different methods for importing data:

- **Using the Import Data Wizard** in the classic web interface
- **Importing from Excel** in model-driven apps
- **Getting data** using Power Query in the Power Apps maker portal

The tools provided by Microsoft are, by design, fairly limited in their capabilities. There are third-party tools for importing data for more complex or high-volume imports.

We will start by looking at the Import Data Wizard, which is useful for importing small sets of clean data.

Using the Import Data Wizard

The Import Data Wizard is available in model-driven apps from the classic user interface; you cannot access it from the unified interface directly.

In the classic user interface, the Import Data Wizard is available from the action bar in most views.

If you have a unified interface app, you access the Import Data Wizard by clicking on **Advanced Settings** | **Data Management** | **Imports**.

You can also access the Import Data Wizard from the Power Platform admin center. Select an environment, open **Settings**, expand **Data management**, and select **Data import wizard**.

To start the wizard, you click on the **Import Data** button. The first page of the wizard will open as shown in the following figure:

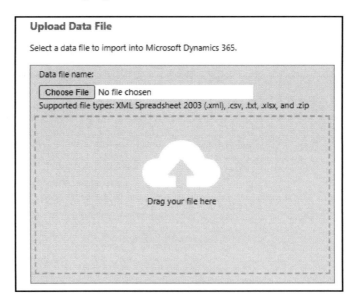

Figure 6.1 – Import Data Wizard step 1

You can either browse to a file on your local computer or drag and drop the file where indicated.

The following file types are supported:

- Comma-separated value (`.csv`)
- Text (`.txt`)
- XML spreadsheet 2003 (`.xml`)
- Excel workbook (`.xlsx`)

You can also have a ZIP file containing multiple related files of these types to import as one job.

 A file has a maximum size of 8 MB. A ZIP file can be up to 32 MB.

The following screenshots will show the steps for importing a comma-separated value file called `People.csv` into the `Contact` record type. After you select a file and click on **Next**, the wizard moves to the next step as shown in the next figure:

Figure 6.2 – Import Data Wizard step 2

On this page, you specify the field and data delimiters. Clicking **Next** moves to the next step as shown in the following figure:

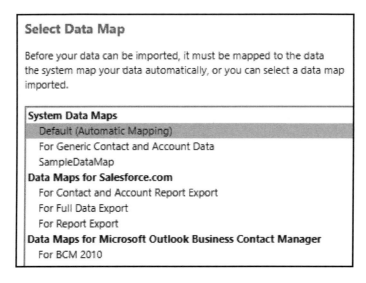

Figure 6.3 – Import Data Wizard step 3

This page of the wizard allows you to select a data map. A **data map** is a mapping from columns in the file to fields in the entity. Using a data map saves you time on the regular import of the same file structure. Maps you create will appear at the bottom of the list. If you do not have a data map, you should select the top option, **Default (Automatic Mapping)**, and click **Next**. This will open the next page of the wizard as shown in the following figure:

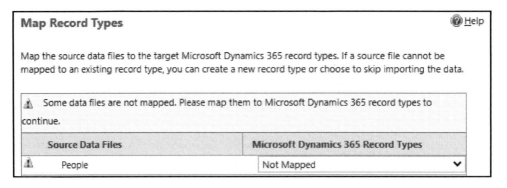

Figure 6.4 – Import Data Wizard step 4

On this page of the wizard, you should select the record type you want to load the data into and click on **Next**. This will open the next page of the wizard as shown in the following screenshot:

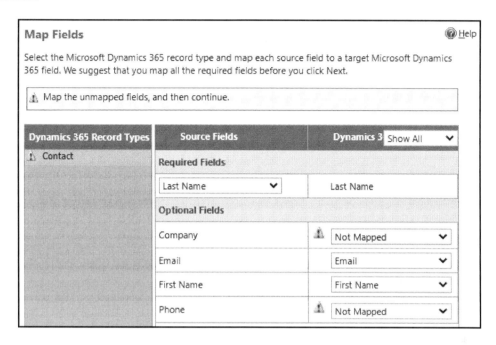

Figure 6.5 – Import Data Wizard step 5

As **Default (Automatic Mapping)** was chosen in *Figure 6.3*, the import wizard has matched the names in the column headings of the file with the display names for the fields on the entity. **First Name**, **Last Name**, and **Email** have mapped. The **Company** and **Phone** columns in the file have not mapped. You need to manually map the fields by selecting the field name from the drop-down list.

You should select **Business Phone** or **Mobile Phone** to map the **Phone** column.

The **Company** column is set to **Company Name**. On the **Contact** entity, the **Company Name** field is a lookup field. When you select a lookup field to map to, a pop-up dialog appears as shown in the next screenshot:

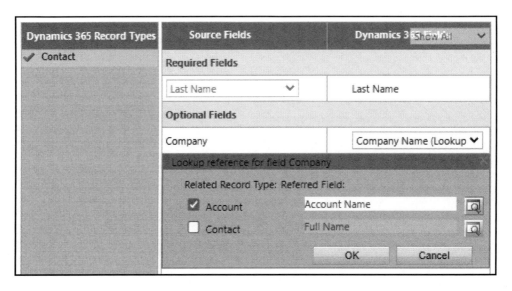

Figure 6.6 – Lookup reference field in the Import Data Wizard

Company Name is a customer lookup; this means it can either be an account or a contact. You should select the entity you want to map to and then choose the field. In the `People` file, the **Company** column holds the account name, but for another file, it could be the account number; you can change which field is used to match the data that the column holds.

 If you map a column to an `option set` field, there is a similar pop-up window that allows you to map to the labels in the option set.

Once you have mapped all columns, you click on **Next**. This will bring up a confirmation page, where you click on **Next** again. This will open the next page of the wizard as shown in the next figure

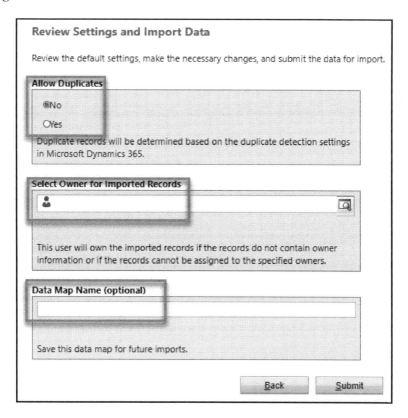

Figure 6.7 – Import Data Wizard final step

On this page, you have a few options:

- **Allow Duplicates**: Setting this to **No** will reject any row in the file that matches existing records using duplication detection. We discuss duplicate detection later in this chapter.
- **Owner**: The user will own the records imported.
- **Data Map Name**: You can save the field mappings to a data map for reuse on future data imports.

To import the data, you click on **Submit** and you will see the following figure:

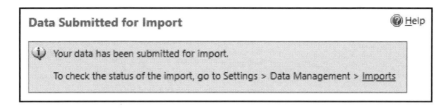

Figure 6.8 – Import Data Wizard submitted

The import will run in the background and you can review the results in **Imports**.

Monitoring import data jobs

All imports created by the Import Data Wizard create an import job record. You can monitor job records in **Imports**.

In the classic user interface, **Imports** is available from **Data Management** in **Settings**. In a unified interface app, **Imports** is available from **Data Management** in **Advanced Settings**. In the Power Platform admin center, **Imports** is available from **Data management** in **Settings**. All these options open the same screen, as shown in the following figure:

Figure 6.9 – Import jobs

You will see the jobs and their status. The status will change from **Submitted**, to **Parsing**, to **Transforming**, to **Importing**, and finally to **Completed**.

The job will show the number of records that were successfully imported, with errors if any. You can open the job to see the details of the errors. Common errors that you see when importing using the wizard are as follows:

- A record was not created or updated because a duplicate record was detected – this shows as an error even if you selected **No** for **Allow Duplicates** in the wizard.
- The lookup references could not be resolved – in the `People` file used in the preceding screenshots, this would occur if there was no account with the file's company name.

You need the Data Import and Data Map privileges to use the Import Data Wizard.

You can delete the records imported by selecting one of the delete options when you have an import job selected, as shown in the next figure:

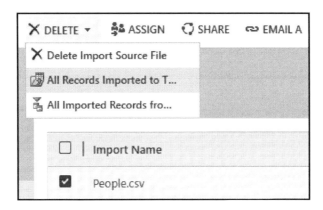

Figure 6.10 – Deleting an import

You can delete the job and leave the imported records in your environment, or you can delete the job and all the records. This is useful if you have failures in the import and need to start again.

As well as using data maps to improve the ease of importing data with the wizard, you can use data templates.

Using data templates

Data templates are spreadsheets that you can download to increase the success of data imports. They are useful for getting data into the correct columns in manual imports, as the spreadsheet has the data types and values for the columns defined, so you reduce the chances of errors on import. Using a data template will mean the columns in the file are automatically mapped to the correct fields.

The data templates are available in **Advanced Settings** under **Data Management**, as shown in the following screenshot:

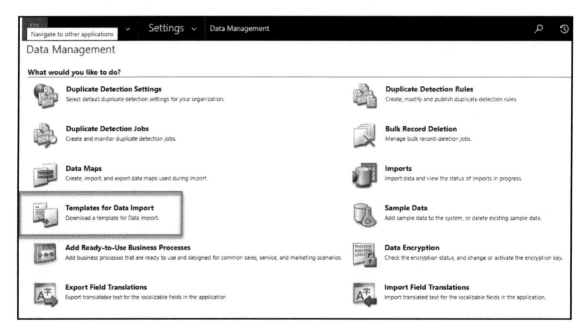

Figure 6.11 – Data Management settings

Clicking on **Templates for Data Import** opens a new window, as shown in the following figure:

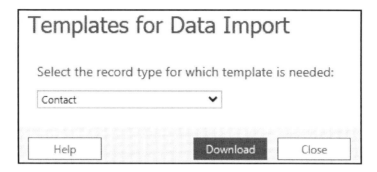

Figure 6.12 – Templates for Data Import settings

You select the entity you want to import into and click on **Download**. An Excel spreadsheet is downloaded to your local computer containing all the fields on the entity, as shown in the following screenshot for **Contact**:

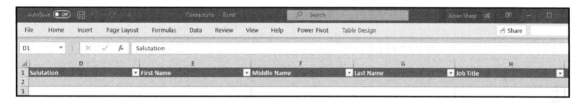

Figure 6.13 – Data template

There is a set of sample data that you can import. This sample data uses the Import Data Wizard functionality to add the sample data to your environment.

Adding sample data

Common Data Service comes with a set of sample data to use for trials and testing. This sample data is small, with around 10 accounts, 15 contacts, and some opportunities, products, cases, and activities.

You can add this sample data from the Power Platform admin center. Open the settings for the environment and expand **Data management** as shown in the next screenshot:

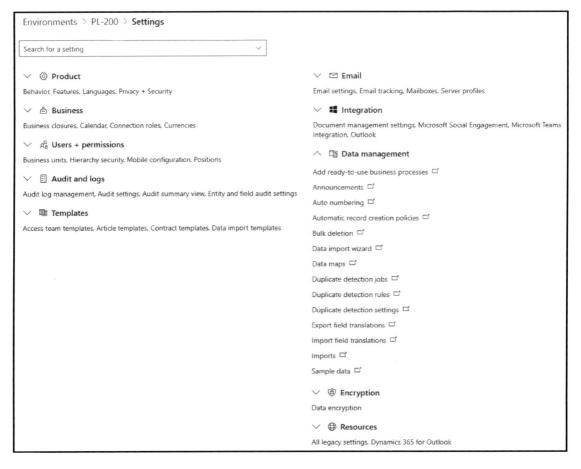

Figure 6.14 – Data management settings

Clicking on **Sample data** will open a new window as shown in the following figure:

Figure 6.15 – Installing sample data

Clicking on the button will start a series of import jobs that you can monitor for success, as shown in the next figure:

Import Name	Status Reaso...	Successe...	Partial Failure...	Errors	Total Pr...
Sample Data Product Substitute	Completed	30	0	0	30
Sample Data Price Level	Completed	2	0	0	2
Sample Data Subject	Completed	6	0	0	6
Sample Data Task	Completed	14	0	20	34
Sample Data Goal	Completed	4	0	0	4
Sample Data Article	Completed	4	0	0	4
Sample Data Incident Resolution	Completed	0	9	0	9
Sample Data Product Price Level	Completed	0	0	13	13
Sample Data KnowledgeArticle	Completed	11	0	0	11
Sample Data Email	Completed	0	0	9	9
Sample Data Category	Completed	6	0	0	6

My Imports

Figure 6.16 – Sample data import jobs

If you want to remove the sample data, then you can click on **Sample data** and the window is shown in the following figure will open:

Figure 6.17 – Removing sample data

You can click on the **Remove Sample Data** button to trigger the deletion of the sample data records.

The Import Data Wizard is not available in the unified interface. Unified interface apps use the **Import from Excel** option, which has many similarities to the Import Data Wizard.

Using Import from Excel

In the unified interface, Import from Excel is available from the action bar in most views. This import tool allows you to import Excel workbooks, CSV files, and XML files.

Import from Excel has many similarities to the Import Data Wizard but has a more modern user interface. Clicking on the **Import from Excel** button gives the two options shown in the following figure:

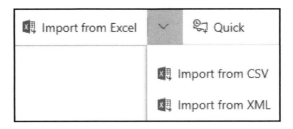

Figure 6.18 – Import from Excel

Instead of a separate window, this wizard opens in a pane on the right-hand side of the screen. You can browse and select a file. The rest of the steps are similar to the Import Data Wizard; for instance, the mapping of columns to fields is shown in the next figure:

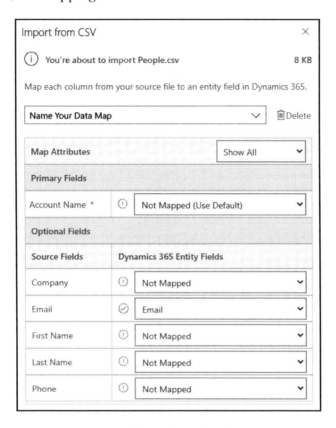

Figure 6.19 – Import from Excel mapping

An import job is created, and you can monitor this job in the same way that you did for the Import Data Wizard.

> You can import only one file at a time. To import more files, you need to run the wizard again.

If you have other data sources, you can use the import functionality in the Power Apps maker portal.

Using Power Query

Power Query is a data extract and transforms tool that is used in many different Microsoft products and services, from Excel to Azure Data Factory and Power BI. Power Query can extract data from a wide variety of data sources. Power Query is available in the Power Platform to import data into Common Data Service.

The Power Apps maker portal has options for importing data:

- **Get data**: Uses Power Query to transform and import data.
- **Get data from Excel**: Import one or more Excel or CSV files.

To be able to import data using these options, you need to expand the **Data** area in the maker portal and select **Entities** as shown in the next screenshot:

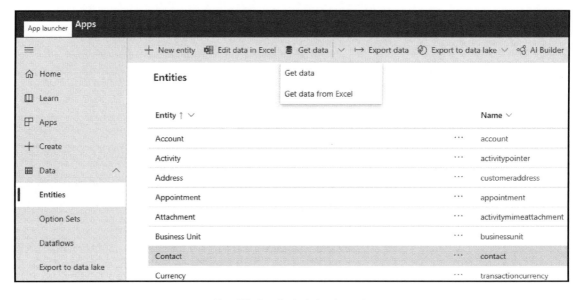

Figure 6.20 – Importing data in the maker portal

The following screenshots will show the steps for importing a CSV file called `People.csv` into the **Contact** record type. Clicking on **Get data from Excel** shows the following screen:

Figure 6.21 – Selecting entities

You should select the entities you want to upload and click on **Next**. The **Get data from Excel** option allows you to upload Excel workbooks or CSV files from your local computer. After uploading the files, you will see the screen shown in the following figure:

Figure 6.22 – Getting data from Excel

Clicking on **Map fields** on the right-hand side allows you to change the column to field mappings, as shown in the next figure:

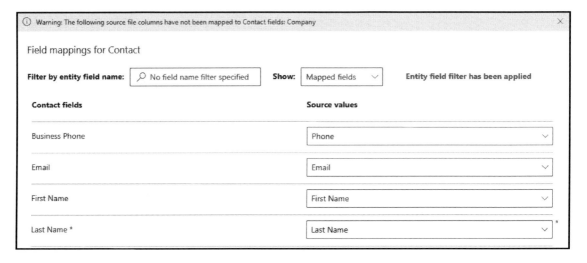

Figure 6.23 – Map fields when getting data from Excel

You can select the fields in the file to map to the fields on the entity.

 At the time of writing, the **Get data from Excel** option does not support lookup fields.

Clicking on **Import** submits the import, and you see a message when it's complete, as shown in the following figure:

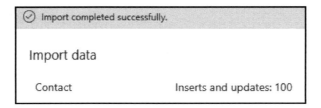

Figure 6.24 – Get data from Excel completed

An import job is not created. Instead, a project is created in **Data integration** in the Power Platform admin center, as shown in the next screenshot:

Figure 6.25 – Data integration

The more powerful option for importing data is accessed by clicking on **Get data**. This launches Power Query as shown in the following screenshot:

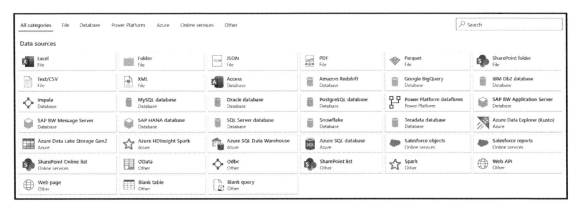

Figure 6.26 – Power Query data sources

Over 30 data sources are available with Power Query. Power Query is used in many Microsoft tools, including Power BI, and some of its capabilities include the following:

- Filtering data
- Combining data
- Adding calculations
- Transforming data
- Automatically refreshing data

The next screenshot shows the Power Query editor where columns have been transformed:

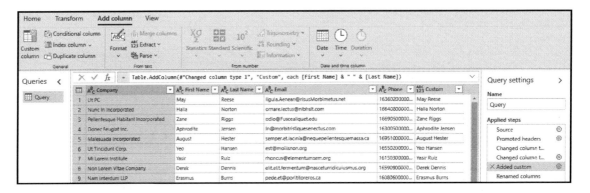

Figure 6.27 – Editing queries

The Power Query editor in the screenshot shows the records from the query and allows you to perform many transformations on the data, from changing the data type to adding calculated columns using the **Transform** and **Add Column** tabs. Power Query allows you to cleanse the data, remove duplicates, and replace values. Each transformation is recorded as a step in the right-hand pane.

Creating queries and manipulating data with Power Query is outside the scope of the PL-200 exam, but knowing that this option is available is within the scope of the exam.

You have seen several different options for importing data. Well done if you have gotten this far. As a reward, here is a summary of the import options and the differences between them:

Tool	Import Data Wizard	Import from Excel	Get data from Excel	Get data
User Interface	Classic interface	Unified interface	Power Platform Admin Center	Power Platform Admin Center
Data Sources	CSV, TXT, XML, XLS, ZIP	CSV, Excel, XML	CSV, Excel	30+ cloud data sources
Target entity	Single record type Multiple related records supported with zip file	Single record type	Single or multiple record types	Single or multiple record types
Monitor jobs	Import jobs	Import jobs	Data Integration	Data Integration
Transform data	No	No	No	Yes
Create/Update	Create only	Create only	Create or Update	Create or Update
Duplicate Detection	Yes – can be overridden	Yes – can be overridden	Yes	Yes

Figure 6.28 – Comparison of data import tools

As well as third-party data integration and migration solutions, Microsoft is enabling other services to integrate data with Common Data Service. One of these is Azure Data Factory, enterprise-grade service for integrating data. You can use Azure Data Factory to import data into Common Data Service with copy and lookup activities supported.

Now that we have learned how to import data, let's look at the options for exporting data.

Exporting data

Common Data Service is a data store used by apps and processes. There is often a need to extract data from Common Data Service for importing into other systems or to produce reports and analyses. In this section, we will look at how data can be exported from the Common Data Service.

As with the importing of data, there are several different options to export data:

- Microsoft Excel
- Maker portal
- Export to Data Lake
- Replicate to Azure SQL
- Power Automate

We will start by looking at the Excel options in the user interface.

Exporting to Excel in model-driven apps

Export to Excel is available from the action bar in most views. This import tool allows you to export the data in the view to an Excel file. Clicking on **Export to Excel** shows the export options as shown in the next figure:

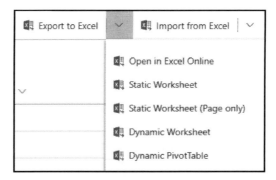

Figure 6.29 – Export to Excel options

The options for exporting to Excel include the following:

- **Static Worksheet**: A snapshot of the records in the view. The data is copied to a worksheet on your local computer.
- **Static Worksheet (Page only)**: Only the records on the first page of the view (up to 250 records based on the setting in your personal options) are copied to the local computer.
- **Dynamic Worksheet**: Creates an Excel worksheet on your local computer with a query based on the current view definition. No data is stored. When you open the worksheet, a connection is made to Common Data Service and the latest data is loaded into the spreadsheet. The query respects your security access. Another user opening a dynamic worksheet will see the data that is relevant to them.

- **Dynamic PivotTable**: Similar to a dynamic worksheet, a query is created but instead of a list of records, a PivotTable is created in the Excel file.
- **Open in Excel Online**: Opens Excel Online with the data from the current view. A user can edit the records and save them back to Common Data Service. We will look at this option later in the chapter as it has some beneficial uses.

These Excel options are extremely popular with users but should not be used for large volumes of data as the number of records exported is limited. If you need to export your data for analysis in other systems, then you should look at the other export options. Next, we will look at exporting data from the Power Apps maker portal.

Exporting data in the maker portal

You can also export data from the Power Apps maker portal. In the Power Apps maker portal, you can access all the entities in your Common Data Service environment. You can view the data, import new data, and export data.

The Power Apps maker portal has two options for exporting data:

- **Export data**: Copies one or more entities into a CSV file
- **Export to data lake**: Copies one or more entities to Azure Data Lake

To be able to export data using these options, you need to expand the **Data** area in the maker portal and select **Entities** as shown in the following screenshot:

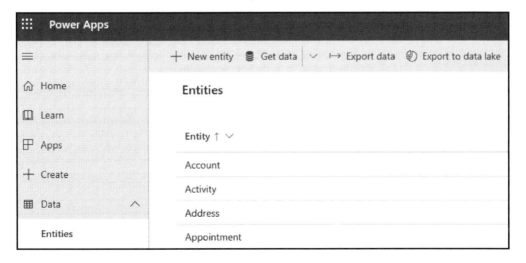

Figure 6.30 – Exporting data in the Power Apps maker portal

The following screenshots will show the steps for exporting the records in the **Account** entity into a CSV file. Clicking on the **Export data** button opens a page where you can select the entities to be exported, as shown in the next figure:

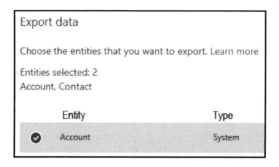

Figure 6.31 – Selecting entities to export

After selecting the entities, click on **Export data**. After a while, the following page will be displayed:

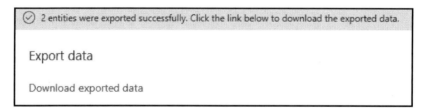

Figure 6.32 – Downloading the exported data

Click on the **Download exported data** link to download the file. The file downloaded will be a CSV file containing all fields for all records in the entity.

 You cannot filter records or choose the fields to be exported with **Export data**.

The other option in the Power Apps maker portal, **Export to data lake**, starts a continuous export of data from Common Data Service to Azure Data Lake Storage Gen2.

Export to data lake is used for analytics services to use the data from your Common Data Service environment. Power BI, Azure Data Factory, Azure Databricks, and Azure Machine Learning will be able to use this data.

The following screenshot shows the first step after you click on **Export to data lake**. You will need to provide the connection details for the Azure Data Lake storage account:

You haven't linked the Common Data Service environment to a data lake

Before you can export to data lake, link the Common Data Service environment to a data lake

New link to data lake

Figure 6.33 – Exporting to a data lake

 You require an Azure subscription and must have created an Azure Data Lake Storage Gen2 account to export to a data lake.

Before this service was available, you could configure the replication of Common Data Service data to an Azure SQL database.

Replicating data to Azure SQL

Data Export Service replicates data from Common Data Service into an Azure SQL database or SQL Server instance running in an Azure virtual machine.

The replication is ongoing and continuous. It utilizes the change tracking feature to pull delta changes of data from Common Data Service, so it is highly efficient.

Replicating Common Data Service to an Azure SQL database enables real-time reporting with Power BI, allows your data to be added to a data warehouse, or allows your data to be combined with data in other systems for reporting.

The Data Export Service is an add-on available from Microsoft AppSource. Here is a screenshot of the **Data Export Service** page in AppSource:

Figure 6.34 – Data Export Service

There is a set of prerequisites for configuring Data Export Service:

- Install the solution from AppSource.
- Get access to an Azure subscription.
- Create an Azure SQL database.
- Create an Azure key vault.
- Enable change tracking on entities in Common Data Service.

Export profiles specify the entities that should be replicated. You can create multiple export profiles.

 The replicated database does not have any of the security associated with the records when it is in Common Data Service. Anyone who has access to the replicated database has access to all the data.

There is another option that can be used to export small sets of data, **Power Automate**.

Using Power Automate

Power Automate flows can be used to retrieve a set of records using the **Get Records** action. A flow can loop through these records and write the data to an Excel or CSV file.

The Get Records action can have an OData query to filter the records for the entity. The flow can then retrieve other data as necessary to create its output.

Using Power Automate in this way enables many scenarios, for example, providing an extract of today's records in a file and sending that file to a supplier.

Many solutions use reference data that needs to be copied between development, test, and production systems. Manually exporting and importing can cause problems where records have changed as importing from Excel only imports new records. The **Configuration Migration tool** solves this problem.

Configuration Migration tool

One of the challenges faced when working on a system is keeping reference data synchronized across environments. The Configuration Migration tool assists in the copying of configuration and reference data from one environment to another.

Scenarios where you might use the Configuration Migration tool to synchronize data are as follows:

- Reference data, such as countries or keywords
- Currencies
- Product catalog
- Portal configuration

The Configuration Migration tool allows you to do the following:

- Export sets of data
- Import sets of data, keeping the same references on all environments
- Import sets of interrelated data

The Configuration Migration tool is contained in the **SDK Core Tools** package, which can be downloaded from NuGet.

The process of using the Configuration Migration tool is as follows:

1. Run the Configuration Migration tool to create the schema file of entities to be exported. This is an XML file.
2. Run the Configuration Migration tool to export the data. The schema file and the data files are combined into a ZIP file.
3. Run the Configuration Migration tool to import the data, selecting the ZIP file.

A system is nothing without its data. Many systems need to have the same reference and configuration data in each environment. The Configuration Migration tool enables you to keep environments in sync with each other.

Summary

In this chapter, we learned about loading data into Common Data Service and extracting data with Common Data Service.

You should now understand how to use the many different methods of importing and exporting data. These are key skills used in the implementation of new systems that use the Power Platform.

In the next chapter, we will look at some of the settings for Common Data Service environments.

Questions

After reading this chapter, test your knowledge with these questions. You will find the answers to these questions under Assessments at the end of the book:

1. Which two file types can you import data from within a model-driven app?

    A) CSV
    B) TXT
    C) XML
    D) ZIP

2. What should you use to ensure that the correct data types are used when creating a file to import data?

    A) Power Query
    B) Data template
    C) Import Data Wizard
    D) Excel template

3. Which tool is used to copy reference data from one environment to another?

    A) Configuration Migration tool
    B) Package Deployer
    C) Solution Packager
    D) App Checker

4. Which tool can transform data and import it into Common Data Service?

    A) Import Data Wizard
    B) Import from Excel
    C) Get data from Excel
    D) Power Query

Further reading

For more details on topics in this chapter, use these resources:

- Import data (all record types) from multiple sources: `https://docs.microsoft.com/power-platform/admin/import-data-all-record-types`
- Import data: `https://docs.microsoft.com/powerapps/user/import-data`
- Import or export data from Common Data Service: `https://docs.microsoft.com/powerapps/maker/common-data-service/data-platform-import-export`
- Add data to an entity in Common Data Service by using Power Query: `https://docs.microsoft.com/powerapps/maker/common-data-service/data-platform-cds-newentity-pq`
- Copy data from and to Dynamics 365 (Common Data Service) or Dynamics CRM by using Azure Data Factory: `https://docs.microsoft.com/azure/data-factory/connector-dynamics-crm-office-365`

- Export entity data to Azure Data Lake Storage Gen2: `https://docs.microsoft.com/powerapps/maker/common-data-service/export-to-data-lake`

- Replicate data to Azure SQL Database using Data Export Service: `https://docs.microsoft.com/power-platform/admin/replicate-data-microsoft-azure-sql-database`

- *Move configuration data across environments and organizations with the Configuration Migration tool*: `https://docs.microsoft.com/power-platform/admin/manage-configuration-data`

Dataverse Settings 7

In the previous chapter, we discussed importing and exporting data. Once you have data, you must configure your **Dataverse** (formerly known as the **Common Data Service** or **CDS**) to be able to enhance the quality of your data and manage how the data is used.

In this chapter, we will discuss the features for managing data once it is in the Dataverse, including finding duplicates, cleansing data, how to remove data when it is no longer required, and how to monitor and control data volumes.

 At the time of publishing, Microsoft Dataverse (formerly known as the Common Data Service) was undergoing a branding change. This name change has not yet been applied to all the tools, connectors, and user interfaces in the Power Platform. You will see the use of Common Data Service and the abbreviation of CDS throughout this chapter.

The topics covered in this chapter are as follows:

- Configuring duplicate detection
- Cleansing data
- Managing data growth
- Configuring auditing
- Configuring search

By the end of this chapter, you will be able to configure duplicate detection, use bulk delete to manage data growth, and configure key features, such as auditing and search. Knowing how to use these features is a key skill of a functional consultant in getting a Power Platform solution ready for use and in terms of ongoing management of the solution.

Configuring duplicate detection

In many systems, it is important for records to be unique. Having multiple records referring to the same object or person can cause users to miss vital information. The Dataverse has a feature to identify duplicate records and prevent them from being created. This is called **duplicate detection**.

Duplicate detection has three components:

- **Duplicate detection settings**: Enable and disable duplicate detection.
- **Duplicate detection rules**: Define how records are matched.
- **Duplicate detection jobs**: Create scheduled jobs to detect duplicates.

You can access the duplicate detection feature from the Power Platform admin center. Select an environment, open **Settings**, and then expand **Data management**. You will see the three duplicate detection components (**settings**, **rules**, and **jobs**), as shown in the following screenshot:

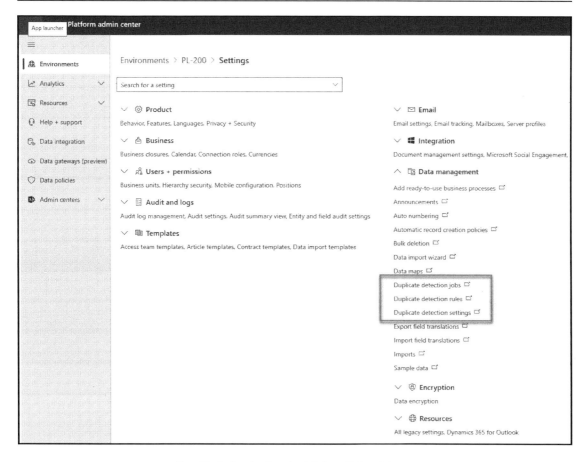

Figure 7.1 – Duplicate detection options in the Power Platform admin center

You need to decide where duplication detection is used in your application. **Duplicate detection settings** control how duplicate records are identified and shown to users.

Duplicate detection settings

Duplicate detection settings allow you to turn off duplicate detection entirely, or to just disable it when creating/updating records., or during data import, as shown in the following screenshot:

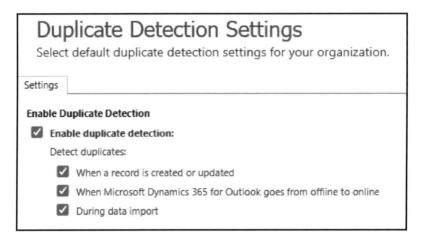

Figure 7.2 – Duplicate Detection Settings

All duplicate detection settings are *enabled* by default.

To use duplicate detection on an entity, you first need to enable the entity for duplicate detection in the entity properties. The following screenshot shows how to enable duplicate detection for an entity in the maker portal:

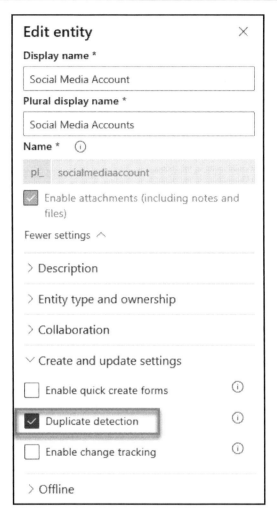

Figure 7.3 – Enabling entity for duplicate detection

Once you have enabled the entity, you can create duplicate detection rules that identify duplicate records.

Duplicate detection rules

The duplicate detection rules define the entities and fields to compare when performing duplicate detection. Each rule defines the entity that wants to find duplicates. The rule then has one or more fields to match together with the criteria for matching values.

Clicking on **Duplicate detection rules** in the Power Platform admin center opens a new page showing the list of rules already in the environment, as shown here:

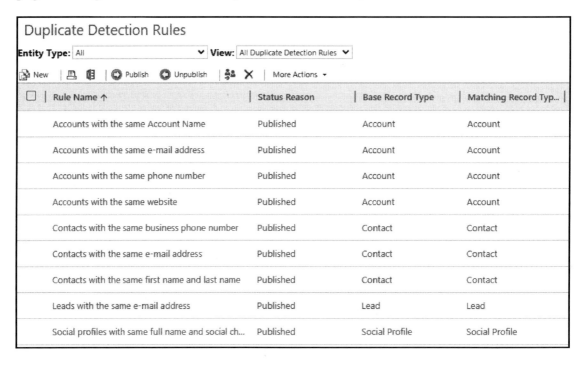

Figure 7.4 – Duplicate Detection Rules

There are rules for **Account**, **Contact**, and **Lead** included. You can edit these rules and create new rules. To create a new rule, click on **New** in the toolbar. This will open a new window, as shown in the following screenshot:

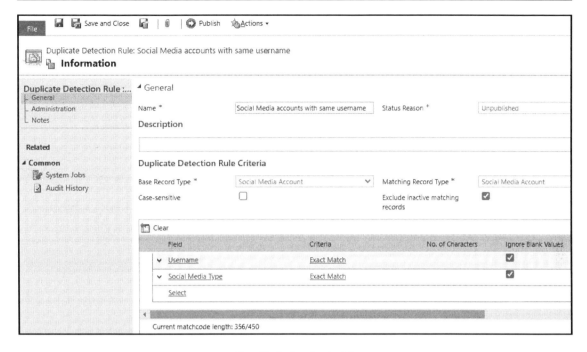

Figure 7.5 – Duplicate Detection Rule

The duplicate detection rule first defines the entity, or record type, to check duplicates against. Select the entity from the drop-down list. The entity will automatically be selected as the matching record type.

If your entity does not appear in the drop-down list, you need to enable the entity for duplicate detection.

You can choose whether the matching record type is case-sensitive and whether the duplicate detection should match deactivated records. Typically, you would choose not to be case-sensitive and to exclude inactive records.

You can change the matching record type to another entity to match across records, for example, checking whether a new lead already exists as a contact.

After selecting the entities, you define the fields to use for matching. Select a field from the drop-down list and then choose the matching criteria. You can specify these criteria:

- Exact match
- The same first number of characters
- The same last number of characters
- To ignore blank or null values

Ignoring blank values prevents the rule from generating false matches where the field is blank.

You can add more than one field to a rule to combine the fields to prevent false matches. For instance, in some countries, some first and last names are very common, and you need to include other fields, such as phone number or email address, to prevent false-positive matches.

Adding multiple fields to a rule means all the fields must match. This is the equivalent of an AND operation. If you need to perform an OR operation, such as matching on the email address or phone number, you need to create separate rules, one for matching on the phone number and one for matching on the email address. You can have five duplicate detection rules per entity.

A duplicate detection rule is unpublished when created. You must publish the rule in order for duplicates to be detected. Publishing a rule changes its status to **Publishing**. The CDS will start a system job to generate a matchcode for every record in the entity. **Matchcodes** are a separate table containing all the fields you specify in the rule. Matchcodes are used to improve performance, so duplicate detection processing does not have to scan all the records in your entity. Depending on the number of records in your entity, generating the matchcodes could take several hours.

The following screenshot shows the rule with the publishing status:

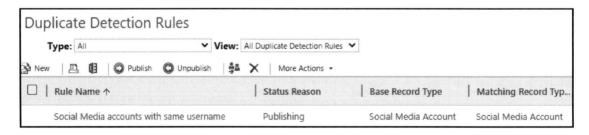

Figure 7.6 – Publishing a duplicate detection rule

Once the rule has been published and matchcodes generated, duplicate records will now be detected when users create or edit records. The following screenshot shows what the user will see when they create a record that matches the rules:

Figure 7.7 – Duplicate detected

The user chooses whether to create the duplicate record. Users are not always able to determine whether a record is a true duplicate, and so will often ignore the warning and save the record.

You can use duplicate detection jobs to find all duplicate records.

Duplicate detection jobs

Duplicate detection jobs are used to find all duplicate records so that an administrator who understands the data can make an informed decision as to whether the record is a true duplicate. The administrator can merge and deactivate duplicate records.

Duplicate detection jobs are system jobs created by a wizard. Clicking on **Duplicate detection jobs** in the Power Platform admin center opens a new page showing the list of jobs already in the environment, as shown in the following screenshot:

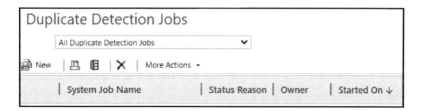

Figure 7.8 – Duplicate Detection Jobs

Clicking on **New** opens the wizard, as shown in the following screenshot:

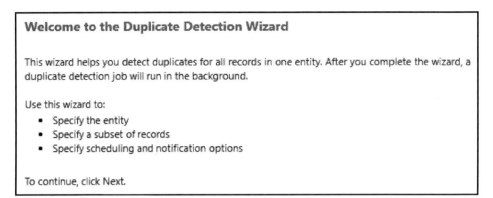

Figure 7.9 – Duplicate detection job wizard step 1

Clicking on the **Next** button reveals the next step in the wizard:

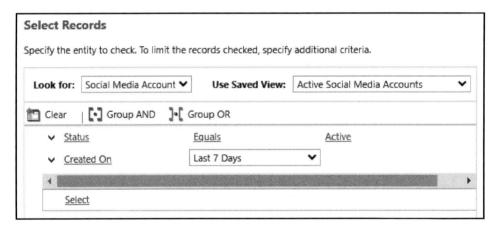

Figure 7.10 – Duplicate detection job wizard step 2

On this page, you select the entity you wish to find duplicates for. You also select the records you want to check. You can use a view or add additional selection criteria. In the following screenshot, the job looks only at active records created in the previous 7 days. Clicking on **Next** shows the next step in the wizard:

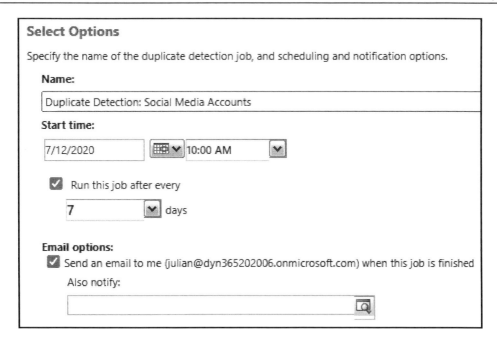

Figure 7.11 – Duplicate detection job wizard step 3

On this page, you name the job and specify the date and time when it should start. You can also schedule the job to run every 7, 30, 90, 180, or 365 days. Clicking on **Next** opens the final page of the wizard:

Figure 7.12 – Duplicate detection job wizard final step

Click on **Submit** to run the job. After the job has completed, you can view the job to see all the duplicate records, as shown in the following screenshot:

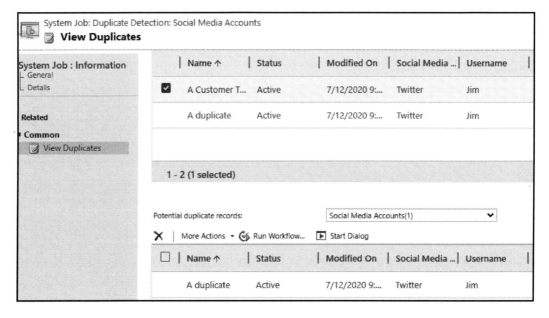

Figure 7.13 – Duplicate detection job results

 Duplicate detection rules cannot be included in solutions.

Duplicate detection is one way of cleansing data in your environment. Let's now look at other ways to cleanse data.

Cleansing data

When migrating or importing data, the quality of the data can be lower than if the data was entered in your apps. The import tools will not fail if data is missing from fields. This can lead to issues when accessing imported data.

There are a number of problems that are commonly encountered when importing data:

- Users are unable to save records as the required fields are blank.
- Errors are processed due to invalid or missing data.

There are several approaches that you can take to cleanse data:

- Cleanse before import: If the data is in Excel or CSV format, you can use Excel to examine the data, correct errors, and add missing values.
- Use Power Query to import the data: Power Query has the functionality to filter records, transform data, and add or calculate missing values. Power Query is an **ETL (Extract, Transform, and Load)** tool.
- List data to be cleansed: Create views that list the missing values of records and let users fix the data using the forms in the app.
- Cleanse outside of the system: Export the data, cleanse it outside of the CDS, and re-import the updated records.
- Cleanse after import: Use **Advanced Find** to select the records with issues and then use Excel Online to edit the records in bulk.

> Create views for missing data, and then create a dashboard called **Data Quality** containing these views. Users can then easily see any data issues and resolve them.

Excel Online is a way to quickly correct data. You can use Excel Online from the **Export to Excel** button in the **Action** bar. The current view of data is opened in Excel Online, as shown in the following screenshot:

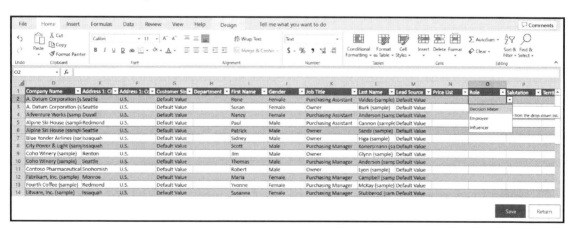

Figure 7.14 – Excel Online

You can then complete the missing data and correct the values pertaining to the records. When you have finished, click on **Save** and the changes will be submitted as an import job and records created and updated in the background.

The other aspect of cleansing data is to remove data you no longer need, such as the following:

- Data that is no longer relevant
- Data that is stale – activities older than the data retention policies
- Merged records
- Deactivated records
- Test data

You can use the bulk delete feature to clean up data by deleting records on a scheduled basis. Bulk delete jobs have the same steps as duplicate detection jobs. First, you select the entity and define the query for the records to delete. Then you specify the date and time, and the frequency for the bulk delete jobs to run.

 To use bulk delete, you must have the Bulk Delete privilege and the Delete privilege on the entity and with the access level for the records selected.

Bulk delete is the main method by which you can manage data growth. We will talk about this in the next section.

Managing data growth

In the CDS, storage is a premium resource. Each tenant has a capacity allowance for the CDS, shared between the environments. Capacity is calculated from the number and type of licenses purchased. You can buy additional storage allowance if you exceed the capacity.

Additional storage is expensive and so you must monitor your storage use and take steps to reduce the storage used. You can monitor the capacity from within the Power Platform admin center, as shown in the following screenshot:

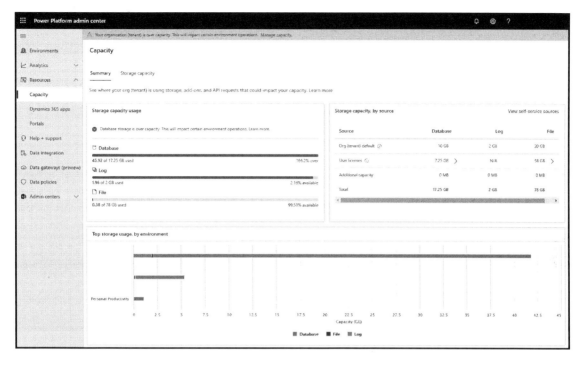

Figure 7.15 – Storage capacity

The preceding capacity report shows that the storage used exceeds the capacity allowance from licenses. To bring this tenant back into compliance, the organization will have to do one of the following:

- Purchase additional capacity.
- Use bulk delete to reduce the amount of data.

As we know that purchasing additional capacity is an expensive option, we will look at how to use the bulk delete feature.

Using bulk delete

In the user interface, a user can only delete up to 250 records at a time. If you have more records to delete, you can use the bulk delete feature.

Bulk delete is found in the user interface by clicking the arrow to the right of the **DELETE** button, as shown here:

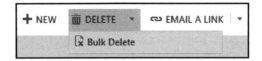

Figure 7.16 – Bulk Delete option

The following screenshots will show the steps in the bulk delete wizard to create a bulk delete job in order to delete completed tasks over 3 months old.

Bulk delete is a privilege in security roles. If you do not have the privilege, then you will not see the Bulk Delete option.

To start the wizard, click on the **Bulk Delete** button. The first page of the wizard will open, as shown in the following screenshot:

Figure 7.17 – Bulk delete wizard step 1

On this page, you select the entity in relation to which you want to delete records. In this example, **Tasks** has been chosen. Bulk delete uses a query to delete records that are created in a comparable way to **Advanced Find**. You can either reuse a query from a view or create your own query. The following screenshot shows how to find all completed tasks over 3 months old:

Figure 7.18 – Bulk delete wizard step 2

After you click on **Next**, the wizard moves to the next step, as shown in the following screenshot:

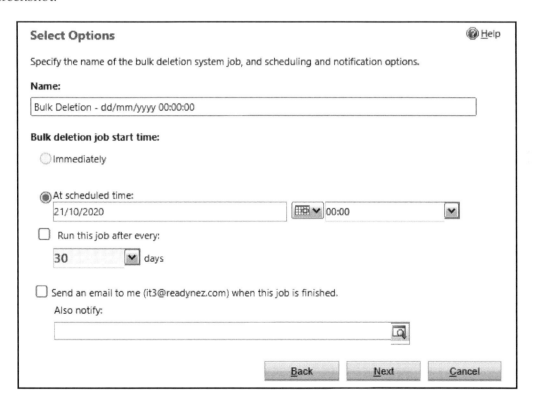

Figure 7.19 – Bulk delete wizard step 3

On this page, you specify the name of the bulk delete job, and when the job should be run. You can either run immediately or at a future date. You can also schedule the bulk delete job to run on a regular occurrence either every 7 days, 30 days, 90 days, 180 days, or 365 days. When the job has finished, you can request that an email be sent to you with a link to the details of the completed job.

Clicking **Next** moves to the final step, as shown in the following screenshot:

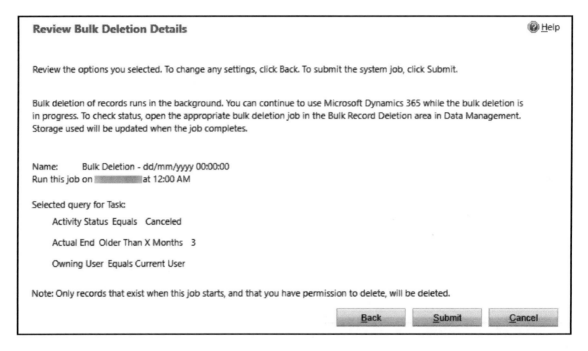

Figure 7.20 – Bulk delete wizard step 4

On this page, a summary of the bulk delete job is displayed. Clicking **Submit** will schedule the bulk delete job to be run.

Bulk delete jobs are run in the background. You can view the progress of the jobs in the **System Jobs** area, as shown in the following screenshot:

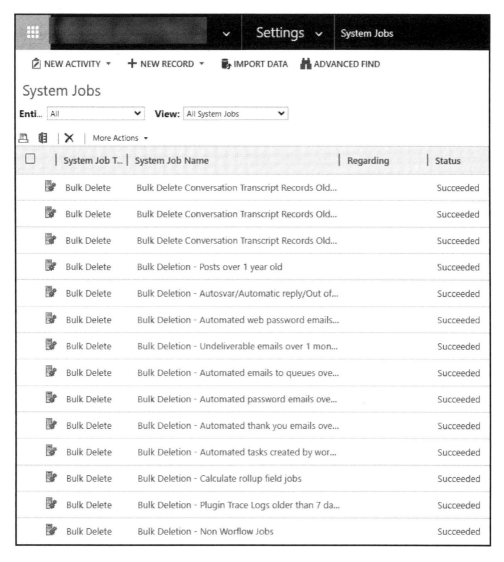

Figure 7.21 – Bulk delete jobs

Bulk delete is an effective way to meet your organization's data retention rules. You can schedule multiple jobs to delete old and stale data on a weekly or monthly basis. Bulk delete can be used to prevent your storage capacity from growing unnecessarily high.

Tracking the changes users have made to data is often required by organizations. The CDS has inbuilt data auditing.

Configuring auditing

The CDS has auditing features to help you meet compliance and security requirements. Auditing shows who made changes to the data, settings, and security configurations, as well as some customizations.

Auditing can help you to understand how users work and can be used to verify whether users are working to the defined business processes.

The changes are logged in audit logs. The audit logs show both the before and after values of changes to data fields.

For changed data, you can use the values that are stored before the change to help you revert to these values if a field has been changed in error.

Enabling auditing creates an additional load for the CDS. Microsoft has made auditing as efficient as possible and users will not normally be aware of the auditing processing, but you should only use auditing to identify and track specific concerns, or data where you need to ensure compliance.

Audit settings are configured in the Power Platform admin center, as shown in the following screenshot:

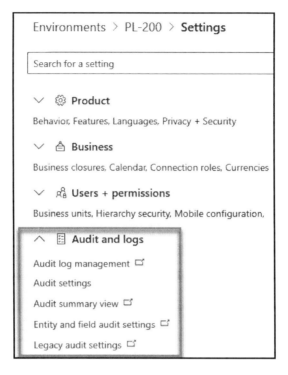

Figure 7.22 – Audit options in the Power Platform admin center

Clicking on **Audit settings** opens the global audit settings, as shown in the following screenshot:

Environments > PL-200 > Settings > **Audit settings**

Auditing

Manage logging for Common Data Service data

- ☑ Start Auditing
- ☐ Log access ⓘ
- ☐ Read logs ⓘ

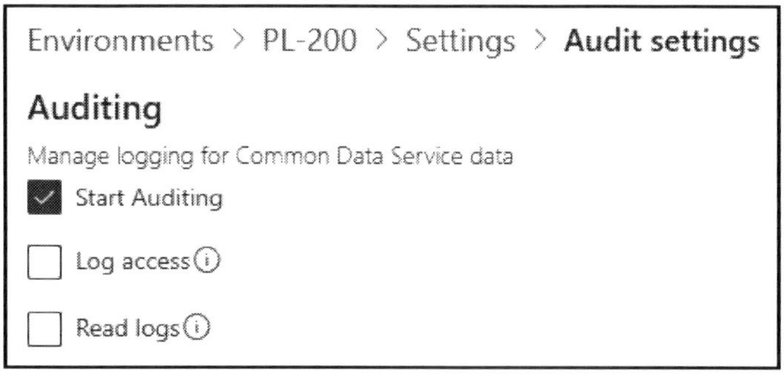

Figure 7.23 – Audit settings

In the audit settings, there are three options:

- **Start Auditing**: Enables or disables auditing for the entire organization
- **Log access**: Tracks when users or services access the environment
- **Read logs**: Sends audit log information to the Office 365 Security and Compliance Center

Starting auditing is not enough to audit data changes.

Understanding how auditing works

Auditing creates a log record for every change to a field value on a record. This audit history is a log of all user data changes. By default, the auditing feature is disabled, and no changes are logged.

To enable auditing, you must enable auditing at three levels:

- **Organization**: *Off* by default. **Start Auditing** in **Audit settings** turns auditing *on* for the organization.
- **Entity**: *Off* by default. Each entity must be enabled for auditing. This cannot currently be done in the Power Apps maker portal; you must switch to the classic solution explorer.
- **Field**: *On* by default. Fields can be enabled and disabled for auditing in the Power Apps maker portal.

To enable an entity for auditing, choose the **Auditing** option in the properties for an entity. The following screenshot shows how to enable an entity for auditing:

Data Services

☐ Allow quick create
☐ Duplicate detection
☑ Auditing
By default, all fields for this entity are enabled for auditing. Choose the Fields tab to enable or disable specific fields for auditing.

Figure 7.24 – Enabling an entity for auditing

Enabling an entity for auditing is not yet available in the Power Apps maker portal and you need to switch to classic to access the preceding options.

To enable a field for auditing, you choose the **Enable auditing** option in the field properties. The following screenshot shows how to enable a field for auditing:

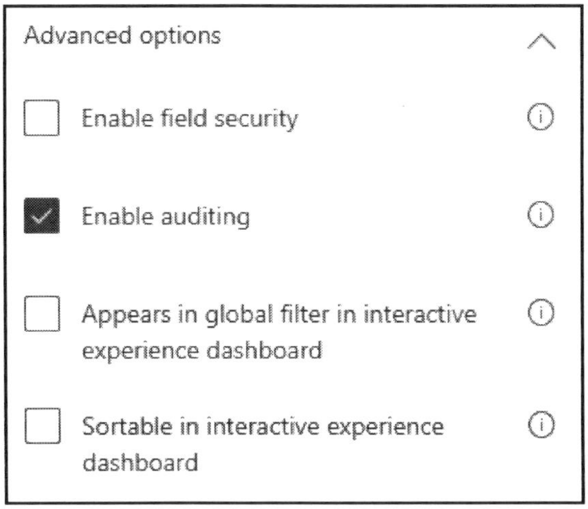

Figure 7.25 – Enabling an auditing field

After auditing is enabled, the following changes are recorded in the CDS audit logs:

- Creation of records
- Update of records
- Deletion of records
- Association and disassociation of records in many-to-many relationships
- Changes to auditing settings
- Deletion of audit logs
- Changes to security roles
- User logins (if log access is enabled)

The following changes are not recorded in the CDS audit logs:

- Reading records
- Querying records
- Changing metadata, for example, making a field required
- Changes to attachments

Changes to data are stored in audit logs. You can view audit logs in two ways.

Viewing audit records

The audit feature is designed not to affect performance. Auditing does not store the audit details in standard CDS entities. This means that you cannot access the details of the changes made in the same way as a standard entity.

Audit transactions can be viewed from the following two places in the user interface: **Audit History** and **Audit Summary**.

Audit History is a view of all the changes made to a record. The old and new values are listed for each change with the date and time, and the user who made the change. **Audit History** is available from an entity form under related records. The following screenshot shows an example of **Audit History** for a record:

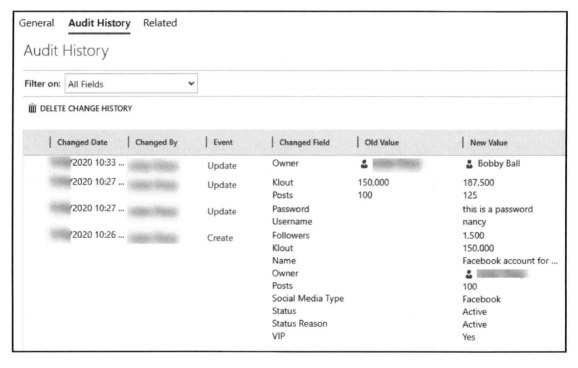

Figure 7.26 – Audit History

Audit Summary is the view of all audit events for the environment. The summary shows the user who made the change, the date and time, the record changed, and the data operation made. **Audit Summary** is available from the Power Platform admin center. The following screenshot shows the **Audit Summary** page:

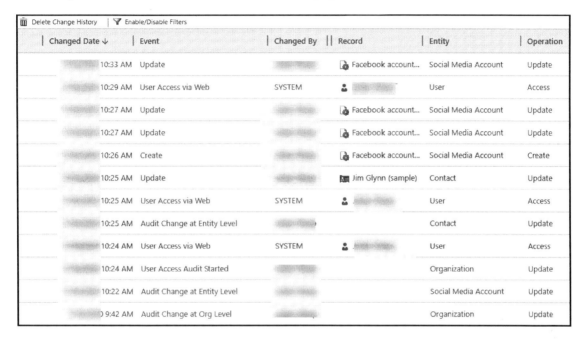

Figure 7.27 – Audit Summary

 You can delete individual audit records in this view with the **Delete Change History** button.

Enabling auditing stores additional data. The storage of audit logs needs to be managed.

Managing audit logs

There is a separate capacity allowance for audit logs. The default capacity is 2 GB. It will be necessary to delete old audit logs to reduce the space used.

A new audit log is created every 90 days. Clicking on **Audit log management** in the Power Platform admin center opens a list of the logs, as shown in the following screenshot:

Figure 7.28 – Audit logs

You can delete audit logs from this screen. Deleting an audit log deletes all history for the time period covered by the audit log.

 You can only delete the oldest audit log. The current log cannot be deleted.

Access to all auditing features is managed by privileges in security roles.

Managing audit security

Access to the auditing features is controlled by security. Typically, users will not have access to audit data and will not be aware of data changes being logged in auditing.

There are four privileges in security roles related to auditing:

- **View Audit History**: View the audit history within an entity form.
- **View Audit Summary**: View the audit summary page.
- **View Audit Partitions:** View the audit logs.
- **Delete Audit Partitions**: Delete the audit logs. This capability should only be given to an administrator.

These privileges are at the bottom of the general tab in the security role, as shown in the following screenshot:

Figure 7.29 – Audit privileges

These privileges are either *on* or *off*. Users do not need any privileges to create audit records as auditing is performed by the system automatically.

The main deficiency of auditing in the CDS is the lack of auditing of data reads. Tracking who is accessing records without updating them is a common compliance request. Microsoft makes all audit logs available from the Microsoft 365 Security and Compliance Center with the added benefit of including *reads* and other data viewing activities, such as exporting to Excel.

Enabling read logging

In **Audit settings**, there is the option to enable read logging. This option logs events in Microsoft 365 alongside other applications and services.

The activities that are logged in Microsoft 365 are more extensive than those in the CDS. Some of the activities that are logged include the following:

- Reads of individual records
- Queries of multiple records
- Export to Excel
- Adding a user to a team

There are some restrictions:

- A Microsoft 365 Enterprise E3 or E5 subscription is required.
- Only Power Platform production environments are supported.

The activity logs can be viewed in the Microsoft 365 Security and Compliance Center at `https://protection.office.com`, as shown in the following screenshot:

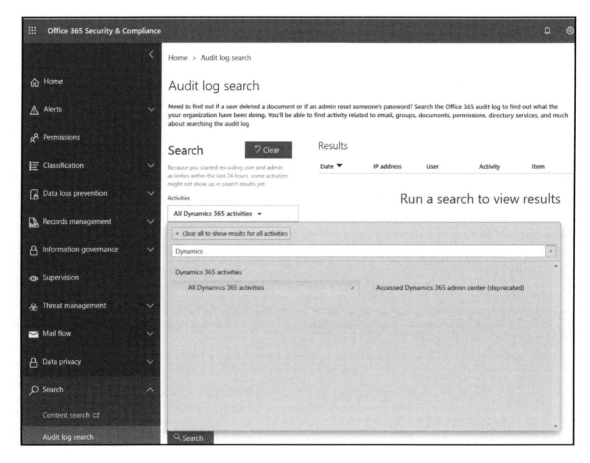

Figure 7.30 – Search activity logs

One of the most beneficial configurations you can do for users is to make it easier to find their data.

Configuring search

Users need to be able to search for and find records from within the user interface of an app. There are several typical search requirements, such as finding a specific record, or finding all similar records, to be able to create complex queries to find a set of records.

There are several different ways to search for data in a model-driven app:

- **Quick Find**: Each entity has a search field in the top right of the view that searches specified fields in that entity.
- **Advanced Find**: A tool to create and run complex queries.
- **Categorized Search**: Searches across up to 10 entities using the fields defined for **Quick Find**.
- **Relevance Search:** Searches across multiple entities and fields utilizing the Azure Search functionality.

An example of using **Quick Find** is shown in the following screenshot:

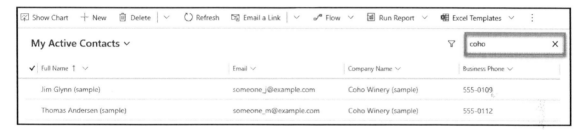

Figure 7.31 – Quick Find

The fields searched on can be changed in the Power Apps maker portal by customizing the Quick Find view in the entity. The following screenshot shows the view editor for the **Contact Quick Find** view:

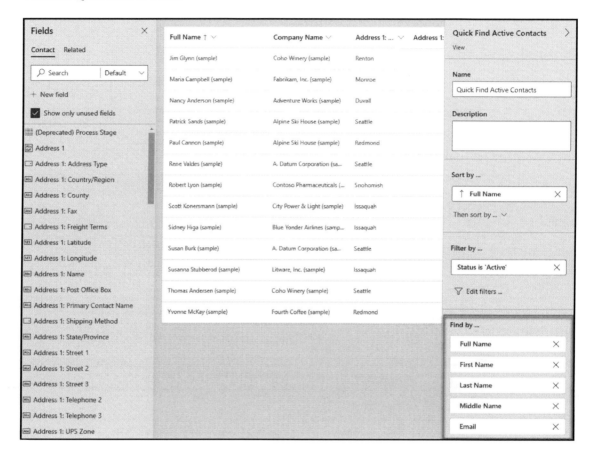

Figure 7.32 – Customizing the Quick Find view

Advanced Find is a powerful tool that allows queries to be built and saved. An example query is shown in the following screenshot:

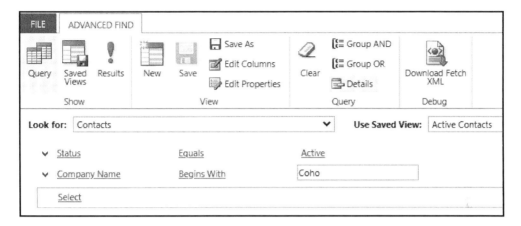

Figure 7.33 – ADVANCED FIND

 Mastering Advanced Find is a key skill for functional consultants.

Categorized Search is available from the search icon in the application toolbar at the top of the app, as shown in the following screenshot:

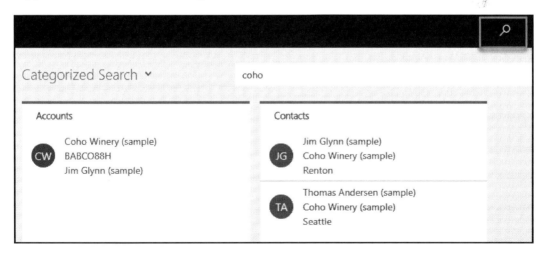

Figure 7.34 – Categorized Search

Categorized Search uses the fields defined in the **Quick Find** view for the entities selected in **System Settings**.

Relevance Search performs an intelligent search of data and attachments using the Azure Search functionality. **Relevance Search** must be enabled in the Power Platform admin center, as shown in the following screenshot:

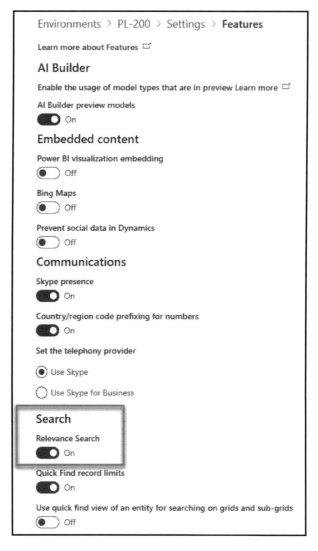

Figure 7.35 – Enabling Relevance Search

Once enabled, **Relevance Search** is available from the same icon as **Categorized Search**. An example of the results of the relevance search is shown in the following screenshot:

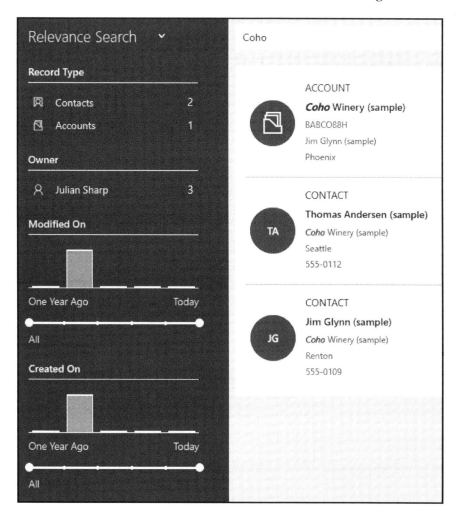

Figure 7.36 – Relevance Search

Relevance Search is the preferred method for finding records as it searches more fields than the other methods and searches in notes and the contents of attachments. **Relevance Search** understands inflections and ranks the results. A user can use the facets on the left-hand pane to filter the search results.

Summary

In this chapter, we learned about some of the key settings in the CDS.

You should now understand how to monitor data volumes and manage data growth using the capacity reporting in the Power Platform Admin Center and Bulk Delete to delete stale data. You should be able to implement and monitor auditing and configure a search. These are key skills employed in both the implementation of new systems that use the Power Platform and in the ongoing day-to-day operation of the system.

In the next chapter, we will look at the security features of the CDS.

Questions

After reading this chapter, test your knowledge with these questions. You will find the answers to these questions under `Assessments` at the end of the book:

1. Which of the following should you create to ensure that unique records are created when importing data?

   A)A bulk delete job
   B) A duplicate detection rule
   C) A duplicate detection job
   D) A data integration project

2. Which three levels do you need to enable auditing for?

   A) Business unit
   B) Entity
   C) Field
   D) Organization
   E) Tenant

3. How often are audit logs created?

   A) Every 7 days
   B) Every 30 days
   C) Every 90 days
   D)Every 180 days

4. Which of the following isn't audited by the CDS?

   A) Who deleted a record
   B) Who performed a query on records
   C) Who changed the ownership of a record
   D) Who changed the privileges on a security role

Further reading

For more details on the topics covered in this chapter, please refer to the following resources:

- System Settings Auditing tab: `https://docs.microsoft.com/power-platform/admin/system-settings-dialog-box-auditing-tab`
- Audit data and user activity for security and compliance: `https://docs.microsoft.com/power-platform/admin/audit-data-user-activity`
- Enabling and using Activity Logging: `https://docs.microsoft.com/power-platform/admin/enable-use-comprehensive-auditing`
- Configuring Relevance Search to improve search results and performance: `https://docs.microsoft.com/power-platform/admin/configure-relevance-search-organization`

8
Security

Apps that you build require access to data in the **Common Data Service** (**CDS**). You need to understand how to apply security to restrict a user's access to data and functionality. You can also control access to environments and apps through the different layers of security.

Security is a broad topic, and the CDS has a wide set of security features that are discussed in this chapter. The chapter will begin with an overview of the available features and will then concentrate on the security features you are likely to employ within your systems.

In this chapter, we will cover the following topics:

- Overview of the available security features
- Security in the CDS
- Users and teams
- Hierarchical security
- Field-level security

By the end of this chapter, you will be able to employ the appropriate security features, create and manage security roles, enable field-level security, enable hierarchical security, and manage user and team security.

Overview of security features

The control of access to data and functionalities is extremely important in any system. The CDS has a powerful and flexible security model that can be configured to meet many different security requirements.

Security is controlled by different products, such as the following:

- **Azure Active Directory** (**AD**) handles the authentication of users.
- **Office 365** and **Azure AD** manage users and their licenses.

- Access to environments can be restricted in the **Power Platform admin center**.
- **CDS databases** manage security, authorizing the use of data and services within applications.

Security in the Power Platform and CDS is provided by multiple layers, all aimed at ensuring users can only access the apps, features, and data they need and no more. The following diagram shows the layers of security in the Power Platform:

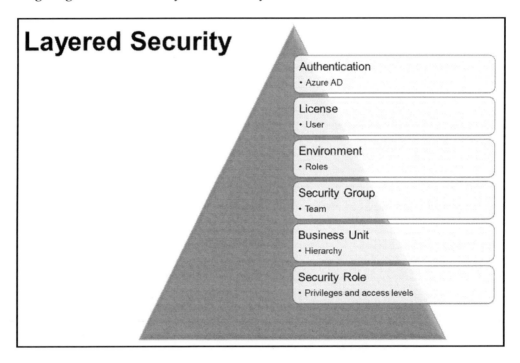

Figure 8.1 – Layered security model

Before we look at these capabilities and features of security in the CDS, we need to consider the security aspects of the cloud.

Cloud security

The CDS runs on the Microsoft cloud as a service on top of Azure. The CDS inherits security, privacy, and compliance protections from Azure, leverages other security features to protect your data and apps, and assists in your compliance with the **General Data Protection Regulation** (**GDPR**) and other privacy initiatives.

Because the CDS runs in the cloud, Microsoft has enabled multiple security protections for your apps and data.

Securing data with encryption

Your data is encrypted at rest using SQL Server **Transparent Data Encryption** (TDE). There is a default encryption key generated for each CDS database that you should manage and make a safe copy of.

All data is secured in transit between the Microsoft data centers and your devices.

Authenticating apps

The authentication for your apps, maker portal, and admin portals is handled by Azure AD. This means you inherit all the capabilities of Azure AD for your apps including multi-factor authentication, Conditional Access policies, identity protection, **Business-to-Business (B2B)** access, and **Single Sign-On (SSO)**.

> Refer to https://docs.microsoft.com/azure/active-directory/ conditional-access/overview for more information on Conditional Access.

SSO adds both security and convenience for users. SSO enables users to access apps by logging on only once to their PC and Azure AD. Users are not prompted to access Dynamics 365 or Power Platform apps again, with SSO handling authentication on your behalf. Once authenticated, the Power Platform then authorizes access to your environments.

Environment security

An environment is a container for your data, apps, and flows; you first learned about environments in Chapter 2, *Power Platform*.

Each environment is controlled by the security functionalities to restrict who can access the environment. The access to such security functionalities is different depending on whether there is a CDS database in the environment or not.

Environments can be linked to an Azure AD security group. Once linked, only users in that security group will be able to access that environment.

Without a CDS database, access is controlled by users being given either of the following roles on the environment:

- Environment Maker
- Environment Admin

 For more details on security in environments, see `https://docs.`
`microsoft.com/power-platform/admin/environments-`
`overview#environment-permissions`.

Once a CDS database has been added to an environment, access is controlled by CDS security roles. Users must have a security role to be able to access data in the CDS database.

Security in the CDS

The CDS is not just a data store for your apps to read and write data. The CDS has a comprehensive set of security features that you can employ in your Power Platform system.

This section will describe the various features so that you can decide which feature(s) map to your security requirements. As shown in the following diagram, the CDS has a set of complementary security features that control access to data, features, and apps:

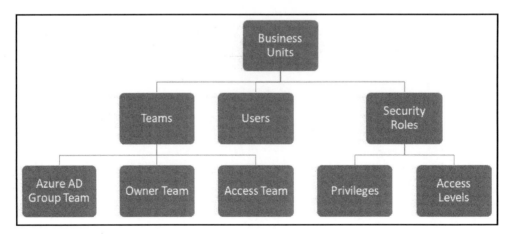

Figure 8.2 – CDS security features

You will learn about these features in the following sections. First, we will look at the cornerstone of security, business units.

Business units

Business units provide the basis for security within the CDS. A business unit is a security boundary used to control access to data.

Business units can be arranged in a hierarchy such as in the following diagram:

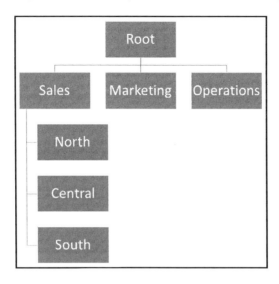

Figure 8.3 – Example business unit hierarchy

Every CDS database has a business unit automatically created when the database is created. This is known as the root business unit and is normally named after the environment's name. The root business unit cannot be disabled or deleted.

You can create business units, but these child business units must always have a parent business unit; only the root business unit cannot have a parent. Unlike the root business unit, child business units can be disabled and deleted.

You manage business units from your environment's settings in the Power Platform admin center. The following screenshot shows an example list of business units:

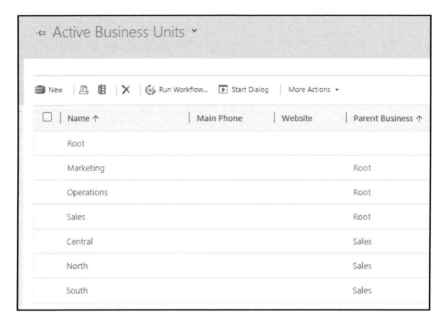

Figure 8.4 – Business units

The business hierarchy reflects your organization's internal structure. However, you should not simply replicate your org chart; instead, you should create your business unit hierarchy to meet the needs of your security requirements. Users will never see business units in model-driven apps and should not be aware of them. It may be sufficient for your needs to just have the single root business unit, or you may require multiple business units to control access by functional areas or by geography, or even a combination of function and region, as shown in the preceding diagram.

Business units work with security roles to determine a user's access to data.

Security roles

The CDS employs the concept of **Role-Based Access Control (RBAC)**. Note that roles within the CDS are referred to as **security roles**. A security role is a collection of privileges and access levels. There are several security roles provided to enable you to get started quickly, for example, the **Common Data Service User** role shown in the following screenshot:

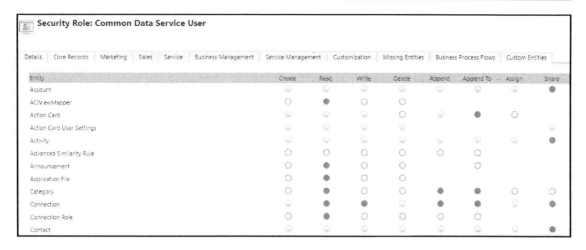

Figure 8.5 – Common Data Service User security role

There are two types of privilege contained in a security role:

- **Record-level**: For entities and records
- **Task-based**: For specific features or operations

The following screenshot shows some of the record-level privileges in a security role:

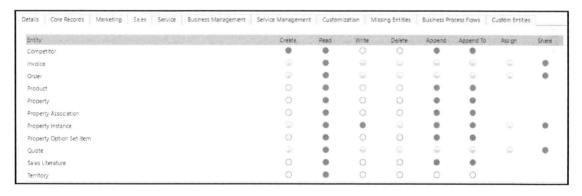

Figure 8.6 – Record-level privileges

As shown in the previous screenshot, record-level privileges define the operations that a user can perform for each entity, and for the records of that entity:

- **Create**: Used to create a new record.
- **Read**: Used to view records.
- **Write**: Used to edit or update records.
- **Delete**: Used to delete records.
- **Append/Append To**: These work in combinations of one-to-many and many-to-many relationships to control whether one record can be attached to another record.
- **Assign**: To change the ownership of a record to a different user or team.
- **Share**: To share a record with another user or team.

 Entities can either be user-, team-, or organization-owned. Entities that are organization-owned do not have the **Assign** and **Share** privileges as these privileges are concerned with record ownership – records for organization-owned entities do not have an owner.

These privileges affect the user interface for model-driven apps, such as in the following examples:

- If a user does not have at least read access on an entity, then that entity will not be shown in the model-driven app; it will not be shown in the navigation or appear in **Advanced Find**.
- If a user does not have the **Create** privilege for an entity, then the **+ NEW** button will not be shown in the action bar.
- If a user does not have the **Delete** privilege on a record, then the delete icon will not be shown in the form for that record.
- If a user does not have the **Append To** privilege on a record, then they will be unable to attach other records to it such as phone calls, tasks, emails, and other types of activity.

 Security roles provide access to records. If a user has access to a record, then they have access to all fields for that record.

The following screenshot shows some of the task-based privileges in a security role:

Privacy Related Privileges

Enabling these privileges will allow users to extract customer data from Microsoft Dynamics 365. For more information, review the corresponding user documentation.

Document Generation	●	Dynamics 365 for mobile	●
Export to Excel	●	Go Offline in Outlook	●
Mail Merge	●	Print	●
Sync to Outlook	●	Use Dynamics 365 App for Outlook	●

Miscellaneous Privileges

Act on Behalf of Another User	○	Approve Email Addresses for Users or Queues	○
Assign manager for a user	○	Assign position for a user	○
Assign Territory to User	○	Bulk Edit	●
Change Hierarchy Security Settings	○	Dynamics 365 Address Book	●
Enable or Disable Business Unit	○	Enable or Disable User	○
Language Settings	○	Merge	●
Override Created on or Created by for Records during Data Import	○	Perform in sync rollups on goals	○
Read License Info	●	Reparent Business unit	○
Reparent team	○	Reparent user	○
Send Email as Another User	○	Send Invitation	○
Update Business Closures	○	Web Mail Merge	●

Figure 8.7 – Task-based privileges

As shown in the previous screenshot, task-based privileges permit a user to perform specific tasks, such as exporting to Excel, merging records, or using the app for Outlook. Typically, these privileges will be buttons in the action bar of a view or a form. If a user does not have the privilege for a task, the related button will not be shown on the action bar.

You will have noticed that in the previous screenshots, each privilege is represented by a circle and that the circles have assorted colors.

Access levels

Access levels are where the privileges are combined with the business unit hierarchy to determine the privileges for each record. The following screenshot shows how access levels are represented on the security role page:

Figure 8.8 – Access levels

As shown in the previous screenshot, there are five access levels:

- **None**: An empty circle with a red boundary. This means the user will not have this privilege.
- **User**: A quarter-filled yellow circle. If a user owns the record, they will have this privilege.
- **Business Unit**: A yellow semi-circle. If a user is in the same business unit as the record, they will have this privilege.
- **Parent: Child Business Units**: A three-quarter-filled green circle. If a record is in the same business unit as the user, or in a business unit in the hierarchy underneath the user, they will have this privilege.
- **Organization**: A green solid circle. This means the user will have this privilege on all records.

This is easier to understand with an example:

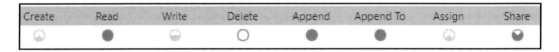

Figure 8.9 – Example access levels for an entity

In the preceding example, the security role has the following access levels for an entity's privileges:

- **Create User**: The user will be able to create a record, but they will not be able to change the owner of the record before saving; that is, they will be the owner of the record.
- **Read Organization**: The user will be able to see all records for the entity, no matter who owns the records, or where the user is in the business unit hierarchy.
- **Write Business Unit**: The user will be able to update records they own, and any record owned by users in the same business unit.
- **Delete None**: The user will not be able to delete any records for the entity even if they own the record.
- **Append Organization**: The user will be able to link this record to a parent record, that is, for a many-to-one relationship.
- **Append To Organization**: The user will be able to link other records for entities in a one-to-many relationship.

- **Assign User**: The user will be able to change the ownership, but only on records where they are the owner.
- **Share Parent: Child Business Units**: The user will be able to share records they own, records owned by users in the same business unit as the user, and records owned by business units in the hierarchy underneath the user's business unit.

 Assign and Share privileges do not control to whom a user can assign or share to; that is controlled by the Append privilege on the entity combined with the Append To privilege they have on the User and Team entities. The Assign and Share privileges control which records you can assign and share.

Where there is a many-to-many relationship between two entities, the Append and Append To privileges are required on both entities in the relationship. Organization-owned entities have only the None and Organization access levels; that is, they are on/off or all/nothing.

Business units, users, and security roles

Business units are the cornerstone of security in the CDS. All users must belong to one, and only one, business unit. A user's access to records flows from their place in the business unit hierarchy.

This section explains how business units, users, and security roles come together to give users access to data. Security starts from the hierarchy of business units and the location of a user within this hierarchy. The following diagram shows an example business unit hierarchy with users assigned to different business units:

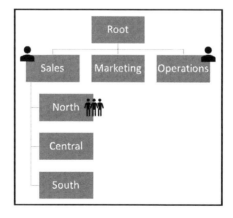

Figure 8.10 – Users and business units

Let's look at the Read Account privilege for a security role using the business unit hierarchy in the preceding diagram:

- A user in the **North** business unit with a Read Account privilege access level set to **Business Unit** will be able to view accounts that they own and accounts that are owned by the other users who are in the **North** business unit.
- A user in the **Sales** business unit with a Read Account privilege access level set to **Parent: Child Business Units** will be able to view accounts that they own, accounts owned by the other users who are in the **Sales** business unit, and all accounts owned by users in the **North, Central,** and **South** business units.
- A user in the **Operations** business unit with a Read Account privilege access level set to **Organization** will be able to view any account, no matter who owns it or where the owner is in the hierarchy.

 A user must be assigned a security role before they can access the system.

 If you change a user's business unit, they will lose all their security roles. The User Summary report generates a list of users, the business units, and their security roles, and is a useful tool when reorganizing to make sure you reallocate the correct roles.

Now that you have seen how security roles work with access levels and privileges, you need to know how to create security roles and change the access levels.

Creating or modifying security roles

There are several security roles provided out of the box to enable you to get started quickly. You can edit these roles, copy and edit the roles, or create new custom roles from your environment's settings in the Power Platform admin center:

Figure 8.11 – Copying a role

When you copy a role, you give it a name and all the access levels are copied for each privilege.

You cannot create new privileges yourself but when you create a custom entity, create, read, write, and other privileges are created for you. When you edit a security role you are restricted to just changing the access levels on each privilege.

To change an access level for a privilege, you simply click on the circular icon and it will rotate through the access levels from **None** to **User** to **Business Unit** to **Parent: Child Business Units** and then to **Organization**. If you click again, the access level will change to **None**.

If you click on the entity name, all the access levels will change together. This is a very quick way to turn an entity on or off from its security role.

If you click on **Create** or **Read** in the header above the privileges, then all the access levels for all the entities in the tab will change. This is extremely dangerous as it can change many different entities in ways you did not intend.

The out-of-the-box roles are named after job roles, for example, **Salesperson**, and are aimed at providing all the privileges that the job requires. You can follow this model of roles for specific job roles, but you may end up with many security roles that are similar and that you must maintain. For example, adding a new custom entity means editing many, if not all, the roles.

A more modern model is to use a layered security model. In this model, you would copy an out-of-the-box role, such as Salesperson or Common Data Service User, and change the access levels to the common, or minimal, levels that all users require. You might name this role **Base**, or **All Staff**. You would then create new roles and just set the access levels for the few privileges that each group of users would need in addition to the base role.

The following diagram shows how layered security roles function. All users will be assigned the **All Staff** role. Salespeople will also be assigned the **Sales** role with sales managers also having the **Manager** role. Salespeople who need to travel to customers can also be assigned the **Mobile** role. Operations staff will have the **Operations** role assigned, with operations managers also having the **Manager** role:

Figure 8.12 – Layered security roles

This model is much easier to manage; for example, adding a new custom entity may just require you to edit the base role.

You assign the base role and additional roles to each user. When you add multiple roles to a user, you need to understand how the privileges and access levels are combined.

Assigning multiple security roles

When you assign multiple roles to a user, the effective security a user has is cumulative. It is a union of least restrictive privileges.

You need to work out effective security practices on a privilege-by-privilege basis. There is no tool provided that performs this analysis for you.

The None access level is not the same as Deny. This behavior is different to the behavior in AD that you might be familiar with.

For example, three security roles have the following access levels on the Update privilege for the Contact entity:

- None
- User
- Business Unit

The effective privilege is the least restrictive of these, that is, Business Unit.

In another example, three security roles have the following access levels on the Assign privilege for the Activity entity:

- User
- Business Unit
- Organization

The effective privilege is the least restrictive of these, that is, Organization.

 Determining effective privileges is much easier with the layered approach previously outlined than using *full* job roles.

In the following screenshot, you can see the result of the combined security roles:

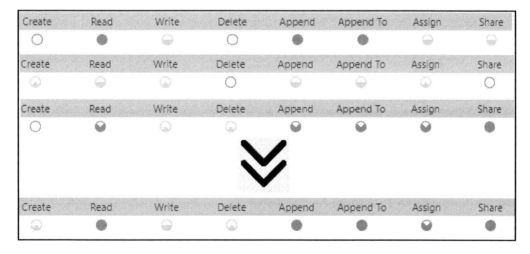

Figure 8.13 – Combined security roles result

Security roles also have a purpose outside of a user's data and functionality access – they can be used to restrict access to apps and user interface components.

Roles in model-driven apps

Model-driven apps must be associated with one or more security roles before they can be run by users.

In the classic interface, you added one or more security roles to your app after creating the app by clicking on **Manage roles**.

In the maker portal, the new method is to share the app with one or more security roles. This matches the model for distributing canvas apps. In either method, you are associating the app with one or more security roles.

Users will then be able to see and run an app if they have one of the same roles as the app.

Roles in other components

Security roles can be used to restrict access to the following user interface components in the CDS and model-driven apps:

- Forms
- Dashboards
- Business process flows

You cannot control access to the following components with security roles:

- Fields
- Charts
- Views

Now that we have identified all the security features, you need to learn how these features are applied to users.

Users and teams

All users of the Power Platform are authenticated by Azure AD, as described earlier in the chapter. You will now discover how users are set up.

Users in Microsoft 365

Microsoft 365 uses Azure AD to manage users and handle authentication and authorization when a user attempts to access an app or data in the Power Platform. You can use either the Microsoft 365 admin portal (`https://admin.microsoft.com/Adminportal/Home#/homepage`) or the Azure AD portal (`https://aad.portal.azure.com`) to create and manage users. A user must be assigned a license in Azure AD.

Managing users in Microsoft 365 or Azure AD is out of scope for the PL-200 exam. A functional consultant will not be responsible or have permission for this level of administration.

Users in the CDS

Users in a CDS database are created automatically when a user is given a license. Users are created in the root business unit and, except for users with administration roles, are not given a security role and are therefore prevented from accessing the CDS.

After creating a user, you will need to do the following:

- Change the user's business unit so that they are in the correct place in the hierarchy.
- Apply one or more security roles to the user.

If there is only one business unit, the root, then you will not need to change the user's business unit.

You manage users, along with the other security features covered in this chapter, from the **Settings** window for your environment in the **Power Platform admin center**, as shown in the following screenshot:

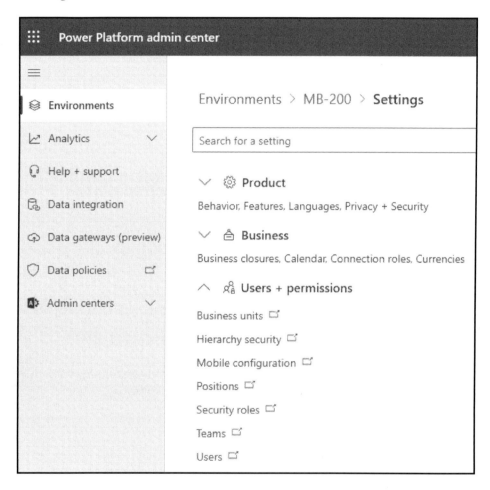

Figure 8.14 – Environment settings

 You can create an application user in the CDS. Application users are used for integrating with apps registered in Azure AD.

You can now associate your new user with one or more teams, but first, you need to understand how teams are used in the CDS.

Record ownership

When you create an entity in the CDS it can either be user-, team-, or organization-owned.

Entities that are user- or team-owned have the additional Assign and Share privileges compared with organization-owned entities. The Assign privilege is concerned with record ownership. When you create a record, you become the owner of that record.

If you own a record, the record also belongs to the business unit that you are in. This is how the business unit/security role model works. If you change your business unit, your records move with you, and their business unit is changed also.

> The owner of a record can be a user or a team. It is common for teams to own records, such as accounts not being managed by a salesperson but handled by all salespeople in a department, or in marketing, where marketeers do not have responsibility for individual contacts.

You can change the record to a different user or team using the **Assign** button in the user interface; *assign* here means changing the owner. If you do not have the Assign privilege on a record, the **Assign** button will be disabled or even hidden in the user interface.

> A record cannot be assigned to a user or a team if that user/team does not have at least user-level access for that entity. If you haven't applied a security role to a team then you will be unable to assign a record to that team.

It is common to set up security so that users can only access their own records, or records in their department, using business units and security roles. In some circumstances, a user may need access to a record they do not have rights to – this is what the Share privilege is for.

Sharing

In the security model, the concept of sharing has been provided so that a record can be accessed by a user who does not have access through the security model. You can share a record with other users and teams.

The Share privilege permits a user to share a record. If a user does not have the Share privilege on a record, the **Share** button will either be disabled or even hidden in the user interface.

When a user shares a record, the user specifies the privileges the other user or team will have, out of **Read**, **Write**, **Delete**, **Append**, **Assign**, and **Share**:

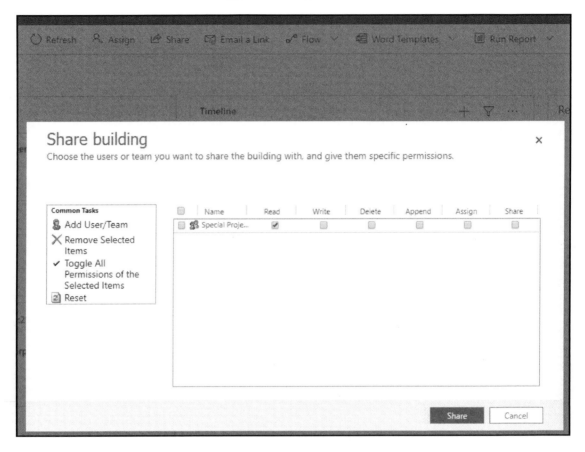

Figure 8.15 – Sharing a record with a team

 You cannot give another user a privilege you do not have; that is, if you do not have the Delete privilege on a record, you cannot select **Delete** while sharing the record.

You can also share the following:

- Personal views
- Personal charts
- Excel templates
- Word templates

It is better to share with teams as it reduces the management overhead.

Teams

There are several reasons to create teams. A team could be a group of people who work together for a long time, for example, a department; or temporarily, for example, a project team.

There are three types of teams:

- Owner teams
- Access teams
- Azure AD security group teams

Owner teams

Owner teams can have security roles applied and can therefore own records and have records shared with the team. You create owner teams manually and add users as members of the team.

 Every business unit has a team. This is known as the *default team,* and all users who belong to the business unit are automatically added as members of the default team. You cannot edit the default team or change its membership.

Teams must belong to a business unit but can have members from other business units. This is the method by which we can breach the strict hierarchy of the business unit/security role model. For instance, an owner team can be created for the Central business unit, but it might contain members from the Operations business unit. A record owned by this team will be accessible by members of the Operations business unit even if their security role provided only the business unit access level to the entity.

Sharing a record requires the user to access a non-intuitive user interface and understand the privileges shown. Most users struggle with this and access teams exist to make the action of sharing a record as simple as possible.

Access teams

Access teams are created automatically by the system when you add a user to a special sub-grid on a form; in Dynamics 365 Sales there is an example of such a sub-grid on the Opportunity form, called Sales Team.

When you add a user to such a sub-grid, the system does the following:

- Creates an access team
- Adds the user as a member of the new team
- Shares the record with the new team

The main benefit of access teams is that the user does not have to specify the privileges to be shared; instead, an administrator creates an access team template that specifies the privileges provided. All the user has to do is add another user to the sub-grid on the form.

 Only users can be added to an access team sub-grid.

The process to add a sub-grid is as follows:

1. Enable the entity for access teams.
2. Create an access team template.
3. Add a sub-grid of users to the entity form.
4. Select the access team template.

 Access teams cannot have security roles applied and cannot own records.

One of the advantages of access teams is that you can query and see what records are shared with which users. It is not possible to find out what records are shared with owner teams.

Azure AD group teams

You can connect a team to an Azure AD security group. This has many advantages for user management, as the membership of a team in the CDS is managed by the Azure AD group membership.

Azure AD security groups operate like owner teams; they can have security roles applied and can own records.

> You can use Azure AD security group teams to manage app and data access.

The security model is based on the business unit hierarchy, and although you have seen how we can bypass the hierarchy with teams, there are still business needs that require different hierarchies, which is confusingly called hierarchical security.

Hierarchical security

Hierarchical security is an alternative to the strict business unit and security role model. Instead of using business units and security roles, security is based on who reports to whom.

In this model, your user has read and write privileges on all records for the users who directly report to you. Your direct reports have read and write privileges for the users who report to them and you have read privileges on those users' records as well.

To summarize, with hierarchical security you have the following options:

- Read and write privileges for one level below you
- Read privileges for the levels beneath that

This is a common model for sales teams, where sales managers need to have full access to their team's data. It is even more useful where you have people working across different regions and you have to set up your business units based on geography.

You have two options:

- **Manager**: Based on the manager field on each user record
- **Position**: Based on a position that is assigned to users:

Figure 8.16 – Hierarchical security

Hierarchical security is off by default and must be enabled. Then you can choose one of the security hierarchy options, either **Manager** or **Position**.

Manager hierarchy

The manager hierarchy is restrictive as it works within the business unit structure.

The rule for allocating a manager to a user is that the manager must reside in the same business unit as the user, or in one of its parent business units. So, in our example business unit structure, a user in the Central business unit can only be managed by a user in the Central, Sales, or Root business units.

The manager hierarchy is useful if you already use the manager field, for example, in your workflow.

Position hierarchy

The position hierarchy is much more flexible; it ignores the business unit structure so you can easily apply this model alongside your existing business unit structure without complications.

There is an entity called **Position**. You create your positions and their hierarchy and then assign those positions to users. Positions allow the spanning of business units so a user in one business unit can access the records of a user in a subordinate position, no matter which business unit that user is in.

Another benefit of the position hierarchy is that a user can only have one manager; with positions, you can have more than one person in a position, thus allowing greater access where there are shared management responsibilities.

All the security models so far have been concerned with access to records; the read or write privileges are for the record and all fields in the record, but you may require certain fields within an entity to be restricted. Field-level security is the method by which we can control access to fields.

Field-level security

In the CDS, once you have access to a record via security, you have access to all fields for that record. Even if the fields are not on the form, you can access the fields using Advanced Find or using the Web API.

The CDS supports setting fields to *secured* to restrict access to the field's contents.

Secured fields

Setting a field to secured will prevent users from being able to view or set the value of the field. You enable fields for field-level security when creating or editing a field. The following screenshot shows you how to secure a field:

 Field-level security (at the time of writing) is not available in the maker portal, so you will need to switch to Classic to enable or disable a field for field-level security.

Figure 8.17 – Securing a field

You can set most fields to `secured`, including system and custom fields. Exceptions are fields such as `createdon`, `statecode`, and `ownerid`.

 Setting a field to secured does not hide the field; the field will still be on the form or in the view. The contents of the field will return a null value.

On the form, the field will appear with a key symbol next to the label and the contents will be shown as empty or masked with asterisks:

Figure 8.18– A secured field in a form

After a field is enabled for field-level security, only users with the System Administrator security role will be able to set and view the contents of the field. To allow other users to access the contents of a secured field, you will need to create a field security profile.

Field security profiles

Field security profiles simplify the setting of permissions on secured fields by grouping secured field permissions into a profile that can be assigned to users and teams. This eliminates the need to set the permission on each secured field for each user.

Field security profiles control which users can access which secured fields. A field security profile contains the following:

- **Field permissions**: The permissions on all secured fields
- **Service principals**: Users and teams that belong to the field security profile

Field security profiles are components that can be added to solutions. You create a field security profile from within a solution in the maker portal.

For each secured field, you can set three permissions:

- **Read**: Allows the user to read or view the contents of the field
- **Update**: Allows the user to change or overwrite the contents of the field for an existing record
- **Create**: Allows the user to set the contents of the field when creating a record

The field permissions are illustrated in the following screenshot:

Figure 8.19 – Field permissions

Common combinations for permissions are as follows:

- **Read-only**: **Allow Read** set to Yes, **Allow Update** and **Allow Create** set to No
- **Password/PIN**: **Allow Read** set to No, **Allow Update** and **Allow Create** set to Yes

Once you have set the field permissions, you add the user(s) and/or team(s) as members of the field security profile.

Just like security roles, a user can belong to more than one field security profile. When a user has more than one profile, the user has the least restrictive combination of permissions. That is, if one profile has a secured field set to **Not Allow Read** and another profile has the field set to **Allow Read**, then you will have **Allow Read** permission.

 All users with the System Administrator role are automatically added to a built-in field security profile called **System Administrator**. You cannot edit the field permissions in this profile.

Congratulations on reaching the end of this chapter. As you will have seen, there are many security features provided by the CDS. Which options you choose will depend on the security requirements for your data and user access. You will not likely use all these features, but will be able to select the most appropriate features to meet your scenario.

Summary

In this chapter, we learned about the capabilities of the security model in the CDS, primarily business units and security roles. We also discussed alternative security approaches with teams, field security, and hierarchies.

We covered how to add a user and then apply security features to the user to ensure they have access to the necessary data and functionalities to do their job.

You will now be able to identify the appropriate security features to meet your requirements, and then be able to configure environments and security settings as needed.

In the next chapter, we will introduce model-driven apps and how to build them, and in doing so we will compare them with canvas apps.

Questions

After reading this chapter, test your knowledge with these questions. You will find the answers to these questions under the `Assessments` section at the end of the book:

1. Your users report that they are not seeing your model-driven app. What should you do?

    A) Share the app.
    B) Publish the app.
    C) Run the app checker.
    D) Run the solution checker.

2. You have a business unit hierarchy. The user has been created in the root business unit and has been assigned a security role with **Read Account** set to **Business Unit**. Which accounts can they see?

    A) Accounts they own
    B) Accounts in their business unit
    C) Accounts in their business unit and the child business units one level beneath it
    D) Accounts in their business unit and all child business units beneath it

3. A user is assigned three security roles. The first security role has **Read Account** set to **Parent: Child Business Units**, the second security role has **Read Account** set to **User**, and the third security role has **Read Account** set to **None**. What is the effective access level on accounts for this user?

    A) None
    B) User
    C) Business Unit
    D) Parent: Child Business Units
    E) Organization

4. You have created a new model-driven app. Your users are unable to see the app, but you can. What should you do?

    A) In the app designer, run **Validate**.
    B) In the app designer, click **Publish**.
    C) Export the app and tell the users to import the app.
    D) Share the app and select the appropriate security role.
    E) Tell the users to use the classic interface.

5. You have assigned a user two security roles. The user's access level for a specific entity will do which of the following?

 A) Reflect the most restrictive level of access for that entity across both security roles.
 B) Reflect the highest level of access for that entity across both security roles.
 C) Automatically default to read privileges for organization access.
 D) Be determined by the user's field-level security profile.

6. Before a user can be assigned a security role, they must be assigned to which of the following?

 A) A region
 B) A business unit
 C) An access team
 D) A security group
 E) A field security profile

7. Which of the following technologies is used as the primary authentication method for Dynamics 365?

 A) Windows Hello
 B) Azure Multi-Factor Authentication
 C) Azure AD
 D) Azure Conditional Access
 E) Dynamics 365 security profiles

Further reading

Here are a few links if you wish to read more:

- Security in the CDS: https://docs.microsoft.com/power-platform/admin/wp-security
- Manage the encryption key: https://docs.microsoft.com/power-platform/admin/manage-encryption-key
- Manage teams: https://docs.microsoft.com//power-platform/admin/manage-teams
- User service admin roles to manage your tenant: https://docs.microsoft.com/power-platform/admin/use-service-admin-role-manage-tenant

- **Share a model-driven app:** `https://docs.microsoft.com/powerapps/maker/model-driven-apps/share-model-driven-app`
- **System and application users:** `https://docs.microsoft.com/power-platform/admin/system-application-users`
- **Create a team template to control access rights for automatically created teams:** `https://docs.microsoft.com/power-platform/admin/create-team-template-add-entity-form`
- **Field-level security:** `https://docs.microsoft.com/power-platform/admin/field-level-security`

3
Section 3: Power Apps

Section 3 is concerned with creating apps on top of the data captured in *Section 2*. By the end, the reader will be able to create solutions for users that enhance the user experience.

This section contains the following chapters:

- Chapter 9, *Model-Driven Apps*
- Chapter 10, *Canvas Apps*
- Chapter 11, *Portal Apps*

9
Model-Driven Apps

Model-driven apps allow you to create apps for the data stored in Microsoft Dataverse (formerly the Common Data Service). Model-driven apps leverage the data model you created in `Chapter 3`, *Data Modeling*, and a component-based framework to create no-code apps built on top of Dataverse.

This chapter explains the components in model-driven apps and how to configure these components, including forms, views, and charts. The chapter then shows you how to bring the components together to create an app. Using model-driven apps allows you to quickly build apps to manage business processes.

The following topics will be covered in this chapter:

- Introducing model-driven apps
- Configuring forms and controls
- Configuring views
- Creating charts and dashboards
- Understanding reporting options

By the end of this chapter, you will be able to create and modify the user interface components for model-driven apps, including forms, views, charts, and dashboards. You will be able to assemble these components into a model-driven app.

Introducing model-driven apps

Users require apps to manage their data through their business processes. Model-driven apps allow users to create and update their data while observing defined business process steps and rules.

Model-driven apps are one of the types of Power App that you can create. They are based on the entities in the Common Data Service.

Model-driven apps require an environment with a Common Data Service database.

This section provides an overview of model-driven apps, their components, and how you create a model-driven app.

The term *model* in model-driven apps is explained by the apps being based on top of the data model in the Common Data Service. You can think of model-driven apps as *forms over data*, with the app showing the records in each entity and users being able to edit a record for the entity.

 At the time of publishing, Microsoft Dataverse (formerly known as the Common Data Service) was undergoing a branding change. You will see the use of Common Data Service and the abbreviation CDS throughout this chapter. There are several changes to terminology such as tables (formerly entities), columns (formerly fields), rows (formerly records), choices (formerly option sets), and yes/no (formerly two options). These terminology changes will be applied to the user interface, documentation, and exam over time. You should be aware that the terms used in this chapter may not match the tools and documentation.

There is another aspect to model-driven apps and that is that the components of the app work within a defined framework. You do not have control over many aspects of the user interface, such as fonts and colors. You do not need to create buttons to create records or create controls to show data. You work within the framework; the framework handles how the components work together in the app.

Model-driven apps provide the following benefits:

- Reusable component-oriented design
- No-code development approach
- Single responsive design for desktop, tablet, and mobile client devices
- Focus on the components, not the interaction between components
- Solution-aware, so can be deployed to test and production environments

The types of components in a model-driven app are as follows:

- **Entities**: A model-driven app contains a subset of the entities in the Common Data Service environment. Entities were discussed in `Chapter 3`, *Data Modeling.*
- **Forms**: Each entity has multiple forms used in the model-driven app to view, create, and edit records for the entity. You can create and edit these forms and decide whether to include them in the app.
- **Views**: The views show lists of records for an entity. Each entity has multiple views. You can create and edit these views and decide whether to include them in the app.
- **Charts**: Charts are a visual representation of an entity's data.
- **Dashboards**: A collection of views, charts, and other components to provide the user with an overview of their work and data.
- **Business process flows**: Guide the user through a business process, informing the user as to where they are in the process and controlling when data is to be entered. Business process flows are explained in `Chapter 13`, *Business Process Flows.*
- **Site map**: Controls the application-level navigation of the app.

Model-driven apps also provide access to other features of the Common Data Service, including the following:

- **Duplicate detection**: Duplicate detection is explained in `Chapter 7`, *Dataverse Settings.*
- **Import and export of data**: Import and export are explained in `Chapter 6`, *Managing Data.*

Model-driven apps utilize other features of the Power Platform:

- **Business rules**: Validate data, perform calculations, and manipulate fields on forms. Business rules are explained in `Chapter 4`, *Business Rules.*
- **Security model**: Model-driven apps observe the security configured in the Common Data Service. Security controls the user interface. For example, if a user does not have read access to an entity in the app, that entity will not be visible to that user. If a user does not have create privileges on an entity, the **Add new** button to create a record will not be displayed. If a user does not have write privileges on an entity, the form will be read-only when the user attempts to edit a record for that entity. Features such as **Export to Excel** are controlled by security; if the user does not have the privileges for the feature, the feature is hidden in the user interface. Security is explained in `Chapter 8`, *Security.*

You can also initiate Power Automate flows (explained in `Chapter 12`, *Power Automate Flows*) and classic workflows (explained in `Chapter 5`, *Classic Workflows*) from a model-driven app.

In this section, we will explore how to create a model-driven app, how to configure the left-hand navigation bar in the app, and sharing the app with users.

Now that you know what components are used to compose an app, let's look at creating a model-driven app.

Creating a model-driven app

Model-driven apps are created by assembling components from the Common Data Service. You customize the individual components and then select the appropriate components to meet your business requirements.

Model-driven apps are created from the Power App maker portal (`https://make.powerapps.com`). To create an app, click on the **+ Create** button in the maker portal and click on **Model-driven app from blank**, and then click on **Create**. The following page will appear:

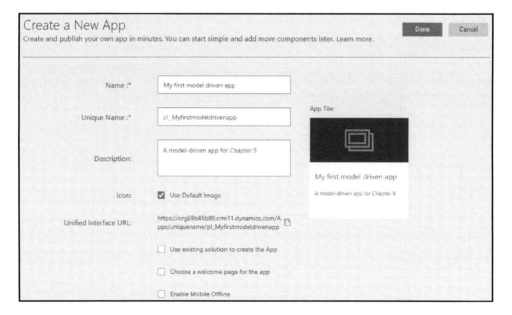

Figure 9.1 – Creating a model-driven app

In the **Create a New App** page, enter the name of your app. **Unique Name** is automatically populated. Click on **Done**.

> If you are using solutions, you can check the **Use existing solutions to create the App** option. You will then be able to select a solution and the components in the solution will be added to the app.

After clicking **Done**, the **App Designer** page will open, as shown in the following screenshot:

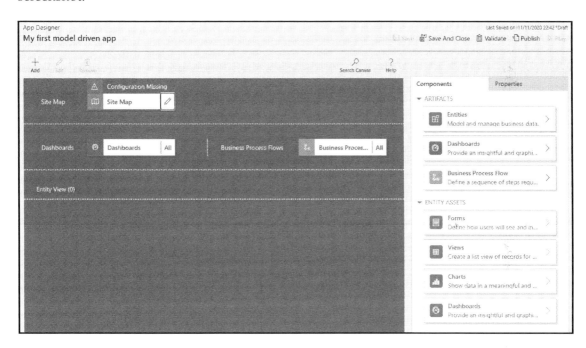

Figure 9.2 – App Designer

The designer shows the selected components in the main area. In *Figure 9.2*, no components have been added to the app. The right-hand pane is used to add components to the app.

The component at the top of the canvas is **Site Map**, which controls the app navigation. Editing the site map is the first step in configuring your app.

Configuring the site map

The site map controls the left-hand navigation pane in a model-driven app. You can specify how this navigation pane is organized and the order of the entities in the app.

To edit the site map, click on the pencil icon next to the site map tile. This opens the **Sitemap Designer** page, as shown in the following screenshot:

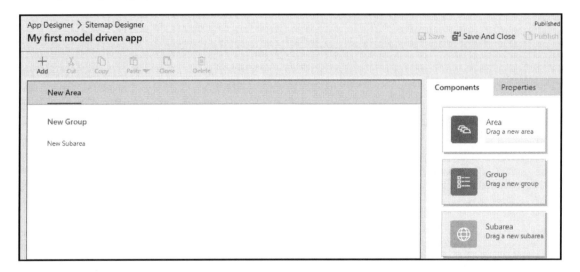

Figure 9.3 – Sitemap Designer

A site map has three elements:

- **Area**: Areas are the top level of the site map. If you have more than one area, the user can switch from one area to another from the bottom left of a model-driven app.
- **Group**: Groups are the second level of the site map and belong to an area. Groups are simply a way to combine subareas together into common groups and have a title that appears in the navigation.
- **Subarea**: Subareas are the components that can be displayed, such as entities and dashboards.

When you edit a new site map, a single area, group, and subarea are included. To edit these, simply click on them and the **Properties** pane. In the **Properties** pane, you select the type of component. You can choose an entity from the list of entities. For areas and groups, you can change the name used in the navigation.

You can add any of the elements either by dragging a tile from the right-hand pane or by clicking on **+ Add** and selecting the element to add. When you have completed adding elements to the site map, click on **Save**, followed by **Publish**. You should then click on **Save and Close** to return to the app designer.

The following screenshot shows a site map with multiple areas, groups, and subareas:

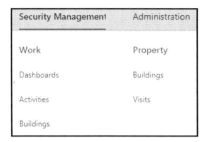

Figure 9.4 – Site map

The site map from *Figure 9.4* will create the navigation in a model-driven app shown in the following screenshot:

Figure 9.5 – Model-driven app navigation

In the previous screenshot, you can see the selection of the area at the bottom, with the groups and subareas above.

Configuring the site map is straightforward. When you have added the entities and dashboard, you can select the components for the app.

Selecting components for an app

After creating a site map, the entities you included in the site map are automatically added to the app. You can now add additional components and assets, including entities, forms, views, charts, dashboards, and business process flows.

You can use the **Components** and **Properties** tabs on the right-hand side of the app designer, as shown in *Figure 9.2*, to select components for the app. For each entity, you can choose which entity assets, such as forms, views, or charts, will be available in the app.

 You can create new components from within the app designer.

Once you have completed selecting the components and entity assets, click on **Save**, then **Validate**, followed by **Publish**. You can use the play button to open and test your model-driven app.

Users will not be able to run your app until you share the app with them.

Sharing a model-driven app

Model-driven apps rely on security roles to control access to the app. The app must be assigned to one or more security roles. If a user does not have the security role that has been assigned to the app, they will not be able to use the app.

After creating the app, you should select the app in the maker portal and click on **Share**. You then select the security roles for the app and click on **Share** again. You can now share the app with users and teams.

In this section, you have learned how to create an app, configure the sitemap, add components and assets to the app, and then share the app so that the app can be run by users.

We will now look at customizing the components, starting with forms.

Configuring forms and controls

Forms are used to view, create, and edit data for an entity. Each entity has multiple forms that can be used in a model-driven app to view, create, and edit records for the entity. Some forms are created automatically when you create an entity. You can customize these forms and create new forms.

In this section, we will explore the types of forms, how to customize forms, and adding controls to forms.

There are four types of entity form in the Common Data Service:

- **Main**: The form used for creating and editing records. This form is used on all clients. The form contains the fields for the entity and other controls, such as the timeline. The main form will show business process flows along the top of the form.
- **Card**: The card form is used with interactive dashboards. The card form is also used to display columns in views when the view is in a compact format, for subgrids, and on mobile clients.
- **Quick create**: Allows users to create new records without navigating away from the existing form or view.
- **Quick view**: Shows a subset of read-only fields on the form for records from lookup fields. The quick view form is also used for the tile in hierarchical views.

We will look at each of these form types, starting with the main form.

Configuring the main form

The main form is used when creating and editing records. It is the form most users will interact with in a model-driven app. Forms are an asset of an entity. Each entity has at least one main form.

The same form definition is used for web applications, Outlook clients, and the mobile apps for tablets and phones. The form automatically adjusts to the screen's orientation and size. The form can be rendered very differently in different clients.

You edit a form in the maker portal from within the entity. To edit a form, click on **Solutions**, open your solution, and select the entity, and then click on the **Forms** tab. You will see a list of forms, as shown in the following screenshot:

Figure 9.6 – Forms

In the previous screenshot, you can see three forms, including the main form. To edit a form, click on the name of the form. The form editor will open, as shown in the following screenshot:

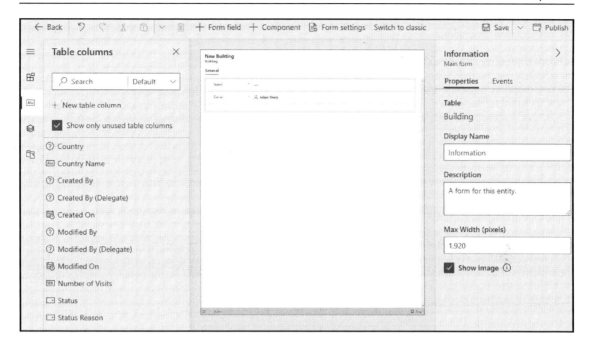

Figure 9.7 – Form editor

In the form editor shown in *Figure 9.7*, there are three panes. The left-hand pane lists the fields in the entity, the middle pane is a **WYSIWYG (what you see is what you get)** view of the form, and the right-hand pane shows the properties of the selected element. You can also use the left-hand pane to add other form components.

 To create a new form, use the **Add form** button shown in *Figure 9.6*. You will need to choose the form type to create.

To add a field to the form, simply drag the field from the left-hand pane onto the form in the middle pane. You cannot simply add a field anywhere on the form. The form has a structure that you need to understand before you can add fields.

Understanding the form structure

The main form can include many fields and other form components. Unlike canvas apps, you cannot add a control anywhere; there is a layout to the form that you must observe.

The main form is structured like so:

- **Header**: Contains up to four fields. These are usually important fields that the user should see if the form scrolls. Fields in the header can be edited using the flyout control.
- **Body**: Contains fields and other controls. There is a hierarchy for the layout of the body:
    - **Tabs**: The body has at least one tab. A tab has a label that is displayed above the tab. A tab's layout can have 1, 2, or 3 columns. Tabs can be hidden.
    - **Sections**: Each column of a tab must have at least one section. Sections can only be contained within a tab. A section has a label that is displayed above the section. Sections can have up to four columns. Sections can be hidden. Sections are a way of grouping similar fields together.
    - **Controls**: Controls are added within sections. Controls include fields, subgrids, timeline, IFrames, web resources, Bing maps, and spacers.
- **Footer**: Contains read-only fields. The footer does not scroll.

For a form to be responsive, you should use multi-column tabs and single-column sections. The form will then be rendered correctly on mobile devices.

You can add tabs and sections to the form by selecting the components icon in the left-hand pane and dragging the component to the form, as shown in the following screenshot:

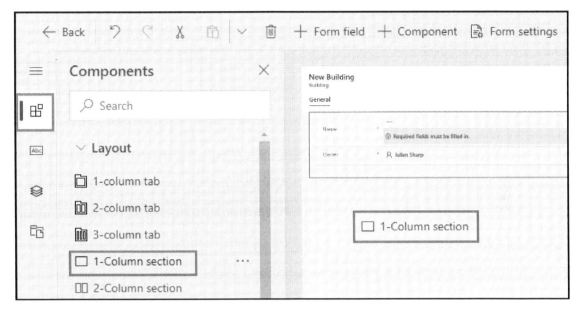

Figure 9.8 – Adding a single-column section to a form

In the previous screenshot, the components icon has been selected, changing the left-hand pane to a list of components. **1-Column section** is in the process of being dragged onto the form.

This form editor does not yet contain all the capabilities of the classic form editor and for some customizations, such as controlling which entities to display under related records, you need to switch to classic.

Showing related records

The main form has an additional tab not shown in the form editor, called **Related**. This tab allows you to view related records in one-to-many and many-to-many relationships.

You can only currently change which related entities are shown when the user uses this tab from the classic form editor, as shown:

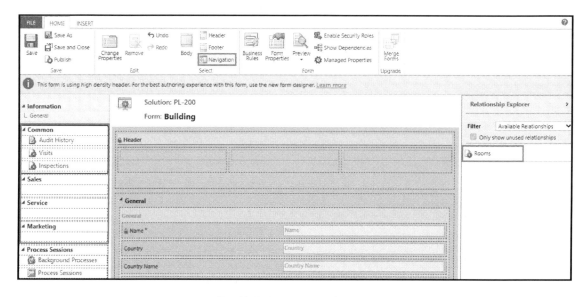

Figure 9.9 – Navigation in the classic form editor

In the previous screenshot, the **Navigation** button in the toolbar has been selected. This shows the related entities on the form in the left-hand pane and the available related entities in the right-hand pane. You can drag the entity from the right-hand pane and place it in the left-hand pane. You can also re-arrange the entities in the left-hand pane. You must save and then publish the form.

Now that you have structured your form with tabs, sections, and navigation, let's look at adding and configuring the controls on the form.

Adding controls to forms

Controls is the generic term for fields and other visual elements that you can add to a form. There are many different controls:

- **Fields**: You can only add fields from the entity. The control used for the field will depend on the data type of the field.
- **Canvas app**: You can embed a Power Apps canvas app in a model-driven form.

- **Quick view form**: You can embed a quick view form for any of the entities that have a many-to-one relationship. The fields in the quick view form are read-only.
- **Subgrid**: A list of related records. You can add a subgrid for one-to-many and many-to-many relationships.
- **Timeline**: The activities. The timeline is added to the form automatically if you check the **Enable for activities** property when creating an entity.

There are controls that you can only add using the classic form editor:

- **Spacer**: Controls are added next to or beneath another control. Spacers allow you to create a blank space between controls.
- **Web resource**: Web resources contain HTML and image files. You cannot add an image to a form directly; you need to create a web resource component and upload the image to the resource. You can then add the web resource to the form to embed HTML and images.
- **IFrame**: An IFrame displays the web page defined in the URL properties of the control embedded in the form.
- **Bing Maps**: Displays a visual map for an address. This control only works with accounts and contacts and some other Dynamics 365 entities.
- **Timer**: Displays a countdown timer on the form. The timer requires a date/time field.

Let's look at adding and configuring some of these important controls to the form, starting with fields.

Adding fields to a form

The form editor shows a list of fields on the entity that have not already been added to the form, the unused fields. You can show the used fields in this list by unchecking **Show only unused fields**.

The fields are also filtered by a dropdown with the **Default**, **All**, and **Custom** options. If you have a lot of fields on the entity, you can search by field name.

The **Default** option hides fields you may need. A useful option is to choose **Custom**, which shows any custom fields you have created.

You can drag and drop a field from the left-hand pane onto the form, or you can select an existing field on the form, click on **+ Form Field**, and then click on the field in the left-hand pane. The field will be added underneath the existing field.

Fields added this way will be simple data entry fields. You can change the input controls to be visual.

Configuring fields

Fields display controls that users use to view or edit data in a record. Some field controls can be changed from simple fields into visual controls. You can switch the control used by selecting a field on the form, and in the form field's properties, expand **Components** and click on **+ Component**, as shown in the following screenshot for a numeric field:

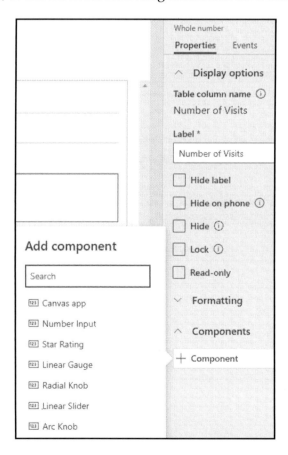

Figure 9.10 – Adding a visual component to an input field in the field properties

Depending on the data type for the field, you will see different controls. For a whole number field, you can choose from the controls shown in *Figure 9.10*. For a two-options field, you can choose between a toggle and flip switch. The following screenshot shows the field controls in a model-driven app:

Figure 9.11 – Visual components in a form

There are other properties for field controls that you can configure. These properties are shown in *Figure 9.10*:

- **Label**: The label defaults to the display name of the field. You can edit the label used on this form.
- **Hide label**: Does not display the label.
- **Hide on phone**: Does not display the field on the mobile phone client.
- **Hide**: Several types of form elements have the option to be shown or hidden by default, including tabs, sections, and fields.
- **Lock**: This prevents the field from being removed from the form accidentally. To remove this field, you would need to clear this property first.
- **Read-only**: A field can be made read-only so that the contents of the field cannot be edited.

 You can use business rules to change a field's read-only and visibility properties to create a dynamic form and provide a user interface that adapts to the data in the form.

There are some additional properties for some fields and controls.

Configuring lookup fields

A lookup field allows users to select the parent record in a many-to-one relationship. Users can search or browse the parent entity using this field. The Lookup view is used by default. You can change which view is used by default and can allow the user to choose from a subset of the views on the entity.

Configuring subgrids

Subgrids are one of the most useful components you can use on a form. Subgrids are lists of records, typically the child records in a one-to-many relationship. By using subgrids, a user can see all the relevant information for a record without having to navigate to another form.

To add a subgrid, select the components icon in the left-hand pane and click the **Subgrid** component. The window shown in the following screenshot will be displayed:

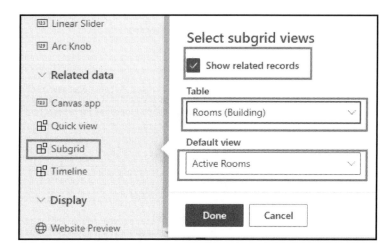

Figure 9.12 – Adding a subgrid to a form

Select the entity you want to show data for and select a view to use for the columns to be displayed, and then click on **Done**.

Subgrids are read-only by default but can be editable. Editable grids are discussed later in the chapter.

Configuring the timeline

The **Timeline** control displays notes, activities, activity feed posts, Yammer posts, and knowledge articles. The timeline is typically displayed in the middle pane of a three-column tab on a form.

You can configure which entities can be included in the timeline. Records are sorted by the last updated date. You can change the sort order to use the created date, which will not change when records are updated or assigned.

You can use the card form to control which fields are displayed within the timeline.

You are now able to customize the main form. The other form types are customized using the same tools but have some restrictions on what components can be used. We will start with the quick view form.

Using quick view forms

Quick view forms can be added to another form as a quick view control. The quick view control provides the capability to view information about a many-to-one-related record. Adding a quick view form means that users do not need to navigate to a different record form to see the information they need to complete their work.

Quick view controls are associated with a lookup field. If the lookup field value is not set, the quick view control will not be visible. The fields shown in quick view controls are read-only and cannot be edited.

Quick view forms have a simple structure. They are a single one-column tab with one or more one-column sections. You cannot add more tabs, but you can add more one-column sections.

Only fields, spacers, and subgrids can be added to quick view forms. The ability to use subgrids is especially useful as when the quick view form is added to another form, the user can see the details of the parent record and other related records.

To add a quick view control, select the components icon in the left-hand pane and click the **Quick view** component. The window shown in the following screenshot will be displayed:

Figure 9.13 – Adding a quick view to a form

Select the **Lookup** field you want to show data for and then select a quick view form to display, then click on **Done**.

The quick create form is used to create records without disrupting the user's current work process.

Using quick create forms

Quick create forms are designed to appear on the right-hand side of the screen to create new records without having to navigate away from the current form or view. The purpose is to quickly create a new record without the user having to navigate back to continue their work.

Quick create forms appear when you click the **+** button in the application bar at the top of the screen or when you click on **+ New** when creating a new record from a lookup field or subgrid.

 A quick create form is not created when a custom entity is created. You need to create a new form.

Quick create forms have a simple structure. They have a single three-column tab, each with a single section. You cannot add further tabs or sections. Only fields and spacers can be added to quick create forms.

 To use Quick Create, you must first enable the entity for Quick Create in the properties for the entity and create a quick create form.

The card form is the last type of model-driven app form.

Using the card form

Card forms are used to display information for a record in a condensed format. The card form can be used in many places in the user interface of a model-driven app:

- In the streams in interactive dashboards
- On mobile devices
- As the read-only grid control for views

- For views instead of a grid when the width of the view is small – for example, on subgrids in on-column sections
- In the timeline control

You should limit the number of fields on a card form.

You can create multiple forms of each type and use different forms for different users and in different situations.

Using multiple forms

Different users interact with the same data in different ways. Managers may need to be able to quickly scan information in a record, users may require a form that streamlines data entry, and admins may need access to fields not required by users and managers. You can create different forms for each of these sets of users.

Each of the four types of form can have multiple forms. You can create a new form either by editing an existing form and using the **Save As** button, or by clicking on the **Add form** button when editing an entity.

If there are multiple forms, a user will be able to switch between forms in the model-driven app, as shown in the following screenshot:

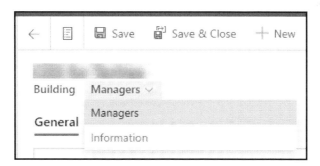

Figure 9.14 – Switching forms

A user can only switch main forms, not the other form types.

The order of the forms listed can be configured by assigning the form order. To change the form order, click on the ellipses (**...**) next to a form and select **Form settings** and then **Form Order**. The following window will open:

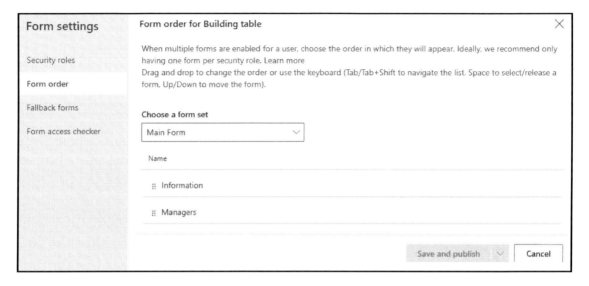

Figure 9.15 – Form settings

In the previous screen, you can drag the forms into order. When you have finished ordering the forms, click on **Save and publish**.

Change the name of existing forms and change the name of newly created forms. This will make it easier to order your forms.

The form order determines which of the available forms will be shown after security roles have been evaluated. You can ensure that users only see the forms that are relevant to them by assigning security roles to main forms.

You can assign security roles to a main form in the form editor by clicking on **Form settings**, as shown in the following screenshot:

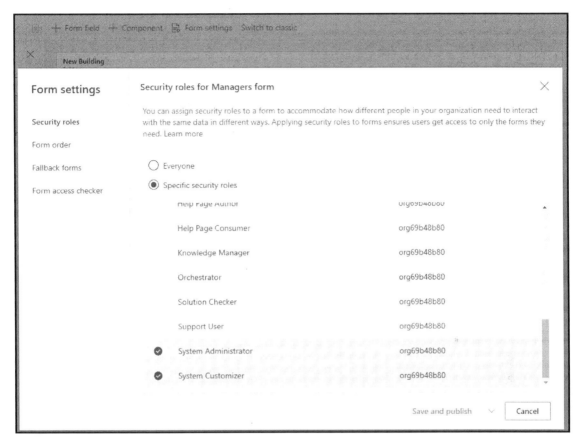

Figure 9.16 – Assigning security roles to forms

You should select the appropriate roles and click on **Save and publish**.

 By default, new forms are only available to System Administrators and System Customizers.

You must ensure that all users see at least one main form. You can choose which form is the fallback form, the form that is used if the user does not have a form through their security roles.

You can set the fallback form in the form editor by clicking on **Form settings** and then **Fallback forms**, as shown in the following screenshot:

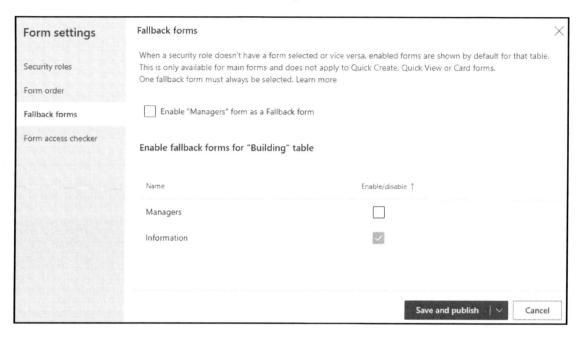

Figure 9.17 – Fallback forms

You must have at least one form enabled for fallback.

You also need to consider other client devices, especially mobile phones, where the screen is smaller.

Configuring forms for mobile

Model-driven apps running on mobile devices use the same form layouts as the web interface. For tablets and phones that have smaller screens, the forms adjust automatically to the size and orientation. The forms are responsive.

The controls on the forms can be changed from simple entry fields into touch-friendly controls. The forms can be customized to hide user interface components when running on a mobile phone. Each form component has the **Hide on phone** property, as shown in the following screenshot:

Figure 9.18 – Hide on phone

Tabs, sections, and fields can be turned *on* or *off* for phones. This property is *off* by default and all components are displayed.

Web resources, IFrames, and dashboards have a similar property, **Enable for mobile**. This property is off by default.

 Enable for mobile refers to both phone and tablet. You will notice that some properties are for mobile, which means both types of device, and others are for phone only.

For both entity lists and individual fields, controls can be added to render the component in a more user-friendly way. For example, you can change the view layout from a read-only grid into a calendar or **Kanban** view, as shown in the following screenshot:

Control	Web	Phone	Tablet
Read-only Grid (default)	◉	○	○
Kanban	○	◉	◉

Figure 9.19 – Entity controls

You can have different options for the web client, when running on a tablet, and when running on a phone.

In the following screenshot, you can see how to change the way a field is rendered for web, phone, or tablet:

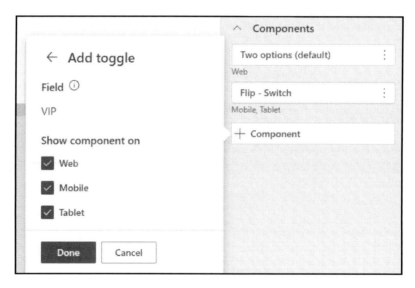

Figure 9.20 – Show component on clients

In this section, you learned about the types of forms, how to add and configure the controls on the forms, how to handle multiple forms, and applying security on forms.

The other major visual component that displays data in a model-driven app is views.

Configuring views

When a user selects an entity in the site map of a model-driven app, they will see a grid of records. This grid is a view. You can change which views are shown by default and can customize the view definition.

Views define how a list of records for an entity is displayed. Views are a fundamental part of the user interface and one that is often overlooked.

In this section, we will explore the types of views, how to customize views, and adding controls to forms.

A view definition consists of the following:

- The entity the view will display records for
- The fields to display as columns in the list
- The order of columns in the list
- The query (filter) to restrict which records will be displayed
- The sort order

Each entity has its own set of views that are displayed in various places in the user interface. Users utilize views to focus on the records that they need to work on. You should put careful thought into the number, and design, of views. If users have to go into the record form to find a piece of information, then the view definition is incorrect. If there are too many similar views, then users might choose the wrong one.

Views are used within dashboards to show lists of records that users should be interested in. Another major use of views is to display related data in subgrids on the form. It is not unusual to create views specifically for use in subgrids. Views also define the data used by charts.

There are three types of views:

- **Public**: The views seen by all users when a user selects an entity in a model-driven app
- **System**: Specialist views used in specific circumstances in an app, the view used for a lookup field
- **Personal**: Views created by a user

You can edit views and create new views from the **Views** tab of the entity in your solution, as shown in the following screenshot:

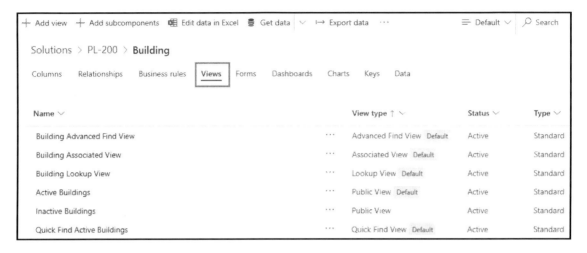

Figure 9.21 – Views

In the previous screenshot, you can see the public views and the four system views for a custom entity.

We will look at types of views and then how to customize views, starting with public views.

Using public views

Public views are the views that are displayed when a user selects an entity from the application navigation.

> In the model-driven app user interface, public views are referred to as system views.

Public views are a component of an entity and are created and edited from the **Views** tab of the entity in your solution.

When a custom entity is created, two public views are created, called the following:

- **Active <Entity plural name>**
- **Inactive <Entity plural name>**

You cannot delete these views created for you, the standard views, but you can edit and rename them.

You cannot restrict public views with security. If you need to prevent users from accessing a view, you can either deactivate the view or remove it from entity assets in the app designer.

Views that you create are custom public views. These views can be edited, deactivated, and deleted.

Each entity has a default public view; this is the view that is displayed by default when a user selects an entity from the application navigation. You can change the default public view by clicking on the ellipses (…) next to a view name and selecting **Set as default view**.

You should ensure that the default view only returns a small subset of records and fields in order to improve the overall system performance.

Users can override the default view and set their own default by pinning a view in their app.

Public views are used when you select an entity in the app navigation. Public views are also used in subgrids and can be added to dashboards.

Let's now look at the system views, what they are, and where they are used.

Using system views

System views are views that the application uses in special circumstances. Each entity has its own set of these views, which are created automatically for custom entities.

These views have specific purposes and some additional capabilities:

- **Quick Find**: The view used when searches are performed using **Search this view** in the user interface of an app. This view defines which fields are searched in lookup fields and in the categorized search.
- **Advanced Find**: The default view for Advanced Find.
- **Associated**: The view that is used when a user clicks on **Related** in a form and selects the entity.
- **Lookup**: The view used when a user clicks on the search icon in a lookup field. It also defines which fields appear in the form when you click into a lookup field.

These four views do not appear in the list of system views when a user selects an entity from the app site map navigation.

 System views cannot be deleted or deactivated. You cannot create new system views.

Public and system views are customized in the same way using the **view designer**.

Customizing a view

Views are used in many places in the user interface to display lists of records. Ensuring the view shows the correct records and the most appropriate fields is a key focus of a functional consultant. Just as the form layout can make a significant difference to how a user works with your app, the configuration of views is just as, if not more, important. A well-designed system makes careful use of views to show the user exactly the right information in the right order.

You edit a view in the maker portal from within the entity. To edit a form, click on **Solutions**, open your solution, and select the entity, and then click on the **Views** tab, as shown in *Figure 9.21*. To edit a view, click on the name of the view. The view editor will open, as shown in the following screenshot:

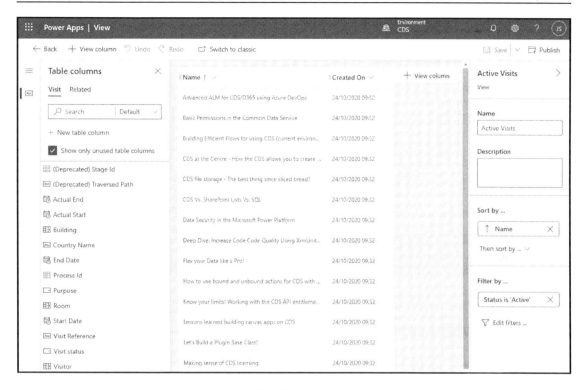

Figure 9.22 – View editor

In the view editor shown in *Figure 9.22*, there are three panes. The left-hand pane lists the fields in the entity, the middle pane is a WYSIWYG layout of the view, and the right-hand pane shows the properties of the view. The name and created on fields are added to new views by default.

You can make several changes to the columns in the view:

- **Add column**: Drag and drop a field from the left-hand pane onto the view, or you can click on **+ View column** and select a field. The field will be added to the right of the existing columns.
- **Remove column**: Click on a column heading and select **Remove**.
- **Move column**: Rearrange the order of the columns by dragging and dropping or by clicking on a column heading and selecting **Move Left** and **Move Right**.

- **Column width**: Change the size of column by dragging the column or by clicking on the column heading, selecting **Edit properties**, and entering the number of pixels.
- **Filter**: Click on a column heading and select **Filter by**, and then specify the value to filter the records on.
- **Sort**: Click on a column heading and sort by ascending or descending.

You are not restricted from adding fields from the entity. You can add fields from all entities that have a many-to-one relationship with the view's entity. Adding related entity fields to a view will often make the view more relevant and useful for users.

In the view's properties, as shown in *Figure 9.22*, you can specify the name of the view. View names are important as they inform the user as to the purpose and content of the view.

The view properties show the **Sort by** columns. If you click on a column heading and select a sort option, this column replaces the columns specified in the **Properties** pane. You can add and remove fields from **Sort by** in the **Properties** pane.

You can only sort by fields that have been added to the view. You can only sort by columns for the entity and not columns from related entities.

Along with the columns displayed in the view, the filter is a critical part of the value provided by the view defining the records that will be included in the view. If you click on a column heading and use **Filter by**, then the columns are added to the **Filter by** columns in the **Properties** pane. You can edit the filter in the property pane, as shown in the following screenshot:

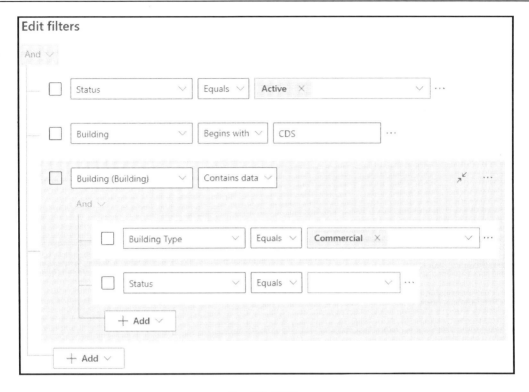

Figure 9.23 – Edit filters

You can use AND and OR clauses to specify and group the criteria. You can add joins to related entities to create complex filter conditions to just show the records needed for the view.

For the quick view form, there is an additional section in the **Properties** pane, **Find by**. Fields added here will be searched for. You can only include fields from the entity to search on. You cannot add fields from other entities.

If you need additional views, you can create new views by editing an existing view and clicking on **Save As**, or you can click on the **+ Add view** button shown in *Figure 9.21*.

Public and system views are created in the maker portal. Users can create their own personal views in a model-driven app.

Sharing personal views

Personal views are created by users within the user interface of a model-driven app. Personal views can be created using Advanced Find or by clicking on **Create view** from the action bar of any entity in the app.

Personal views are owned by the user that created them and are only visible to their owners. Personal views appear under **My Views**, as shown in the following screenshot:

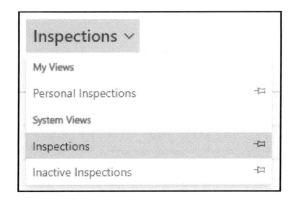

Figure 9.24 – Personal views

Users can pin the personal view to make it their default view. Users can share their personal views with other users and teams. If you share a view with another user, the view will appear under **My Views** for the other user.

 Personal views cannot be included in a solution and cannot be converted into a public view. Personal views cannot be exported or imported like charts.

Views are read-only by default, but you can configure them so that users can edit the records in the list.

Enabling editable grids

Editable grids allow the user to edit a record in a list without having to open the form for the record. Editable grids are especially useful in subgrids when the user has to perform a set of updates to child records.

Editable grids have the following features:

- **Grouping**: Group by a column.
- **Sorting**: Sort by any column in the view.
- **Filtering**: Users can filter the records in the view.
- **Support for business rules**: Business rules can perform actions on the fields in the view.

You do not configure a view to be editable; you configure the component showing the view. You can configure the entity so that views are editable when the entity is selected in the site map, and you can configure subgrids in forms to be editable. You cannot currently configure editable grids in the maker portal. You need to switch to classic.

For an entity, you need to click on the **Controls** tab for the entity, click on **Add Control...**, and select **Editable Grid**, as shown in the following screenshot:

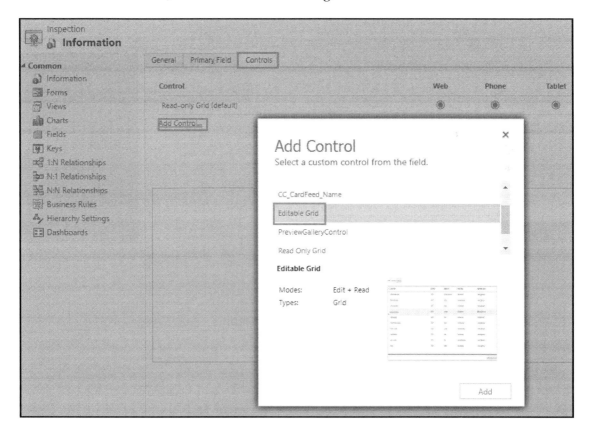

Figure 9.25 – Adding an editable grid control to an entity

Clicking on **Add** in the previous screenshot will add the control to the entity. You then must select which client from **Web, Phone,** and **Tablet** will use the editable grid and which will use the read-only grid.

The process for configuring a subgrid to be editable is similar. You edit the form and add the editable grid control to the subgrid.

There are some limitations of editable grids. You cannot edit the following:

- Address composite fields
- Calculated fields
- Rollup fields
- Status or status reasons
- Fields from a related entity

In this section, you learned about the types of views and how to create and configure views.

The other visual components that display data in a model-driven app are charts and dashboards.

Creating charts and dashboards

Charts and dashboards visualize data stored in entities in the Common Data Service so that users can have an overview of their data and decide on the actions to take.

A chart is a single visualization for an entity that can be displayed alongside a view, embedded in a form, or added to a dashboard. A dashboard is a single pane that displays views and charts from one or more entities.

In this section, we will learn about the capabilities of charts and dashboards and see how to create and configure both charts and dashboards.

Let's look at charts and how to create them.

Understanding charts

Charts provide a visual representation of an entity's data. Typically, charts show aggregated data. They are easy to create.

You can edit charts and create new charts from the **Charts** tab of the entity in your solution, as shown in the following screenshot:

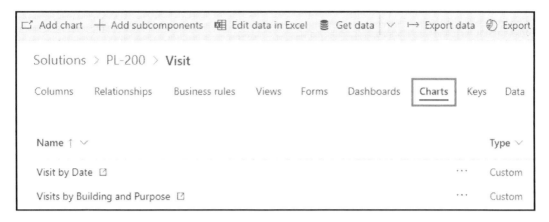

Figure 9.26 – Charts

In the previous screenshot, you can see two custom charts. No charts are created when you create a custom entity. The Account and Contact entities have a series of charts provided.

There are a limited set of chart types that you can create:

- Column
- Bar
- Line
- Area
- Pie
- Funnel
- Tag
- Doughnut

 The Tag and Doughnut charts are used with interactive dashboards.

The following screenshot shows an example of a bar chart:

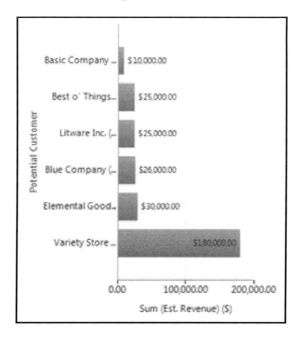

Figure 9.27 – Bar chart

Charts share the query functionality used in Advanced Find and views, FetchXML. FetchXML supports grouping and aggregation.

 You cannot restrict charts with security. If you need to prevent users from accessing a chart, you can either deactivate the chart or remove it from the entity assets in the app designer.

Let's look at how to create a chart.

Creating a chart

You can create a new chart from the **Charts** tab of the entity in your solution by clicking **Add chart**, as shown in *Figure 9.28*. This opens the chart designer, as shown in the following screenshot:

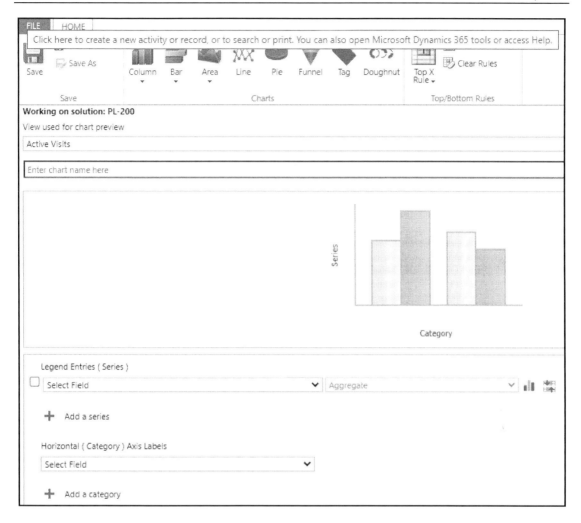

Figure 9.28 – Chart designer

In the previous screenshot, you can configure the following:

- **View used for chart preview**: You can use any public view to select the records to be used in the chart. The view is not saved with the chart definition. It is just for illustration.
- **Chart type**: Click on the type of chart. You can change this at any time.

- **Name**: This will be populated automatically from the fields selected.
- **Series**: The field(s) you want to aggregate (summarize).
- **Aggregate**: The function you want to aggregate with.
- **Categories**: The field(s) that you want to group the data by. If you use a date field, then you can group by day, week, month, quarter, and year.

If you have multiple series in your chart, you can have different chart types for each series. Column, line, and area charts can be combined.

Sharing personal charts

Personal charts are created by users within the user interface of a model-driven app. Personal charts are owned by their creator and are only visible to their owners. Like personal views, personal charts can be shared with users and teams.

Users can also export their chart to an XML file and pass the file to an administrator to import as a system chart. Charts are the only component you can convert from a personal component into a system component.

 It is often difficult to work out how a chart will appear once you have lots of data. One way to create a chart is to create the chart in the live system as a personal chart, export the chart to XML, and then import the chart into your solution in your development environment.

Charts show data in real time and are useful to show users their current workload. Charts are very often added to dashboards.

Understanding dashboards

Dashboards provide an overview of data from multiple entities on a single page.

There are two types of dashboards in a model-driven app:

- **Standard**: A collection of components from different entities, such as charts and lists, where the data is displayed
- **Interactive**: Displays visualizations and lists of records that can be filtered and acted upon

Let's look at standard dashboards first.

Configuring standard dashboards

Dashboards are useful for providing a user with an overview of their workload, or for a manager to see how their team is functioning. Dashboards show the data in the Common Data Service in real time.

A dashboard is a single pane showing components from one or more entities. The components are not linked and are not refreshed automatically.

Dashboards can have the following components:

- Charts
- Lists (views)
- IFrames
- Web resources
- Relationship assistant cards (for Dynamics 365 Sales)
- Power BI tiles (personal dashboards only)

You create a standard dashboard from your solution by clicking **+ New** and then selecting **Dashboard**. You choose a layout and then select the charts and views you want to use.

 There is a maximum of six components that can be included on a dashboard.

Interactive experience dashboards have more functionality and are aimed at providing a centralized workspace for a user.

Configuring interactive experience dashboards

Interactive experience dashboards are useful for users who need to manage work that is constantly changing. A user can sort and filter the data in the dashboard and take action on the data. Interactive experience dashboards are linked to an entity.

There are two field properties related to the interactive experience:

- **Appears in the global filter**
- **Sortable**

The following screenshot shows these fields enabled in the maker portal:

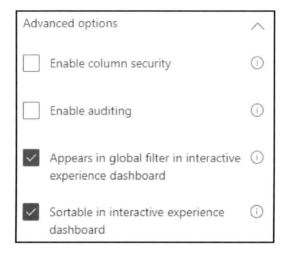

Figure 9.29 – Field properties for an interactive experience

You create an interactive dashboard from the **Dashboards** tab of your entity in a solution.

After a dashboard is created, it is available to all users by default. You will need to control which users have access to a dashboard.

Securing dashboards

Dashboards are typically aimed at sets of users. It is a good idea to restrict a dashboard to just the users who need that dashboard.

You can restrict dashboards by security role. By default, all users can see new dashboards. You can change which security roles are associated with a dashboard by clicking on the ellipses (**...**) next to the name of the dashboard in your solution and selecting **Enable security roles**.

 You can add and remove dashboards in the app designer.

Dashboards are not available by default for mobile clients. You should edit the dashboard properties and set **Enable for mobile**, as shown in the following screenshot:

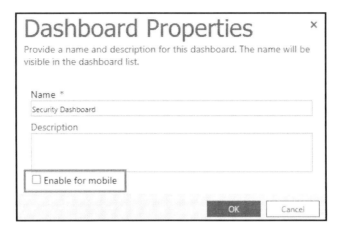

Figure 9.30 – Dashboard properties

As with views and charts, users can create their own personal dashboards.

Sharing personal dashboards

Personal dashboards are created by users within the user interface of a model-driven app. Personal dashboards can be created by clicking on **+ New** from the action bar when viewing dashboards in the app.

Personal dashboards are owned by the user that created them and are only visible to their owners. Users can share their personal dashboard with other users and teams.

 Personal views cannot be included in a solution and cannot be converted into a public view. Personal views cannot be exported or imported like charts.

You can also add a Power BI dashboard to a model-driven app. A Power BI dashboard can be added as a personal dashboard. You can add a Power BI tile to a personal dashboard. You must enable the **Power BI virtualization embedding** option in the settings in the Power Platform admin center.

In this section, you learned how to create charts and dashboards. Charts and dashboards provide visualizations of data. There are other options for reporting data from the Common Data Service.

Understanding reporting options

Users need to be able to produce analyses of their data and produce formatted reports to their management and external stakeholders. The Power Platform provides a number of options to assist in analyzing, prioritizing, and viewing data. The options have been increased with each new release:

- Views
- Export to Excel
- Charts
- Dashboards
- Word and Excel templates
- Report wizard
- SQL Reporting Services
- Power BI

Views, charts, and dashboards have been explained earlier in this chapter but there are a few issues when it comes to generating formatted output:

- Chart results cannot be exported or printed. The only option, if you want to share a picture of a chart, is to take a screenshot. Charts are not accessible except from within the app.
- Dashboards cannot be exported or printed. Dashboards can only be accessed by a licensed user.
- Dashboards show current data, not trends. For trend analysis, time series, and deeper analysis, you should consider the use of Power BI.
- The data listed in a view can be exported to Excel. Exporting to Excel is explained in Chapter 6, *Managing Data*. There is a limit to the number of rows that can be exported. That limit is currently 100,000 rows.
- Word and Excel templates can be used to created formatted output. These templates are explained in Chapter 19, *Microsoft 365 Integration*. Word templates are used with a single record. Excel templates have the same limit as Export to Excel.

The report wizard allows you to create a report for an entity using a step-by-step wizard. The layout is simple but can include grouping and totals.

If you need to create complex reports containing multiple tables, you should consider developing reports with SQL Reporting Services or using Power BI.

Congratulations on completing one of the most important chapters in this book! Understanding how to create model-driven apps is a fundamental skill for a functional consultant. You will have seen from the section on introducing model-driven apps the number of references to the other chapters in the book, from business rules to managing data.

Summary

In this chapter, you were introduced to model-driven apps and the components that are configured and assembled to make the app. You should now understand all the components and how to create and modify the user interface components for model-driven apps, including forms, views, charts, and dashboards. You should now be able to assemble these components into a model-driven app.

The skills you have learned will allow you to build effective apps for users who have to manage a business process. The apps you build will allow access to many different entities and present a coherent user interface, allowing users to focus on their business process.

In the next chapter, we will learn how to create canvas apps, apps aimed at users who require an app as part of their job role or to perform a task.

Questions

After reading this chapter, test your knowledge with these questions. You will find the answers to these questions in the Assessments section at the end of the book:

1. You create a model-driven app containing a custom entity named Visit. In which two ways can you prevent the Inactive Visits public view from being selected by a user?

    A) Edit the entity assets.
    B) Deactivate the view.
    C) Delete the view.
    D) Unshare the view.

2. Which three form components can be hidden for the mobile phone client?

   A) Tabs
   B) Sections
   C) Fields
   D) Timeline
   E) Timer

3. Which form can be used in the timeline?

   A) Main
   B) Quick create
   C) Quick view
   D) Card

4. Where do you add dashboards in the site map?

   A) Area
   B) Group
   C) Subarea
   D) Entity assets

5. Which of the following is used when a user clicks on **Related** in a form?

   A) Quick find view
   B) Default public view
   C) Associated view
   D) Lookup view

Further reading

For more details on the topics in this chapter, refer to these resources:

- Understand model-driven app components: `https://docs.microsoft.com/powerapps/maker/model-driven-apps/model-driven-app-components`
- Add or edit model-driven app components in the Power Apps app designer: `https://docs.microsoft.com/powerapps/maker/model-driven-apps/add-edit-app-components`
- Share a model-driven app using Power Apps: `https://docs.microsoft.com/powerapps/maker/model-driven-apps/share-model-driven-app`

- Types of model-driven app forms in Power Apps: `https://docs.microsoft.com/powerapps/maker/model-driven-apps/types-forms`
- Overview of the model-driven form designer: `https://docs.microsoft.com/powerapps/maker/model-driven-apps/form-designer-overview`
- Add, configure, move, or delete components on a form: `https://docs.microsoft.com/powerapps/maker/model-driven-apps/add-move-configure-or-delete-components-on-form`
- Set up the timeline control: `https://docs.microsoft.com/powerapps/maker/model-driven-apps/set-up-timeline-control`
- Add and configure a quick view component on a form: `https://docs.microsoft.com/powerapps/maker/model-driven-apps/form-designer-add-configure-quickview`
- Add and configure a subgrid component on a form: `https://docs.microsoft.com/powerapps/maker/model-driven-apps/form-designer-add-configure-subgrid`
- Embed a canvas app in a model-driven form: `https://docs.microsoft.com/powerapps/maker/model-driven-apps/embed-canvas-app-in-form`
- Create a card form: `https://docs.microsoft.com/powerapps/maker/model-driven-apps/create-card-forms`
- Understand model-driven app views: `https://docs.microsoft.com/powerapps/maker/model-driven-apps/create-edit-views`
- Create and edit public or system model-driven app views: `https://docs.microsoft.com/powerapps/maker/model-driven-apps/create-edit-views-app-designer`
- Make model-driven app grids (lists) editable using the Editable Grid custom control: `https://docs.microsoft.com/powerapps/maker/model-driven-apps/make-grids-lists-editable-custom-control`
- Create a model-driven app system chart: `https://docs.microsoft.com/powerapps/maker/model-driven-apps/create-edit-system-chart`
- Create and configure model-driven app interactive experience dashboards: `https://docs.microsoft.com/powerapps/maker/model-driven-apps/configure-interactive-experience-dashboards`
- Create a report using the report wizard: `https://docs.microsoft.com/powerapps/user/create-report-with-wizard`
- Add reporting features to your model-driven app: `https://docs.microsoft.com/powerapps/maker/model-driven-apps/add-reporting-to-app`

10
Canvas Apps

This chapter will explain how to create canvas apps, accessing data held in the **Common Data Service (CDS)** and other data sources, to create task- or role-based web and mobile applications for users.

We will begin with an introduction to canvas apps, then we will cover where and how to create them by adding controls to the app. We will look at accessing data sources, in particular the CDS, with canvas apps. We will finish by understanding how to deploy these apps.

In this chapter, we will cover the following topics:

- Introducing canvas apps
- Creating canvas apps
- Adding visual controls to apps
- Using connectors to access data
- Deploying apps to users

By the end of this chapter, you will be able to create and manage canvas apps, understand how to use the App Checker to spot errors and potential issues when running your apps, and learn to use entities and fields you created in the CDS within your canvas apps.

Introducing canvas apps

A key component of the Power Platform is the capability to create low-code/no-code apps. There are three types of power app: canvas apps, model-driven apps, and portal apps. The next two chapters will look at model-driven apps and portal apps, and this chapter will focus on canvas apps.

Canvas apps are small apps created around a specific task or role, normally as an app that someone uses as a part of their job, in contrast with an app that they use all day. A typical example of a use case for a canvas app is a mobile user who needs to capture information while performing part of their duties, for example, recording the results of an inspection:

Figure 10.1 – An example canvas app

Canvas apps run in a browser or on a mobile device using the Power Apps app, which can be downloaded from your mobile phone's app store. Further, a canvas app has access to the resources of your device, such as, for example, the camera, GPS location, and whether the device is connected to a network or not. Using these capabilities, you can create an app that runs on your employees' iOS and Android phones to track their locations. A utilities company can use this information to direct the nearest technician to any outage so that the problem is resolved more quickly.

Canvas apps have been formulated so that you do not need to be a developer to create the app; no code is required. The techniques needed to build an app are inherited from how we build visual designs in PowerPoint and the use of functions in Excel. Microsoft uses the term "maker" in place of "developer" when talking about the people creating canvas apps, to reinforce the ease of creating these apps.

The use of the word "canvas" reflects that the app maker has full control over every element of the app's screens. So much control, in fact, that canvas apps are sometimes referred to as pixel-perfect apps.

Now that you know what a canvas app is used for, let's look at how to create one.

Creating canvas apps

Canvas apps are created in a web browser; there is no need for Visual Studio or any local software installation.

A maker navigates to the Power Apps maker portal at `https://make.powerapps.com`. In this portal, you can view and edit existing apps and create new apps. With Microsoft, there is never one way to do something; this is just as true when creating apps.

Creating an app

When you access Power Apps, the home page looks as follows:

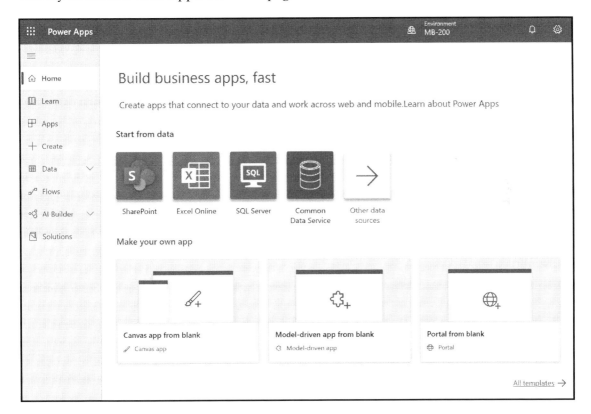

Figure 10.2 – Power Apps maker portal

There are several ways to create an app:

- **Start from data**: Connect to a data source and use an existing entity or table. Starting from data is an excellent choice for a straightforward app that just needs to list data from your data source and provide create, read, write, and delete functionalities on data records.
- **Canvas app from blank**: You can also start with a blank canvas, adding connections and controls. You start from blank when you need to create a richer user interface, or you want to use non-tabular data. This will be the choice for most apps that you will build.
- **Templates**: You can additionally use one of many prebuilt app templates.

 There are many templates, but I would suggest these as examples of how to build apps rather than a starting point for your app, as changing them to meet your needs will likely take longer than creating your app from scratch.

 You can also create apps directly from within SharePoint, but we will not look at this method in this book.

The quickest way to build an app is to create an app from data. When you select this option, you are prompted to select a data source and then an entity from that data source. A simple three-page app is created for you:

Figure 10.3 – List screen from a three-page app

The three pages are as follows:

- A list screen containing a list of records from your entity
- A view page showing the fields from your entity

- An edit page that can be used to edit records and create new records

This auto-generated app has search and sort functions. You can easily amend the layout of the list of records, change which fields are shown for view and edit screens, add a background image, and change the color scheme. You can then use the app as the basis for the rest of the functionality that you need.

Alternatively, you can start from a blank canvas by clicking on the **Canvas app from blank** option and adding your controls.

Adding controls to your app

The Power Apps canvas studio is a web application and has been designed to be familiar to users of Office applications.

The studio has three panes, a ribbon for commands, and a function bar where you enter Excel-like formulas, as shown in the next screenshot:

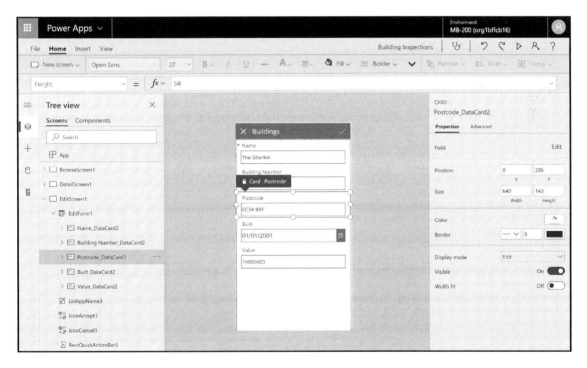

Figure 10.4 – Canvas studio

As you can see, the three panes are as follows:

- **Left-hand pane**: This shows the screens, controls, and data sources in your app.
- **Middle pane**: This shows your app in a true WYSIWYG layout.
- **Right-hand pane**: This is where you can change the properties of controls.

When you start from blank, you just have a single empty screen added to your app. You then use the menu options in the tabs at the top of the screen to build your app:

Figure 10.5 – Tabs in the canvas studio

As shown in the previous screenshot, the different available tabs are as follows:

- The **Home** tab: Contains the formatting commands for changing the appearance of any element in your app.
- The **Insert** tab: This tab is for adding controls to your app.
- The **View** tab: This tab handles data sources, media, variables, and collections.
- The **Action** tab: This tab is a quick way to control what happens when a user clicks on a control.

Canvas apps start with a screen that you can build your app on top of.

Understanding what screens are

No matter which way you create an app, there will always be at least one screen. A screen is a canvas on which you add controls and change the color, background image, and other aspects of the app's appearance. You can add multiple screens to your app and then navigate between them.

We have previously mentioned controls, but what are they exactly?

Understanding what controls are

Controls are the prebuilt visual components that you add to your apps that allow your users to view and interact with data. Some of the more common controls are the following:

- Labels
- Buttons
- Forms
- Checkboxes
- Galleries

You add controls using the **Insert** tab of Canvas Studio, selecting the appropriate control, dragging it into place in the middle pane, and setting its properties in the right-hand pane and in the formula bar:

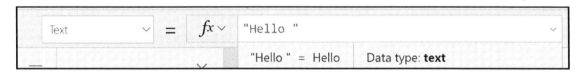

Figure 10.6 – Properties and the formula bar

Let's look at a few of the controls in more detail.

The gallery control

The gallery control is used to display lists of records. When you build an app from data, the first screen is a gallery showing the records for the entity you chose:

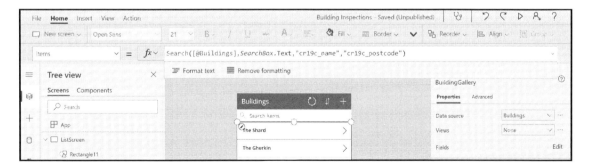

Figure 10.7 – Gallery control

In the properties of the gallery, you can select the following:

- Data source.
- Entity.
- Fields.
- For the CDS, you can also reuse a view.

This will display records from the entity. You can use the **Items** property of the gallery to restrict the records listed using the filter and search functions.

The button control

A button control is an area on the screen that a user clicks on, which then performs an action. A button does not have to look like a traditional button; it can be an icon or an image:

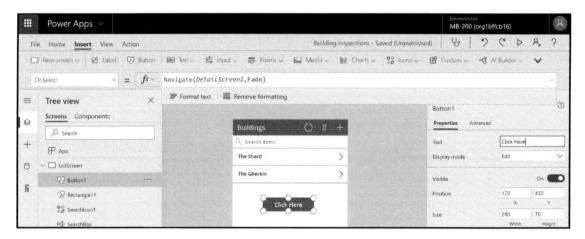

Figure 10.8 – Button control

The **OnSelect** property defines what happens when a user clicks on the button; for example, the `Navigate` function changes to a different screen.

The form control

The form control is used to display and edit a set of fields from an entity. Using a form makes it easier to read and save records.

The form control is associated with entity data. You will often use a form with a gallery; the form showing the data for the selected record in the gallery.

The `SubmitForm` function, as shown in the following screenshot, saves the contents of the form to your data source:

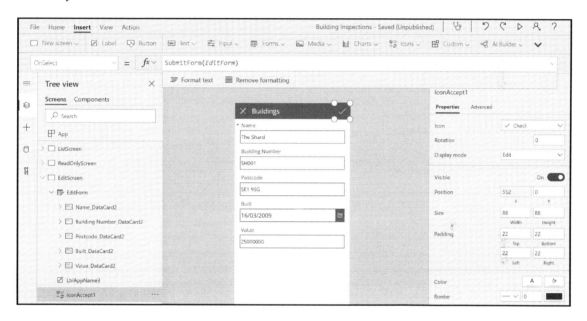

Figure 10.9 – Form control

Building apps is simply the process of adding components to screens, arranging them, changing their properties, and defining key properties.

Where there isn't a control available, you can create your own controls.

Reusable components

There are two types of reusable components:

- Canvas components
- The **Power Apps Component Framework (PCF)**

Any app maker can create a reusable canvas component using the existing controls provided. A simple example is a standard screen header and logo that all your other apps will use to engender a common look and feel for all the apps in your organization.

When you need a visual control that is different to the controls provided, a developer can use TypeScript and HTML to create components with the PCF. There are examples in the PCF gallery (`https://pcf.gallery`).

We have looked at controls – the other important criterion for building a canvas app is to connect to data.

Exploring connectors and data sources

Canvas apps can connect to many different data sources. They share the connectors used by Power Automate, with over 400 connectors to Office 365, Dynamics 365, Azure, and third-party services.

A canvas app can connect to multiple data sources in a single app, being able to mash up data from the different connectors on a single screen or read from one data source and write to another. The possibilities are endless.

Using the on-premises data gateway, canvas apps can read and write data in an on-premises SQL server or access an on-premises SharePoint list. Depending on the data source you connect to, you may have to set more properties and handle more steps in your app.

Although many different data sources can be used by canvas apps, the PL-200 exam focuses on the CDS connector.

Using the Common Data Service

The CDS is one possible connector for use with canvas apps. The CDS connector has a number of advantages over other connectors due to its built-in capabilities that can be leveraged by your apps; the Power Platform tools have been designed to work together, with the whole being greater than the sum of its parts.

Some advantages of using the CDS over a SharePoint list are as follows:

- **Metadata**: Common Data Service entities and fields have metadata that a Power App can use to set, for instance, the data type on fields, the length on string fields, or whether to automatically reuse option sets.
- **Scale**: The CDS can scale to large record sets, whereas you may find issues with query delegation using SharePoint.
- **Logic**: Business rules in the CDS can perform data validation, simplifying your apps.

Some advantages of using the CDS over an Azure SQL database are the following:

- **Metadata**: The range values for fields, such as min and max, are stored in metadata and used by Power Apps. With SQL Server, a maker would need to handle this validation explicitly.
- **Security**: Row-level security is handled by the CDS; users will not be able to access data they are not entitled to access, with no effort required by the app maker. In contrast, with SQL Server the app will need to handle record-level access.
- **Logic**: Calculated and rollup fields reduce the need for processing and calculations in your apps.

 Building apps using the CDS is faster and will have fewer issues than any other data source.

In the Canvas Studio, when you add a gallery or a form, you are prompted for a data source. If you have a CDS database in your environment, the entities will be available for you to select from, as seen in *Figure 10.10*. Working with CDS databases is very straightforward in canvas apps:

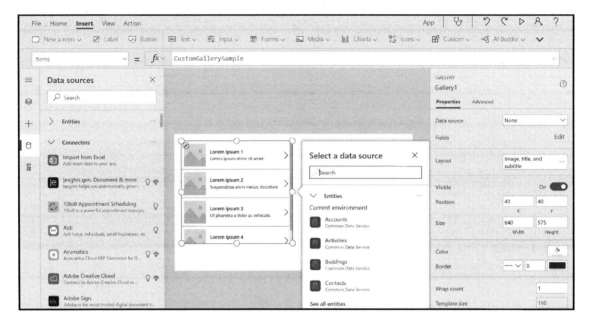

Figure 10.10 – Adding a data source

Now that you have built your app, you need to deploy it to your users.

Deploying canvas apps

Now that your app is ready, you need to deploy it so that it can be run by your target user community. You do not compile or build a canvas app or package it.

Before you give access to users, you should check for any errors with the App Checker tool.

App Checker

The App Checker tool runs a set of rules to find errors and identify potential issues when running your app. The rules cover the following areas:

- **Formulas**: Are there missing brackets, missing quotes, or invalid references?
- **Runtime**: Will the app pose a reliability risk, or is the app using deprecated functionality?
- **Accessibility**: Will the app cause problems for keyboard or screen reader tools?
- **Performance**: Are there any likely performance issues when running the app?

You can run the App Checker by clicking on the stethoscope icon in the toolbar of the Canvas Studio.

> The App Checker can also be run as a DevOps task when exporting solutions. For more information, see `Chapter 20`, *Application Life Cycle Management*.

The App Checker runs automatically in the background while you are editing your app. If the App Checker finds an error, a red dot will appear next to the stethoscope icon in the toolbar as shown in the next screenshot. Clicking on this icon will expand the App Checker pane and the issues will be listed as shown in the following screenshot:

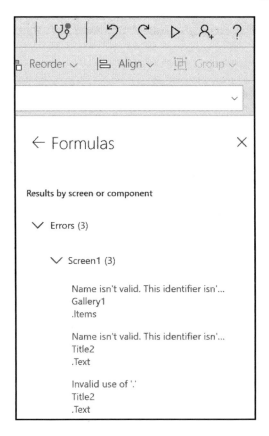

Figure 10.11 – App Checker

Once you have resolved the errors, you can now test your app.

Testing an app

Testing is an important part of developing apps. You should test your app to make sure it works as expected. You should use different sets of data to test your app, including data that is incomplete and incorrect, to make sure all errors are handled correctly.

Test Studio is a browser-based automated user interface test system for canvas apps. Test Studio enables you to create and run a set of tests. You can re-run the tests after each change you make to the app. This is known as regression testing.

Test Studio contains the following components:

- **Test cases**: The set of steps to be performed
- **Test suites**: Groups of test cases
- **Test assertions**: Assertions that evaluate the expected results with a pass or fail expression

The following screenshot shows Test Studio in a browser:

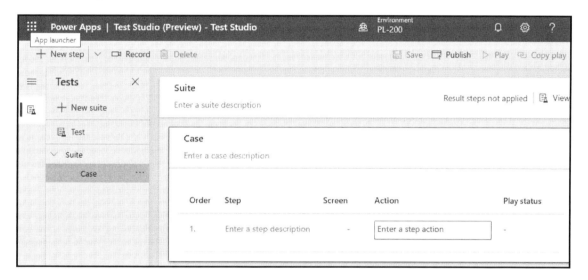

Figure 10.12 – Test Studio

Test Studio is a useful tool that improves the quality of your app. Once you have completed testing, you can now deploy your app.

Publishing and sharing an app

To deploy an app, all you do is publish the app and then share it with the user(s).

You do not need to install any software to run a canvas app; all apps can be run from a browser or from the Power Apps player app on mobile devices:

Figure 10.13 – Sharing an app

 Microsoft has deliberately used document-centric terminology around creating and sharing apps.

To run an app, a user must be authenticated and authorized.

User authentication

To access a Power App, the user must belong to your **Azure Active Directory** (**AD**) tenant.

 Office 365 users are managed by Azure AD, so adding a user to Office 365 is sufficient.

Azure AD provides a great deal of functionality around authentication, including the following:

- **Multi-Factor Authentication** (**MFA**): This is a form of authentication where you need something you *know* (such as a password), something you *have* (for example, a mobile device), and something you *are* (a biometric signature, for instance).
- **Conditional Access**: This restricts access based on rules your administrator defines, such as location, method of access, or the device used, based on rules defined by your organization.

Azure AD also monitors for unusual access to protect your systems and data.

Canvas apps benefit from the capabilities of Azure AD, which helps give canvas app makers access to enterprise-level security control and governance.

 Canvas apps support the use of guest users in your tenant if you require people outside of your organization to be able to run your app.

Authentication verifies who you are, and authorization allows you access to the appropriate resources.

User authorization

You have already seen that you share an app to deploy it. Sharing an app with a user authorizes that user to run the app.

 Share apps with groups and add users to AD security groups to make deployment and management easier.

 Along with the authorization to use the app, you will also need additional authorization to use any data sources the app connects to; users may be forced to sign into the data sources when they run the app.

Users need to be licensed for Power Apps. Licenses for Power Apps are included with Office 365 E3/E5 and Dynamics 365, but these subscriptions only cover the Office 365 and CDS connectors. If you want to use other connectors, then you may need to purchase and allocate separate Power Apps licenses.

Sharing an app allows a user to run the app. You need to allow others to edit and change the app separately.

Managing changes

When you create an app, only you can edit it. If you want others to be able to edit your app, you need to make them a co-owner of the app. To do so, you share the app and check the **Co-owner** box in *Figure 10.13*.

 Guest users cannot be made co-owners of canvas apps.

You can export your app into a ZIP file and import the app to other environments; a better way is to include your app in a solution. We will look at solutions and application life cycle management in `Chapter 20`, *Application Life Cycle Management*.

There are some limitations with canvas apps that you need to be aware of.

Limitations of canvas apps

Currently, canvas apps are not responsive, that is, they will not adjust to the orientation and screen size of your device. You create apps using the phone layout (portrait) or the tablet layout (landscape).

 The best practice is to make all control positions relative to each other using formulas rather than explicitly setting their X and Y values.

To provide access to data offline access from your network is not natively supported, an app maker must detect the loss of a network connection, store data locally, and then save back once connected.

The `Connection.Connected` function returns false if you lose your network connection. You can use the `Collections` and `SaveData` functions to store data locally on the device and retrieve it using `LoadData` when the connection is restored.

Performance

Similarly, for canvas apps, there are several techniques and options you can use to improve app performance:

- **Controls**: Keep the number of controls on a form as low as possible and make use of galleries instead of cards. The more controls you have, the slower the app will be.
- **Use delegation**: Check that queries are executed on the server, not in the app. If queries are not delegated, you will see poor performance when opening your app.
- **Data connections**: Limit the number of connections.
- **Caching**: Use the `ClearCollect` function to cache data during `OnStart`.
- **Delayed load**: Enable this option if you have multiple screens. It will only populate a screen when the screen is accessed rather than at startup.
- **Delay output**: Enable this option on text input fields so formulas are not evaluated on each keystroke.
- **Formulas**: Reduce the number of times a formula is used by setting a variable once and then referencing the stored result elsewhere.

Summary

In this chapter, you were introduced to canvas apps, how they are created, how the Canvas Studio is used, and details around some of the controls used to build the apps. You should now understand how to create and deploy canvas apps, and why you should use the CDS as the data source for your apps.

In the next chapter, we will introduce portal apps and how to build them, and in doing so we will compare them with canvas apps.

Questions

After reading this chapter, test your knowledge with these questions. You will find the answers to these questions in the `Assessments` chapter at the end of the book:

1. Your users report that they are not seeing the latest version of the app. What should you do?

   A) Share the app.
   B) Publish the app.
   C) Run the App Checker.
   D) Run the solution checker.

2. Which connector should you use in a canvas app with Dynamics 365 Sales?

   A) Azure SQL
   B) Common Data Model
   C) CDS
   D) Dynamics 365 Customer Engagement

3. A user reports that they cannot see the app on their mobile device. What should you do?

   A) Share the app.
   B) Export the app and email it to the user.
   C) Export the app and import it into the user's environment.
   D) Run the App Checker.

4. A user requires an app that shows a subset of records. What control do you add?

   A) A form
   B) A media control
   C) A combo box
   D) A gallery

5. You are an administrator with responsibility for the deployment of canvas apps to many different sets of users. How should you best manage the deployment?

   A) Use Azure AD Conditional Access rules.
   B) Use Azure AD security groups.
   C) Use the Power Apps for App Makers Connector.
   D) Use the Azure AD connector.

Further reading

- Create an app from scratch: `https://docs.microsoft.com/powerapps/maker/canvas-apps/data-platform-create-app-scratch`
- App Checker: `https://docs.microsoft.com/powerapps/maker/canvas-apps/accessibility-checker`
- Share app: `https://docs.microsoft.com/powerapps/maker/canvas-apps/share-app`
- Test Studio: `https://docs.microsoft.com/powerapps/maker/canvas-apps/test-studio`
- Optimize canvas app performance in Power Apps: `https://docs.microsoft.com/powerapps/maker/canvas-apps/performance-tips`
- Understand delegation in a canvas app: `https://docs.microsoft.com/powerapps/maker/canvas-apps/delegation-overview`
- Performance considerations with Power Apps: `https://powerapps.microsoft.com/blog/performance-considerations-with-powerapps`

11
Portal Apps

Portal apps allow you to expose the data in **Common Data Service** (**CDS**) to external users using a website built on the basis of a no-code approach.

This chapter will explain how to create portal apps to expose data in CDS to external users. You can quickly create a portal website and easily customize the pages and layout, and add content to meet your customers' needs.

The following topics will be covered in this chapter:

- Introducing portal apps
- Creating portal apps
- Adding web pages and entity forms
- Securing portal apps

By the end of this chapter, you will be able to create a portal app and configure it by applying themes and adding pages. You will also be able to secure access to the portal app.

Introducing portal apps

Customers demand to interact with your organization using many different channels. The web is one such channel. Customers need to view the data you hold on them, for example, the status of their service requests, and to submit new service requests over the web. Portal apps address this requirement.

Other than model-driven and canvas apps, portal apps are the third type of Power App that you can create. Portal apps are external-facing websites that users outside of your organization can browse anonymously, or sign in to, in order to access data stored in the CDS.

Portal apps require an environment with a CDS database.

This section provides an overview of the portal and how external users can access the portal. The following screenshot shows a portal website:

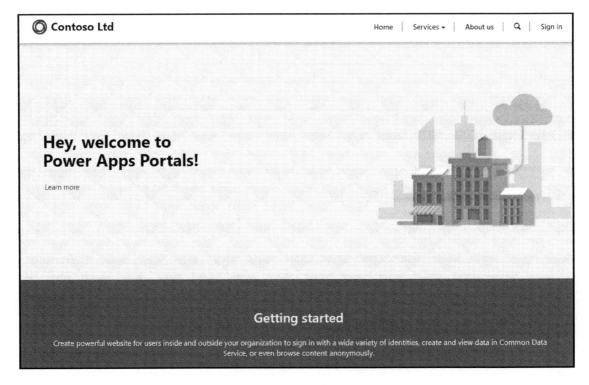

Figure 11.1 – Starter portal

The starter portal website shown in the preceding screenshot has a **Home** page, a **Services** page with two child pages, an **About us** page, and a **Sign in** page.

Before we begin configuring the portal, you need to understand how external users can be given access to it.

Inviting users to the portal

Portal websites are available on the internet to the public and users can anonymously browse the website. To gain access to data, a portal user must be associated with a contact record in the CDS.

You can invite a user to the portal by completing these steps from their contact record form:

1. **Contact**: Open the contact record form in a model-driven app.
2. **Invite the user**: Click on **Create Invitation** in the action bar on the contact record. This opens a new page where you can specify the details of the invitation. Click **Save** and a unique invitation code is generated.
3. **Add a web role**: Each portal user needs a web role that contains the privileges and data access settings. Under **Assign to Web Roles** in the invitation record, click on **Add Existing Web Role** and select the **Authenticated Users** web role.
4. **Send invitation**: Click on **Flow** in the action bar on the invitation record, select **Send Invitation**, and then click **OK**.

The user receives the email with a URL to the portal containing the unique invitation code. Clicking on this link will direct the user to the portal where they can redeem the invitation code under the **Sign In** page.

You have learned the purpose of portal apps and how external users can be authorized to access data in the portal app. Now let's look at how you can create a portal app.

Creating portal apps

If you need to expose your CDS data to customers and partners, you need to create a portal app and then configure the entities and forms to expose. Creating a portal app is easy. You create portal apps from the Power Apps maker portal (`https://make.powerapps.com`).

To create an app, click on **+ Create** in the maker portal and then click on **Portal from blank**. The following window will appear:

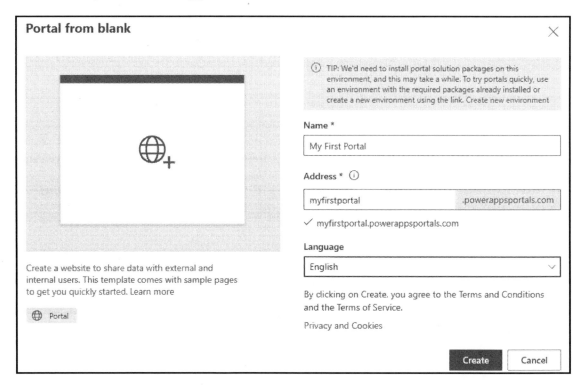

Figure 11.2 – Creating a portal app

In the fields shown in *Figure 11.2*, enter the name of your portal, the URL address for your portal, select a language, and then click on **Create**.

 The address must be unique for all Power Apps portals worldwide. If it is unique, you will see a tick. If you do not see a tick, change the address until a unique name is available.

Provisioning a portal can take a few hours. Clicking on **Apps** in the maker portal will show you the status of your portal app. When the portal has been provisioned, you will see two apps, as shown in the following screenshot:

	Name		Modified ↓	Owner	Type
	My First Portal	...	7 min ago	SYSTEM	Portal
	Portal Management	...	10 min ago		Model-driven

Apps

Apps Component libraries (preview)

Figure 11.3 – Portal apps

You can only create one portal app per CDS environment.

The first app in *Figure 11.3* is the portal app itself. You can browse to the portal website or edit the portal app using Power Apps portals Studio, a visual editor for customizing the portal website. The second app is a model-driven app, named Portal Management, which provides access to the records that hold the configuration of the portal website. You can use either of these to customize your portal website.

The **Portal from blank** option uses the starter kit template. There are also other templates you can use to create portal apps if you have Dynamics 365.

Creating portals for Dynamics 365 apps

Portals were originally an add-on component for the Dynamics 365 Sales, Dynamics 365 Customer Service, Dynamics 365 Field Service, and Dynamics 365 Marketing apps. Dynamics 365 portals are now Power Apps portal apps. You create a portal for a Dynamics 365 app using a template supplied by Microsoft.

To create a portal for a Dynamics 365 app, you create a portal from the Power Apps maker portal and select one of the following templates:

- **Community**: A community portal for customers to share information with each other, using forums, the knowledge base, and providing feedback with comments and ratings.
- **Customer self-service**: A self-service portal for customers to view and submit cases, search the knowledge base, and share with others on forums and feedback.
- **Partner**: A portal for partner organizations such as resellers and suppliers. The portal for the Dynamics 365 Field Service app requires the partner template.
- **Employee self-service**: A self-service portal for employees with forums, search, knowledge base, and feedback.

You must have a Dynamics 365 app installed in your environment in order to be able to choose one of these templates.

You can also create a portal using the **Portal from blank** option in an environment containing a Dynamics 365 app. This is a starter portal with a few sample pages. It is the same template that is used if you create a portal app for an environment that does not have a Dynamics 365 app installed.

As well as being able to customize the portal website, there is a dedicated administration center.

Administering a portal

The configuration for the portal app is held in entities in the CDS. This configuration needs to be synchronized to the actual portal website that is running inside Azure. The portal website caches the data from the CDS. It can take a few minutes for the portal website to reflect any changes made to its configuration.

To control the portal website, you need to access the **Power Apps Portals admin center** page. In the Power Apps maker portal, click on the ellipses (**...**) next to the portal app and select **Settings** and then **Administration**. The following window will open:

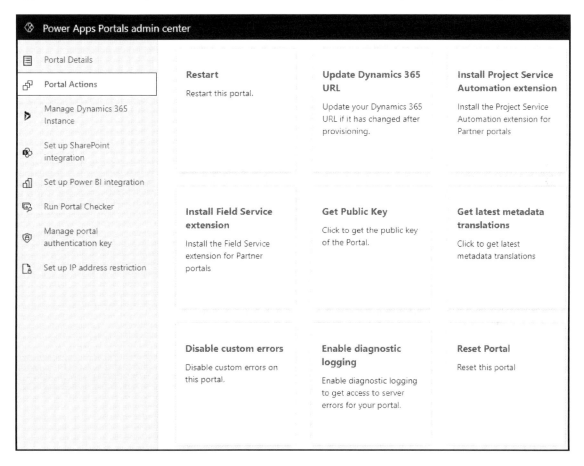

Figure 11.4 – Power Apps Portals admin center

In this admin center, there are maintenance and configuration tasks that you can perform, including the following:

- **Change base URL**: Changes the URL address for your portal.
- **Restart**: Restarts the portal. If your changes to the portal are not being shown in the portal website, restarting the portal will normally resolve any issues.
- **Reset Portal**: This portal action deletes the portal site and removes all configuration.

In this section, you have learned how to create a portal app and the different tools for managing and customizing the portal website. We will now look at adding pages and exposing data in your portal app.

Adding web pages and entity forms

The website for a portal app is generated from the configuration data held in entities in the CDS. You can add a page to the website by simply creating a record in the **Web Pages** entity in Portal Management app. However, it is easier to use the Power Apps portals Studio to add pages and change the website navigation.

You open Power Apps portals Studio by clicking on the ellipses (**...**) next to the portal app and selecting **Edit**. Power Apps portals Studio will open, as shown in the following screenshot:

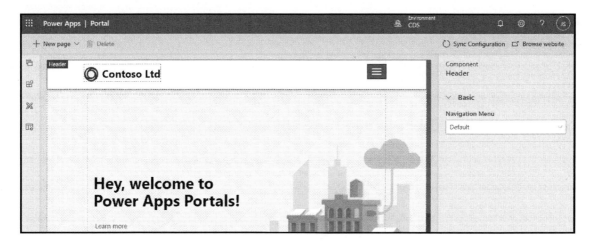

Figure 11.5 – Power Apps portals Studio

Power Apps portals Studio is a WYSIWYG visual editor for customizing the portal website by adding and configuring components on the web pages. To add a web page, click on **+ New page**, as shown in the preceding screenshot. You then select a web page template that controls the basic layout of the page.

 Web page templates can be customized. You can also add Liquid tags in the source code editor for advanced configuration. Liquid is an open source template language that can add dynamic content to web pages in the portal.

You can add portal components to the page. Two of the components are entity lists and entity forms that expose CDS data on the portal website.

Exposing data in the portal

To display or manage data in the portal, you only to need to specify the entity in the CDS. To show a list of records, you select the entity and then a public view for that entity. You can choose to add the create, edit, and delete options, as shown in the following screenshot:

Figure 11.6 – Entity list

To create or edit a record, you need to create a web form by selecting the entity, a system form, and select the edit mode, as shown in the following screenshot:

Figure 11.7 – Configuring an entity list

The portal app inherits its list and form layouts from the views and forms in the CDS. To change which fields are included in the portal lists and forms, you need to customize the view and forms for the entities in the Power Apps maker portal.

 Portal apps can only expose data held in the CDS. If data is held in other data sources, you must import the data into the CDS to display on the portal.

Portal apps allow for simple addition of pages, lists, and forms, as shown in this section. There are deeper configuration options available through JavaScript, **Cascading Style Sheets (CSS)**, and Liquid templates.

Applying a theme to a portal

Portal apps are built using the Bootstrap frontend framework using CSS and JavaScript. The use of this common framework means that you can leverage bootstrap to brand your portal website.

The appearance of portal apps can be changed in the following scenarios:

- When switching between preset basic themes
- When creating a new basic theme and changing the colors
- When editing the CSS under **Themes** in Power Apps portals Studio
- When uploading custom themes

With these options, you can make simple changes, or you can employ a professional designer to create a highly customized theme for your portal app.

 Portal apps use Bootstrap v3.3.

In this section, you have learned to customize portal pages and display data from the CDS in your portal. You now need to secure access to the pages and the data.

Securing portal apps

Your portal website is available on the internet for anyone to browse. If you expose data on web pages, you will need to secure the website and require users to authenticate. Once a user is authenticated, portal apps can apply security to pages, entity lists, and forms.

In the following sections, we will look first at the authentication of users, and then how to control access for authenticated users.

Authenticating a portal app

For a user to be able access data, the user must be authenticated. By default, there are two ways in which to authenticate a user. You can use the local sign-in, which is handled by the portal and uses the email address and password on the contact record, or you can use Azure **Active Directory** (**AD**) for internal users.

You can configure additional identity providers such as LinkedIn and Facebook. The benefit of using an external identity provider is that you do not need to manage passwords, thereby reducing the overhead of user management.

The user's password is held as a hashed value in a secured field on their associated contact record. You can change a user's password by clicking on **Change Password** in the action bar on their contact record. This opens a pane on the right-hand side. Enter a password, click on **Next**, and then click on **Done.**

Once a user is authenticated, you can control access for that user to web pages and data.

Managing entity permissions and web roles

To secure an entity list or an entity form, check the **Enable entity permissions** checkbox on the entity form list record. You can see this checkbox at the bottom of *Figure 11.7.*

Once you have enabled this option for a list or form, users will not be able to access these portal components. You will need to create an entity permissions record for the entity in the form or list in the Portal Management app, specifying the privileges on the records.

You then need to associate the entity permissions record with each of the relevant web roles. An authenticated user must be assigned a web role to access the portal. Once you have added entity permissions to the web roles, a user with that web role will be able to access the data.

In this chapter, you have learned how to create a portal app and configure it by applying themes and adding pages. You have also learned how to secure access to the portal app.

Summary

This chapter described how you can create and configure portal apps to expose data in the CDS to external users.

You should now understand how to create and manage portal apps. You should be able to add pages, entity lists, and entity forms. You should understand how to secure the data on your portal website. You can quickly create a portal website and configure the pages, layout, and add content to meet your customers' needs.

In the next chapter, we will learn how to use Power BI Automate to automate steps within the Power Platform and the CDS.

Questions

After reading this chapter, test your knowledge with these questions. You will find the answers to these questions under Assessments at the end of the book:

1. What should you assign to authenticated users to allow access to pages and data?

   A) Web pages
   B) Web roles
   C) An entity list
   D) Entity permissions

2. Which template should I use if I want to have blogs in my portal app?

   A) Starter kit
   B) Customer self-service
   C) Employee self-service
   D) Community

3. You send a request to a contact to use your portal app. What should they enter when signing up to the portal to link their user to their contact record?

   A) Email address
   B) Full name
   C) Invitation code
   D) Web role

4. You add an entity list to a web page. What should you do to prevent access by anonymous users?

    A) Enable the entity permissions option
    B) Create an entity permissions record
    C) Create a web role
    D) Restart the portal

Further reading

- **Invite contacts to your portals:** https://docs.microsoft.com/powerapps/maker/portals/configure/invite-contacts
- **Portal templates:** https://docs.microsoft.com/powerapps/maker/portals/portal-templates
- **Create a Common Data Service starter portal:** https://docs.microsoft.com/powerapps/maker/portals/create-portal
- **Power Apps portals Studio anatomy:** https://docs.microsoft.com/powerapps/maker/portals/portal-designer-anatomy
- **Managing portals from the Power Platform admin center:** https://docs.microsoft.com/powerapps/maker/portals/admin/power-platform-admin-center
- **Power Apps Portals admin center:** https://docs.microsoft.com/powerapps/maker/portals/admin/admin-overview
- **Power Apps Portals FAQ:** https://docs.microsoft.com/powerapps/maker/portals/faq
- **Creating and managing web pages:** https://docs.microsoft.com/powerapps/maker/portals/create-manage-webpages
- **About entity lists:** https://docs.microsoft.com/powerapps/maker/portals/configure/entity-lists
- **About entity forms:** https://docs.microsoft.com/powerapps/maker/portals/configure/entity-forms
- **Working with templates:** https://docs.microsoft.com/powerapps/maker/portals/work-with-templates
- **Overview of themes in Power Apps portals:** https://docs.microsoft.com/powerapps/maker/portals/theme-overview
- **Controlling web page access for portals:** https://docs.microsoft.com/powerapps/maker/portals/configure/webpage-access-control
- **Creating web roles for portals:** https://docs.microsoft.com/powerapps/maker/portals/configure/create-web-roles

Section 4: Automation

4

Section 4 is concerned with automating business processes using the data captured in *Section 2*. By the end, the reader will be able to automate solutions and guide users through business processes.

This section contains the following chapters:

- Chapter 12, *Power Automate Flows*
- Chapter 13, *Business Process Flows*
- Chapter 14, *UI Flows*

12
Power Automate Flows

Power Automate has a point-and-click user interface that makes the process of creating flows straightforward. It is built on top of Azure Logic Apps, an enterprise application integration service, and so is scalable and robust.

This chapter will explain how to use **Power Automate**, a key component of the Power Platform for automating steps within Dynamics 365 and Common Data Service, and for automating, integrating, and orchestrating across cloud systems including Office 365, Azure, and third-party services.

We will begin with an introduction to Power Automate flows; then we will move on to where and how to create them by adding connections, triggers, and actions all controlled by logic. We will look at using connectors, in particular at the Common Data Service connector with flows. We will finish by learning how to monitor flows.

In this chapter, we will cover the following topics:

- Creating Power Automate flows
- Using connectors
- The different types of trigger
- How to use actions to read, update, and create records
- Controlling flows with logic and expressions
- Administering and monitoring flows

By the end of this chapter, you will be able to create and manage flows and create connections, understand how to trigger a flow from a data change, use conditional logic to control the actions taken by a flow, and create records in Common Data Service.

Introduction to Power Automate flows

A key component of the Power Platform is the capability to create low-code/no-code workflows. **Power Automate flows** are workflows that automate repetitive tasks and streamline processes both within and across systems.

You can use Power Automate for the following:

- Personal productivity
- Sending notifications
- Handling approvals
- Gathering data
- Automating processes
- Integrating systems
- Orchestration across systems

The following screenshot shows the flow editor with a simple approval flow:

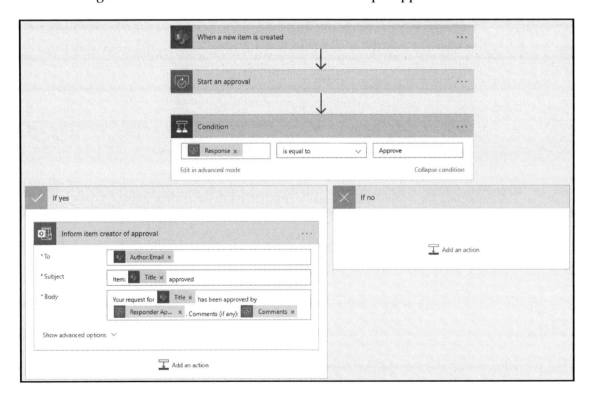

Figure 12.1 – Flow editor

Power Automate has been formulated so that you do not need to be a developer to create flows; no code is required. The techniques needed to build an app are inherited from building visual designs in Visio and the use of functions in Excel.

Now that you know what a Power Automate flow is used for, let's look at how to create one.

Creating Power Automate flows

Power Automate flows are created in a web browser; there is no need for Visual Studio or any local software installation.

A maker navigates to the Power Automate portal, `https://flow.microsoft.com`. In this portal, you can view and edit existing flows, examine templates, create new flows, and monitor flows.

A maker can also navigate to the Power Apps maker portal, `https://make.powerapps.com`. In this portal, you can view and edit existing flows and create new flows. The maker portal focuses on flows that use the Common Data Service connector.

With Microsoft, there is never one way to do something; this is true when creating flows.

Ways to create a flow

There are several ways to create a flow:

- Creating from a **template**: Use a *pre-built* flow template.
- Creating from a **Visio** template: Use a *Visio diagram* as a template.
- Creating from **blank**: Start with a blank canvas, adding connections, actions, and logic.

Templates allow you to create your flow quickly if there is a template that fulfills your requirements. The blank option allows you to create flows to meet your specific requirements.

There are many templates that you can use as a starting point and then edit to meet your requirements.

To create a flow, you need to access either the Power Apps maker portal or the Power Automate portal. The home page of the Power Automate portal looks as follows:

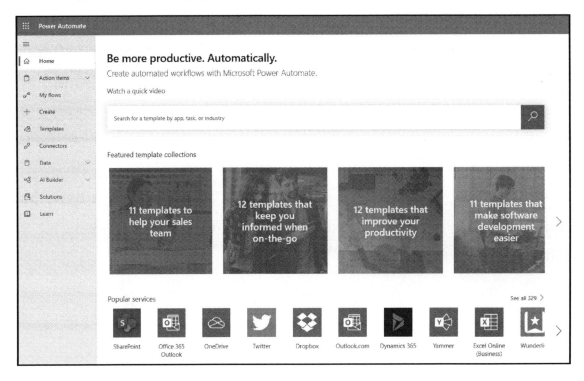

Figure 12.2 – Power Automate portal

To create a new flow, you click on **+ Create** in the left-hand navigation. This will expose the different options for creating a flow.

 You can also create flows directly from within SharePoint, but that is beyond the scope of this book.

The quickest way to create a flow is by using a template. When you select the **Create from a template** option, you can search for a template, and relevant templates are listed for you to choose from:

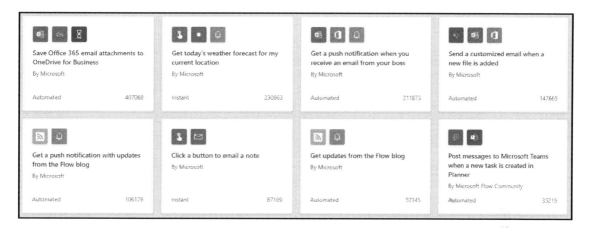

Figure 12.3 – Example flow templates

When you select a template, you are prompted to create connections and the flow is created for you:

Figure 12.4 – Creating connections for a selected template

Alternatively, you can start from a blank canvas, selecting a connector and a trigger:

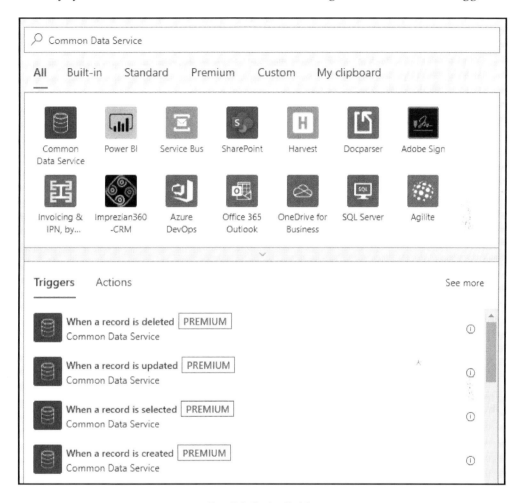

Figure 12.5 – Creating a blank flow

When you search, Power Automate looks for both **connectors** and their **triggers**. You can select a connector and then select a trigger. Triggers define when a flow is initiated and are explained later in this chapter.

You don't need to select a connector; selecting a trigger implicitly selects the connector. It is easier to select the connector first as then only the triggers for the selected connector are displayed.

After selecting a trigger, the flow editor is opened with your trigger as the first step in the flow at the top of the screen:

Figure 12.6 – Trigger step

You need to provide the details for the trigger step.

Each trigger has its own set of information that it requires.

Once you have added your trigger step, you need to add action steps to your flow.

Adding steps to your flow

The first step in a flow is the trigger that initiates the flow. To control the logic and structure, and to perform actions, you need to add steps to the flow.

To add steps to a flow, do the following:

1. You can click on the **+ New step** button under the last step, or hover your mouse between two steps and click on the + icon that appears:

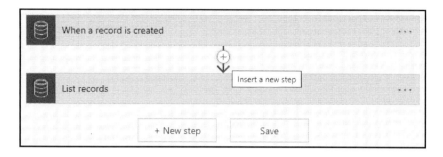

Figure 12.7 – Add step

2. You then need to select a connector and an action:

Figure 12.8 – Choose an action

3. You can select the same connector as the previous steps or any other connector. You may need to sign in to the service of the connector and provide your credentials if you haven't used this connector before.

You don't need to select a connector; selecting an action implicitly selects the connector. It is, however, easier to select the connector first as then only the actions for that connector are displayed.

The selected action is added to your flow. You need to provide the details for the action step:

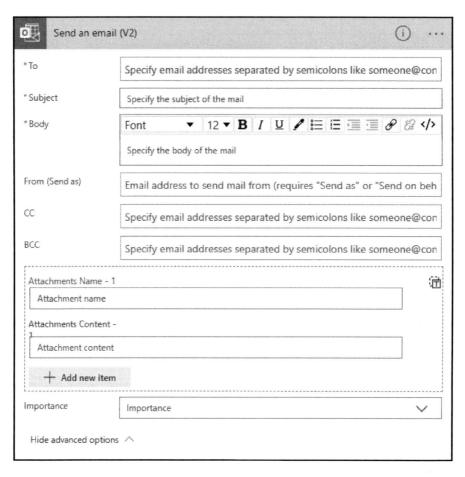

Figure 12.9 – Configuring an action step

Clicking **Show advanced options** displays all the fields that the action requires.

Each action defines the set of information that it requires.

To add details to the step, sometimes you select from a drop-down list, while sometimes you can just enter values, and you can also use details from previous steps.

Using input from the previous step

Each step defines its inputs and its outputs. You can use the output of a previous step as input to a step using the **Dynamic content** tool:

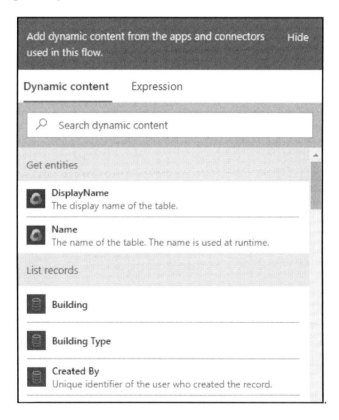

Figure 12.10 – Dynamic content

You can search for dynamic content for outputs. The outputs are grouped by the name of the previous steps.

If you do not see **Dynamic content**, then zoom out in your browser until **Dynamic content** appears.

Clicking on the output field adds that output to the action step:

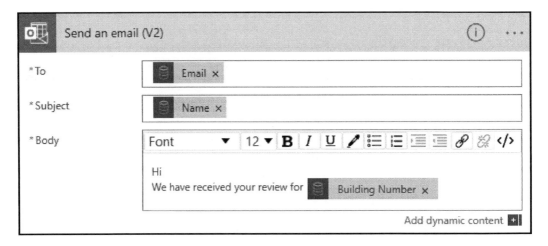

Figure 12.11 – Dynamic content added to an action

Dynamic content operates like a mail merge in Word, with the field stubs appearing as shown in the preceding screenshot.

You may need to combine the outputs, convert, for example, text to a number, perform a calculation, or apply an offset to the date. To do this, you need to use expressions.

Expressions

With expressions, you can perform operations on strings, dates, and numbers. You can convert data from one type to another, perform mathematical operations, parse data, and manipulate data to obtain what you need.

There is a second tab next to the **Dynamic content** tool, called **Expression**. The following screenshot shows the **Expression** tab:

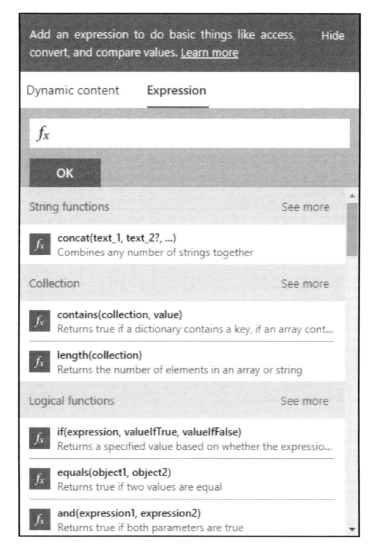

Figure 12.12 – Expressions

The following screenshot shows an expression that concatenates the first name and last name:

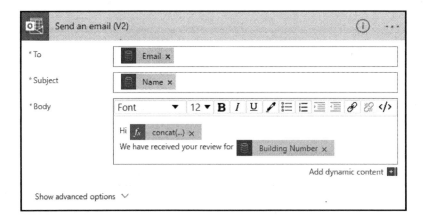

Figure 12.13 – Expression added to an action

You build a flow by adding steps, taking the output from one step and using it as the input for another step:

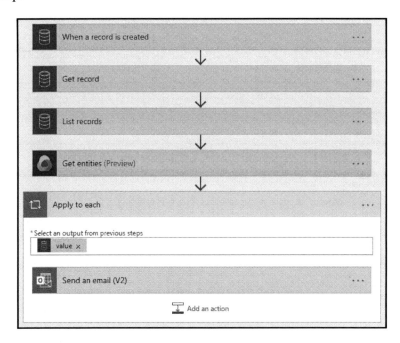

Figure 12.14 - Multiple steps in a flow

Before looking at using Power Automate with Common Data Service, we need to learn about the different ways to initiate flows using the different types of triggers.

Trigger types

There are three different types of triggers for initiating Power Automate flows:

- **Automated**: A flow that is started by an event defined in a connector, such as a record being created or a file being added to a file location
- **Instant**: A flow that is run manually by a user, such as a button being pressed
- **Scheduled**: A flow that is run on a recurring basis, such as at 9 a.m. every workday, or every hour

These three trigger types are presented in the following screenshot:

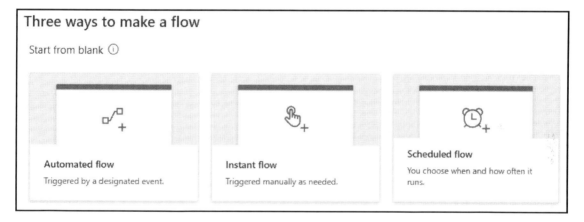

Figure 12.15 – Three ways to make a flow

The triggers in each connector will be one of these three types. Most triggers are for automated flows, where an event in the service the connector is for can be used to start flows.

The **Scheduled flow** option creates a flow with a trigger called **Recurrence**. The **Recurrence** trigger is as follows:

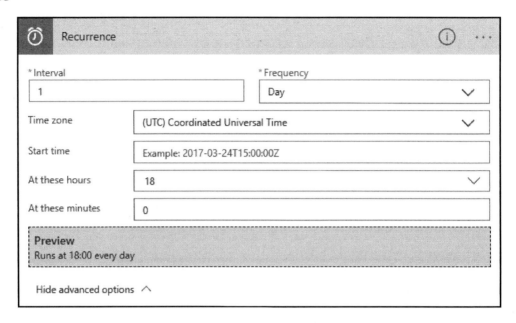

Figure 12.16 – Recurrence trigger

In the **Recurrence** trigger, you specify when and how often the flow will be run.

There are several instant triggers. For example, you can have a flow started by a user pressing a button on the Power Automate mobile app, for a document selected in OneDrive for Business, and for a record selected in a model-driven app. The following screenshot shows some of the available instant triggers:

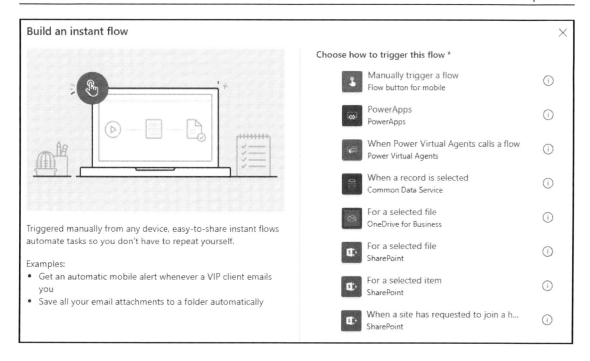

Figure 12.17 – Instant triggers

You can run a flow from within a canvas app, by creating an instant flow with the Power Apps connector. This technique allows your app to perform actions that are difficult or not possible in the app itself.

Now that you have seen how to create the different types of flows, we will look in more detail at connectors.

Connectors and data sources

Power Automate can connect to many different data sources. These connectors are used across the Power Platform, and there are over 400 connectors to Office 365, Dynamics 365, Azure, and third-party services.

A Power Automate flow can connect to multiple data sources in a flow, allowing a flow to copy data and files from one service to another, or to combine data from two services and write it to a third.

Using the on-premises data gateway, a Power Automate flow can read and write data in an on-premises **SQL server** or access an on-premises **SharePoint list**.

Although many different data sources can be used by Power Automate, the PL-200 exam focuses on the Common Data Service connector.

The Common Data Service connector

Common Data Service is one possible connector for use with Power Automate. The Common Data Service connector has many advantages over other connectors due to its built-in capabilities that can be leveraged by your flows; the Power Platform tools have been designed to work together, with the whole being greater than the sum of its parts.

There is more than one connector for Common Data Service, and you need to know when to use each connector.

Available connectors for Common Data Service

As Power Automate and Common Data Service have evolved, several different connectors have been created for accessing Common Data Service. The connectors have similar capabilities, but you need to know which one to use in different circumstances.

There are three connectors that can access Common Data Service:

- Dynamics 365
- Common Data Service
- Common Data Service (current environment)

 The Dynamics 365 connector is deprecated and should not be used.

With the Common Data Service connector, you will need to provide the environment and entity, whereas Common Data Service (current environment) uses the same environment the flow is in, and you only need to provide the entity. The Common Data Service (current environment) connector is only available when creating flows from within a solution.

The Common Data Service connector can be useful when you are synchronizing data between two environments as you can specify each environment in each step of your flow.

> If you are using solutions to transport flows between environments, use the Common Data Service (current environment) connector in your flow.

The difference between the connectors is that the triggers and actions vary for each of the connectors and you need to know the pros and cons of each connector.

Triggers for the Common Data Service connectors

The main difference between the three connectors is the triggers provided by each connector.

The Dynamics 365 connector has the following triggers:

- When a record is created
- When a record is updated
- When a record is deleted
- When a record is created or updated

The Common Data Service connector has the following triggers:

- When a record is created
- When a record is updated
- When a record is deleted
- When a record is selected

The first three triggers are automated triggers. When a record is selected is an instant trigger that allows a user to select a record in a model-driven app and run the flow manually.

The Common Data Service (current environment) connector has a single trigger–when a record is created, updated, or deleted.

In the trigger step, you have to specify the trigger condition:

- Create.
- Create or update.
- Create or delete.
- Create or update or delete.
- Delete.
- Update.
- Update or delete.

The advantage of having a single trigger with multiple trigger conditions is that it can have one flow that handles both the creation and update of records. With the Common Data Service connector, you need two separate flows for creation and update. This approach also allows you to change your flow from create to update without having to delete and recreate your steps.

 Common Data Service (current environment) does not have an instant trigger for when a record is selected.

There are differences in the actions that each of these connectors provides.

Common Data Service connector actions

When looking at the different actions that are available in each connector, the newer Common Data Service (current environment) connector is more flexible and can perform many more actions than the other two connectors.

The Dynamics 365 connector and the Common Data Service connector have the following actions:

- Create a new record.
- Get record.
- List records.
- Update a record.
- Delete a record.

These actions are shown as follows:

Figure 12.18 – Common Data Service connector actions

The Common Data Service (current environment) connector has the same actions but also many more:

- Create a new record.
- Get a record.
- List records.
- Update a record.
- Delete a record.
- Relate records.
- Unrelate records.
- Execute a `changeset` request.
- Get file or image content.
- Upload a file or image content.
- Perform a bound action.
- Perform an unbound action.
- Predict.

The Common Data Service (current environment) connector can also allow the creation and use of child flows.

Common Data Service (current environment) has many advantages over the other connectors and should be your first choice with Power Automate.

When creating a connection to a connector, you provide credentials for the connection to use when accessing the service.

Connecting using a service principal

An issue with using your own user credentials in a flow that will run unattended is that there are a few complications that can arise. Some examples are as follows:

- What happens if you leave the organization and your user account is removed?
- What happens if your access to the environment is removed?
- You are likely to be an administrator with more privileges than required and thus are a potential security risk.

You should consider creating a service principal to connect to Common Data Service in Power Automate. This has many advantages, but the most significant is that it allows you to tightly define the privileges that the flow can use. You would create a security role specifically for the service principal user to achieve this.

The steps to use a service principal in the Common Data Service connector are as follows:

1. Register an app in Azure Active Directory with a client secret.
2. Create an application user in Common Data Service using the client's secret.
3. Assign a security role to the application user.
4. Configure the Common Data Service connection to use a service principal using the application user.

The following screenshot shows the link to connect to a service principal:

Figure 12.19 – Connect with a Service Principal link

When you create flows for Common Data Service, there are common patterns that you use. One common flow pattern is to retrieve all the child records in a one-to-many relationship and then loop through each child record. Another common pattern is to retrieve a single record and check whether a field has a specific value and split your flow logic based on this value. There are steps you can add to your flow to handle branching, looping, and logical control.

Controlling flows with logic and expressions

Triggering a flow when a record is updated is straightforward, but what if you need to query other records to perform a calculation, or what if the record had a null value and the following step will not accept that null value? In Power Automate, you can check values and perform different steps depending on the values.

The **Control** connector contains actions that you can use to control your flow:

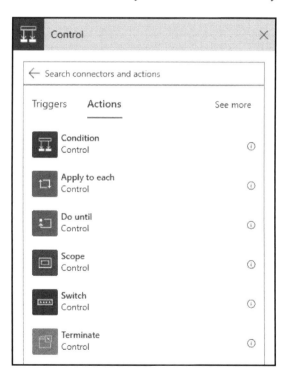

Figure 12.20 – Control actions

Let's look at the key actions for this connector.

Conditions

A **condition** is a step in the flow that evaluates a statement as either true or false. If the statement is true, then the flow will follow the left-hand path; otherwise, the flow will branch to the right-hand path, as shown in the following diagram. A condition performs if-then-else logic. You can refer to the following screenshot for a better understanding:

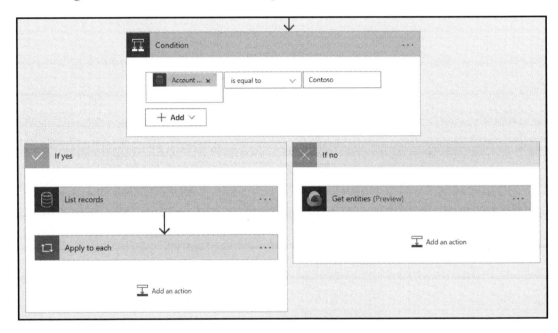

Figure 12.21 – Condition step with a yes and no branch

With a condition, you can compare two items. An item could be output from previous steps that you add in with dynamic content, or a constant value that you have typed in, or a result of an expression.

If the result of the condition is true, then the flow follows the **If yes** path. If false, the flow follows the **If no** path. You can add steps to either of the **yes/no** paths.

 Use the **Terminate** action to stop further processing.

If you need more than two paths, then consider the **Switch** action. A condition has two yes and no branches; the **Switch** action supports multiple branches using a case statement.

If you have a list of records, you may need to loop through the records.

Loops

There are two actions that perform looping: **Apply to each** and **Do until**.

The **Do until** loop repeats until a condition is met.

Apply to each is commonly used after running a query to retrieve a list of records – for example, the **List records** action on the Common Data Service connector:

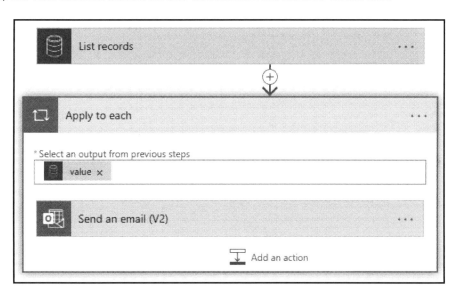

Figure 12.22 – Apply to each

In the **Apply to each** loop, you can add steps. In the preceding example, an email will be sent for every record retrieved.

Variables

You can define variables in flows. There is a connector named **Variable** that has steps to initialize and set variables.

Variables are useful to help simplify flow logic but are often used with loops–for example, as a loop counter, or a string that is appended to.

You will need to check your flows to verify that they are running correctly.

Administering and monitoring flows

Power Automate flows execute in the background. You are notified if a flow fails, so it is imperative that you check flows regularly to see whether they are running and operating without error.

Microsoft provides the ability to monitor the execution of flows with several tools:

- The Power Automate portal
- Microsoft Teams
- The Power Automate mobile app

Monitoring flows

In the Power Automate portal, `https://flow.microsoft.com`, you can view and monitor flows.

If you select a flow, you can see the flow runs and the status of each run. You can filter the runs to just see the failed runs. The following screenshot depicts a sample run history:

Device approval request > **Run history**

Start time	Duration	Status
Oct 11, 10:36 AM (2 d ago)	00:01:23	Succeeded
Oct 7, 03:41 PM (5 d ago)	00:00:44	Test canceled
Oct 7, 10:55 AM (6 d ago)	00:01:22	Succeeded
Oct 3, 10:53 AM (1 wk ago)	10d 03:56:42	Running
Sep 30, 08:55 PM (1 wk ago)	6d 11:33:28	Succeeded

Figure 12.23 – Run history

You can click on a flow run and see how the flow progressed and, if the flow failed, see the step at which the error was detected and the details of the error.

You can edit the flow from within the flow run, fix the error, and save. You can then re-run the flow by clicking on the **Resubmit** button.

If several flow runs failed, you can click on the test icon, then select each failed run and click on **Test** to re-run the flow. The following screenshot shows the list of previous flow runs from which you can select and test:

Figure 12.24 – Test flow

When you create a flow, you are the owner, and others cannot see and monitor flows. You need to share the flow with others to manage the flow.

Sharing flows

Automated and scheduled flows are owned by the user who created them and are not visible to other users. You give access to your flow by sharing it with other users or making them co-owners of the flow.

After sharing, the flow will not appear under **My flows**, but in the **Team flows** tab next to it, as shown in the following screenshot:

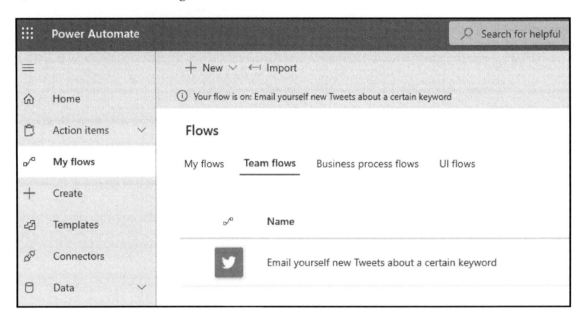

Figure 12.25 – Team flows

All owners of a team flow can do the following:

- View the flow's run history.
- Turn the flow on or off.
- Add other users as owners.
- Edit the flow.
- Delete the flow.

Button flows are only visible to the user who created them. To enable other users to run the button flow, you share and invite others to use your flow. You will see all flow runs for all users.

Before sharing a flow with others, you should check that there are no errors in your flow.

Power Automate checker

The **Power Automate checker tool** is like the Power Apps checker tool. The **Flow checker** feature is available when editing a flow, with the same stethoscope icon that adds a red dot when an error is detected.

Clicking on the flow checker icon will show a list of errors and warnings, as shown in the following screenshot:

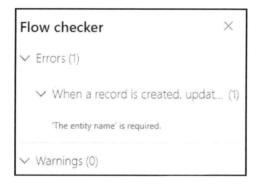

Figure 12.26 – Flow checker

Power Automate is a key component of the Power Platform and can be used to meet many different requirements.

Summary

In this chapter, you were introduced to Power Automate flows, how they are created, how the flow editor is used, and details around some of the logic used. You should now understand how to create flows and why you should use the Common Data Service (current environment) connector.

You can now create flows, using data from Common Data Service, to automate repetitive processes, send emails and other notifications, and synchronize data.

The next chapter is about guiding users through a business process. The chapter will explain how to use business process flows to indicate the stage that a process has reached, and the next steps a user should take.

Questions

After reading this chapter, test your knowledge with these questions. You will find the answers to these questions under Assessments at the end of the book:

1. You are creating a new Power Automate flow. What should you use to find any errors in your flow?

   A) The flow run history
   B) Resubmit
   C) The flow checker
   D) Test

2. You have created a flow and you need colleagues to monitor it. What should you do?

   A) Export the flow to Azure Logic Apps.
   B) Export the flow as a ZIP file.
   C) Send a copy.
   D) Share it.

3. You have added a **List records** step. You need to process all the records in the step's output. What action should you add?

   A) Apply to each
   B) Do until
   C) Switch
   D) Scope

4. You have created an instant button flow. You share the button flow with other users. Who can see the run history for your button flow?

    A) Each user can see their own run history.
    B) You, and only you, can see the run history for all users.
    C) Environment admins can see the run history for all users.
    D) All users can see the run history for all users.

5. You are creating a flow but are unable to find the Common Data Service (current environment) connector. What should you do?

    A) Create the flow from the Power Apps maker portal.
    B) Switch to the default environment.
    C) Create the flow from inside a solution.
    D) Create a service principal.

6. You need to create a flow that runs for a selected record in a model-driven app. Which connector should you use?

    A) Dynamics 365 Customer Engagement
    B) Common Data Service
    C) Common Data Service (current environment)
    D) Power Apps
    E) Flow button for mobile

7. You need to create a flow that runs repeatedly. What type of flow should you create?

    A) Automated
    B) Instant
    C) Scheduled
    D) Business process

Further reading

- Automation of tasks with Microsoft Power Automate https://docs.microsoft.com/power-platform/admin/wp-task-automation-flow
- Design an automated workflow in Visio: https://support.microsoft.com/en-us/office/design-an-automated-workflow-in-visio-35f0c9a9-912b-486d-88f7-4fc68013ad1a

- Design flows in Microsoft Visio: `https://docs.microsoft.com/en-us/power-automate/visio-flows`
- Add multiple actions and advanced options to a flow: `https://docs.microsoft.com/power-automate/multi-step-logic-flow`
- Reference guide for using functions in expressions for Azure Logic Apps and Power Automate: `https://docs.microsoft.com/azure/logic-apps/workflow-definition-language-functions-reference`
- *CDS vs CDS: What Connector should I use in Power Automate?*: `https://saralagerquist.com/2019/12/15/cds-vs-cds-what-connector-should-i-use-in-power-automate/`
- The Common Data Service (current environment) connector: `https://docs.microsoft.com/connectors/commondataserviceforapps`
- Use the `apply to each` action in Power Automate to process a list of items periodically: `https://docs.microsoft.com/power-automate/apply-to-each`
- Use expressions in conditions: `https://docs.microsoft.com/power-automate/use-expressions-in-conditions`
- Create teams flows: `https://docs.microsoft.com/power-automate/create-team-flows`
- Share button flows in Power Automate: `https://docs.microsoft.com/power-automate/share-buttons`

13
Business Process Flows

Business process flows are a capability of the Power Platform that helps users observe a defined business process, find out where they are in the process, and know what data is required to complete the next stage. Business process flows are used within model-driven apps to help guide the user through multiple steps and stages.

This chapter will explain how to create **business process flows** to guide users through an end-to-end process. Many organizations have specific business processes that users must follow; processes such as onboarding a new customer, or responding to a data protection inquiry. These processes typically involve different users and teams over their lifetime.

We will begin with an introduction to business process flows, then look at where and how to create them by adding stages, steps, and conditions. We will look at branching, security, and how business process flows work with other components of the Power Platform.

In this chapter, we will cover the following topics:

- Understanding business process flows
- Creating business process flows
- Conditional branching in business process flows
- Securing business process flows
- Business process flow considerations

By the end of this chapter, you will be able to create business process flows, use stages, employ branching, run classic workflows, and run Power Automate flows from a business process flow.

Understanding business process flows

A business process flow is a straightforward way to guide a user through a process that involves one or more Common Data Service records. It informs users where they are in the process and what they need to do next.

The business process flow control appears as a strip along the top of the form. In the following screenshot, the business process flow is controlling the creation and approval of a social media post:

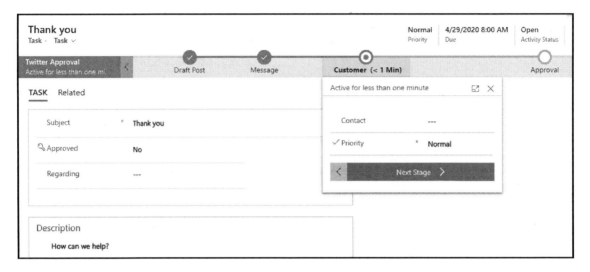

Figure 13.1 – Example of a business process flow

A business process flow breaks a process into stages and steps that logically match how a user thinks about what they are trying to do.

In the previous screenshot, there are four stages shown in the business process flow:

- **Draft Post**
- **Message**
- **Customer**
- **Approval**

The red target icon indicates that the business process flow is currently at the third stage, **Customer**. By clicking on the red target icon, the user can see the steps that they have to complete before they can click on **Next Stage** and move to the final **Approval** stage.

The main benefit of business process flows is that the user paradigm switches from **form-centric** to **process-centric**. Users no longer need to understand which record type or form to use, and in which sequence. In essence, business process flows hide the complexity of the underlying data model from users, so that users can focus on getting their job done.

Moreover, business process flows control what data needs to be captured at each stage and can prevent the process from moving on to the next stage without this data. Controlling the stage in the process when data needs to be entered reduces the need for fields to be defined as *business required* and also improves data quality.

Further, you can run classic workflows, actions, and Power Automate flows from a business process flow stage to automate tasks.

Now that you know what a business process flow is used for, let's look at how to create one.

Creating business process flows

Business process flows are now a part of Power Automate. This means you can create a business process flow with just a web browser!

You can use the Power Automate portal (`https://flow.microsoft.com`) or the Power Apps maker portal (`https://make.powerapps.com`) to create and edit business process flows. There is no difference between these two portals as far as business process flows are concerned.

When you access the Power Automate portal and select the **Business process flows** tab, it looks as follows:

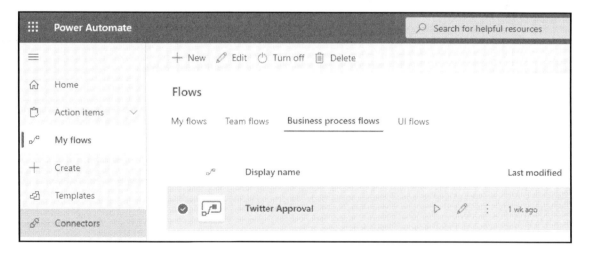

Figure 13.2 – Business process flows in the Power Automate portal

To create a new business process flow, click on the **+ New** button and the following pop-up window will be displayed:

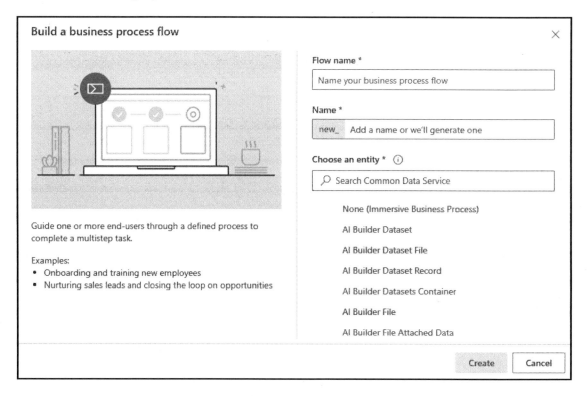

Figure 13.3 – Build a business process flow

In the previous screenshot, you can see that you need to give your business process flow a name. This is important as users will see this name on the left-hand side of the business process flow control.

When you create a business process flow, a custom **entity** is created using the **Name** field. Hence, the name must be unique. The new custom entity is used to track the progress of business process flows, that is, what the current stage is and how long the business process flow has been in each stage. Moreover, you can use this entity to analyze how your processes are being used.

You must also select an entity for the business process flow; the business process flow will start when users create records for the selected entity. After you click on the **Create** button, you will not be able to change the selected entity. The following screenshot shows the business process flow editor:

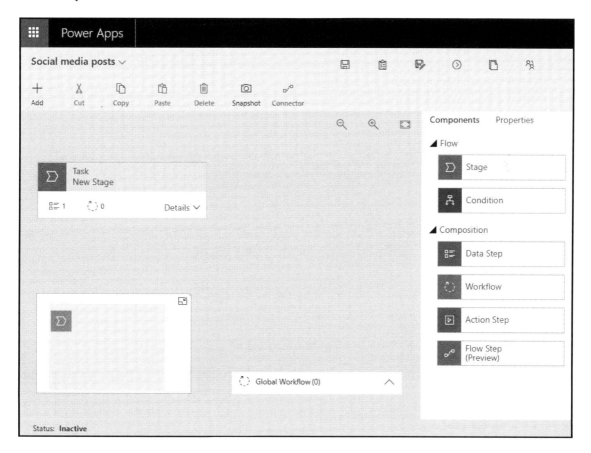

Figure 13.4 – Business process flow editor

After you click on **Create**, the business process flow editor is opened, as shown in the previous screenshot. The editor offers the following:

- A toolbar on the left to add components to and remove components from the business process flow
- A toolbar at the top to perform actions on the business process flow, such as saving it
- A **Components** pane to add components to the business process flow

- A **Properties** pane to set names and other properties for components
- A central canvas where you place components
- A mini-map at the bottom left to allow you to see the entire business process flow
- A tile at the bottom right to add global workflows
- An empty first stage called **New Stage**

 You can use both the toolbar and the **Components** pane to add components to the business process flow. You can click and point with the toolbar and drag and drop with the component pane.

Stages are a core component of business process flows and you first need to add further stages before adding other components.

Adding stages to a business process flow

A business process flow consists of several stages, with each stage containing several steps. Stages are the major parts, or milestones, of a business process. Steps are the data to be collected, or actions performed, in each stage.

You should start by defining the stages needed for your business process. You should consider the following:

- **Milestones**: Specific points in the process – intermediate events – that can be used to monitor progress. Milestones often signify the end of a stage.
- **Transitions**: The work being undertaken either passes from one team to another or moves into a different phase. Transitions are usually pointers to adding a stage to a business process flow.
- **Entities**: A stage can only have data steps for a single entity. If you need to access a different entity in a business process flow, then you will need to add a new stage to the process.
- **Progress reporting**: How you want to report on the progress of your business process. You need to balance the number of stages with how long it takes for your process to complete. Too few stages on a long-running process will not provide the monitoring you need; conversely, too many stages on a short process may be sub-optimal for the user.

You can add a stage in two ways. The first method is to drag the **Stage** tile from the **Components** pane and drop it over the indicated area to the right of a stage as shown in the following figure:

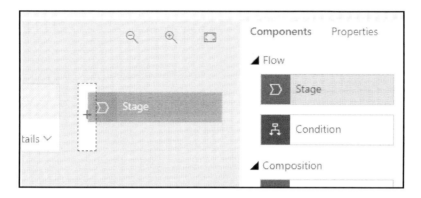

Figure 13.5 – Add a stage with drag and drop

The other method is to click on **Add Stage** in the action bar and then click on the canvas where you want to add the stage as shown in the next figure:

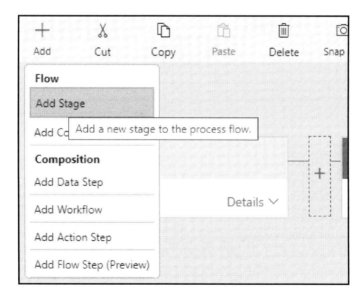

Figure 13.6 – Add a stage from the action bar

A business process flow can have a maximum of 30 stages.

Defining a stage involves specifying the following:

- **Name** of the stage: This will appear above the stage in the business process flow control.
- **Category**: A global option set used for grouping stages for reporting purposes.
- **Entity**: A stage can only be associated with one record type. All data steps can only be fields for the selected entity.
- **Relationship**: If the entity is different from the previous stage, then you should specify the relationship between the two entities to ensure that the related records are used in the process flow.

The following screenshot shows the stage properties, illustrating the details specified for each stage:

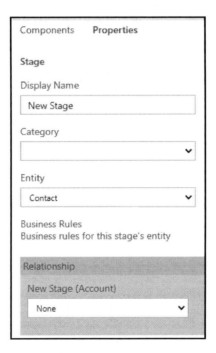

Figure 13.7 – Stage properties

If your process is going to span multiple entities, you should ensure that you have linked the stages to the correct entities before adding steps.

Adding stages is simple and takes little effort.

Creating a business process flow for multiple entities

Each stage can only be associated with a single entity.

The first stage is locked to the primary entity, the entity you selected when creating the business process flow. You cannot change the primary entity after you have clicked on **Save**.

However, you can add entities other than the primary entity to the business process flow. You should specify the entity for the stage before adding any steps, as subsequently changing the entity on a stage will invalidate the steps in the stage.

A business process flow can span a maximum of five entities.

If you select an entity that is different from the entity in the previous stage, then a relationship dropdown will appear. There is no restriction as to which entity you can select. A relationship does not need to exist between the two entities.

If there is a one-to-many (1:N) relationship available, then you should select that relationship. In this way, the business process flow will respect field mappings and relate the records correctly.

Many-to-many (N:N) relationships are not supported by business process flows.

Amending the Stage Category option set

The **Stage Category** option set can be set on each stage. It is optional and has no functional impact on the business process flow, but it can be used for grouping stages together for reporting.

As shown in the next figure, this option offers seven values out of the box; four for the sales category (**Qualify**, **Develop**, **Propose**, and **Close**) and three for the service category (**Identify**, **Research**, and **Resolve**):

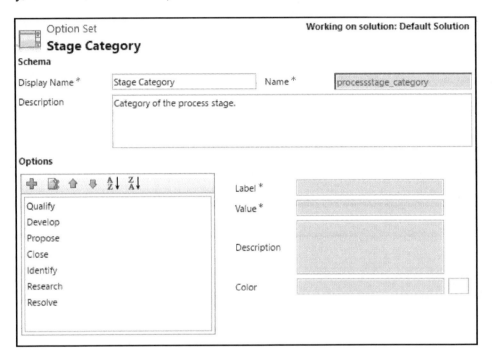

Figure 13.8 – Stage categories

Stage Category is a global option set and you can edit and add items for your own purposes. Once you have defined your stages, you are ready to add steps to each stage.

Adding steps to stages

Steps are the elements the user will interact with within the business process flow. Steps are displayed under a stage when the user clicks on the circular icon for the stage. Steps represent the data that should be captured or actions that should be performed before the user can progress to the next stage.

There are different types of steps, as follows:

- **Data steps**: Fields that users can enter data into
- **Action steps**: Buttons that can execute action and workflow processes
- **Flow steps**: Buttons that can trigger Power Automate flows
- **Workflows**: Workflow processes executed when the stage transitions

You can add a step in two ways. The first method is to drag the **Data Step** tile from the **Components** pane and drop it over the indicated area within the stage. The second method is to click on **Add Step** in the action bar and then click on the stage where you want to add the step:

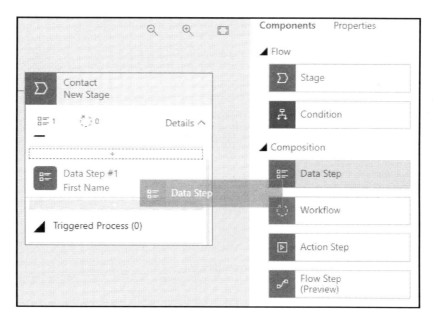

Figure 13.9 – Add a step with drag and drop

The preceding figure shows a maker dragging a data step onto a stage.

A stage can have up to 30 steps.

Data steps

After a step has been added, you will need to set its properties. For a **Data Step**, as shown in the next figure, you need to select a **Data Field**. The field list will contain fields for the entity associated with the stage. **Step Name** will default to the display name of the field. The name can be changed to suit your process flow:

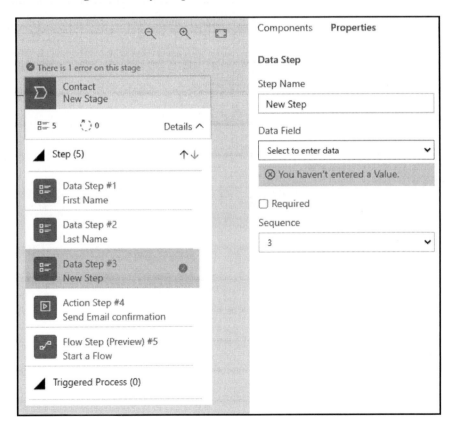

Figure 13.10 – Step properties

You can mark a step as required so that users must enter some data for the step before they can proceed to the next stage. This is commonly called **stage-gating**.

 A field does not have to be on the form to be used as a step in a business process flow. If a field is on the form as well as in the process flow, then entering data in the step updates the field on the form and vice versa.

Action steps

If you use an action step, then the process must be defined for the same entity as the stage. To use an action in a business process flow, you must set the action to be **As a Business Process Flow action step** as shown in the following figure:

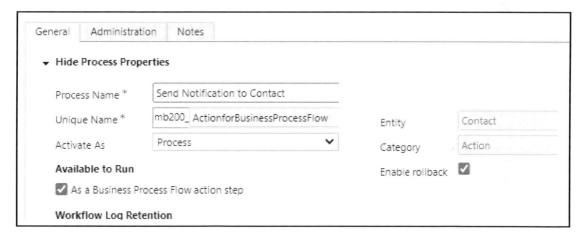

Figure 13.11 – Configuring an action for use in a business process flow

If you use a classic workflow as an action step, the workflow must be configured to be available on demand.

Flow steps

If you use a flow step, the Power Automate flow must have an instant trigger. You should use the Common Data Service connector and the **When a record is selected** trigger.

The following screenshot shows how to add the **When a record is selected** trigger to a Power Automate flow:

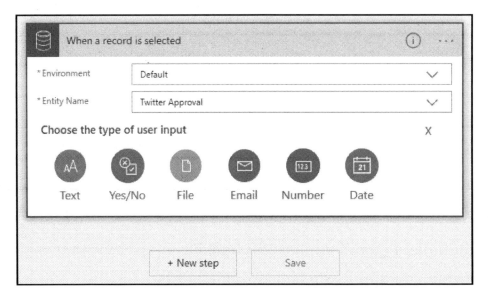

Figure 13.12 – Configuring a flow for use in a business process flow

You must specify in the trigger the entity that was created when you created the business process flow, and not the primary entity, nor any of the entities used in the stages of the business process flow.

 Only solution-aware flows can be added as a flow step.

Classic workflows

Along with using **classic workflows** as an **action step**, you can also set **classic workflows** to run on **stage transition**. Stage transition is the process of ending one stage and starting the next.

The stage transition triggers are as follows:

- Stage entry
- Stage exit

Imagine having two stages; that is, Stage A, followed by Stage B. When Stage A transitions to Stage B, the workflows set to trigger on exit of Stage A and the workflows set to trigger on entry to Stage B will both be executed.

 A classic workflow must be active, available on demand, and be configured for the same entity as the stage.

A workflow set to trigger on stage entry on the first stage in a business process flow, or a workflow set to trigger on stage exit on the final stage in a business process flow, will never be executed. Therefore, you should use a global workflow in such scenarios.

Global workflows

Global workflows are processes that are executed when a business process flow starts or ends.

There are four different triggers:

- **Process applied**: When a process business flow is started, which can be either when the record is created or when a user starts a new business process flow manually.
- **Process abandoned**: When the user abandons the business process flow. The business process flow will be shown under archived processes.
- **Process reactivated**: When a user restarts a previously abandoned business process flow.
- **Process completed**: When the user clicks on **finished** on the final stage of the business process flow to end the business process flow.

You must use **process applied** to execute a workflow in place of a workflow triggered on stage entry of the first stage in the business process flow.

You must use **process completed** to execute a workflow in place of a workflow triggered on stage exit of the final stage in the business process flow.

When a user switches from one business process flow to another, the existing business process flow is abandoned, and a new business process flow is applied.

A global workflow must be active, available on demand, and be configured for the same entity as the primary entity of the business process flow.

A business process flow may not be linear and may require different stages for different circumstances. Business process flows achieve this by branching. Let's now see how branching works in business process flows.

Conditional branching in business process flows

Branches are conditions you add between stages. The conditions are **if-then-else** statements. If the statement is true, the business process flow continues to the stage to the right of the condition. If false, the business process flow continues using the stage under the condition, as shown in the following figure:

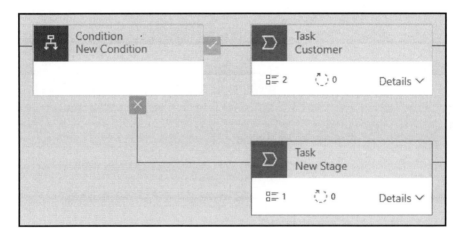

Figure 13.13 – Conditional branching

To add a branch, you first need to add a condition to the business process flow.

Adding a condition

As discussed before, a condition must first be added if you need to add a branch to your process flow:

1. To add a branch, click on **Add Condition** in the action bar, or drag a **Condition** tile from the **Components** area and drop it over the plus (**+**) sign, and set the **Properties**.

2. In the **Properties** pane, enter the **Display Name** of the condition, select a **Field** to evaluate, choose the appropriate **Operator**, and select the **Type**, which can be a **Value**, another **Field**, or a formula, and then complete the rule:

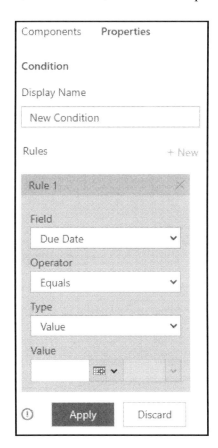

Figure 13.14 – Condition properties

The **Operator** options will change depending on the data type of the selected field.

3. You can click on **+ New** to add further rules. After adding a rule, you can use either **AND** or **OR** logic as shown in the next figure:

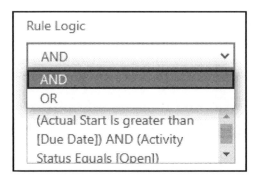

Figure 13.15 – Combining rules

4. Branches are evaluated in real time; you can see stages appear and disappear when you amend the values on the field(s) used in the branch condition.

You can only reference a data step from the previous stage in the condition rules.

A business process flow can loop back to a stage for a previous entity in the business process flow, including the primary entity.

Connecting stages

When you add a condition, the business process flow will link back to the main path, as shown in the following screenshot:

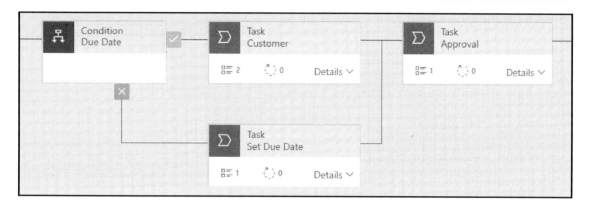

Figure 13.16 – Branching after adding a condition

You can change how the stages are linked by removing and adding connectors using the **Connector** button in the action bar, as shown in the following figure:

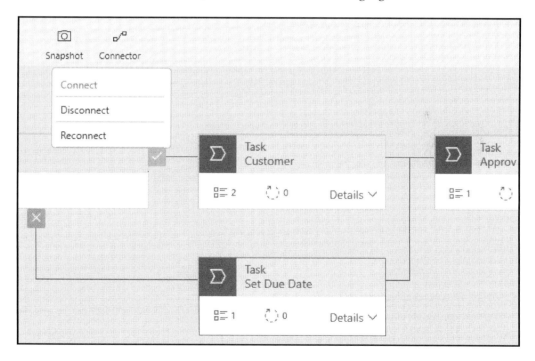

Figure 13.17 – Connector button

You can loop a business process flow back by adding and removing connections between stages.

Using the connector functionality can be tricky at first. To change the branching shown in the preceding screenshot to connect to a stage later in the flow, as shown in the following screenshot, you will need to perform the steps listed beneath this screenshot:

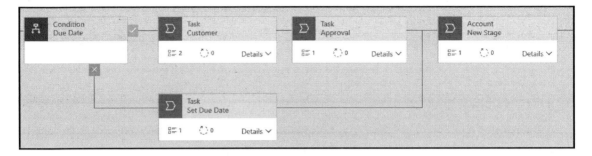

Figure 13.18 – Branching after adding a connector to a later stage

To make these changes as illustrated, you need to perform the following:

1. Select the **Source stage**, **Set Due date**.
2. Click on **Connector** and then click **Disconnect**.
3. Select the **Source stage**, **Set Due date** again.
4. Click on **Connector** and then click **Connect**.
5. Select the **Target stage**, the second point in the connection.

You can add up to five levels of conditions in your business process flow. The following figure illustrates the mini-map for a business process flow with two conditions:

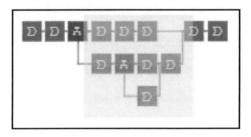

Figure 13.19 – Nested conditions

A common issue with business process flows is that most people forget to set up the security on their business process flows, causing users to not see the business process flow when they create or view records.

Securing business process flows

When you create a business process flow, an entity is created. This entity tracks the progress of the business process flow on each record. The entity holds the current stage and how long the business process flow has been in each stage.

Users require full access to this entity to be able to use the corresponding business process flow. The entity requires privileges and access levels defined as described in Chapter 8, *Security*.

By default, the access levels on the entity privileges are all set to none as shown in the following figure. This means that users will not be able to use the business process flow:

Figure 13.20 – Default security privileges on the business process flow entity

You need to change the access levels on the entity as follows:

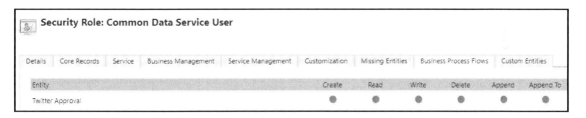

Figure 13.21 – Required security privileges on the business process flow entity

In the previous screenshot, the access levels for all privileges have all been changed to **Organization**. A user requires full privileges on the business process flow entity to be able to use the business process flow.

Monitoring business process flows allows you to gain insight into how users are using the business process flows, how many business process flows are in progress, and the stages they are currently at.

Business process flow performance

You can use the business process flow entity to analyze how your processes are progressing. For example, you can create charts to view the number of active business process flows by stage.

You can also install the **Process Analytics Power BI template**, which contains the dashboard shown in the following figure:

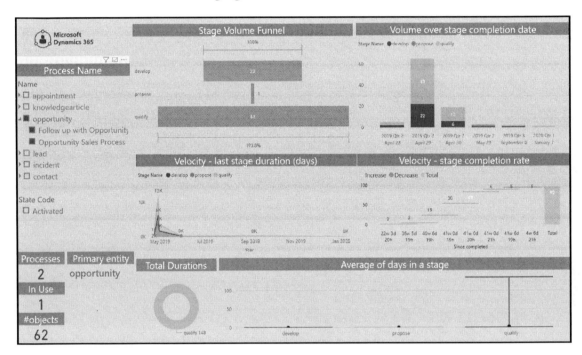

Figure 13.22 – Process Analytics Power BI dashboard

This dashboard provides insights into how your business process flows are performing.

> You can download and install the Power BI template from `https://appsource.microsoft.com/product/power-bi/microsoftd365.d365processanalytics`.

So far, we have seen how business process flows are used in model-driven app forms. We will now learn how business process flows are used with other Power Platform components.

Business process flow considerations

Business process flows can interact with and utilize other Power Platform capabilities. In this section, we will look at how the business process flows operate with forms, flows, business rules, and field-level security.

Forms and business process flows

We have already seen that the business process flow appears at the top of a form.

Fields that are steps in a business process flow do not have to be on the form or in the form header. If you use business process flows, you can simplify forms by removing fields that are in the business process flow. The values in the data steps are saved along with form field data.

If you do have a field in both the form and as a data step in the business process flow, then the field and step work together. If a value is entered in the data step in the business process flow control, then the value from the step appears in the form field immediately.

Flows and business process flows

Any Power Automate flows, or classic workflows triggered by changes to the fields used as data steps in a business process flow control will be applied when the data in the form is saved.

If the classic workflow is a real-time workflow, the changes will be immediately visible to the user when the data in the form is refreshed after the record is saved. However, to see the effect of background workflows and Power Automate flows, the user will need to refresh the form to see the changes.

Business rules and business process flows

When a user enters a data step in a business process flow control, the data changes are also applied to the form fields and this will trigger the business rules and JavaScript for those form fields.

Changes applied by business rules and/or JavaScript are automatically applied to the business process flow control as follows:

- If you hide a field in a form, the corresponding step will also be hidden in the business process flow control.
- If you make a form field business-required, the corresponding step will be set to required.
- If you set a value in a form field, that value will be set in the corresponding data step within the business process flow.

This only applies to actions performed by business rules and JavaScript. If, in the field properties on the form, you uncheck the **Visible by default** box, then this does not affect the business process flow control.

Field-level security and business process flows

You can use a combination of field-level security and a required data step to create an approval step for a stage. This is commonly called stage-gating.

If a data step is marked as required, and the field that is used by the step has field-level security enabled, then users who do not have a **field security profile** that grants them write permissions to the field cannot complete the step and they cannot continue to the next stage.

For example, you might have a field named **Budget** that is enabled for field security with the field security profile set so that only one group of managers can enter a value for the **Budget** field. This field security is applied to the data step in the business process flow. Therefore, a manager must enter a budget value before any user can continue to the next stage of the process.

You must always ensure that all users have a field security profile that grants read privilege to the secured field. If a data step has field security enabled and the user does not have read permission on the field, then the value of the field cannot be viewed by the user or by the process. In this circumstance, the business process flow will treat the field as if it contained a value, and allows the user to move to the next stage.

Model-driven apps and business process flows

Business process flows are components that can be added to model-driven apps. You will need to ensure that the business process flow is included in the app, as shown in the following screenshot:

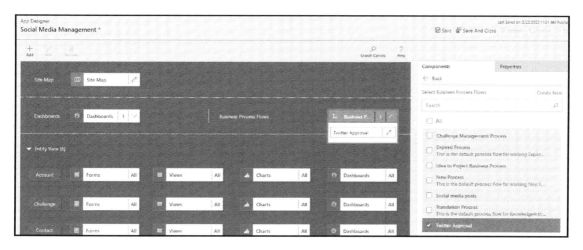

Figure 13.23 – Business process flows in App Designer

In the preceding screenshot, the **Business Process Flows** tile is selected and in the **Components** pane, the business process flow for this app is selected. The other business process flows are not selected and will not be available in this app.

Congratulations on reaching the end of this chapter on business process flows. Business process flows are one of the key components in making your model-driven app usable. Business process flows are well liked by users as they let the user know where they are in the process, and what data and actions they are required to perform next.

Summary

In this chapter, you were introduced to business process flows, how they are created, how the editor is used, and how to add stages, steps, and conditions. You should now understand how to create business process flows, use branching, and understand how the business process flows work with other components of the Power Platform.

You are now able to create and use business process flows to guide users through an end-to-end process.

In the next chapter, we will learn how to automate legacy applications that do not have an API using UI flows.

Questions

After reading this chapter, test your knowledge with these questions. You will find the answers to these questions in the Assessments chapter at the end of the book:

1. You are creating a new business process flow. Users report that the business process flow does not appear when they create a record. What two actions should you take?

   A) Share the business process flow.
   B) Add the business process flow to the app.
   C) Update the security roles for the business process flow.
   D) Set the business process flow to be available on demand.

2. You need to prevent a user from being able to move to the next stage if the data steps are not completed. What should you do?

   A) Set the field to be business required.
   B) Add a condition with a rule for when the data step is empty.
   C) Create a business rule to show an error if the field is empty.
   D) Set the data step to be required.

3. How many stages can you have in a business process flow?

   A) 5.
   B) 25.
   C) 30.
   D) There is no limit.

4. You add a condition to a business process flow and an error is shown for the field you have selected. What should you do?

   A) Add the field as a data step in the previous stage.
   B) Add the field as a data step in the next stage.
   C) Set the data step to be required.
   D) Change the type to a formula.

5. You want to add a classic workflow to execute on a stage transition. You cannot select the workflow. What should you do?

    A) Change the workflow to run in the background.
    B) Change the workflow to be available to run on demand.
    C) Recreate the workflow using the business process flow entity.
    D) You can't use a classic workflow and should instead create a Power Automate flow.

6. You create a business process flow called **Onboarding** on the **Account** entity, and add stages for the **Contact** and **Task** entities. You want to create a chart to show the business process flow by stage. Which entity should you create the chart for?

    A) Account.
    B) Contact.
    C) Onboarding.
    D) Task.

7. You have two entities that have a 1:N relationship. You create a business process flow using the first entity, add a stage, and select the second entity. When users create the first record and click on the next stage to create the second record, the second record is not linked to the first record. What should you do?

    A) Edit the relationship and click on **Generate mappings**.
    B) In the stage, select the relationship.
    C) Create a classic workflow and add it as a stage entry on the second stage to link the two records.
    D) Add an action step to the second stage.

Further reading

- Using Power Automate flows in business process flows: `https://docs.microsoft.com/power-automate/create-business-process-flow#instant-flows-in-business-process-flows`
- Branching in business process flows: `https://docs.microsoft.com/power-automate/enhance-business-process-flows-branching`

14
UI Flows

In Chapter 12, *Power Automate flows*, you learned how to create automations using connectors. UI flows are for automations where there is no connector or API available to use. There are many legacy applications that do not have a method for accessing their data or functionality except through their user interface. UI flows use **Robotic Process Automation (RPA)** techniques to automate user actions on these legacy applications.

UI flows is the name of the RPA functionality in Power Automate. This chapter describes how to create and run UI flows. By using UI flows, you can create automations that span modern and legacy applications.

The following topics will be covered in this chapter:

- Introducing UI flows
- Recording business tasks
- Using attended and non-attended flows

By the end of this chapter, you will be able to differentiate between the distinct types of UI flows and be able to record tasks and create and run UI flows. We will start with the software requirements for creating, editing, and running UI flows.

Technical requirements

Unlike the rest of the Power Platform tools, UI flows require software to be installed on your local computer. You need this software because you need to interact with software applications that are not accessible from the cloud.

You will need a computer running Windows 10 Pro, Windows 10 Enterprise, Windows Server 2016, or Windows Server 2019.

The following software is required for UI flows:

- **A modern browser**: The latest version of the Google Chrome browser or the latest version of Microsoft Edge.
- **Selenium IDE**: An open source tool that records and plays back interactions on a website. Selenium IDE is a browser extension that is installed from the Chrome web store.
- **The Power Automate Desktop app**: A Windows application to create, edit, and run UI flows. You can download this tool from `https://go.microsoft.com/fwlink/?linkid=2102613`.
- **An on-premises data gateway**: This tool allows UI flows to be triggered by a Power Automate flow. You can download a gateway from `https://docs.microsoft.com/data-integration/gateway/service-gateway-install`.

The following screenshot shows the setup screen for Power Automate Desktop:

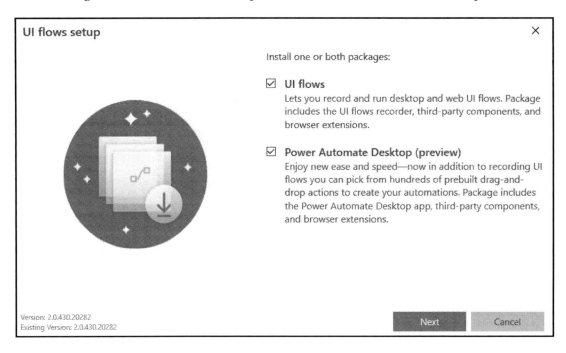

Figure 14.1 – Power Automate Desktop setup screen

UI flows require a Power Platform environment with a Common Data Service database.

Once you have installed this software, you can start exploring UI flows, but before you start, there are some concepts that you need to understand about UI flows.

Introducing UI flows

UI flows are a tool for creating automations using the user interfaces of applications. There are many legacy applications that do not have a programmatic interface. The only way to retrieve data or enter data is to use the user interface that the application provides. Users often work with multiple disjointed systems and must transpose data from one system to another. RPA tools like UI flows aim to automate such repetitive actions.

UI flows can automate the extraction of data from both desktop and web applications as well as the entering of new data into those same applications.

First, we will look at the types of UI flow and then discuss where UIs can be used.

Types of UI flow

UI flows can be created for either Windows desktop applications or applications that run in a web browser. UI flows record the mouse clicks and keyboard strokes made by a user and play these back to repeat the user's interactions.

There are separate tools for desktop apps and web applications. The Power Automate desktop app is used for Windows desktop applications and Selenium is used for web applications.

The following screenshot is an example of Power Automate Desktop editing a Desktop UI flow:

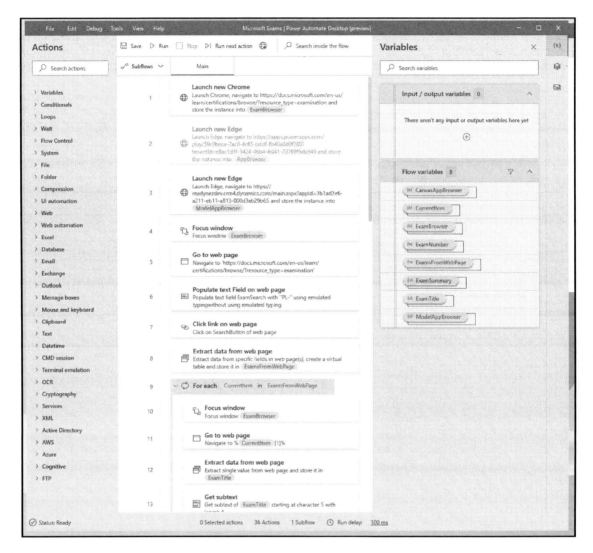

Figure 14.2 – Power Automate Desktop flow designer

The flow designer in the previous screenshot shows the actions available in the left-hand pane, the variables used in the right-hand pane, and in the center pane, a series of actions that have been recorded and edited to automate the copying of data from one web application that does not have an API into another web application.

This UI flow accesses a web page and extracts the links from the page. It then loops through each of the pages linked. Data is extracted from selected places on each page. The data is entered into another system. The example in the previous figure extracts the data from `https://docs.microsoft.com/learn/certifications/browse/` and the individual exam pages for the Power Platform exams.

Selenium is a set of open source tools for recording and playing back interactions with browsers. Selenium WebDriver was originally created for the automated testing of web applications. The Selenium IDE tool records test cases and then plays the tests back. Power Automate Web UI flows are based on Selenium IDE.

 Easy Repro is an automated tool for testing model-driven apps and is based on Selenium WebDriver.

The following screenshot shows Selenium IDE editing a Web UI flow:

Figure 14.3 – Selenium IDE

The IDE in the previous screenshot shows the record button that captures user actions is at the top right of the window. The middle pane shows the commands. Clicking on a command allows you to edit the command.

There are some limitations of Web UI flows:

- Right-clicking on the mouse button is not supported.
- Some Selenium IDE commands are not supported.

 To see all the limitations of Web UI flows,
visit `https://docs.microsoft.com/power-automate/ui-flows/create-web`.

Both the Power Automate Desktop and Selenium IDE tools create UI flows that can be run manually or integrated with Power Automate flows using the UI flows connector.

Now, let's look at where you could use UI flows.

Use cases for UI flows

UI flows automate repetitive tasks and there are many scenarios that UI flows can be employed in. Some of the uses for RPA are as follows:

- **Invoice processing**: Processing invoices includes many repetitive tasks, which, if performed incorrectly, cause incorrect payments. There are many challenges with invoice processing that require human intervention. For instance, invoices need to be validated against the details on purchase orders and thus data in systems needs to be looked up and verified. UI flows can process invoices, automatically performing validation checks, reducing the need for human intervention.
- **Email processing**: Many customer service centers process a high volume of incoming emails. UI flows can automate much of the initial sifting and routing of emails to the correct part of the organization, reducing the handling time and improving the speed of response to customers.
- **Recruitment**: UI flows could collate applications from multiple job portals into a single list of applicants with their relevant details.
- **New user onboarding**: New joiners to an organization must be set up with many systems. While you can use tools such as PowerShell to perform some setup, there are some applications for which there is no automation available. UI flows can be used to add users and configure their settings automatically through the application user interface.

There are many more uses for UI flows. You can consider any scenario where there is the processing of forms, extracting data from systems, or processing claims where the data needs to be verified for automation with UI flows. If you have rule-based processing, UI flows are a viable candidate for automating those processes.

Now that you know what UI flows are, let's discover how to record a user's interactions.

Recording business tasks

UI flows must capture a user's interactions so that the actions can be played back. UI flows need to be able to recognize the components of the application user interface such as buttons and fields. It is not enough to record the x and y values of a component as the window might be moved.

With UI flows, you can identify the components one by one yourself to create a series of actions but both Power Automate Desktop and Selenium IDE have recorder tools that you can use to capture an entire series of user interactions to complete a process.

After recording, you can edit these actions to remove unnecessary clicks and replace data inputs with variables passed into the UI flow. You will then have a UI flow you can run with different data values.

Recording actions

At the top of Power Automate Desktop, there are two buttons for recording desktop and web usage, as shown in the following screenshot:

Figure 14.4 – Recorder buttons

Starting the recorders opens a new pane that captures each keypress and mouse click. The following screenshot shows a list of the interactions captured using the Desktop recorder:

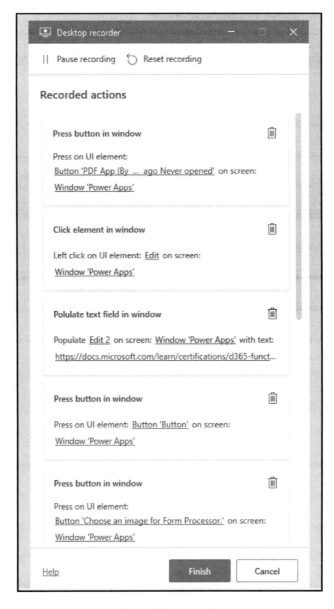

Figure 14.5 – Desktop recorder

Clicking on **Finish** saves the actions to the Power Automate Desktop flow designer, where they can be edited.

Editing actions

Once you have captured actions either manually by using the UI components or directly by using the recorder tools, you can go ahead and edit the steps. You can make changes to actions including the following:

- Dragging and dropping to reorder actions
- Disabling actions
- Inserting new actions
- Editing an action

You will normally need to edit actions and replace data with a variable. The following screenshot shows an action where the text has been entered into a field:

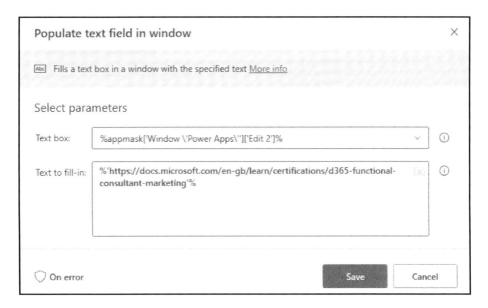

Figure 14.6 – Edit action

The text entered during the recording is between the % symbols. You can create a variable as shown in the next screenshot:

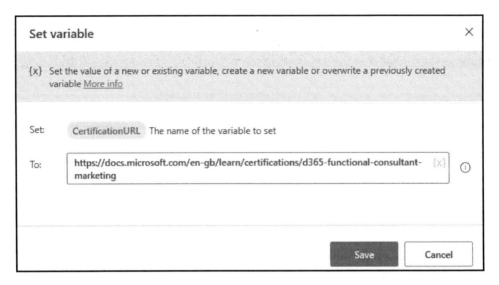

Figure 14.7 – Create a variable

Variables start and end with the % symbol. Variables can be internal variables, flow variables – such as counters, or input or output variables. Input variables can be passed to the UI flow from a Power Automate flow. Output variables are passed from the UI flow to a Power Automate flow.

You can edit the action and replace **Text to fill in** with the variable.

The process for Selenium IDE is like the process for Power Automate Desktop. Recorded steps are edited and, when saved, a UI flow is created.

Once you have completed your changes, you can test your UI flow. When you click on **Save** in *Figure 14.7*, a UI flow is created. The following screenshot shows the list of UI flows in the Power Automate flow portal:

Figure 14.8 – UI flows

You can run these flows manually, but you can initiate these UI flows from a Power Automate flow.

Using attended and non-attended flows

UI flows contain a series of actions required to perform a task. You can run UI flows individually, but for automation, you need to run UI flows as part of a Power Automate flow.

The UI flows connector allows you to initiate a UI flow on a computer. When you select the UI flows connector, you can choose to run either a Desktop UI flow or a Web UI flow as shown in the next screenshot:

Figure 14.9 – UI flows connector

When you choose one of these actions, you need to select the gateway to the computer that will run the flow along with the credentials for logging into the computer.

You then select the UI flow to run and select **Run Mode**:

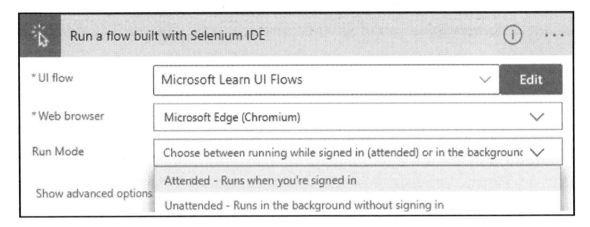

Figure 14.10 – Running a UI flow step in a Power Automate flow

Run Mode is how the UI flow will be run. There are two modes:

- **Attended**: The UI flow runs while the user is sat watching the screen. Attended flows are used for a part of a process that is very repetitive. The user monitors the actions and can handle errors or complete additional steps such as providing credentials to access systems.
- **Unattended**: The UI flow runs on a separate computer, normally a virtual machine running in Azure. The UI flow will perform all the actions in a process.

 Use an instant flow, for example, a button flow, to call a UI flow run in Attended mode. The user can then manually start the UI flow processing.

The advantage of unattended flows is that you can scale the number of machines and run many UI flows in parallel. An automated or scheduled flow is typically used to call the UI flow in unattended mode.

Summary

In this chapter, you were introduced to the RPA capabilities of Power Automate: UI flows. You learned how to install and configure the desktop and web UI flow tools. You should now understand the different tools for desktop and web, and how to record and edit tasks and create variables. You will now be able to differentiate between the distinct types of UI flows, create UI flows, record tasks, and run UI flows.

In the next chapter, we will learn how to create chatbots using the fourth component of Power Platform: Power Virtual Agents.

Questions

After reading this chapter, test your knowledge with these questions. You will find the answers to these questions under `Assessments` at the end of the book:

1. You need to create a variable called `var` in a UI flow. How should you reference the variable in an action?

    A) `$var`
    B) `_var`
    C) `%var%`
    D) `&var&`

2. A user needs to run a UI flow manually to complete a part of a process. Which type of Power Automate flow should they create?

    A) Automated
    B) Instant
    C) Scheduled
    D) Business process

3. Which two of the following operating systems are supported to run UI flows?

    A) Windows 10 Home
    B) Windows 10 Pro
    C) Linux
    D) Windows Server 2016

4. You place a competition on your website. You need to automate each competition entry into a legacy marketing system. You are expecting many thousands of entries per day. What should you create?

   A) An attended UI flow
   B) A business process flow
   C) An instant Power Automate flow
   D) An unattended UI flow

Further reading

- Set up UI flows and Power Automate Desktop: `https://docs.microsoft.com/power-automate/ui-flows/setup`
- Power Automate Desktop flow designer: `https://docs.microsoft.com/power-automate/ui-flows/desktop/flow-designer`
- Use variables and the % notation: `https://docs.microsoft.com/power-automate/ui-flows/desktop/variable-manipulation`
- Create and test your Web UI flows: `https://docs.microsoft.com/power-automate/ui-flows/create-web`
- Automate desktop flows: `https://docs.microsoft.com/power-automate/ui-flows/desktop/desktop-automation`
- Run attended and unattended UI flows: `https://docs.microsoft.com/power-automate/ui-flows/run-ui-flow`

Section 5: Power Virtual Agents

5

Section 5 is concerned with creating chatbots using Power Virtual Agents. By the end, the reader will be able to create a guided graphical interface without requiring code.

This section contains the following chapters:

- Chapter 15, *Creating Chatbots*
- Chapter 16, *Configuring Chatbots*

15
Creating Chatbots

Power Virtual Agents chatbots allow users to create chatbots without the need for code. You can deploy Power Virtual Agents chatbots to your website and to other channels, such as Microsoft Teams.

This chapter describes how to create, publish, and monitor Power Virtual Agents bots using the Power Virtual Agents portal. You will learn how to create and deploy a bot before gaining an understanding of some of the key concepts you should implement when building chatbots.

The following topics will be covered in this chapter:

- Introducing Power Virtual Agents
- Creating a chatbot
- Publishing chatbots
- Adding a chatbot to Microsoft Teams
- Monitoring chatbots

By the end of this chapter, you will be able to create chatbots using Power Virtual Agents, deploy them to websites and to Microsoft Teams, and monitor chatbot usage.

Introducing Power Virtual Agents

Power Virtual Agents chatbots are chatbots powered by **artificial intelligence (AI)** that allow users to focus on more complex and higher-value work while the chatbots themselves handle simple repetitive interactions. As with Chapter 18, *AI Builder*, you do not need to be a data scientist or even a developer to create chatbots using Power Virtual Agents.

Power Virtual Agents chatbots interact with customers and employees, answer questions, and provide information. You can deploy Power Virtual Agents chatbots to multiple channels, including your own website, Facebook, and Microsoft Teams.

Microsoft provides an alternative method for building chatbots using Azure Bot Service. The principal difference is that Azure Bot Service uses C# or Node.js to create your bot, while Power Virtual Agents follows the no-code approach of the Power Platform.

In this section, we will look at the scenarios and use cases for Power Virtual Agents chatbots, as well as the best practices for building chatbots. First, we will look at the benefits of using Power Virtual Agents to create your chatbots.

Benefits of using Power Virtual Agents

Using Power Virtual Agents to build your chatbots brings many benefits to you as a non-developer, as well as to your organization. With Power Virtual Agents, you can create chatbots using an easy to use, no-code graphical interface from within a web browser, as shown in the following screenshot:

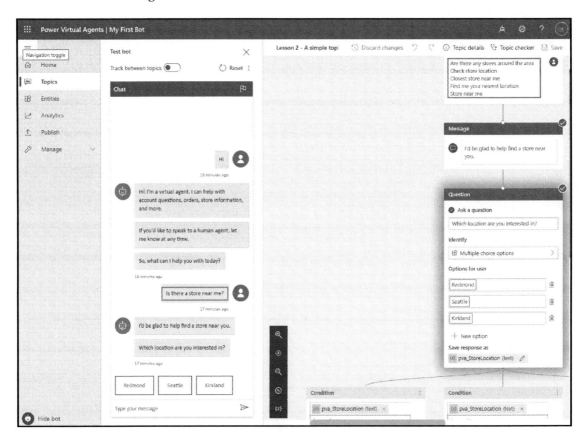

Figure 15.1 – Power Virtual Agents

As shown in the preceding screenshot, Power Virtual Agents has a navigation bar on the left-hand side. The right-hand pane contains the authoring canvas, which is where you can see the questions and messages being relayed. The middle pane allows you to test your bot as you build it.

Power Virtual Agents allows you to understand the questions that are being asked so that customers and users do not have to ask these questions using exactly the same phrases you specified in your chatbot. For example, in the middle pane shown in the preceding screenshot, the question being asked has been phrased differently from the phrases shown in the authoring canvas.

 Power Virtual Agents leverages the natural language processing (LUIS) capabilities of Azure Cognitive Services.

The benefits of using a no-code graphical interface for building chatbots are as follows:

- You can build a bot alongside the **subject matter experts (SMEs)**, thus reducing the time to build the bot and increasing user ownership and adoption.
- The question flow in the chatbot can be adjusted quickly so that it responds to changing circumstances and demands.
- Removes the need for custom code.
- Removes the need to understand Azure AI services.

Power Virtual Agents chatbots come with telemetry built-in so that you can monitor how your chatbots are being used. Once you've done this, you can change your chatbot to increase its effectiveness.

There are many ways to use chatbots that have been created with Power Virtual Agents. We will look at a few common use cases in the following subsection.

Use cases for Power Virtual Agents

Chatbots automate responses to questions and requests. There are many scenarios where chatbots can be used to enhance your organization's productivity. Some of the uses for chatbots are as follows:

- **Customer support**: Automation of customer support using a chatbot on a website. The chatbot can answer simple questions such as *what are your opening hours?*, *when will my order be delivered?*, and *how do I return this item I purchased?* Chatbots can deliver responses promptly and can easily be scaled during peak loads to handle multiple requests. Chatbots can also escalate to a human agent if necessary.
- **Sales help**: Chatbots can be used internally to support sales users by providing information on products, pricing, and availability.
- **Ticket sales**: A chatbot can interact with a customer to inform them of the dates a performer is scheduled for, the ticket types that are available, and their prices. The chatbot can then make the booking for the customer.
- **FAQs**: A common use for chatbots is to get them to provide the answers to frequently asked questions on your website.
- **Employee helpdesk**: Chatbots can be used to answer employee queries about their benefits or leave entitlement.

Chatbots are easy to build, but it is easy to build a chatbot that performs poorly.

Best practices for chatbots

Chatbots can be abandoned if the user of the chatbot cannot obtain the responses they want. The purpose of a chatbot is to handle repetitive tasks and to lower the volume of issues that human agents must handle. If the chatbot cannot fulfill its purpose, then you will have unhappy customers.

You should make sure that you identify the correct reasons for using a chatbot. The best chatbots are clear about what their purpose is and try not to respond to all questions.

There are several principles for conversational AI that you should follow:

- **Transparency**: A customer should know they are interacting with a bot. The purpose of the bot should be clear. The limitations of the bot should be stated.
- **Escalation to a human**: It should be possible to seamlessly transfer to a human agent.
- **Limit the bot**: Reduce the scope of the bot to its purpose.

- **Treat people fairly**: Be aware of bias.
- **Respect privacy**: Chatbots collect customer data, so make sure that this data is handled appropriately.

 Review the guidelines for responsible conversational AI at `https://aidemos.microsoft.com/responsible-conversational-ai/building-a-trustworthy-bot`.

Now that you know what Power Virtual Agents is, let's create a chatbot.

Creating a chatbot

The process of creating a chatbot in Power Virtual Agents is straightforward and only requires a web browser. In this section, we will learn how to create a bot and then how to share it with other users.

Power Virtual Agents requires a license to be built and run. However, you can start a free trial of Power Virtual Agents simply by navigating to the Power Virtual Agents portal (`https://powerva.microsoft.com`). Clicking on **Start free trial** will provision Power Virtual Agents. After a short delay, the following window will be displayed, where you can create a new bot:

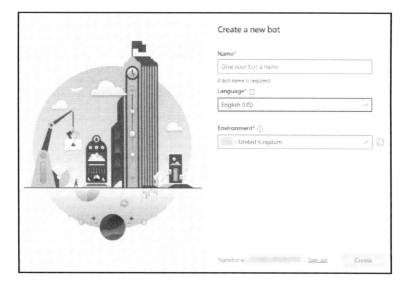

Figure 15.2 – Create a new bot window

When you see the preceding screen, you will need to provide a **Name** for your bot, select the **Language** that the bot will use, and select the **Environment** where the bot will store its configuration and data. If you have permission, you can create an environment from this window.

Power Virtual Agents uses Power Platform environments. The selected environment must have a Common Data Service database.

To create further chatbots, you must click on the bot icon in the top-right of the Power Virtual Agents portal, as shown in the following screenshot. A pane will open on the right-hand side so that you can choose an environment:

Figure 15.3 – Adding a new bot

After clicking on **+ New bot**, the window shown in *Figure 15.2* will appear. Creating a new bot takes a few minutes. You will be provided with sample lessons and system messages to help you get started. From here, you can learn how to author your own bots or simply delete them.

Sharing a bot

You can permit other users to edit your chatbot and access the chatbot's session logs by sharing it with users. From the **Home** page in the Power Virtual Agents portal, click on the **Share** button on the top-right. Clicking on the **Share** button opens a pane on the right-hand side of the portal. To share your chatbot, enter the user's email address and click on the **Share** button.

The user you share the bot with must have been assigned the Environment maker security role, which allows users to create apps in an environment. How to assign security roles to users was covered in Chapter 8, *Security*.

Users can collaborate on chatbots, with different users working on distinct parts of the bot at the same time.

Authoring a chatbot is the process of adding conversation triggers, messages, conditions, and actions. Chapter 16, *Configuring Chatbots*, will explain these concepts and show you how to author your own bot.

We will use the sample topics included with the new bot to publish and deploy a chatbot.

Publishing chatbots

Once you have built and tested your Power Virtual Agents chatbot, you must publish your chatbot so that your customers can interact with it. In this section, you will learn how to publish chatbots and add them to different channels.

Publishing a bot is straightforward. Click on **Publish** in the left-hand navigation pane; the portal will open the publishing page, as shown in the following screenshot:

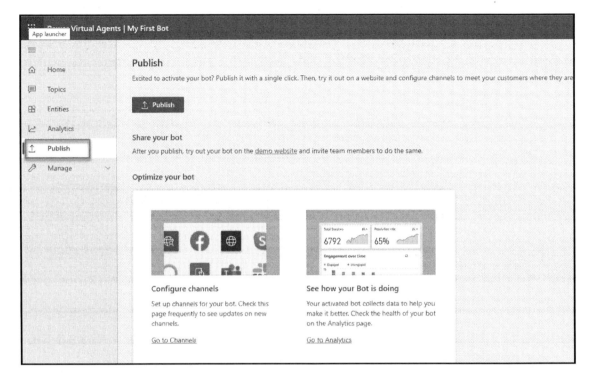

Figure 15.4 – Publishing a chatbot

Clicking on **Publish** and then **Publish** again at the confirmation prompt will make the bot available to others.

 You will need to publish the bot again if you make any changes to it.

Once you have published your chatbot, a link to a demo website will be created, where you can try the bot out yourself or allow your colleagues to test it. You can do this by copying the URL and sending it to them.

Once you are content that the bot is ready for your users or customers, you can add the bot to one or more channels.

Adding the chatbot to channels

Channels are the places where your chatbot can be accessed. The channels that you can select include the following:

- Website
- Microsoft Teams
- Facebook
- Slack

To configure a channel, click on **Manage** in the left-hand navigation and then select **Channels**. You will see a screen similar to the following:

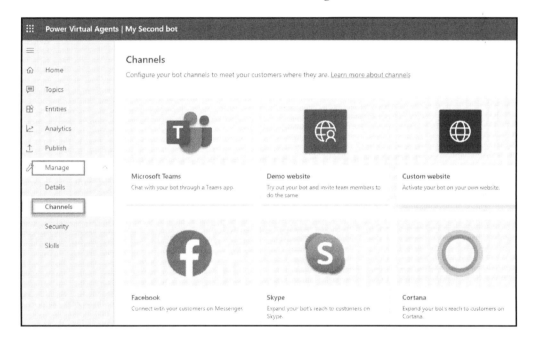

Figure 15.5 – Channels

The configuration for each channel depends on how that service operates. Clicking on **Custom website** will generate some embed code that you can add to your website pages. Clicking on the **Slack** channel generates the IDs you'll need to enter in the Slack application. For Facebook, you need to get the respective IDs and secrets from Facebook and add those details to the Power Virtual Agents portal.

Next, we'll learn how to add a bot to a Microsoft Teams channel.

Adding a chatbot to Microsoft Teams

Chatbots can be used by internal users, as well as external customers. Microsoft Teams is an ideal location to deploy your chatbot as it will operate as a native Teams bot and share Teams' appearance.

Chatbots built using Power Virtual Agents can be used inside Microsoft Teams. You need to select the **Microsoft Teams** channel and click **Turn on Teams.** Once you've done this, the following pane will appear:

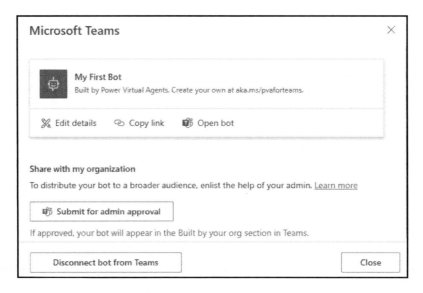

Figure 15.6 – Linking your chatbot to Teams

Clicking on **Open bot** will open Microsoft Teams. A window will appear where you can add the chatbot to Teams:

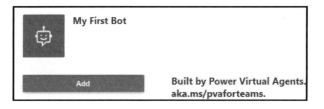

Figure 15.7 – Adding your chatbot to Teams

Clicking on **Add** will add the chatbot to Teams. The following screenshot shows the chatbot working within Teams:

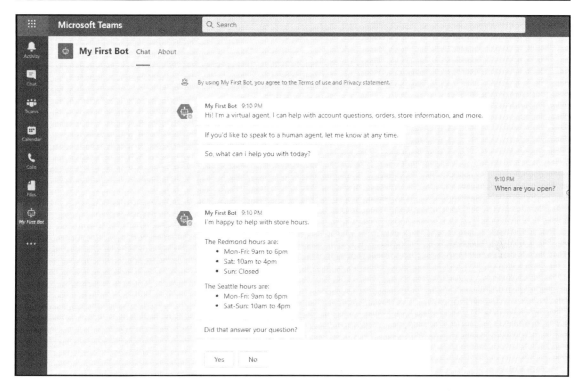

Figure 15.8 – Chatbot in Teams

The chatbot will only be available for your user. To allow other users to add the chatbot themselves, you need to share the chatbot with your organization. The **Submit for Admin approval** button, shown in *Figure 15.6*, allows you to do this. There are two ways you can do this:

- **Download a manifest file**: A `.zip` file must be downloaded. A Teams admin can upload this file to Teams.
- **Submit for admin approval**: The chatbot app will be listed in the Teams Admin portal for a Teams admin to approve.

With that, you have learned how to create chatbots for Microsoft Teams. Your privileges in Microsoft Teams will determine which options are available to you.

Building great chatbots requires monitoring how the chatbot is being used and analyzing where users are failing to get the responses they need. Fortunately, Power Virtual Agents comes with comprehensive monitoring.

Monitoring chatbots

Power Virtual Agents has telemetry built in. This allows you to monitor how your chatbots are being used, where the question flow is causing your chatbot to be abandoned, and which topics are being used. By monitoring your chatbots, you can then optimize your chatbot and increase its effectiveness.

Clicking on **Analytics** in the Power Virtual Agents portal will show the **Analytics** page, as shown in the following screenshot:

Figure 15.9 – Power Virtual Agents analytics

There are four tabs on the **Analytics** page:

- **Summary**: An overview of the bot's performance. The charts use AI to highlight topics that have the greatest impact on escalations, abandons, and resolutions.
- **Customer Satisfaction**: If you capture feedback in your chatbot, **customer satisfaction (CSAT)** scores are shown over time, with the topics that have the greatest impact on CSAT highlighted.

- **Sessions**: The **Sessions** tab allows you to download transcripts of chat sessions.
- **Billing**: The Power Virtual Agents license comes with a set capacity for the number of sessions you can run. This tab allows you to track how many sessions have been billed against your capacity allowance.

 Your capacity allowance is set at the tenant level, but reporting is only available for each chatbot.

You should monitor these analytics for trends and pay attention to abandon rates, as well as which topics are the most influential.

Summary

This chapter described how to build chatbots without using code or having to know certain AI techniques. We used Power Virtual Agents for this purpose.

You should now understand how to create and publish chatbots. You should be able to use channels, including Microsoft Teams, to make your bots available to users and customers. You should also be able to monitor chatbots for performance and analyze where you can improve them. Using these skills, you can create interactive chatbots that will improve customer satisfaction and allow users to concentrate on higher-value activities.

In the next chapter, we will learn how to author your own chatbots by adding conversation triggers, messages, conditions, and actions.

Questions

Now that you've read this chapter, test your knowledge with these questions. You will find the answers to these questions in the `Assessments` section at the end of this book:

1. What must you do before you add a Power Virtual Agents chatbot to a channel?

   A) Share
   B) Publish
   C) Test
   D) Add a skill

2. Which tab in Power Virtual Agents Analytics should you use to find how much of your licensed capacity has been used?

   A) Summary
   B) Customer Satisfaction
   C) Sessions
   D) Billing

3. You need to make your Power Virtual Agents chatbot available to all users of Microsoft Teams. What should you do?

   A) Export
   B) Copy the URL
   C) Share
   D) Submit for admin approval

4. You create a new chatbot in Power Virtual Agents. Which two of the following must you select?

   A) Channel
   B) Environment
   C) Language
   D) Skill

Further reading

- **Power Virtual Agents overview:** https://docs.microsoft.com/power-virtual-agents/fundamentals-what-is-power-virtual-agents
- **Working with environments in Power Virtual Agents:** https://docs.microsoft.com/power-virtual-agents/environments-first-run-experience
- **Creating and deleting Power Virtual Agents bots:** https://docs.microsoft.com/power-virtual-agents/authoring-first-bot
- **Key Concepts – Publishing your bot:** https://docs.microsoft.com/power-virtual-agents/publication-fundamentals-publish-channels
- **Sharing your bot with other users:** https://docs.microsoft.com/power-virtual-agents/admin-share-bots
- **Configuring the demo website and adding the bot to your live website:** https://docs.microsoft.com/power-virtual-agents/publication-connect-bot-to-web-channels

- **Adding a bot to Microsoft Teams:** `https://docs.microsoft.com/power-virtual-agents/publication-add-bot-to-microsoft-teams`
- **Power Virtual Agents app in Microsoft Teams:** `https://docs.microsoft.com/power-virtual-agents/teams/fundamentals-what-is-power-virtual-agents-teams`
- **Analysis in Power Virtual Agents:** `https://docs.microsoft.com/power-virtual-agents/analytics-overview`

16
Configuring Chatbots

Power Virtual Agents chatbots can be configured to identify multiple types of conversation and perform different actions.

This chapter describes how to configure and author your own chatbots. You will learn how to change the questions and responses used in your chatbot so that you can tailor your chatbot to your business scenario. By configuring the conversations your chatbots have, you will be able to handle both simple and complex interactions with users and increase customer satisfaction in relation to your chatbots.

The following topics will be covered in this chapter:

- Defining topics
- Configuring entities
- Defining actions

By the end of this chapter, you will be able to create topics and entities, use a Power Automate flow with Power Virtual Agent chatbots, and use bot variables.

Defining topics

Power Virtual Agents works by identifying the subject that the user is asking about and then having a conversation about that subject.

Topics are the main subjects of the conversation. A Power Virtual Agents chatbot can have up to 1,000 topics. Each topic is a separate conversation path. It is the combination of topics in a chatbot that provides a natural conversational flow. You create topics for the tasks or requests that you need your chatbot to respond to.

Topics define the purpose of your chatbot and are the first step in authoring your chatbot.

A topic has two parts:

- **Trigger phrases**: The keywords, phrases, or utterances that the user will enter
- **Conversation nodes**: How your bot should respond

A topic has its own conversation flow with the bot. When a bot identifies a trigger for a topic, the conversation for that bot is initiated.

Each newly created bot includes predefined user and system topics to help you get started. Clicking on **Topics** in the Power Virtual Agents portal will show the sample user and system topics, as shown in the following screenshot:

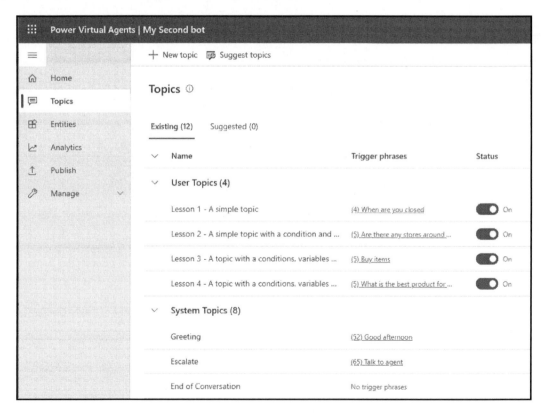

Figure 16.1 – Sample topics

In the preceding screenshot, there are four lessons under **User Topics** that can help you understand how to author chatbot conversations. **System Topics** includes common interactions that can occur during a chatbot conversation.

You can use these to learn how to author your own bots or can adapt or delete them.

In this section, we will learn how to configure topics manually, create topics from existing content, and handle escalations and errors.

Configuring topics

A topic is a part of a conversation a customer has with a chatbot. You will need to create topics to handle each type of request your bot should handle. For instance, you might require a chatbot to respond to employee inquiries concerning travel and expenses.

You can start by collating a list of phrases that an employee might use and then grouping them into similar inquiries.

For example, you might collect the following sets of phrases for an organization's travel and expenses policies:

- **Accommodation**: The policies for overnight hotel accommodation:
    - What level of hotel accommodation am I entitled to?
    - What else is included in my hotel stay?

- **Subsistence**: The level of food and incidental expenses when working away from the office or home:
    - Is breakfast included in an overnight stay?
    - Can I claim for dinner?
    - Do I need a receipt for meals?

- **Car travel**: Allowances for use of a vehicle when traveling to remote locations:
    - What is the mileage allowance for my car?
    - Can I share a car?
    - Can I hire a car?

In this example, the first-level bullets are the topics, and the second-level bullets are the trigger phrases. The end result for this example will be three topics, each having their own conversation flow. To create a new topic, select **Topics** in the Power Virtual Agents portal and then click on **+ New topic**. The following page will be displayed:

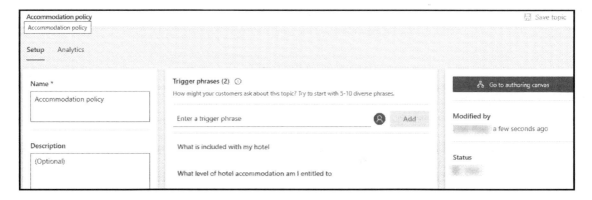

Figure 16.2 – New topic

In the preceding screenshot, enter the topic in the **Name** field, enter the trigger phases, click on **Add**, and then click on **Save topic**.

A topic should have a minimum of 10 trigger phrases to be effective. Include phrases that mean the same thing, but are constructed in different ways. You can find guidance on collecting trigger phrases at `https://docs.microsoft.com/azure/cognitive-services/luis/luis-concept-utterance`.

Once you have added your trigger phrases, click on **Go to authoring canvas**. The authoring canvas is a graphical editor where you can add the conversation nodes for the topic. The authoring canvas starts with the trigger phrases and a welcome message. The authoring canvas allows you to add questions, messages, and other actions, as shown in the following screenshot:

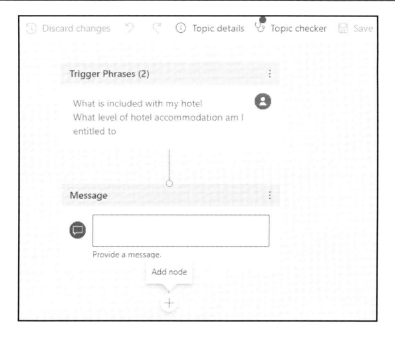

Figure 16.3 – Authoring canvas

In the preceding screenshot, you can see **Trigger Phrases** at the top of the canvas with a blank **Message** field underneath. You need to provide a welcome message and then click on **Add node** to determine the conversation's path.

Clicking on **Add node** gives the following options:

- **Ask a question**: Adds a new question node with the aim of getting a response from the user. The question can be from a string or number as a multiple-choice question, or an entity.
- **Call an action**: Calls a Power Automate flow or an authentication node to force the user to sign in.
- **Show a message**: Displays a message in a textbox.
- **Add a condition**: Available after a question node to control the flow of the conversation.
- **Go to another topic**: Switch to a different topic. Only available on the last node.
- **End the conversation**: There are two options. You can end with a survey or transfer to an agent. Only available on the last node.

The following screenshot shows a question node:

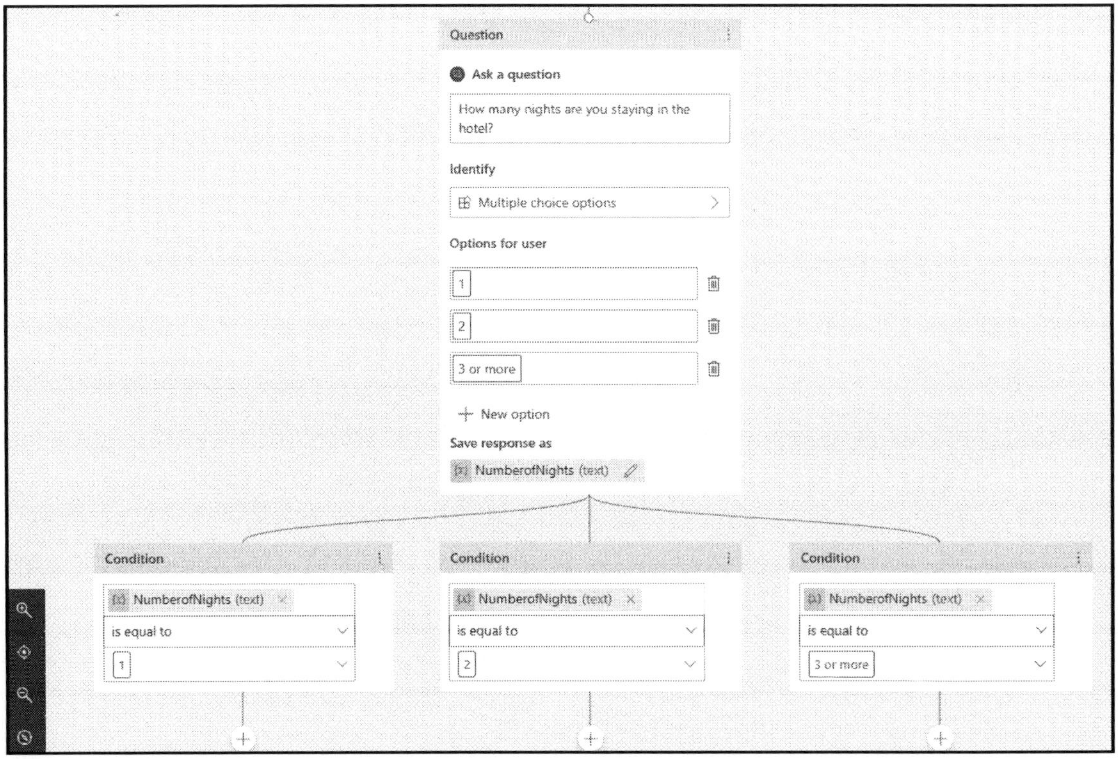

Figure 16.4 – Question node

You add nodes to the canvas to build the topic's conversation path until you have completed your question flow. If you have existing questions and answers, you can extract the details and create new topics automatically.

Extracting topics from existing content

Many organizations will have procedures, product information, frequently asked questions, and other information in documents or on websites.

Power Virtual Agents can extract information and create topics with trigger phrases. Selecting **Suggest topics** from the top of the **Topics** page, as shown in *Figure 16.1*, will open a window where you can specify the URL to your content.

You can only use online content. Files should be added to OneDrive or another cloud service to be used for suggested topics.

After you have extracted the content, you can review the suggested topics and add them to your chatbot.

If you are using Dynamics 365 Customer Service Insights, you can select the topics from within **Customer Service Insights** and add the topics and trigger phrases to your chatbot.

There are several topics that handle conversations, such as **Greetings**, **Thank you**, and **Goodbye**. These are system topics.

Adding greetings and other system topics

A Power Virtual Agents chatbot includes several system topics to improve the usability of your chatbot. For example, there are topics for **Greetings**, **Goodbye**, and **Thank you**.

 You cannot edit the trigger phrases for system topics.

Your chatbot uses the most appropriate topic based on user input. If the chatbot cannot determine which topic to use, then the chatbot will prompt the user again. If the chatbot still cannot determine the user's intent, then the chatbot will use the **Escalate system** topic.

You may want to handle the escalation differently by prompting the user with different questions to try and pinpoint their intent. To change the default escalation behavior, add a fallback topic.

Your chatbot will have multiple topics and Power Virtual Agents will choose the most appropriate topic by matching the phrase entered by the user with the trigger phrases in the topics. You will then start on the conversation path defined in the authoring canvas, prompting the user with questions, and handling the responses.

A significant part of the success of a chatbot is language understanding. Power Virtual Agents includes AI to understand a user's intent and entities that define real-world concepts and objects.

Configuring entities

Power Virtual Agents attempts to extract information from the phrases entered by the user. This extracted information can be used to control the conversation's path. Power Virtual Agents uses entities to identify information in a textual phrase, for instance, names, dates, and numbers. Your chatbot can then use this information to decide on the appropriate next step in the conversation.

Entities are people, places, and things that a chatbot can identify from the phrases entered into a chatbot. Power Virtual Agents includes a set of pre-built entities for the most commonly used objects.

The benefit of entities is to reduce the number of questions asked by the chatbot. The following screenshot shows some of the pre-built entities included with Power Virtual Agents:

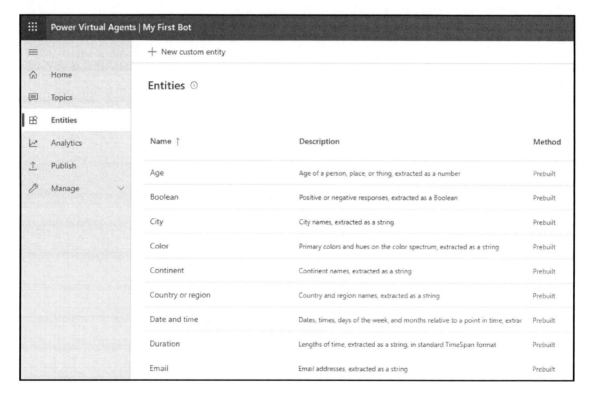

Figure 16.5 – Entities

The pre-built entities include the ability to identify simple things such as colors, or *yes/no* and *true/false*. The **Date and time** entity can identify a date from phrases such as tomorrow, next week, on Friday, as well as first week next year.

You can create custom entities for the domain-specific knowledge of your industry or organization to extend your chatbot's ability to recognize user input.

Creating custom entities

If your chatbot handles a specific process or business scenario, you may need to provide the chatbot with assistance by teaching it the objects and terminology your organization uses. You do this by creating a custom entity.

To create a new entity, select **Entities** in the Power Virtual Agents portal and click on **+ New custom entity**. The following page will be displayed:

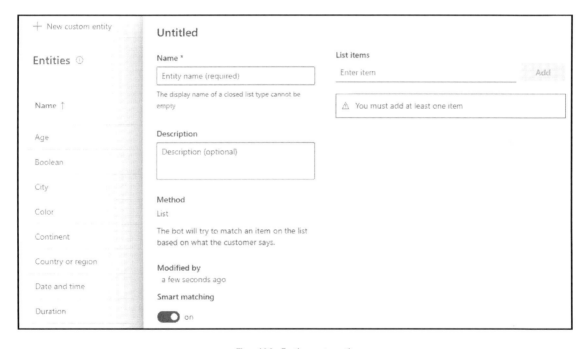

Figure 16.6 – Creating a custom entity

In the preceding screenshot, enter the topic in the **Name** field, enter each of the terms in **List items**, click on **Add**, and then click on **Save**.

You can add synonyms to assist the chatbot in matching. For instance, for travel expenses, you might add *a receipt* as an item and add *the bill* as a synonym.

For example, you might add the following entity for an organization's travel and expenses policies:

- **ExpenseType** with the following items:
    - Mileage
    - Subsistence
    - Train fare
    - Hospitality

The example custom entity can be created as shown in the following screenshot:

Figure 16.7 – Example custom entity

Your entity can be used in the **Ask a question** node in the authoring canvas. Instead of multiple choice, you can select either a pre-built or custom entity, as shown in the following screenshot:

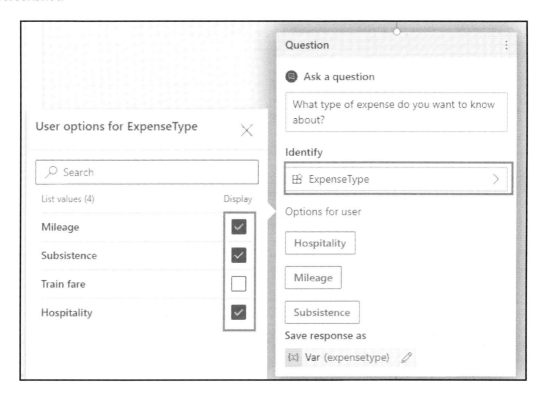

Figure 16.8 – Using a custom entity

In the preceding screenshot, an **Ask a question** node has been added and the custom entity chosen for **Identify**. You can then select which of the list options to use. In this example, three of the options have been chosen. The chatbot will use these list items to prompt the user in the conversation. The advantage of entities is that if the user had already used one of these terms earlier in the conversation, this question will be skipped, improving the conversation flow.

Entities are crucial to your chatbot being able to determine what a user is saying. You can use the many pre-built entities for dates, places, and numbers, and you can create custom entities to teach your chatbot about the terminology used within your organization or industry.

Your chatbot can also perform actions using the **Call an action** node.

Defining actions

A chatbot sometimes needs to perform actions on other systems or to retrieve data from other systems. You use Power Automate flows to perform actions. Power Virtual Agents can pass parameters to a Power Automate flow and receive data back from the flow and use that data in the conversation flow. For instance, a chatbot may handle customer order updates and so will use a Power Automate flow to fetch the order's status from the relevant system. In this section, you will learn how to use Power Automate flows from within a chatbot.

To call a Power Automate flow, use the **Call an action** node and select **Create a flow**, as shown in the following screenshot:

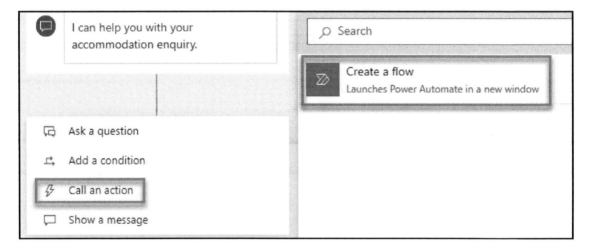

Figure 16.9 – Call an action

Clicking on **Create a flow** will launch the Power Automate editor using the Power Virtual Agents flow template. There is a Power Virtual Agents connector that you use within a Power Automate flow. If there are Power Automate flows that use the Power Virtual Agents connector, they will be listed here and will be available to select.

The responses a user enters and the choices they make can be stored and used in the conversational flow. Variables are used to save the responses. Variables can control the conversational flow or be displayed in messages to users.

Using variables

Variables let you save responses from your users in a conversation so that you can reuse them later in conversations. You can also use variables as input parameters to Power Automate flows and save the output results to parameters.

The response for each question asked in a conversation is stored as a variable. You can then pass the variable to a Power Automate flow or use the variable later in the topic, or even in other topics, to control the questions being asked. For example, you can use a variable to decide to skip a question if you have the information you need at that point.

Variables can be defined as either of the following:

- **Topic**: The variable can only be used within its topic.
- **Bot**: The variables can be used by any topic.

Many chatbots need to interact with other systems, either to record the outcome of the conversation, or to retrieve information and display it to the user. You have learned that a Power Automate flow is the way you achieve these requirements. You have also learned that variables are a good way of making your chatbot simpler and improving the friendliness of your chatbot.

Summary

This chapter described how you can configure chatbots to handle different business scenarios.

You should now understand how to author chatbots. You should be able to add topics with trigger phrases, add entities identifying the customer intent, and then perform actions using Power Automate. Configuring the conversations with these elements will build chatbots that are more relevant to the users' requests and will increase the customer satisfaction of your chatbots.

In the next chapter, we will learn how to use Power BI to create visualizations of your data and use those visualizations with the other components of the Power Platform.

Questions

After reading this chapter, test your knowledge with these questions. You will find the answers to these questions under `Assessments at the end of the book`:

1. Which component of Power Virtual Agents is used to define the conversation path in a chatbot?

   A) Entities
   B) Topics
   C) Actions
   D) Variables

2. What should you define in Power Virtual Agents to identify the intent in the phrases used by customers?

   A) Entities
   B) Topics
   C) Actions
   D) Variables

3. What should you add to your Power Virtual Agents to prevent escalations to a human agent when your chatbot cannot determine the user's intent?

   A) Fallback topic
   B) System topic
   C) Variable
   D) Entity

4. How many times will a Power Virtual Agents chatbot prompt a user by default before escalating to a human agent?

   A) One
   B) Two
   C) Three
   D) Five

Further reading

- Creating and editing topics in your Power Virtual Agents bot: `https://docs.microsoft.com/power-virtual-agents/authoring-create-edit-topics`
- Creating topics from existing online support content: `https://docs.microsoft.com/power-virtual-agents/advanced-create-topics-from-web`
- Creating bot topics from Customer Service Insights: `https://docs.microsoft.com/power-virtual-agents/advanced-create-topics-from-csi`
- Configuring the system fallback topic in Power Virtual Agents: `https://docs.microsoft.com/power-virtual-agents/authoring-system-fallback-topic`
- Managing topics in Power Virtual Agents: `https://docs.microsoft.com/power-virtual-agents/authoring-topic-management`
- Adding actions to a bot using Power Automate: `https://docs.microsoft.com/power-virtual-agents/advanced-flow`
- Smart Entity Extraction and Proactive Slot Filling: `https://powervirtualagents.microsoft.com/blog/smart-entity-extraction-and-proactive-slot-filling/`
- Using entities and slot filling in Power Virtual Agents bots: `https://docs.microsoft.com/power-virtual-agents/advanced-entities-slot-filling`
- Using variables: `https://docs.microsoft.com/power-virtual-agents/authoring-variables`
- Reusing variables across topics: `https://docs.microsoft.com/power-virtual-agents/authoring-variables-bot`
- Using Microsoft Bot Framework Skills in Power Virtual Agents: `https://docs.microsoft.com/power-virtual-agents/advanced-use-skills`

Section 6: Integrations

Section 6 is concerned with integrations with the Power Platform.

This section contains the following chapters:

- Chapter 17, *Power BI*
- Chapter 18, *AI Builder*
- Chapter 19, *Microsoft 365 Integration*
- Chapter 20, *Application Life Cycle Management*

17
Power BI

Power BI is a major component of Power Platform and creates powerful visualizations so that we can analyze data and gain insights into it. Power BI can be used standalone or combined with the various components that Power Platform provides.

In this chapter, you will learn how to use **Power BI** to create powerful visualizations of data that have been captured and held in the Common Data Service. Power BI is a powerful self-service data analysis tool that is a key component of Power Platform. While Power BI can be used with many data sources, this chapter describes how to create Power BI dashboards using Common Data Service data.

In this chapter, we will cover the following topics:

- Introducing Power BI
- Using data with Power BI
- Creating visualizations
- Creating reports and dashboards
- Using Power BI with Power Platform

By the end of this chapter, you will be able to use Common Data Service data with dataflows to create Power BI dashboards. You will also be able to embed Power BI tiles and dashboards within Power Apps.

Introducing Power BI

Power BI is a business analysis tool that can turn data from multiple sources into interactive reports and dashboards that provide insights into your data.

Power BI can be used to create visualizations from a single data source. Alternatively, it can be used as an enterprise business intelligence application for collating data from multiple data sources, cleansing and transforming the data, modeling the data, and creating calculations that can be used to create powerful visuals that allow users create and share their own dashboards.

Power BI consists of three tools:

- **Power BI Desktop:** A Microsoft Windows desktop application used to model data and create visualizations.
- **Power BI Service:** An online service used to create and share reports and dashboards.
- **Power BI Mobile:** A mobile application used to consume dashboards from the Power BI service.

If you are simply creating visuals of your data from a well-formed data source, then you can use the Power BI service to connect to data and create reports and dashboards.

If you need to cleanse or transform data, create KPIs and other calculations, or combine data from multiple sources, then you will need to use Power BI desktop. Once you have added visualizations to your report, you publish the report to the Power BI service. In the Power BI service, you create and publish dashboards.

Power BI Mobile can view dashboards published by the Power BI service. In Power BI Mobile, you can specify rules that notify you when the data in visuals exceeds a threshold value.

There are many preconfigured apps you can install from Microsoft AppSource directly into Power BI service, such as the app to analyze business process flows, as discussed in Chapter 13, *Business Process Flows*. The following screenshot shows the page in AppSource for the Process Analytics app:

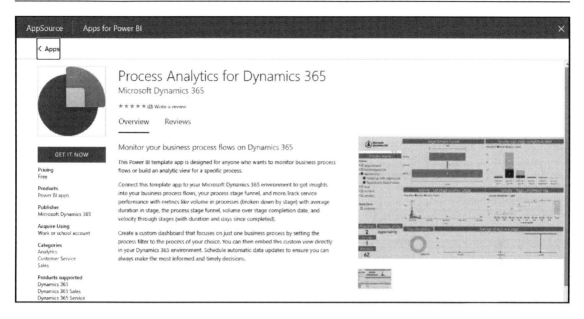

Figure 17.1 – Power BI app in AppSource

The common process of using Power BI is as follows:

1. Connect to data in Power BI Desktop.
2. Cleanse data in Power BI Desktop.
3. Create reports by adding visualizations to Power BI Desktop.
4. Publish the reports to the Power BI service.
5. Create and share reports and dashboards in the Power BI service.
6. Consume dashboards with Power BI Mobile.

 You can create reports by adding visualizations to both Power BI Desktop and the Power BI service, but you can only create dashboards in the Power BI service.

Before you learn how to use Power BI, you need to understand the components that it uses:

- **Data sources**: The source of the data that you want to analyze. Power BI can connect to many different data sources. Power BI does not share the connectors used in Power Apps and Power Automate. The Common Data Service is one of the supported data sources for Power BI.
- **Datasets**: A set of data that is ready for reporting and visualizations. A dataset represents a data model containing data from one or more sources that have been transformed and cleansed.
- **Dataflows**: A cloud-based *extract, transform, and load* processing tool that supports the Common Data Model.
- **Visualizations**: A visual representation of data. There are many types of visuals supported in Power BI, such as pie charts, bar charts, KPI charts, donut charts, and scatter charts.
- **Reports**: One or more pages containing visualizations on a dataset.
- **Dashboards**: A single page containing key visualizations.
- **Tiles**: An individual visual pinned to a dashboard.
- **Workspace**: An environment used to collaborate on creating reports and dashboards.

The following table shows where you can edit and use these components in Power BI Desktop and the Power BI service:

Power BI Component	Power BI Desktop	Power BI service
Dataflows	-	Create and edit
Datasets	Create and edit	Consume
Visualizations	Create and edit	Create and edit
Reports	Create and edit	Create, edit, and share
Dashboards	-	Create, edit, and share
Tiles	-	Create and edit
Workspaces	-	Create, edit, and share

Now that you have learned about the components involved, we will learn how to connect to data.

Using data with Power BI

In many organizations, data is stored in many locations and in many different structures, file types, and databases. You may need to extract data from different sources to create the visuals and reports required.

Before you can create your visualizations and reports, you must extract the data from the various sources, prepare the data by cleansing it, and then shape it so that visualizations can be created properly.

One data source supported in Power BI is the Common Data Service. Using Power BI with the Common Data Service allows data in the Common Data Service to be analyzed. The visuals that are created from the data can then be displayed within the apps that use the Common Data Service.

 There is an exam for the data analyst role, DA-100, that covers using Power BI with many other data sources. The DA-100 exam covers all the capabilities of Power BI. The PL-200 exam is restricted to using Power BI with the Common Data Service, Power Apps, and Power Automate.

Let's discover how to connect to the Common Data Service with Power BI.

Using pre-built Power BI apps

Pre-built apps are a straightforward way to provide visualizations of your data. Using these pre-built apps will allow you to create a set of reports and dashboards that you can share with your users. You can edit these apps in order to add your own visuals without having to start from a blank report page.

You can use the Power BI service or Power BI Desktop to connect to the Common Data Service.

In the Power BI service, you can use the **Get Data** button in the bottom-left corner of the page to access different types of data sources. After clicking on **Get Data**, the following options will appear:

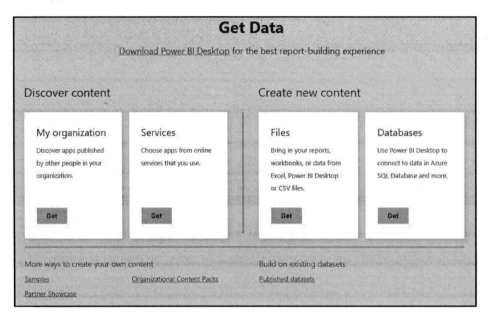

Figure 17.2 – Get Data in the Power BI service

Clicking on **Get** in the **Services** tile makes a list of Power BI apps available from AppSource appear, as shown in the following screenshot:

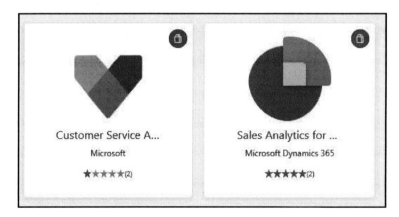

Figure 17.3 – Power BI apps for Dynamics 365

There are two pre-packaged analytics apps available: **Sales Analytics** and **Customer Service Analytics**. To install apps, you must select them from inside AppSource. Once installed, the following page will be displayed:

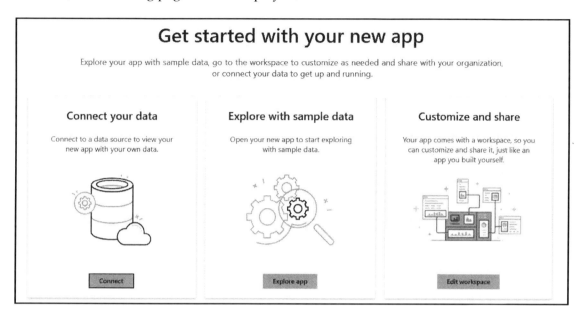

Figure 17.4 – Configuring a Power BI app

Clicking on **Connect** will prompt you to enter the URL for your Dynamics 365 environment. Once you've done this, the reports and dashboard provided will be populated with your data. The app will look like this:

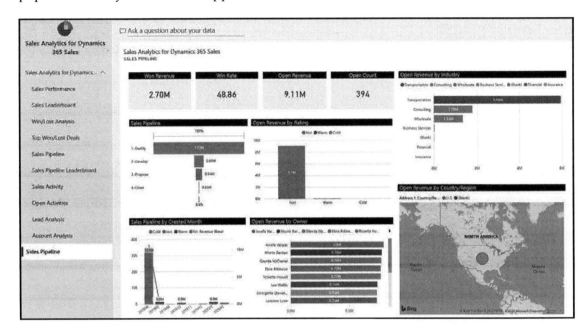

Figure 17.5 – Configure the Power BI app

These pre-built apps are good if you are using the corresponding Dynamics 365 Sales or Customer Service apps. If you have created your own entities and fields, you will need to connect to the Common Data Service.

Connecting to the Common Data Service

If you need to build your own reports with your own entities, you need to connect to the Common Data Service using Power BI Desktop. Starting Power BI Desktop will display the following page:

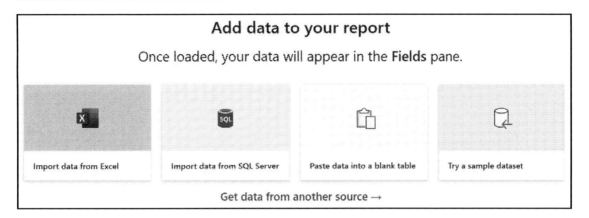

Figure 17.6 – Get Data in Power BI Desktop

Clicking on **Get data from another source** or the **Get Data** button from the Power BI Desktop menu will make the following screen appear. Here, you can select your data source:

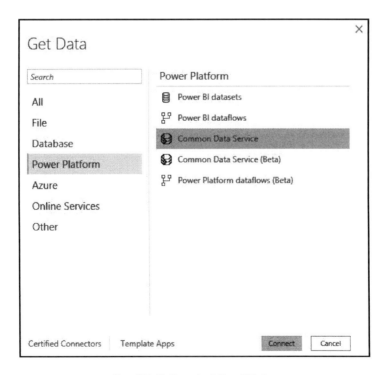

Figure 17.7 – Get Data options in Power BI Desktop

To connect to the Common Data Service, select **Power Platform** | **Common Data Service** | **Connect**. Another popup window will be displayed, prompting you to add the URL of your Power Platform environment:

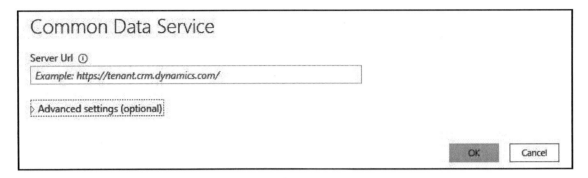

Figure 17.8 – Connecting to the Common Data Service

In the previous window, enter the URL for your environment and click **OK**. Once Power BI has connected to the Common Data Service, the **Navigator** window will be displayed. The **Navigator** window contains a list of entities from the environment you added previously. The following screenshot shows the **Navigator** window containing a list of entities:

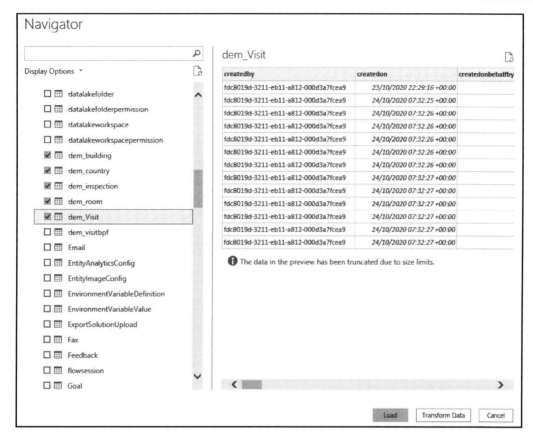

Figure 17.9 – Selecting entities in the Navigator window

In the **Navigator** window, select the entities you want to include in your report and click on **Load** to import the data. After a short while, the data will be loaded into a dataset, and a data model will be created.

You can view the dataset containing the data model and the rows in Power BI Desktop.

Creating datasets

Datasets are created from the data that's been imported from your data sources. You should now cleanse and shape this data so that it is ready for creating visualizations.

The first step is to use Power Query to transform the data. Power Query is a tool that's used in several Microsoft products for extracting and transforming data. We learned how Power Query can be used to import data into the Common Data Service in Chapter 6, *Managing Data*.

Clicking on the **Transform data** button in the Power BI Desktop menu opens Power Query, as shown in the following screenshot:

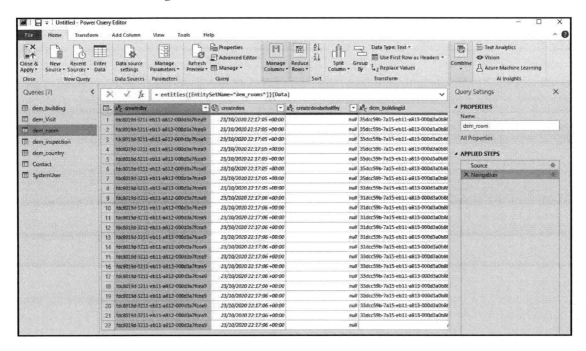

Figure 17.10 – Power Query Editor

As you can see, Power Query Editor shows the records from the query and allows you to perform many transformations on the data, from changing the data type to adding calculated columns using the **Transform** and **Add Column** tabs. Power Query allows you to cleanse the data, remove duplicates, and replace values. Each transformation is recorded as a step in the right-hand pane.

Transforming data with Power Query is outside the scope of the PL-200 exam.

You can filter the rows that have been extracted from the Common Data Service using Power Query. Moreover, you can also exclude records that have been deactivated and other records that you do not need for your visualizations.

Once you have transformed your data, you need to specify the relationships between them in the model tab in Power BI Desktop, as shown in the following screenshot:

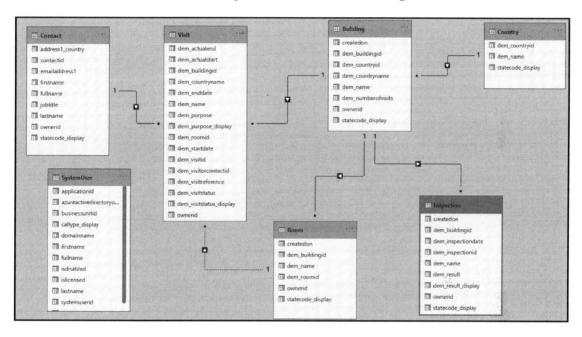

Figure 17.11 – Data model in Power BI Desktop

You are now ready to start adding visuals to reports. However, before we do that, there is another option for preparing dataflows.

Using Dataflows to extract and transform data

Power Platform Dataflows is a cloud-based **extract, transform and load** (ETL) tool that you can use to extract and shape data for use in Power BI.

Dataflows are created in the Power BI service. To create a dataflow, you must click on the **Dataflows** tab in a Power BI workspace:

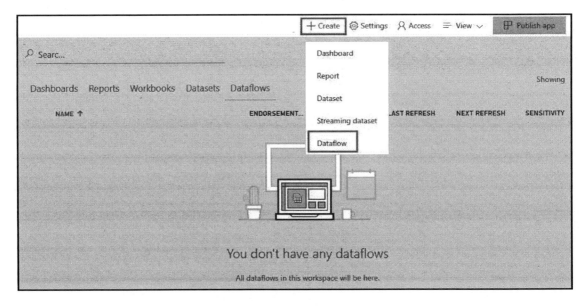

Figure 17.12 – Dataflows in a Power BI workspace

To create a new dataflow, click on **+ Create** in the action bar and select **Dataflow**, as shown in the preceding screenshot. A new dataflow page will be shown that provides four options, as shown in the following screenshot:

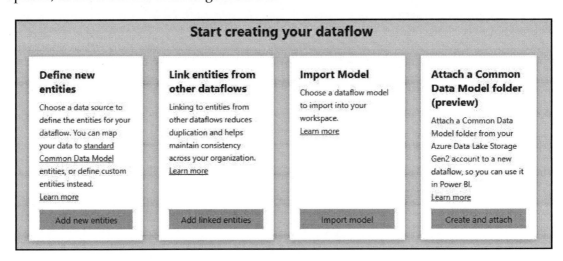

Figure 17.13 – Start creating your dataflow options

To extract data from the Common Data Service, click on the **Add new entities** button. Clicking on this button makes a list of data sources to choose from appear, including the Common Data Service, as shown here:

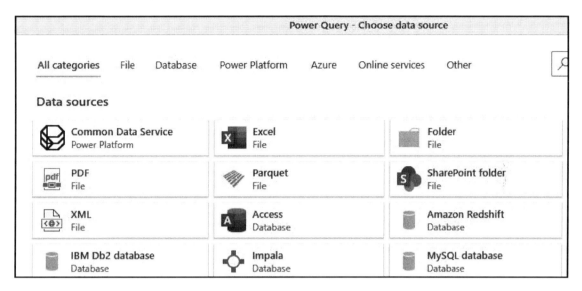

Figure 17.14 – Data sources for dataflows

Choose **Common Data Service** and enter the URL of the Power Platform environment you want to extract data from. The **Navigator** window is shown next. Here, you can select the entities you want to use for visualizations, as follows:

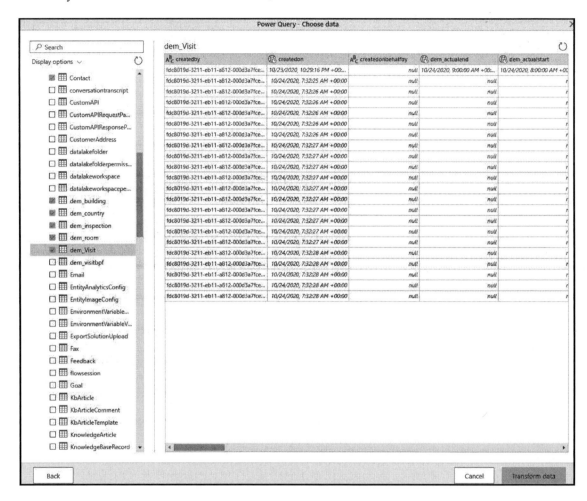

Figure 17.15 – Selecting entities for dataflows

Once you have selected the required entities, click on **Transform data**. This launches the Power Query Editor window, where you can transform the data. When you have finished shaping the data, name the dataflow and click **Save**:

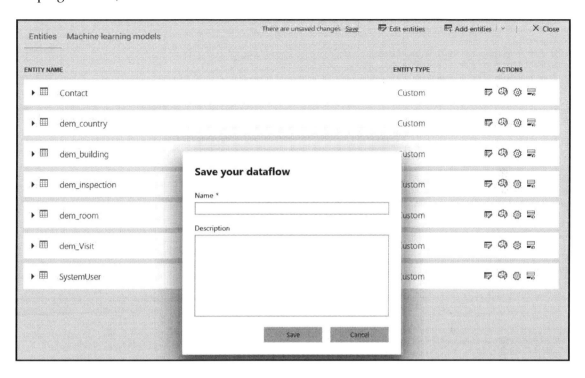

Figure 17.16 – Saving a dataflow

Dataflows, like datasets, can have scheduled runs to refresh their data. In the settings of the dataflow, you can schedule an automatic refresh and specify the time(s) when the dataflow must be run:

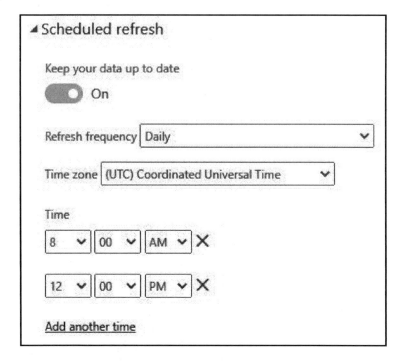

Figure 17.17 – Scheduling a dataflow run

Dataflows feed data into datasets. The advantage of dataflows is that they can be shared across many datasets. You can also enrich data by using AI and machine learning models with dataflows.

The following table summarizes the differences between datasets and dataflows:

Difference	Dataset	Dataflow
Where it's created	Power BI Desktop or the Power BI service	The Power BI service
Can create visualizations with	Yes	No
Purpose	Data modeling	**Extract, Transform, and Load (ETL)**
Share	Yes	Yes
Enrich data with machine learning	No	Yes

You are now ready to create visualizations.

Creating visualizations

Once you have created your dataset, you can add visuals to your reports. You can create reports in either Power BI Desktop or the Power BI service. To add a visual, you need to edit a report page.

There are many ways to create a visual, as follows:

- You can select a visualization and then add fields to the label and value elements.
- You can drag fields onto the report canvas and Power BI will determine the most appropriate visualization.
- You can select the appropriate fields and Power BI will select a visual based on the fields you have chosen.

The following screenshot shows a blank report page with the fields in the right-hand pane and the visualizations in the pane to the left of these fields:

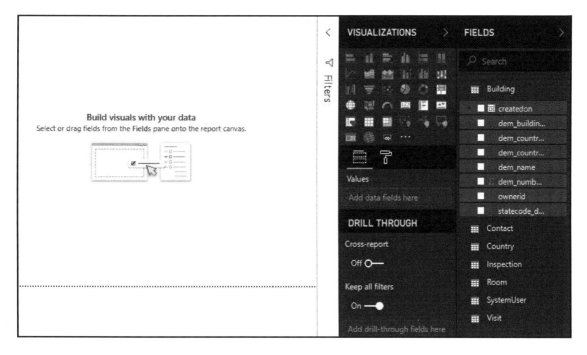

Figure 17.18 – Creating visuals on a report

There are many types of visualization available, and visuals have many properties that affect how they appear on reports. This level of detail is outside the scope of the PL-200 exam.

Reports are created once you've added visuals to your report pages.

Creating reports and dashboards

Reports are a collection of visuals that users can consume to view data. Building reports in Power BI entails choosing the visualizations that will tell the story behind the data you've acquired.

If you have created your report in Power BI Desktop, you need to publish it to the Power BI service.

Dashboards can be created in one of two ways, as follows:

- **Pin a live page**: You can pin a single page of a report as a dashboard. Pinning a page means that any changes that are made to the page are reflected on the dashboard.
- **Pin visuals**: You can pin individual visuals to a dashboard. A dashboard built in this way shows a subset of the important visuals from all the report pages.

Dashboards are created in the Power BI service.

The key difference between reports and dashboards is that a report contains multiple pages containing many visuals, whereas a dashboard is a single page containing key visuals. The following table summarizes the differences between reports and dashboards:

Feature	Report	Dashboard
Pages	One or more	One
Source	Single dataset	Can contain visuals from different reports and datasets
Filtering	Filter pane and slicers	No
Sharing	Yes	Yes
Alerts	No	Yes
Q&A	Q&A visual	Ask a question about your data
View data	Yes	No

Once you have created your reports and dashboards, you can share them with other users, including groups.

> Sharing is necessary if you wish to display Power BI visuals in Power Apps.

You can consume your Power BI dashboards and tiles in Power Apps. Note that Power BI dashboards can interact with apps and Power Automate flows. We will learn how to use Power BI with Power Apps and Power Automate in the next section.

Using Power BI with Power Platform

Power BI can interact with Power Apps and Power Automate. In this section, we will learn these Power Platform components work together.

Using Power BI with Power Apps

Power Apps has its own charting capabilities, but they are quite limited. You can create a better experience for your users by consuming Power BI visuals within Power Apps.

You can embed individual Power BI visuals in a canvas Power App. The following screenshot shows the Power BI control in a canvas app:

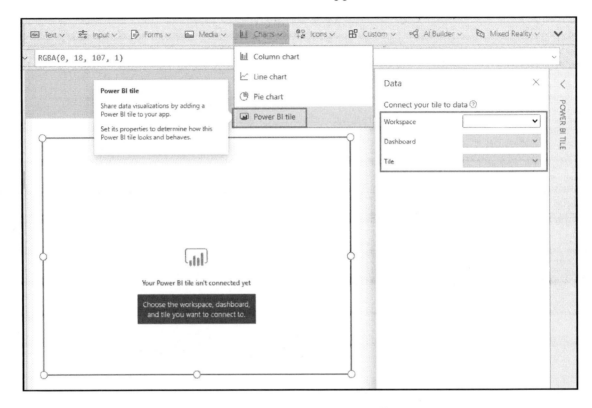

Figure 17.19 – Embedding Power BI in a canvas Power App

To add a Power BI tile to a canvas app, you must add the Power BI tile control, select the Power BI **Workspace**, choose the **Dashboard** you require, and then choose a **Tile** from that dashboard. The visual will then be displayed in the app. The following screenshot shows a tile embedded in a canvas app:

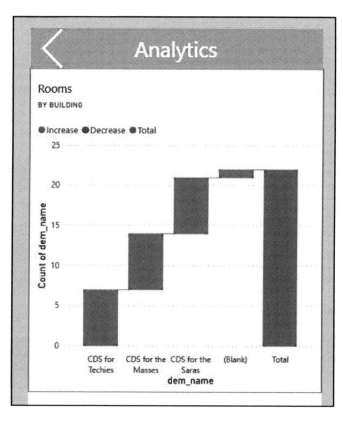

Figure 17.20 –Power BI tile displayed in a canvas Power App

You can also add Power BI to a model-driven app personal dashboard. In a model-driven app, you can add new dashboards, as shown here:

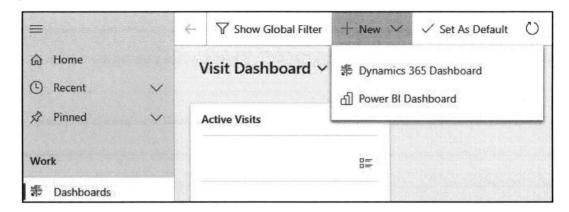

Figure 17.21 – Adding a Power BI dashboard to a model-driven app

You have two options when using Power BI in a model-driven app, as follows:

- **Power BI Dashboard**: Here, you can display an entire Power BI dashboard. You select the Power BI workspace and choose the necessary dashboard.
- **Dynamics 365 Dashboard**: Here, you can add a mixture of model-driven app charts and views. You can also add individual Power BI tiles. You select the Power BI workspace, dashboard, and tile.

The following screenshot shows the process of adding a tile from a Power BI dashboard to a model-driven app dashboard:

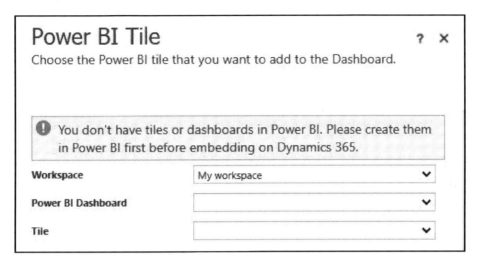

Figure 17.22 – Adding a Power BI tile to a model-driven dashboard

 You need to enable Power BI visualization embedding for your environment in **Features**, under **Settings**, in the Power Platform admin center.

The following table summarizes how you can use Power BI components in Power Apps:

Power BI component	Model-driven app	Canvas app
Dashboards	Consume	Not available
Tiles	Consume	Consume

With that, you have learned how to embed Power BI in Power Apps. You can also embed it in the opposite way by embedding Power Apps in a Power BI report. To do this, you must use an embedded canvas Power App to interact with the visuals in a Power BI dashboard. There is a Power Apps visual that, once added to a report, allows you to create a canvas app within the Power BI report.

To embed a canvas app in Power BI, perform the following steps:

1. Add the Power Apps for Power BI visual to a report page. The following screenshot shows the Power Apps for Power BI visual once it's been added to a report. The steps required to add an app will be explained shortly:

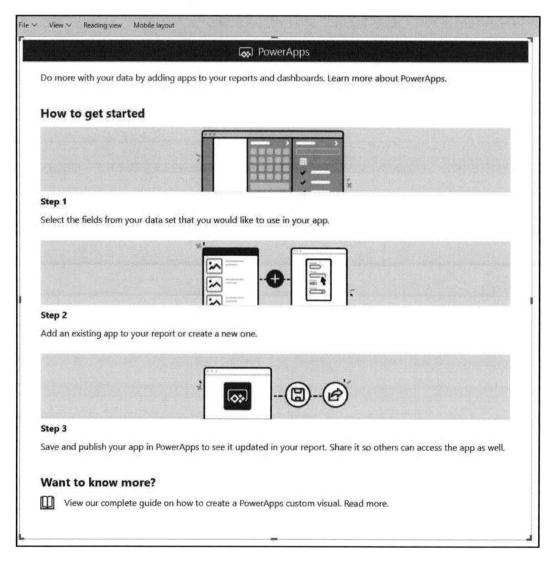

Figure 17.23– Power Apps visual – step 1

2. Next, you should add one or more fields to the data property for the visual. The visual will then prompt you to create a new app or choose an existing app:

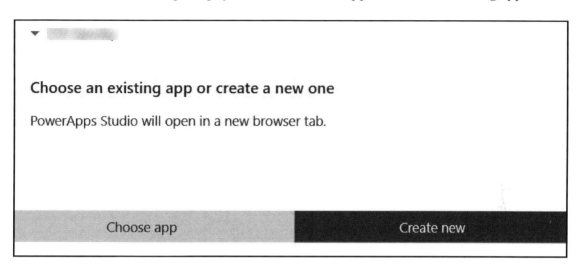

Figure 17.24 – Power Apps visual – step 2

3. Clicking **Create new** launches the Power Apps Studio, where you can create a new app. Once you have created the app, you must save, publish, and share the app so that other users can access the app in Power BI.

We can also use Power Automate with Power BI.

Using Power BI with Power Automate

Power BI can generate alerts when data exceeds the thresholds that you have defined. Alerts appear in a user's notification area and the alert can also be sent by email. You can use Power Automate to perform additional actions over and above email when an alert has been triggered.

 Alerts can only be created for visuals on dashboards.

Clicking on **Manage alerts** on a KPI, card, or gauge visual opens the **Manage alerts** pane as shown in the next image. There is a link at the bottom of the **Manage alerts** window, which, when clicked, will launch Power Automate:

Figure 17.25 – Manage alerts window

Clicking on **Use Microsoft Power Automate to trigger additional actions** will launch a Power Automate flow that uses the Power BI alert template, as shown here:

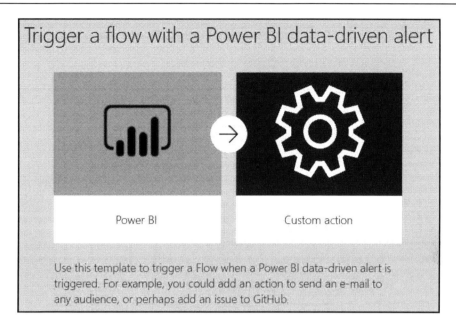

Figure 17.26 – Power BI alert template

In the flow, you can set the trigger to the alert rule you created and then use other connectors to perform any actions supported by Power Automate.

Congratulations on finishing this chapter! Power BI is a key component of Power Platform and understanding how to use Power BI to create visuals in order to provide analytics for the data you've captured is important in your role as a Power Platform functional consultant.

Summary

In this chapter, you were introduced to Power BI, how data is used to create visualizations and reports, and how to use Power BI with other components of Power Platform. You should now understand how to use dataflows, create and share dashboards, and how business process flows work with other components of Power Platform.

With that, you can now create visual representations of your data and display them in your apps.

In the next chapter, we will learn how to use AI Builder to enhance data and make predictions using the artificial intelligence capabilities of Power Platform.

Questions

Now that you've read this chapter, test your knowledge with these questions. You will find the answers to these questions under Assessments, at the end of this book:

1. Which two tools can you use to create a Power BI report?

   A) Common Data Service
   B) Power Apps Maker portal
   C) Power BI Desktop
   D) Power BI Mobile
   E) The Power BI service

2. What can trigger a Power Automate flow?

   A) A comment being added to a dashboard
   B) A Power BI dataset being refreshed
   C) A Power BI alert
   D) A Power BI workspace being shared

3. You need to share visualizations with other users. Which two components should you share?

   A) Dataset
   B) Dashboard
   C) Report
   D) Tile
   E) Workspace

4. You have created a Power BI report and dashboard containing visualizations. You add a Power BI tile to a dashboard in a model-driven app. What should you share with users so that they can see the tile?

   A) Dataset
   B) Dashboard
   C) Report
   D) Workspace

5. You create a dataflow to extract and shape data. What should you create before adding visualizations?

    A) Dataset
    B) Dashboard
    C) Report
    D) Workspace

6. What tool do you use to transform data in a dataflow?

    A) Power Automate
    B) DAX functions
    C) Power Query
    D) T-SQL

7. Which visual do you add to a Power BI report to allow users to take action from within the report and dashboard?

    A) KPI
    B) TreeMap
    C) Power Apps
    D) Scatter

Further reading

- Creating Power BI reports and dashboards with PowerApps Common Data Service: `https://powerapps.microsoft.com/blog/cdsconnectortopowerbi/`
- Power BI data sources: `https://docs.microsoft.com/power-bi/connect-data/power-bi-data-sources`
- Filtering by values in a column: `https://docs.microsoft.com/power-query/filter-values`
- Self-service data prep with dataflows: `https://docs.microsoft.com/powerapps/maker/common-data-service/self-service-data-prep-with-dataflows`
- Configuring and consuming a dataflow: `https://docs.microsoft.com/power-bi/transform-model/dataflows/dataflows-configure-consume`
- Power BI data prep with dataflows: `https://powerbi.microsoft.com/blog/introducing-power-bi-data-prep-wtih-dataflows`
- PowerApps and Power BI, together at last: `https://powerbi.microsoft.com/blog/power-bi-tile-in-powerapps/`

18
AI Builder

AI Builder is a tool within the Power Platform that allows you to add **Artificial Intelligence (AI)** to your apps and flows without needing to be a data scientist or having to write code. AI Builder supports several **Machine Learning (ML)** models that allow you to extract information from text and images to enhance your data and make predictions from your data. With AI Builder, you can gain insights from your data and enable the users of your apps to make better decisions.

This chapter describes how to create AI Builder models based on your data stored in the Common Data Service. By using AI, you can classify new data captured in your apps, and make predictions based on historical data.

The following topics will be covered in this chapter:

- Introducing AI Builder
- Building an AI Builder model
- Preparing data for a model
- Training and testing a model
- Using AI Builder models

By the end of this chapter, you will be able to create AI models, and use those models in Power Apps and Power Automate.

Introducing AI Builder

AI Builder is a component of the Power Platform solution that allows you to easily add AI to predict outcomes to help improve business performance without writing code. You do not need to understand ML or learn Python to use AI Builder. Microsoft makes it easy both to create AI models and then to consume those models in the Power Platform.

ML is a technique used to create predictive models based on relationships in data. Normally, to use ML, you need to understand the different algorithms, how the algorithms can be applied to data, and become an expert at making sure your model performs well with different data. Microsoft Azure provides many tools for AI, including AutoML, ML Designer, Azure Databricks, and Cognitive Services.

The learning curve to be able to use Azure AI tools and services is very steep. AI Builder eliminates this learning curve. AI Builder is a software-as-a-service solution that simplifies building and using ML models in business scenarios. AI Builder addresses common requirements in business applications, such as classifying data and predicting outcomes.

AI Builder lets you add AI capabilities to the flows and apps you create. You can do either of the following:

- Use one of the prebuilt AI models supplied with AI Builder.
- Build and train your own AI model using your own data.

We will first look at the several types of models you can build.

Identifying AI Builder model types

AI Builder addresses some of the common requirements for AI in business applications. You don't need to choose the correct algorithm when using AI Builder; AI Builder uses its own ML functionality to find the best algorithm for your data. You simply choose the type of model and AI Builder then creates an AI model for you.

AI Builder has five model types for prediction, vision, and language:

- **Category classification**: Performs **Natural Language Processing** (**NLP**) on text data. Category classification can be used to identify sentiment or meaning within the text. For instance, you can use category classification to determine the importance of an email message, or whether an email message is a request for action, a complaint, or just an acknowledgment.
- **Entity extraction**: Recognizes specific data in text data. Entity extraction transforms unstructured text into structured data that can be used in apps and flows. You can use entity extraction to identify terms used in your industry or organization.

- **Form processing**: Reads and extracts information from documents such as invoices and purchase orders. Many organizations process documents, re-keying information from the documents they receive. Form processing can be used with Power Automate to remove the need for manual processing of such documents.
- **Object detection**: Finds objects within images. You could use object detection within a repair scenario to identify a piece of equipment from a photograph.
- **Prediction**: Analyzes patterns in historical data to predict the outcome of new data. You can use predictions to forecast the volume of phone calls your call center will receive, or which product a customer might be interested in.

The following screenshot shows the five model types in AI Builder:

Figure 18.1 – AI Builder model types

To use these model types, you will need to provide data and train the model. AI Builder includes trained models that you can just add to your apps and flows.

Introducing AI Builder prebuilt models

AI Builder prebuilt models are ML models that Microsoft has trained with vast amounts of data to meet specific business scenarios. Data scientists at Microsoft have evaluated these models for accuracy and verified that they perform well with a vast range of disparate data. You can use these models without having to prepare data and train the models.

AI Builder has the following pre-trained models:

- **Category Classification (Preview)**: Classifies text into categories associated with customer feedback, such as compliments, issues, and pricing.
- **Entity Extraction**: Recognizes and extracts standard business objects in data, such as dates, countries, names of people, phone numbers, and email addresses.
- **Key Phrase Extraction**: Identifies the main talking points from a piece of text. You could use keyphrase extraction to find important phrases from customer feedback comments.
- **Language Detection**: Identifies the language used in a piece of text.
- **Sentiment analysis**: Detects whether the message in a piece of text has a positive or negative emotional sentiment.
- **Text translation**: Translates text from one language into another language.
- **Business Card Reader**: Extracts information from an image of a business card, including the name, email address, company, and job title.
- **Text Recognition**: Extracts words from documents and images. Text recognition uses **Optical Character Recognition (OCR)** on printed and handwritten documents.
- **Receipt Processing (preview)**: Extracts details from pictures of printed and handwritten receipts. You can use this to extract information from a photo of a receipt and add the data to your expenses system.

The following screenshot shows the prebuilt models in AI Builder:

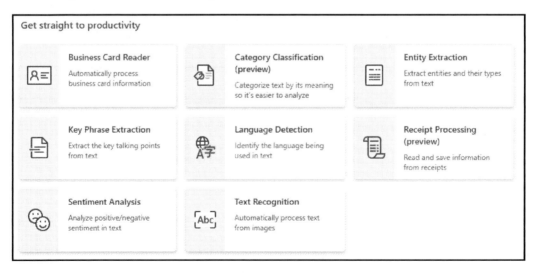

Figure 18.2 – AI Builder prebuilt models

The prebuilt models are aimed at specific business scenarios. If your scenario does not match that of the existing models, you can create your own model using one of the five model types listed in the previous section.

Building an AI Builder model

The prebuilt AI Builder models have been created to meet common business scenarios. You can build and train your own custom model in AI Builder to meet your business scenario if the models included with AI Builder do not support your needs.

You build and manage models from the Power Apps maker portal (`https://make.powerapps.com`). To view and build models, click on **AI Builder** | **Models** as shown in the following screenshot:

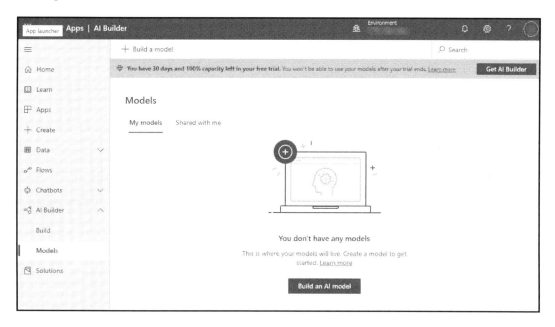

Figure 18.3 – AI Builder in the Power Apps maker portal

AI Builder requires a Common Data Service database in your environment.

A 30-day free trial of AI Builder is available. You can start your trial from the AI Builder area in the Power Apps maker portal.

To build a custom model, click on **+ Build a model** as shown at the top of *Figure 18.3* and choose the type of model from the tiles shown in *Figure 18.1*.

Each model type has slightly different steps when building a model, but they follow the same high-level process:

- Choose the model type.
- Name the model.
- Select or add examples of data or documents.
- Choose the field that you want to analyze/predict.
- Train the model.
- Publish the model.
- Share the model.

AI Builder uses a wizard to assist you in building a custom model. The following screenshot shows the wizard for the object detection model type:

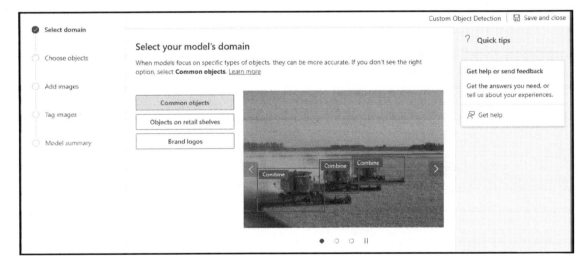

Figure 18.4 – Building a custom object detection model

The preceding screenshot shows the steps for building a model on the left-hand side of the page.

You should review the steps for each model type by creating a model for each type and stepping through the wizard. There is sample data available for each model type.

The key to building a successful model is gathering the data you will use to train and test your model.

Preparing data for a model

ML models are very dependent upon the datasets used to train and test the given model. A frequent problem in ML is overfitting. Overfitting means that the model does not generalize well from training data to unseen data, especially data that is unlike the training data. Common causes include the presence of bias in the training data, meaning the model cannot distinguish between the signal and the noise.

AI Builder implements many techniques to avoid such problems, but you will need to supply AI Builder with enough data to be able to create a model. The more data and the more varied the data, the better the model will behave.

AI Builder requires the training and test data to be stored in entities in the Common Data Service. If the data does not reside in the Common Data Service, you will need to import the data. You may need to create a custom entity for this data.

> AI Builder provides a set of examples and labs with sample data that you can use to learn how to import data and train models. The labs are available at `https://docs.microsoft.com/ai-builder/learn-ai-builder`

After building your model, you must train the model, and then evaluate the model's performance.

Training and testing a model

Before you can use your model, you must train the model. Training is the automated process by which AI Builder analyzes the data for patterns, determines the algorithm to use, and validates the model.

You train the model from the **Model summary** page. The following screenshot shows the model summary for an entity extraction model:

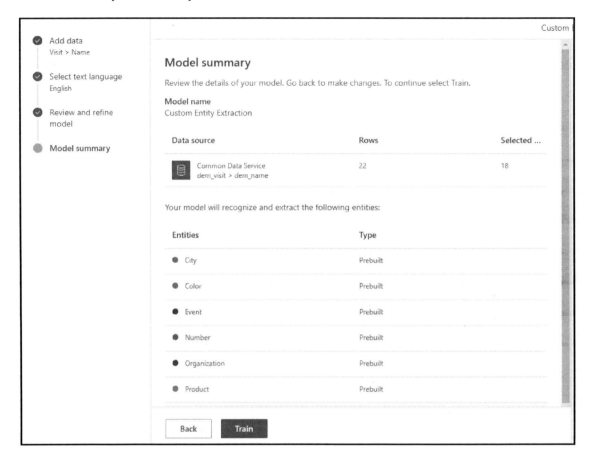

Figure 18.5 – Model summary

To train a model, click on the **Train** button.

 Training a model can take a long time. You can close the portal and view the results later.

When training is complete, you can view the details page for the model, as shown in the following screenshot for an entity extraction model:

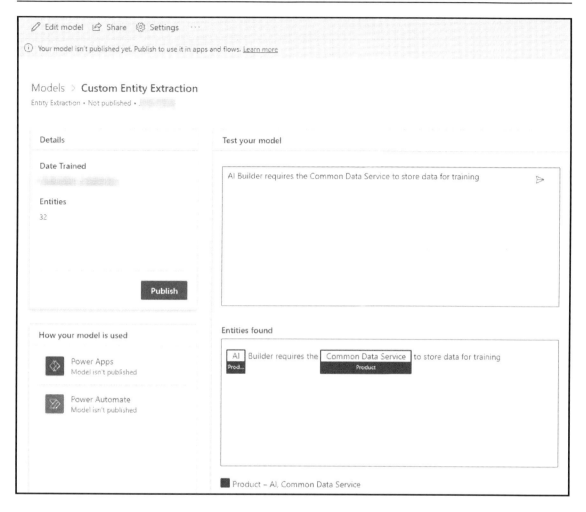

Figure 18.6 – Model details

On the model details page, you can perform your own quick tests on the model. In the previous screenshot, you can see some text entered under **Test your model.** The entity extraction model has identified two products: **AI** and **Common Data Service**.

If your model needs refinement, you can use the **Edit model** button. If you want to use the model, you must publish it first.

After you publish your AI Builder model, only you can use it in your apps and flows. To make your model available to other users, you must share your model. You share the model by clicking the **Share** button as shown at the top of *Figure 18.6*.

Using AI Builder models

AI Builder lets you add AI capabilities to the flows and apps you create. The AI models you build allow you to enhance your solutions with AI to extract data from text, recognize objects, and predict outcomes.

In this section, we will look at how you use both the prebuilt models and your custom models in the Power Platform.

Consuming a model using canvas apps

Canvas apps can use prebuilt models and custom models to enhance data. You could use an AI Builder model to analyze text that a user has entered. You can take a picture with a canvas app and use an AI Builder model to extract the text from the image or to detect objects in the image.

You can use AI Builder models in two ways:

- By adding AI Builder model controls to a screen
- By using AI Builder models through the formula bar

The following screenshot shows the AI Builder models you can add as controls to a canvas app screen:

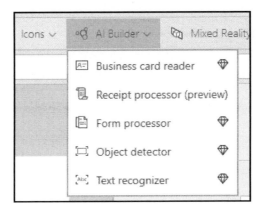

Figure 18.7 – AI Builder controls in Power Apps Studio

These controls are easy to use. The outputs from the controls can be referenced like any other canvas app control.

The following screenshot shows the screenshot from *Figure 18.7* analyzed with the **Text recognizer** control. The control has identified the text instances in the screenshot and drawn a rectangle around them, as shown in the following figure:

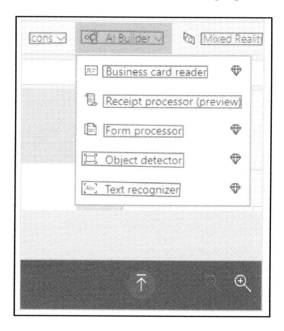

Figure 18.8 – Text recognizer control in a canvas app

The result from the text recognizer control is a list of detected lines of text. To use AI Builder models from the formula bar, use the `AIBuilder` formula, select the model, and then specify the text to analyze. The following example shows how to write a formula to find the sentiment for text entered in a `TextInput` control:

```
AIBuilder.AnalyzeSentiment(TextInput1).sentiment
```

The next screenshot shows results from several of the AI Builder formulas using the text entered in the input control at the top of the screen. The results from sentiment, language detection, category classification, and key phrase extraction models are shown:

> AI Builder requires the Common Data Service to store data for training
>
> Sentiment: neutral
>
> Language: en
>
> Categories: Documentation
>
> Key Phrases: Common Data Service
>   AI Builder
>   training

Figure 18.9 – Text AI Builder formula results in a canvas app

The following table shows where you can use custom models in canvas apps:

Model type	Control	Formula bar
Category Classification	-	Yes
Entity Extraction	-	Yes
Form Processing	Yes	-
Object Detection	Yes	-
Prediction	-	-

 The prediction model cannot be used directly in canvas apps. However, the prediction model sets a field with the prediction value. This outcome field can be displayed in a canvas app.

The following table shows where you can use prebuilt models in canvas apps:

Prebuilt model	Control	Formula bar
Category Classification	-	Yes
Entity Extraction	-	Yes
Key phrase Extraction	-	Yes
Language Detection	-	Yes
Sentiment Analysis	-	Yes

Text Translation	-	-
Business Card Reader	Yes	-
Text Recognition	Yes	-
Receipt Processing	Yes	-

 Text translation is not available with Power Apps. You can use the text translation model with Power Automate.

You can also use a limited set of AI Builder capabilities in model-driven apps.

Consuming a model using model-driven apps

Model-driven apps do not have the same capabilities as canvas apps when it comes to using AI Builder models. Only the Business Card Reader control can be used in a model-driven app.

 The business card reader is available in the Dynamics 365 Sales app, in the **Quick create** form of the **Lead** entity.

The prediction model cannot be used directly in a model-driven app. However, the prediction model sets a field with the prediction value. This outcome field can be displayed in a model-driven app.

 If you need to include AI in a model-driven app, add the AI Builder model to a canvas app and embed the canvas app in a model-driven app form.

Portal apps cannot use AI Builder models, but a data change made to the Common Data Service by a portal user could trigger a Power Automate flow that uses an AI Builder model.

You can use AI Builder with Power Automate to automatically enhance data created and updated in a model-driven app.

Consuming a model using Power Automate

Power Automate can use all the prebuilt models and any custom models in AI Builder to enhance data. You can trigger a Power Automate flow when a record is created, or an image stored. The flow can then use AI models. For example, Power Automate can categorize a new record or predict what will happen to a newly created record.

There is an AI Builder connector that you add to a flow to access the models. The AI Builder connector does not have any triggers but has actions for prebuilt as well as custom models. The following actions are available:

- Analyze positive or negative sentiment in some text.
- Classify text into categories with the standard model.
- Classify text into categories with one of your custom models.
- Detect and count objects in images.
- Detect the language being used in some text.
- Extract entities from the text with the standard model.
- Extract entities from the text with one of your custom models.
- Extract the key phrases from the text.
- Predict.
- Process and save information from forms.
- Process and save information from receipts.
- Read business card information.
- Recognize text in an image.
- Translate text into another language.

The following screenshot shows a Power Automate flow that triggers the creation of a record in the Common Data Service and then uses a custom entity extraction model as a step in the flow:

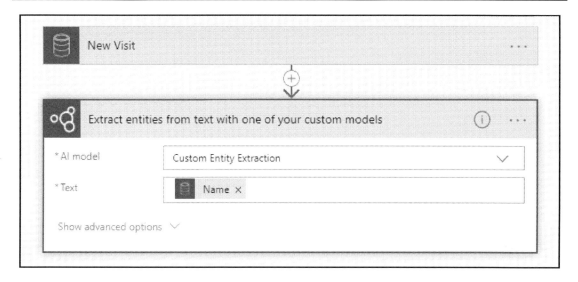

Figure 18.10 – Using an AI Builder model in Power Automate

 You can use any of the dedicated actions for each model in AI Builder, or you can use the Predict action. The Predict action allows you to dynamically choose a model using the output of a previous step in the flow.

Congratulations on finishing this chapter! Using AI with the Common Data Service is a new and exciting capability. As it's an example of new functionality, you should make sure you are familiar with the options and processes associated with AI Builder.

Summary

This chapter described the different model types and showed you how to build AI models with AI Builder.

You are now able to build AI models, and use those models in Power Apps and Power Automate. These skills enable you to enhance your data and make predictions using the models you have created.

In the next chapter, we will look at integrating the Power Platform with Microsoft 365; specifically, Microsoft Teams, Word, and Excel.

Questions

After reading this chapter, test your knowledge with these questions. You will find the answers to these questions in the Assessments chapter at the end of the book:

1. Which of the following is a model type you can use to create a custom AI Builder model?

   A) Business Card Reader
   B) Receipt Processing
   C) Sentiment Analysis
   D) Text Recognition
   E) Form Processing

2. Which AI Builder model type allows you to create a model to forecast a numerical value?

   A) Object Detection
   B) Sentiment Analysis
   C) Prediction
   D) Entity Extraction

3. You have published an AI Builder model and used it in your Power Automate flow. Other users are not able to use the model. What should you do?

   A) Publish the model.
   B) Share the model.
   C) Train the model.
   D) Edit the model.

4. Which AI Builder prebuilt model is available in Dynamics 365 Sales?

   A) Business Card Reader
   B) Receipt Processing
   C) Text Translation
   D) Text Recognition

Further reading

- **What is AI Builder?:** `https://docs.microsoft.com/ai-builder/overview`
- **AI Builder in Power Apps overview:** `https://docs.microsoft.com/ai-builder/use-in-powerapps-overview`
- **Use the business card reader component in model-driven apps:** `https://docs.microsoft.com/ai-builder/business-card-reader-component-model-driven`
- **AI Builder in Power Automate overview:** `https://docs.microsoft.com/ai-builder/use-in-flow-overview`
- **Use the predict action in Power Automate:** `https://docs.microsoft.com/ai-builder/predict-action-pwr-automate`
- **AI Builder labs:** `https://docs.microsoft.com/ai-builder/learn-ai-builder`

Microsoft 365 Integration **19**

Collaboration with Microsoft 365 services is a major feature of the Power Platform, and understanding the capabilities and how to enable these features is a significant skill required by functional consultants. Generating documents from data is often a key requirement.

In this chapter, we will look at integrating Power Apps and Power Automate with Microsoft 365, Word, and Excel.

The topics covered in this chapter are the following:

- Understanding integration with SharePoint
- Using Power Apps with Microsoft Teams
- Using Power Automate with Microsoft Teams
- Integrating Microsoft Teams with the Common Data Service
- Creating Word and Excel templates

By the end of this chapter, you will be able to add a Power App to Microsoft Teams and create templates in Word and Excel.

Understanding integration with SharePoint

Handling documents is a common requirement when creating solutions with the Power Platform. You can add documents directly to the Common Data Service or you can use SharePoint as your document store.

Model-driven apps can upload and attach files to records using Notes. There are some issues with using Notes for document management:

- Files are stored in the Common Data Service and use precious storage capacity.
- There is no capability to open an attached file, edit it, and save it back to the app – you must save it locally and upload it again.

- There are no features such as check-out/check-in.
- There is no version control.

Microsoft provides the ability to integrate the Common Data Service with SharePoint. With SharePoint integration, a document library is created for each record where the entity is enabled for Document Management.

Using SharePoint for managing documents in model-driven apps provides the following benefits:

- Enables the use of SharePoint Document Management features including check-out/check-in and versioning from within a model-driven app
- Allows collaboration with non-Power Platform and non-Dynamics 365 users
- Provides the infrastructure to support OneNote integration in model-driven apps

You can configure SharePoint integration from the Power Platform admin center.

SharePoint integration is known as *server-based integration* to distinguish it from the server-side synchronization that is used for email integration.

The setup and configuration of the SharePoint integration are out of scope for the PL-200 exam because this requires privileges to Microsoft 365 services a functional consultant will not have. If you want to learn more about SharePoint integration, there are links at the end of this chapter that you can refer to.

You will require SharePoint integration to be enabled if you want to use the collaboration features with Microsoft Teams. Microsoft Teams is an effective way of collaborating with other workers. First, we will look at using Power Apps inside of Microsoft Teams, and will then look at the collaboration options.

Using Power Apps with Microsoft Teams

Microsoft Teams is becoming a key collaboration app that is the focus of a user's daily work. To prevent the need for users to switch between applications when accessing their data, it is possible to embed Power Apps in Microsoft Team channels.

First, we will look at adding a model-driven app to a channel.

Model-driven apps with Microsoft Teams

Many organizations create teams and channels to allow users to work together on projects or to manage a particular customer. If you have a model-driven app, you can display data from the Common Data Service in Microsoft Teams. This allows users to access data where they are working and not have to switch and navigate to other applications.

You can add forms and views from a model-driven Power App to tabs in channels.

To add a record from the Common Data Service, you start from a channel in the Microsoft Teams app and click on **Add a tab**. The following page will be shown:

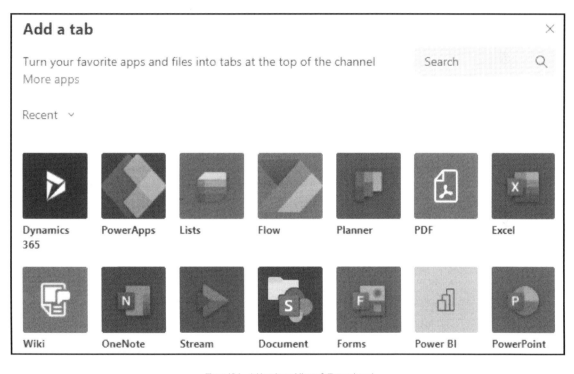

Figure 19.1 – Add a tab to a Microsoft Teams channel

You should select the **Dynamics 365** app and you will see the following page:

Figure 19.2 – Add a form

On the page shown in the preceding screenshot, you should select your environment and a model-driven app by clicking on the **pencil icon** at the top of the page. This will produce the following dialog:

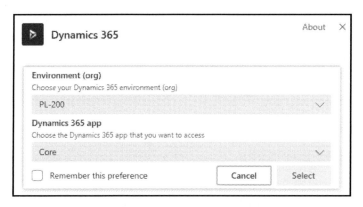

Figure 19.3 – Select an environment and model app

Only entities included in the selected model-driven app can be added as tabs in a channel.

After choosing your environment and model-driven app, you can search for the record you want to add to the channel, as shown in the following screenshot:

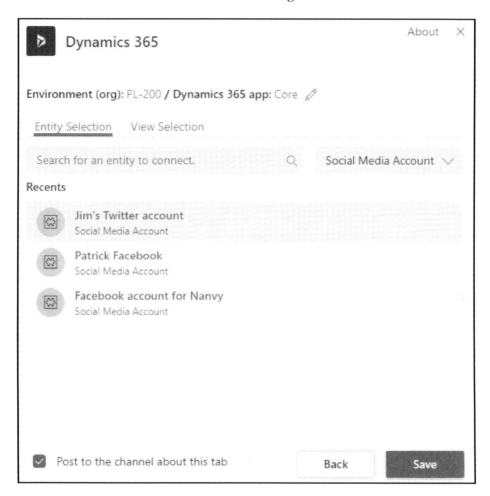

Figure 19.4 – Search for and select a Common Data Services record

After clicking on **Save**, a new tab is added to the channel showing the main form from the model-driven app, as shown in the following screenshot:

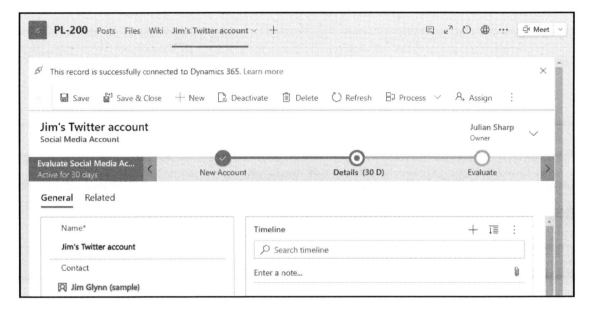

Figure 19.5 – Model-driven app form embedded as a tab

 If all you need to do is display and edit a record in a tab, you do not need to enable the integration between the Common Data Service and Microsoft Teams described later in this chapter.

You can add a view as a tab by selecting **View Selection** on the page displayed when adding the Dynamics 365 app, as shown in the next screenshot:

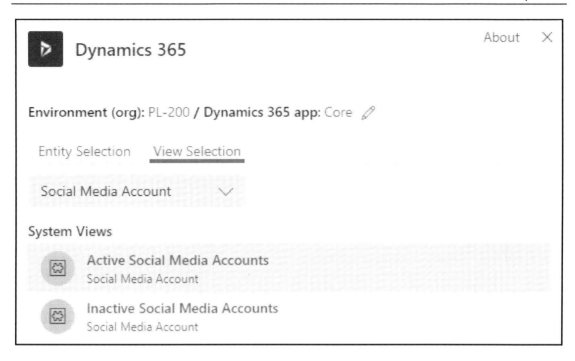

Figure 19.6 – Selecting a view

You should select the entity and view you want to use. After clicking **Save**, a new tab is added to the channel showing the main form from the model-driven app, as shown in the following screenshot:

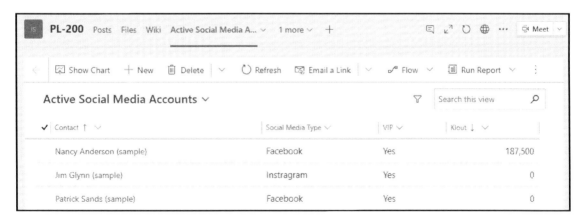

Figure 19.7 – Model-driven app view embedded as a tab

By default, only the first-party model-driven apps supplied by Microsoft can be selected. If you have a custom model-driven app, you need to enable the model-driven integration with Microsoft Teams from the settings in the Power Platform admin center, as shown in the following screenshot:

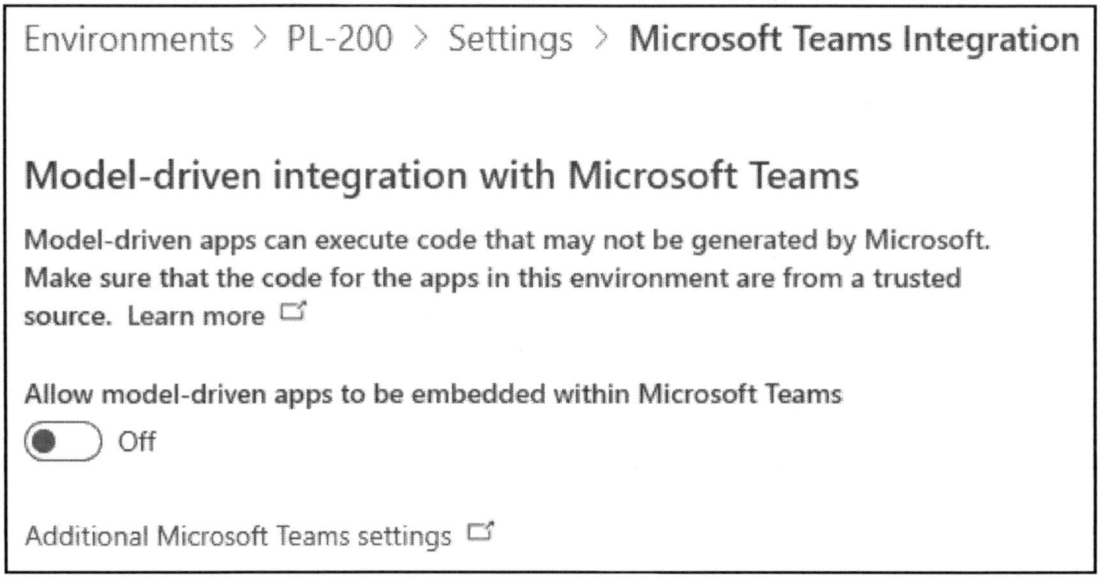

Environments > PL-200 > Settings > **Microsoft Teams Integration**

Model-driven integration with Microsoft Teams

Model-driven apps can execute code that may not be generated by Microsoft. Make sure that the code for the apps in this environment are from a trusted source. Learn more ⊡

Allow model-driven apps to be embedded within Microsoft Teams

(●) Off

Additional Microsoft Teams settings ⊡

Figure 19.8 – Allow model-driven apps to be embedded within Microsoft Teams

As well as adding the Dynamics 365 app to channels, you can add the Dynamics 365 app to Teams by clicking the ellipses on the left-hand rail (in the Teams app bar) in Teams as indicated in this screenshot:

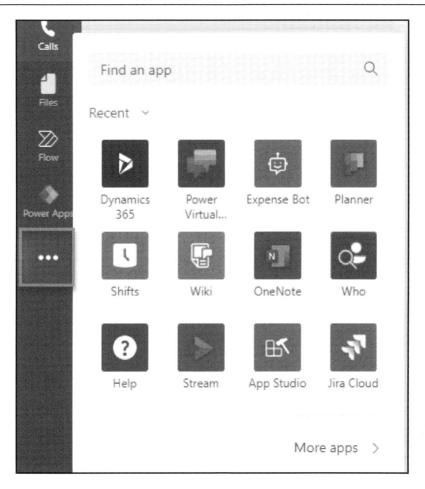

Figure 19.9 – Add a Dynamics 365 app to Microsoft Teams

This will add the model-driven app to Teams, as shown in the following screenshot:

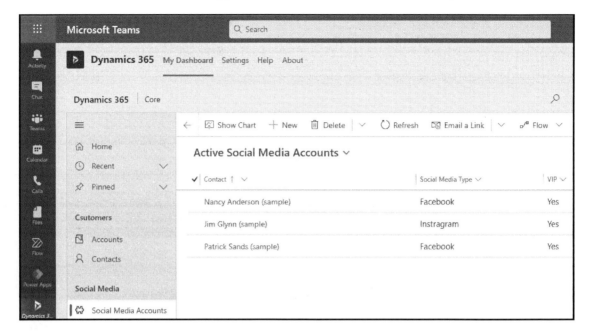

Figure 19.10 – Add a model-driven app to Microsoft Teams

The **Settings** tab allows you to change the environment and model-driven app used. You can pin the app to the navigation bar for easier access.

Displaying Common Data Service records and apps in Microsoft Teams allows users to access their data where they work. You can also embed canvas apps within Microsoft Teams.

Canvas apps with Microsoft Teams

Canvas apps can provide specific functionality to users to perform their roles. Adding a canvas app to a channel is an effective way to deploy canvas apps to users.

To embed a canvas app, you start from a channel in the Microsoft Team app and click on **Add a tab**. The following page will be shown:

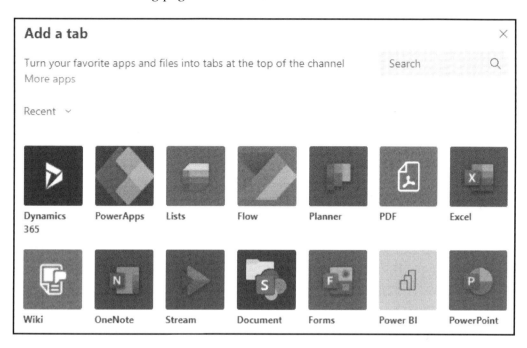

Figure 19.11 – Add a tab to a Microsoft Teams channel

You should select the **Power Apps** app and you will see the following page. You can search for the app you want to add to the channel, as shown in the following screenshot:

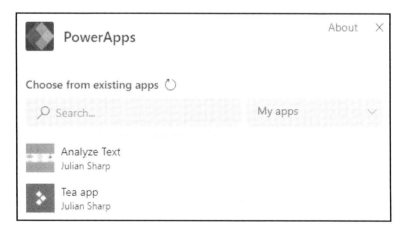

Figure 19.12 – Select a canvas app

After clicking on **Save**, a new tab is added to the channel showing the canvas app, as shown in this screenshot:

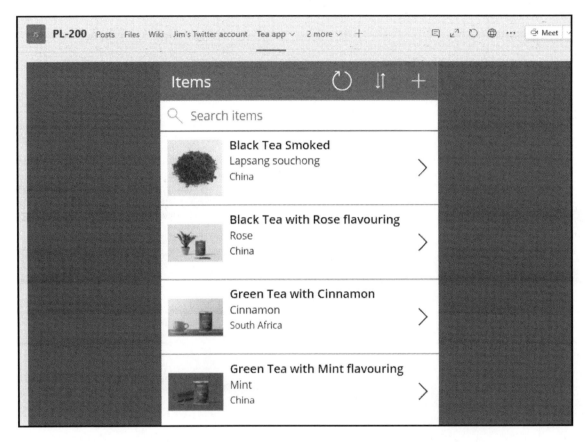

Figure 19.13 – Canvas app embedded as a tab

Only apps that you own or that have been shared with you can be added with the preceding method.

Apps deployed to Teams are also available in the Microsoft Teams mobile app. Users do not need to switch to the Power Apps mobile app to access their apps.

As well as adding a canvas app to a channel, you can add the same canvas app to Teams so it appears on the left-hand rail (the Teams app bar), as shown in the following screenshot:

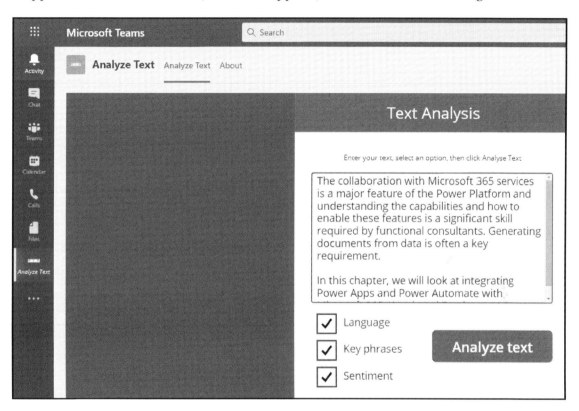

Figure 19.14 – Canvas app as a Teams app

To add a canvas app as a Teams app, you need to navigate to the maker portal and display the app's details page as shown in the following screenshot:

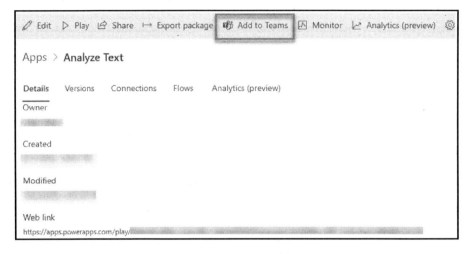

Figure 19.15 – Canvas app details page

On this page, click on the **Add to Teams** button in the toolbar and a pane will open on the right-hand side. The details page is shown in the following screenshot:

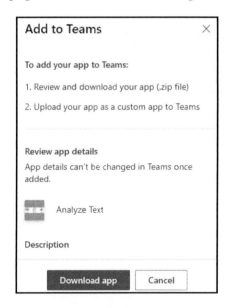

Figure 19.16 – Canvas app details page

You should download the app as a .zip file. In Microsoft Teams, you need to click on **Apps** in the bottom left-hand rail and click on the **Upload a custom app** link. Then, select the .zip file and click on **Add**.

You can upload the app as a personal app, or if you are an administrator you can upload it for your entire organization.

 To add canvas apps as a Teams app, the **Upload custom apps** option must be *enabled* by a Teams admin in the Teams app setup policies.

If you want this app to appear for all users, you need to upload the app for the organization and then, in the Teams admin portal, edit the global app setup policy and add the canvas app to the list of pinned apps:

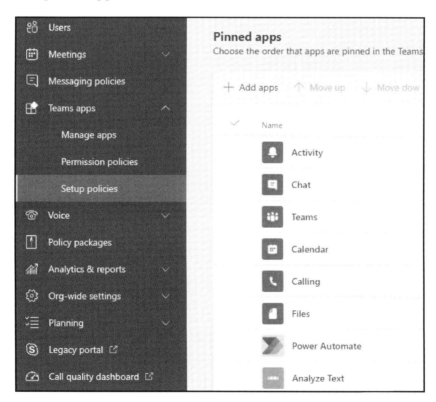

Figure 19.17 – Teams admin center – app setup policy

You can see that there are several options for displaying Power Apps within Microsoft Teams. Microsoft is working to make the use of Power Apps within Teams a lot easier with the introduction of Project Oakdale.

Project Oakdale

Project Oakdale is in public preview at the time of writing; however, it is a major innovation from Microsoft, and you need to be aware of it. Project Oakdale provides the capability to create data models and canvas apps inside of Microsoft Teams. With Project Oakdale you do not need to create an app and go through the steps to install and share the app; instead, you create an app within a team and all members of the team can access the app.

To use Project Oakdale, you need to click on **Apps** in the bottom left-hand rail, then search for and select **Power Apps**. This adds the Power Apps app to the left-hand rail, as shown in the following screenshot:

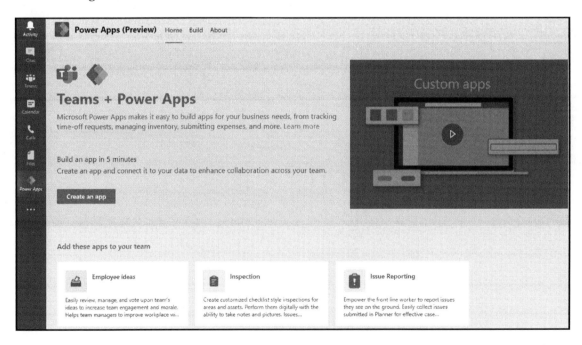

Figure 19.18 – Build Power Apps inside Teams

From this page, you can create tables to store your data and create apps. There are sample apps you can deploy for common business challenges such as inspections and issue reporting.

This ability to combine with Microsoft Teams is not limited to Power Apps; the other parts of the Power Platform can be used with Teams as well. In the next section, we will look at how you can use Power Automate with Microsoft Teams.

Using Power Automate with Microsoft Teams

If you use Power Automate flows in your organization, you can manage your flows from within Microsoft Teams. You can add the Flow app to a tab in a channel, or to the left-hand rail, as shown in the following screenshot:

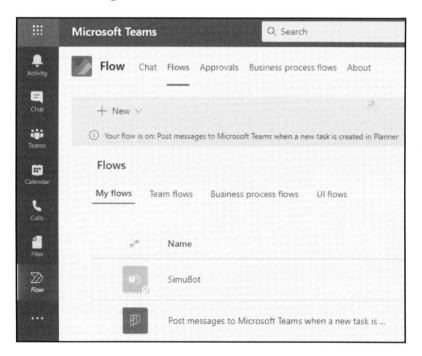

Figure 19.19 – Power Automate inside Teams

From the Flow app, you can create and monitor flows, and manage approvals.

Microsoft Teams has a connector that you can use with Power Automate. This connector has several triggers and actions that can be classified as follows:

- **Messaging**: The posting of messages to a channel
- **Team management**: Creation of teams and channels and management of their memberships

Common scenarios for using Power Automate with the Teams connector include the following:

- Setting up automated replies to messages posted to a channel
- Posting messages to a channel when a task has been added to Planner
- Creating a channel when a record is created in the Common Data Service

We have learned so far about embedding apps within Microsoft Teams. There is a further level of integration between the Common Data Service and Microsoft Teams. This integration concerns the synchronization of files.

Integrating Microsoft Teams with the Common Data Service

The integration between Microsoft Teams and the Common Data Service shares documents between the Common Data Service record and the Microsoft Teams channel:

- Documents show in the **Files** tab in Microsoft Teams.
- Documents show under **Documents** in the model-driven app.

The integration between the Common Data Service and Microsoft Teams is disabled by default. You have two options for integrating with Microsoft Teams:

- **Basic**: Configuration must be performed in Microsoft Teams.
- **Enhanced**: Configuration is driven by a wizard in the model-driven app.

The following screenshot shows the options to enable Microsoft Teams integration in the system settings:

Figure 19.20 – Microsoft Teams integration settings

 If Microsoft Teams integration is not enabled, users can still add a Common Data Service record to a Teams channel, but the common file functionality is not enabled. All the user will be able to do is view and update the record.

There are different privileges required to enable the two options:

- **Basic**: Configuration must be performed by a user with the **System Administrator** role in the Common Data Service environment.
- **Enhanced**: Configuration must be performed by a user with the **Global Administrator** role in the Office 365 tenant.

Upon enabling the **Basic Teams integration**, a **Collaborate** button is added to the model-driven app's forms. The **Collaborate** button does not actually make any changes; instead, it tells the user to open Microsoft Teams and add the Dynamics 365 app to a channel and select a record.

Enabling the **Enhanced Teams integration** can only be performed after the **Basic Teams integration** has been enabled. Similarly, enabling the enhanced integration adds the **Collaborate** button to model-drivel record forms and views. Clicking on the **Collaborate** button starts a wizard that connects the Common Data Service record to a Microsoft Teams channel.

The final part of integrating with Microsoft 365 is using Word and Excel templates to generate output using data stored in Common Data Service entities.

Creating Word and Excel templates

Most systems require formatted output generated from data. You could use the Export to Excel feature to extract data and then format it externally, but often the formatted output needs to be generated regularly. The Common Data Service has templates that can be used to generate formatted output. These templates can be used with the automation capabilities of the Power Platform and the Common Data Service.

There are three types of template that can be used to create formatted output using data in the Common Data Service:

- Email
- Excel
- Word

First, we will look at using email templates to send emails containing data held in the Common Data Service.

Email templates

Email templates can be used manually by a user when creating an email in a model-driven app, or automatically with a classic workflow. You can also use email templates using the campaign functionality in Dynamics 365 Sales.

The email templates are managed from **Templates** under **Advanced Settings**, as shown in the following screenshot:

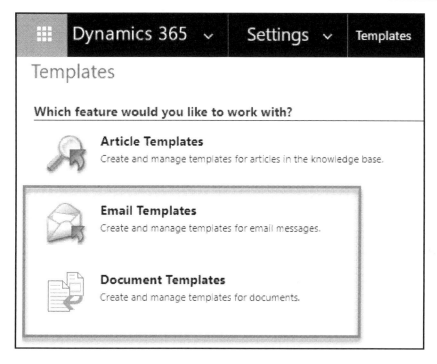

Figure 19.21 – Templates

There are several email templates supplied by Microsoft for automatic notifications about import data jobs and bulk delete jobs. The Dynamics 365 Sales and Dynamics 365 Customer Service apps include some email templates.

You can create personal email templates or organizational templates. A personal email template is created from personal options. A personal email template can be converted to an organizational template. An organizational template can be reverted back to a personal template.

Email templates have many limitations, including the following:

- A limited choice of fonts and other formatting options
- Cannot edit the HTML
- No spell checker
- Cannot embed images
- Can only be created for accounts, contacts, opportunities, leads, quotes, orders, invoices, and cases
- Cannot change the entity once saved

When you select a record type for an email template, you can add in fields from that entity, and from the user who is the owner of the record, using the **Insert/Update** button in the command bar. The next screenshot shows using fields on an email template for a contact:

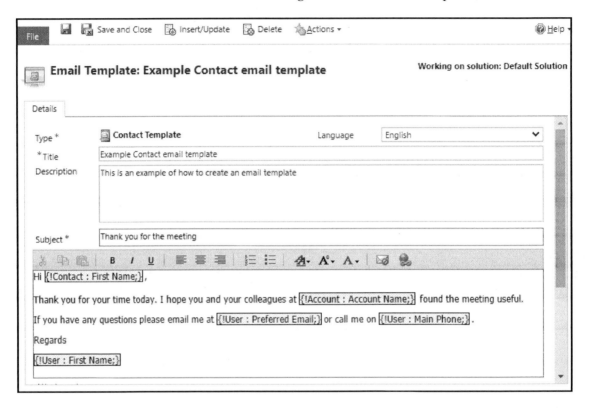

Figure 19.22 – Email templates

You can also create an email template for the Global record type. This means the email is not linked to an entity, but can instead be used with any entity. However, a global email template cannot access any fields except for the record owner.

Email templates can however be included in a solution and migrated through environments as part of application life cycle management. Email templates operate on one record at a time. If you want to process a set of records, then Excel templates are a better choice.

Excel templates

Excel templates are used to produce lists and charts from data held in the Common Data Service. They are used with a list of records in a view.

You can create an Excel template from any view. In the following screenshot, you can see the options you get when you click the **Excel Templates** button:

Figure 19.23 – Excel templates

To create a new template, click on **Download Template** and the following window will appear:

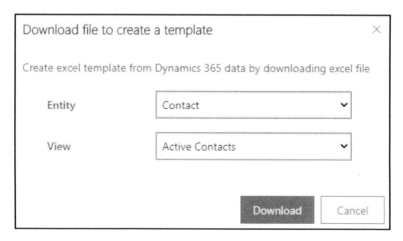

Figure 19.24 – Download an Excel template

You select the entity and view you want to use, and an Excel document will be downloaded to your computer. You can then edit the Excel document, where you will have full formatting, formulas, and charting available.

 You are limited to fields in the view. You can add fields to the Excel document from the entity, and from any entity in a many-to-one relationship with the entity you have selected.

Once you have created your Excel document, upload it by clicking on **Excel Templates**, selecting **Upload Template**, and browsing to your Excel document. It will then be available for selection:

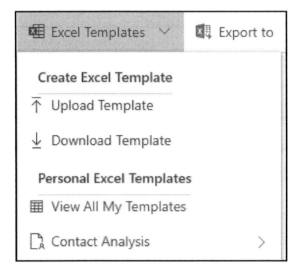

Figure 19.25 – Excel templates

You can open the Excel template in either the Excel desktop app, or by using Excel Online, as shown in the next screenshot:

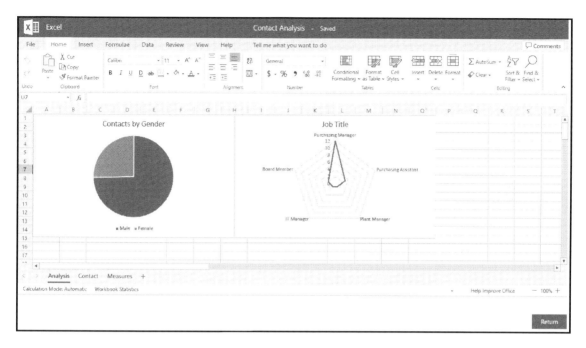

Figure 19.26 – Excel template in Excel Online

Excel templates cannot be added to a solution. You cannot move templates between environments with the functionality provided by Microsoft. A tool in XrmToolBox can move Excel templates between environments.

Excel templates are useful for lists of data you want to show in charts, but if you need a more formal document, Word templates are a better choice.

Word templates

Unlike Excel templates, Word templates can include data from other entities. Word templates are based on a single record but can include records from other entities that are related to it. You can include many-to-one, one-to-many, and many-to-many relationships.

The following screenshot shows how to download a Word template from within a model-driven app form:

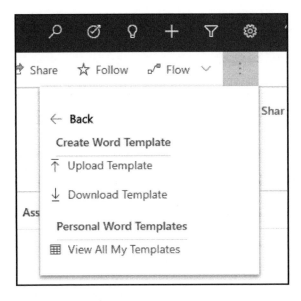

Figure 19.27 – Create a Word template

Clicking on **Download Template** will display the following screen, where you can select the relationships that you want to include in your Word template:

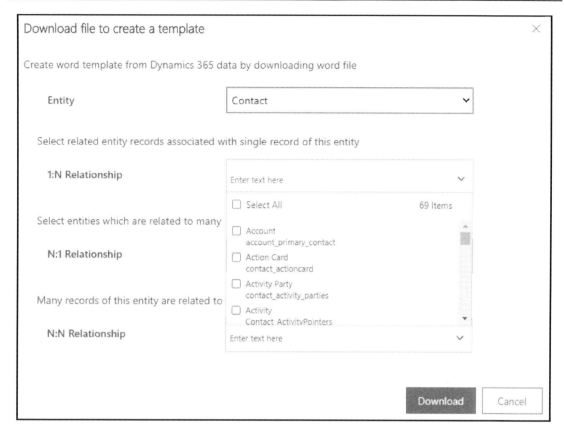

Figure 19.28 – Download the Word template

You select the relationships you want to use, and a Word document will be downloaded to your computer. You can edit the Word document, where you will have full formatting available.

There are some steps you need to undertake to be able to use the Common Data Service fields and add them to the template. You need to do the following:

1. Enable the **Developer** tab in Word.
2. Show the **XML** pane.
3. Select **CRM schema**.
4. Add fields as plain text.

First, you must add the **Developer** tab to Word. To do this, open Word, and in the **File & Options** menu, click on **Customize Ribbon** and enable the **Developer** tab as shown in the following screenshot:

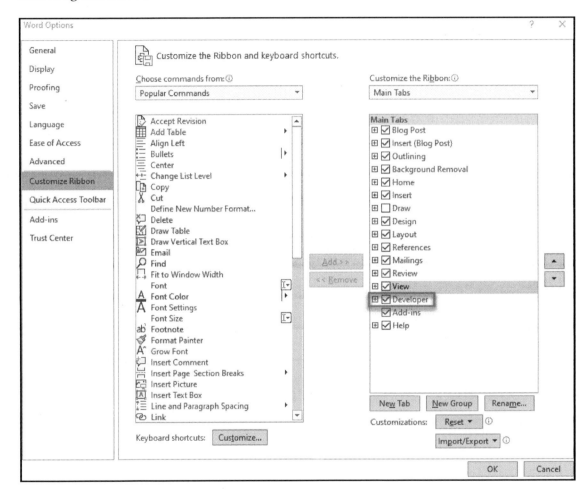

Figure 19.29 – Add the Developer tab to Word

When you open the Word template, you need to expose the CRM schema and fields. You need to do the following:

1. Select the **Developer** tab.
2. Click on the **XML Mapping Pane** tile.
3. This will open the pane on the right-hand side of the Word window. Then you need to select the schema for CRM from the drop-down list.
   When you have done all of this, you will be able to see all the fields for the entity, as shown in the following screenshot:

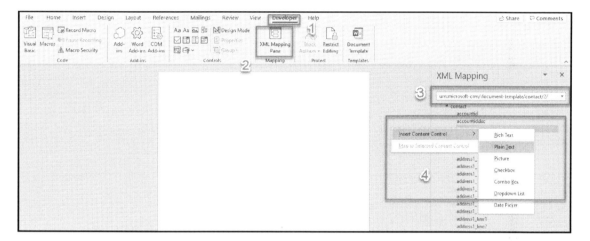

Figure 19.30 – Adding fields to a Word template

4. To add a field, right-click on the field in the XML page, select Insert Content Control, and choose Plain Text.

 Inserting any control other than **Picture** or **Plain Text** will cause Word to throw an error.

Once you have finished editing, you can upload the template and it will then be available for use by clicking on the **Word Template** button. You can also generate documents from a Word template using the `SetDocumentTemplate` action either in Workflow or in a Power Automate flow. With Dynamics 365 Sales, there is the functionality to generate and email quotes formatted as PDFs using Word templates.

Word templates cannot be added to a solution. You cannot move templates between environments with the functionality provided by Microsoft. A tool in XrmToolBox can move Word templates between environments.

Users can create and upload templates, but templates need to be made available to the users who need them. Next, we will look at the security aspects of templates.

Controlling access to templates

You use security roles to control the creating and editing of personal and organizational templates. Word and Excel templates share the same security privileges, as shown in the following screenshot:

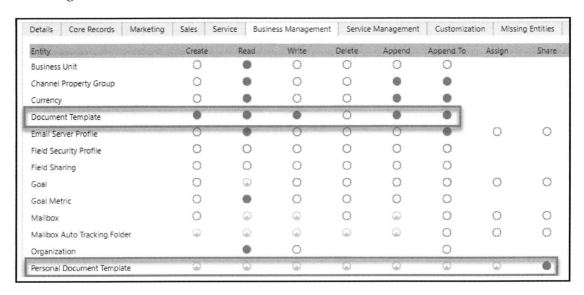

Details	Core Records	Marketing	Sales	Service	Business Management	Service Management	Customization	Missing Entities		
Entity	Create	Read	Write	Delete	Append	Append To	Assign	Share
Business Unit	○	●	○	○	○	○		
Channel Property Group	○	●	○	○	●	●		
Currency	○	●	○	○	●	●		
Document Template	●	●	●	○	●	●		
Email Server Profile	○	●	○	○	○	●	○	○
Field Security Profile	○	○	○	○	○	○		
Field Sharing	○	○	○	○	○	○		
Goal	○	◔	○	○	○	○	○	○
Goal Metric	○	●	○	○	○	○		
Mailbox	○	◔	◔	○	◔	○	○	○
Mailbox Auto Tracking Folder	◔	◔	◔	◔	◔	○	○	○
Organization		●	○			○		
Personal Document Template	◔	◔	◔	◔	◔	◔	◔	●

Figure 19.31 – Document Template security privileges

If you upload a document template from within a view in a model-driven app, the template will be a personal template. You can share a personal document template with users and teams.

If you upload a document template into the **Document** settings under **Advanced Settings**, the template will be an organizational template:

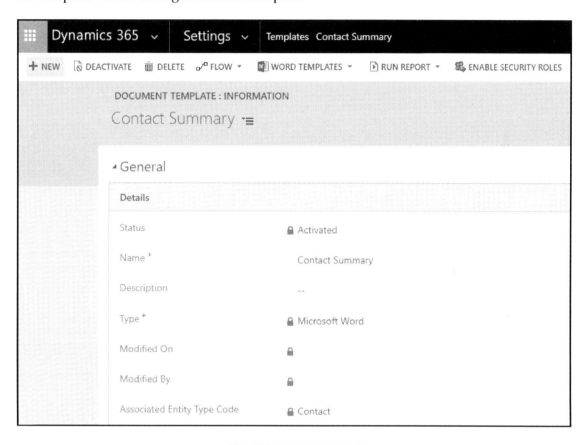

Figure 19.32 – Document template record

By default, the template will be available to all users, but you can restrict a document template to users with specific roles by clicking on **ENABLE SECURITY ROLES** in the command bar and selecting the relevant roles, as shown in the following screenshot:

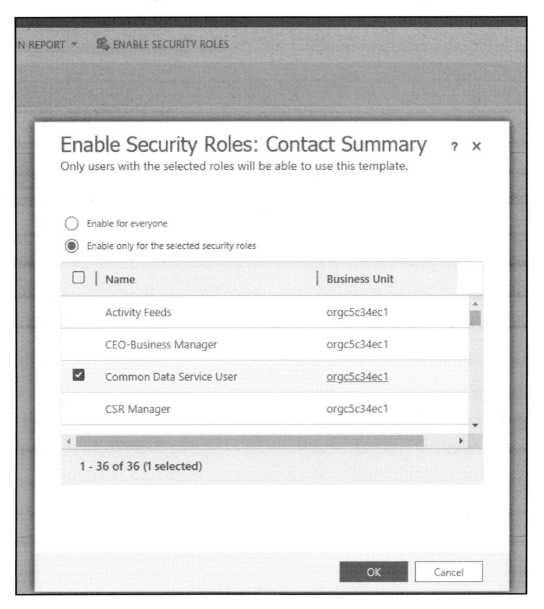

Figure 19.33 – Enable security roles for a document template

Email templates have separate security privileges to Word and Excel templates, as shown in this screenshot:

Figure 19.34 – Security privileges for email templates

Unlike document templates, email templates can't be restricted by security roles.

The following table provides a quick summary of the differences between email, Word, and Excel templates:

Email	Word	Excel
Solution-aware	Not solution-aware.	Not solution-aware.
Account, Contact, Lead, Opportunity, Quote, Order, Invoice, Case, User, or Global	All entities.	All entities.
Single record	Single record with related records (1:N, N:N, N:1 relationships).	A view of records.
Limited formatting	Full formatting.	Full formatting.
Create in classic workflow	Action to generate in classic workflow and flow.	Manual only.
Personal and organizational	Personal and organizational.	Personal and organizational.
Security for email templates	Security for document templates.	Security for document templates.
No individual template security	Templates can be linked to roles.	Templates can be linked to roles.
No PDFs	PDFs for Quote and other sales entities.	No PDFs.

As we have now seen, the Common Data Service, Power Platform, and Microsoft Teams provide a powerful combination of tools and services that can be used to create collaborative experiences for users.

Summary

In this chapter, we learned about the different options for collaborating using the services in Microsoft 365.

You should now understand the integration points between the Common Data Service and Microsoft 365. You will now be able to deploy your apps in Microsoft Teams and can generate documents using Word and Excel templates.

By using the skills you have learned in this chapter, you will be able to create apps that are accessible wherever the user works, and users will be able to share information more easily.

In the next chapter, we will look at the tools and processes around moving changes from development through testing to the production environment using solutions.

Questions

After reading this chapter, test your knowledge with these questions. You will find the answers to these questions in the Assessments chapter at the end of the book:

1. You are a Power Platform Functional Consultant. You use templates within your model-driven app. You need to transport templates between environments. Which template can be included in a solution?

   A) Data maps
   B) Email templates
   C) Excel templates
   D) Templates for data import
   E) Word templates

2. You are a functional consultant. You need to create a Word template that is only accessible by a subset of users. Your solution: create an organizational template and assign a security role to the template. Does this solution meet the goal?

   A) Yes
   B) No

3. You are a functional consultant. You need to create a Word template that is only accessible by a subset of users. Your solution: create a personal template and share it with a team. Does this solution meet the goal?

    A) Yes
    B) No

4. You are a functional consultant. You need to create a Word template that is only accessible by a subset of users. Your solution: in the security role settings, set all privileges for article templates. Does this solution meet the goal?

    A) Yes
    B) No

5. You need to configure the integration with Microsoft Teams. What must you configure before you can configure Microsoft Teams?

    A) Server-side synchronization
    B) OneDrive for Business
    C) Server-based integration
    D) Office 365 Groups connector

6. You need to create a Word template. What should you do?

    A) Install Dynamics 365 for Outlook.
    B) Install the Office Data Connector add-in.
    C) Enable the Developer tab.
    D) Install the Open XML SDK.

7. You need to add a canvas app to the left-hand rail in Microsoft Teams for all users. What should you do?

    A) Share the app with all Team members.
    B) Edit the Teams global app setup policy.
    C) Enable the embedding of model-driven apps within Microsoft Teams.
    D) Enable enhanced Teams integration.

8. From which two places can you run a canvas app in Microsoft Teams?

    A) A team
    B) A channel
    C) The Teams app bar
    D) The Teams admin portal

9. What can you do with Power Automate in Microsoft Teams?

    A) Pin an app to the Teams app bar.
    B) Add a model-driven app as a tab in a channel.
    C) Remove a member from a team.
    D) Create a channel.

Further reading

For more details on the topics covered in this chapter, please refer to the following resources:

- Set up model-driven apps in Dynamics 365 to use SharePoint Online: `https://docs.microsoft.com/power-platform/admin/set-up-dynamics-365-online-to-use-sharepoint-online`
- Enable OneDrive for Business (online): `https://docs.microsoft.com/power-platform/admin/enable-onedrive-for-business`
- Set up OneNote integration: `https://docs.microsoft.com/power-platform/admin/set-up-onenote-integration-in-dynamics-365`
- Deploy Microsoft 365 groups Dynamics 365 (online): `https://docs.microsoft.com/power-platform/admin/deploy-office-365-groups`
- Use the personal dashboard: `https://docs.microsoft.com/dynamics365/teams-integration/teams-personal-use`
- Embed a canvas app as tab app in Teams: `https://docs.microsoft.com/powerapps/teams/embed-teams-tab`
- Embed a canvas app as personal app in Teams: `https://docs.microsoft.com/powerapps/teams/embed-teams-app`
- Create apps in Microsoft Teams by using Power Apps: `https://docs.microsoft.com/powerapps/teams/create-apps-overview`
- Manage app setup policies in Microsoft Teams: `https://docs.microsoft.com/microsoftteams/teams-app-setup-policies`
- Manage your apps in the Microsoft Teams admin center: `https://docs.microsoft.com/MicrosoftTeams/manage-apps`
- Microsoft Teams integration: `https://docs.microsoft.com/power-platform/admin/about-teams-environment#microsoft-teams-integration`

- Microsoft Teams integration with customer engagement apps in Dynamics 365: `https://docs.microsoft.com/dynamics365/teams-integration/teams-integration`
- Install and set up Microsoft Teams integration: `https://docs.microsoft.com/dynamics365/teams-integration/teams-install-app`
- Difference between the Basic and Enhanced Collaboration Experiences with Microsoft Teams: `https://docs.microsoft.com/dynamics365/teams-integration/teams-basic-vs-enhanced-collaboration`
- The Microsoft Teams connector: `https://docs.microsoft.com/connectors/teams/`
- Analyze and share your data with Excel templates: `https://docs.microsoft.com/power-platform/admin/analyze-your-data-with-excel-templates`
- Use Word templates to create standardized documents: `https://docs.microsoft.com/power-platform/admin/using-word-templates-dynamics-365`
- Create templates for email: `https://docs.microsoft.com/power-platform/admin/create-templates-email`

20
Application Life Cycle Management

The customizations you make in Power Platform will need to be deployed from your development environment to your test and production environments. Solutions are the containers for your customizations and allow you to manage the application life cycle changes that you make to your Power Platform systems.

In this chapter, we will cover the activities that a functional consultant performs when deploying solutions. We will then learn about the differences between unmanaged and managed solutions. We'll also learn how to move solutions from one environment to another by using a release life cycle.

In this chapter, we will cover the following topics:

- Working with solutions
- Exporting and importing solutions
- Cloning solutions and patches

By the end of this chapter, you will understand how to use and distribute solutions so that you can manage the customization changes you make from one environment to another. Solutions are the basis for managing your application life cycle management processes.

Working with solutions

You were introduced to solutions in Chapter 3, *Data Modeling*, where we covered using containers to manage the changes we make to components and how we can deploy these changes. Microsoft provides Dynamics 365 apps as solutions. Third-party software vendors (ISVs) provide their products as solutions.

You can work with the following types of solutions:

- **Default**: Contains all the components in your Common Data Service environment.
- **Common Data Service default:** An empty solution. This is used if you customize the data model outside of a solution in the Maker portal.
- **Custom:** A solution you create that holds your customizations.

You can add components to solutions and create components in solutions. So far, the solutions you have created and used are unmanaged solutions. Unmanaged means you can change the components in the solution.

Working with unmanaged solutions

Any solution that you manually create is an unmanaged solution. You can edit, add, and create new components in unmanaged solutions.

There is an especially important concept to understand surrounding unmanaged solutions that is crucial if you wish to understand how solutions work: when you add an existing component to an unmanaged solution, the component is not copied. Instead, a reference is made in the unmanaged solution to the component in the default solution.

In the following diagram, you can see that there are several components in the Default solution. A new solution, *Solution A*, has been created and adds one of the existing components, **Component X**, to the solution. *Solution A* now references **Component X** in the Default solution:

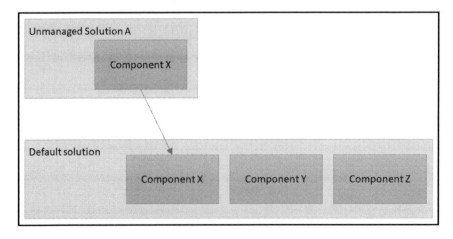

Figure 20.1 – Solution components

If you create a new component in an unmanaged solution, this component is actually created in the Default solution, and in the unmanaged solution, a reference is added to the component in the default solution.

 An unmanaged solution is, effectively, a container for the components that you have added to, and created in, the solution. Your solution only contains references to these components, not copies of them.

There are several operations you can perform on components in a solution. These are as follows:

- If you *edit* a component in an unmanaged solution, then that change is made to the component in the Default solution. You will see the change to the component in your own solution, as well as in the Default solution.
- If you *remove* a component from an unmanaged solution, it simply removes the reference to the component in the Default solution. Any changes you made to the component prior to removing it will be kept in the component in the Default solution.
- If you *delete a component from an unmanaged solution*, two actions are performed. First, the reference to the component in the Default solution is removed, and then the component is deleted from the Default solution. No checks are made if the component is in another solution.
- If you *delete an unmanaged solution*, this removes all the references to the components in the Default solution and then deletes the solution record. All the changes that you made to the components in your solution remain in the Default solution.

The implication surrounding the way unmanaged solutions work is that you need to manage the changes that you make to components carefully if you have multiple people customizing multiple solutions in the same environment.

Working with multiple solutions

Consider a scenario where there are two unmanaged solutions in an environment, both containing the same component. There is just one version of the component, but both unmanaged solutions are referencing the same version.

If that component is changed in one of the solutions, because the change is actually being made to the Default solution, viewing the component in the other solution will allow you to see the changes that were made to the first solution.

Check out the following diagram. **Component X** has been added to both *Solution A* and *Solution B*. Due to this, any changes that are made to **Component X** in *Solution A* are visible from *Solution B* and vice versa:

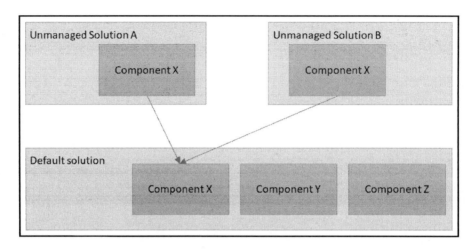

Figure 20.2 – Component in multiple solutions

This situation can lead to the risk of changes being made to one solution being accidentally released by another solution before they have been completed and tested.

There are several approaches you can take to reduce this risk:

- Provide each developer with their own environment. Developers will export and merge their changes to a staging environment.
- Schedule the development work so that there are no conflicts between components.
- Use the Solution Packager tool, export and extract the solution, and store exported components in your code control system.
- Implement Azure DevOps with Build and Release pipelines.

 One way of reducing the risk of accidentally including components that someone else has changed is to include just the components you are changing in your solution.

Adding only the components you need is known as using segmented solutions.

Using segmented solutions

A Common Data Service entity contains not just the entity definition, but also the required fields, views, forms, relationships, business rules, and charts. The fields and forms and so on are sub-components and belong to the entity.

In earlier versions of Dynamics 365, adding an entity included all the sub-components in your solution. You couldn't have a solution just containing the individual sub-component you needed to change. Because of the way unmanaged solutions work, it was easy to accidentally release changes that had been made to other sub-components by other users.

In the Power Platform, you can create a solution that only contains the selected sub-components of an entity. This reduces the risk of accidentally including changes that have been made in another solution.

When you add an existing entity to a solution, you will be presented with a page similar to the following:

← **Selected entities**

Select components to your selected entities.

1 entities will be added to your project

Account

1 forms, 1 fields selected

Select components

☐ Include all components   ☐ Include entity metadata

Figure 20.3 – Adding an entity to an existing solution

In the preceding screenshot, you can see that you have two choices: you can click on **Include all components**, to include all your components, or click on **Select components**, to only add a subset of your components. Clicking on **Select components** allows you to choose individual components, such as fields, forms, relationships, and views. Once you've done this, you can click on **Add**. Once you have chosen all the components, click on **Add** again. This will include only the components you have selected in your solution.

> You should only use **Include all components** when you are including a new custom entity in your solution.

The **Include entity metadata** option does not add components but includes properties of the entity, such as auditing, duplicate detection, and change tracking.

You can control how changes are made to components with a properly controlled life cycle management process. One way you can restrict what someone can customize is by using managed solutions.

Using managed solutions

A managed solution can be created by importing a solution that has already been exported. Its package type must be set to **Managed**.

To create a managed solution, click on the **Export** button in any solution. Then, in the **Export as** column, select **Managed**, as shown in the following screenshot:

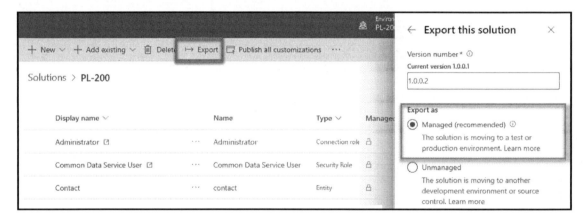

Figure 20.4 – Exporting a managed solution

Managed solutions are used to distribute customizations. Managed solutions allow the developer to control what happens to the solution once it has been deployed and can help protect the developer's intellectual property.

Once you've imported a managed solution, the following rules apply:

- You cannot add components to the solution.
- You cannot remove components from the solution.
- You cannot delete components from the solution.
- You cannot edit the solution record.
- You cannot export the solution.

 You cannot convert an unmanaged solution into a managed solution; you can create a managed solution by exporting an unmanaged solution and selecting the managed solution as the package type. Once it's been imported into another environment, the solution will be managed.

If you delete a managed solution, all the components of the solution will be deleted; any data inside the custom entities of the solution will be deleted, along with any related activities and notes. Any custom fields for other entities will also be deleted and their data will be lost.

 One way you can think about unmanaged versus managed is that providing an unmanaged solution is like providing the source code that can be used and recompiled in any way, whereas providing a managed solution is like providing an installer program that can be configured within the limitations set by the developer, or just uninstalled.

However, you can add components contained in the managed solution to an unmanaged solution, and depending on the managed properties set by the managed solution's developer, you can change those components.

Using managed properties

By using managed properties, the developer of a managed solution can control whether a solution component can be customized once it has been imported. The developer of the solution can restrict the level of change that can be made to the component in the target environment.

You can set managed properties when you're editing a component from the Solutions Explorer, as shown in the following screenshot:

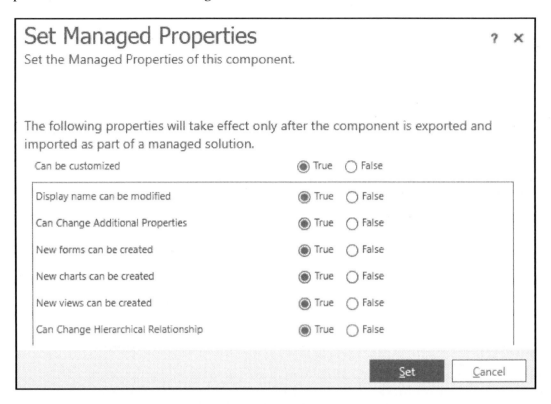

Figure 20.5 – Managed properties for an entity

Here, we can see the managed properties for an entity. The following screenshot shows the managed properties for a field that contains fewer properties that can be restricted:

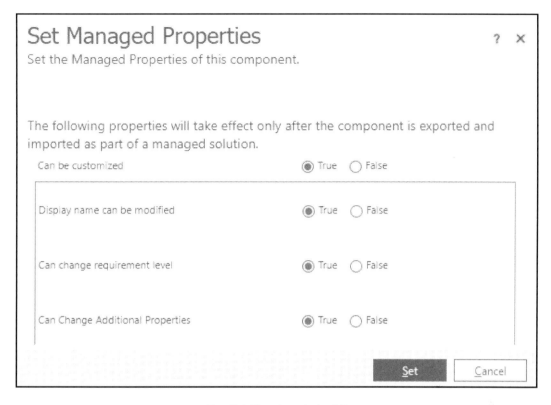

Figure 20.6 – Managed properties for a field

A developer would set a property to *false* to prevent that setting from being edited once it's been imported. For example, a developer might have some processing that is dependent on a field that they have set to `Business required`. The developer does not want the field to be changed to optional as this might cause the processing to fail, so the development team would set the **Can change requirement level** property, as shown in the previous screenshot, to `False`.

Once you have completed your customizations and set your managed properties, you can export your solution. But before you export your solution, you should check for any potential issues within your solution.

Using the Solution checker

The Solution checker tool can be run at any time on your solution from within the Maker portal.

To run the checker, select your solution in the Maker portal and click on **Solution checker** in the toolbar. Then, select **Run**, as shown in the following screenshot:

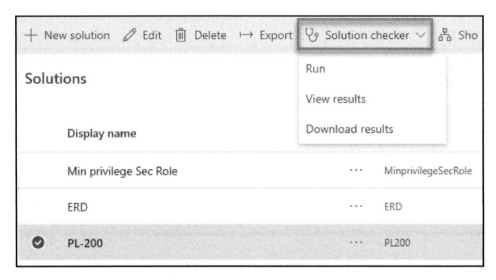

Figure 20.7 – Running the Solution checker tool

The checker applies a series of rules for custom code and JavaScript.

For a list of common issues that the Solution checker might find and how to resolve them, check out the following article: `https://docs.microsoft.com/powerapps/maker/common-data-service/common-issues-resolutions-solution-checker`.

After a short delay, you can view and download the results of the Solution checker. You should resolve any issues that have been reported since these may affect the solution when you import it into the target environment.

You are now ready to export your solution.

Exporting and importing solutions

Solutions, when you create and edit them, are known as unmanaged solutions. You will typically have a separate sandbox environment to perform your customizations. You need to transfer your customizations to your test environment and then to your production, environment.

You can transfer a solution and all its components by exporting the solution from your sandbox environment.

To export your solution, click on the **Export** button when editing the solution in the Maker portal, as shown in the following screenshot:

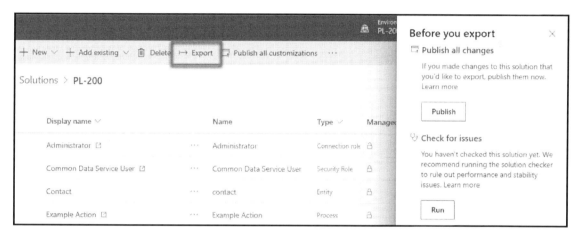

Figure 20.8 – Exporting a solution

The pane shown on the right-hand side of the preceding screenshot will appear and allow you to **Publish** your changes. Now, you can run the Solution checker tool by simply clicking on **Run**:

Figure 20.9 – No issues found in the Solution checker tool

 Only published customizations can be exported.

Clicking on **Next** will make the following screen appear. Here, you can set the version number for this solution and choose how you want to package your solution – either managed or unmanaged:

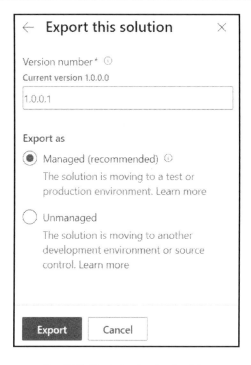

Figure 20.10 – Choosing how to package the solution

The version number is incremented automatically. You can change the version number before clicking on the **Export** button.

 You can only determine whether a solution is managed or unmanaged during the export process.

When you export the solution, the platform packages the solution into a compressed file with a ZIP file extension, as shown in the following screenshot:

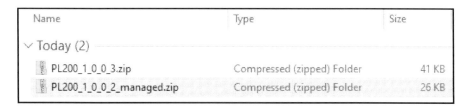

Figure 20.11 – Exported solution files

This `.zip` file contains several XML files and other file types, such as `.xaml`, `.dll`, and `.png`, depending on the components you have included in the solution:

Name	Type	Compressed size	Password ...	Size	Ratio
Workflows	File folder				
[Content_Types].xml	XML Document	1 KB	No	1 KB	38%
customizations.xml	XML Document	28 KB	No	255 KB	90%
solution.xml	XML Document	2 KB	No	8 KB	81%

Figure 20.12 – Contents of an exported solution

You should keep a copy of this solution package as part of your change control process.

If you export a managed solution, you should also export an unmanaged copy of the solution. This ensures that you can recreate your development environment using the unmanaged solution if your development environment is lost or becomes corrupted.

Once you have exported the solution, you can import the solution into another environment. This environment can be in the same Microsoft 365 tenant or a different one.

Importing unmanaged solutions

Once you've exported a solution from your development sandbox environment, you can import the solution into other environments for testing and to deploy it to production.

You can import a solution from the Maker portal. Select the target environment and then click on the **Import** button of the toolbar, as shown in the following screenshot:

Figure 20.13 – Importing a solution

Clicking on the **Import** button opens a new window:

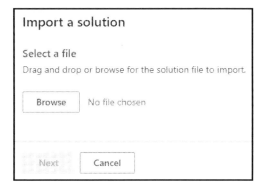

Figure 20.14 – Choosing a solution package file

You should browse to your local computer and select the solution ZIP file you exported from your source environment before clicking on **Next**. This checks that the ZIP file is a valid solution file and whether it is managed or unmanaged. If it is unmanaged, you will see the following screen:

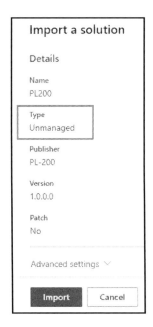

Figure 20.15 – Solution details

When you import an unmanaged solution, all the components in the solution file overwrite the components in the Default solution.

 You cannot uninstall an unmanaged solution.

At this stage, you can decide not to enable any server-side plugins in your solution under **Advanced settings**. Click on **Import** to start importing your solution.

The solution will import in the background and may take several minutes to import, depending on the number of components in the solution. Once the solution has been imported, a notification will be displayed in the Maker portal:

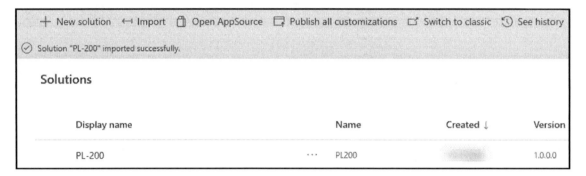

Figure 20.16 – Import complete

 You must publish the solution after importing an unmanaged solution.

You cannot uninstall unmanaged solutions, but you can delete them. However, deleting an unmanaged solution will leave the components as-is; that is, they will remain imported. Deleting an unmanaged solution simply removes the references regarding the solution from the default solution. If you need to undo the import, you need to edit and delete the components manually.

If you import multiple unmanaged solutions that contain changes for the same component, the last solution that was imported will overwrite all the changes in the other solutions. When importing unmanaged solutions, the order you import the files can make a significant difference.

These issues with importing unmanaged solutions are one of the main reasons why managed solutions are preferred for importing into test and production environments.

Importing managed solutions

Managed solutions are stored differently compared to unmanaged solutions. Instead of overwriting the Default solution, the components of a managed solution are held separately, and the platform determines how to merge the default solution components with the components in any managed solution at runtime.

The import process identifies a managed solution, as shown in the following screenshot:

Figure 20.17 – Importing a managed solution

Managed solutions have many benefits, as follows:

- Managed solutions do not need to be published once they've been imported.
- Managed solutions can be uninstalled.
- Version numbering is enforced.

You can uninstall a managed solution by deleting it. When you delete a managed solution, all the components that were imported with it are removed and the environment is left as it was before the solution was imported. You can think of importing a managed solution as installing a compiled software package that you can later uninstall.

You can create new versions of your managed solution and apply these updated versions. With unmanaged solutions, the version numbers are not checked and have no effect, but for managed solutions, the version number must be higher than the existing version.

Updating a managed solution

When you import a later version of a managed solution in the Maker portal, the solution will be updated with no additional steps. If you click **Switch to classic** and import an updated solution file, you will see a message similar to the one shown in the following screenshot:

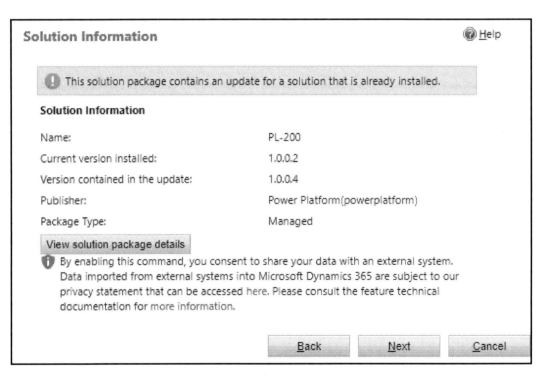

Figure 20.18 – Importing an update for a managed solution

Clicking **Next** will bring up further choices, as shown in the following screenshot:

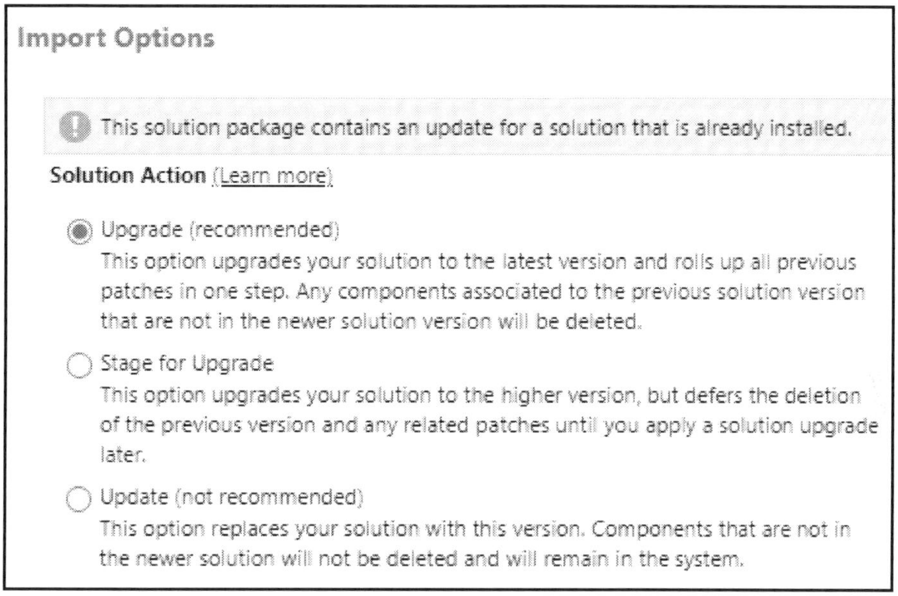

Figure 20.19 – Solution actions

There are three actions you can choose from, as follows:

- **Upgrade (recommended)**: Applies all changes in the solution file; any components not in the solution will be deleted. The result will be as if the previous solution had never been imported and the solution had been imported for the first time.

- **Stage for Upgrade**: Applies the changes in the solution file but does not apply any deletions. You can apply the upgrade later and the missing components will be deleted.

- **Update (not recommended)**: Applies the changes but does not delete any components that have been removed from the source.

You will also be presented with the options shown in the following screenshot. These options control how customizations contained in the updated solution should be applied:

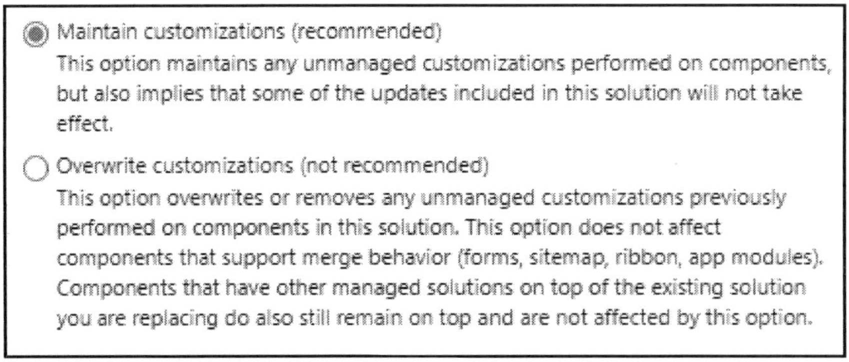

⦿ Maintain customizations (recommended)
This option maintains any unmanaged customizations performed on components, but also implies that some of the updates included in this solution will not take effect.

◯ Overwrite customizations (not recommended)
This option overwrites or removes any unmanaged customizations previously performed on components in this solution. This option does not affect components that support merge behavior (forms, sitemap, ribbon, app modules). Components that have other managed solutions on top of the existing solution you are replacing do also still remain on top and are not affected by this option.

Figure 20.20 – Previous customizations

These options are concerned with changes that have been made to the target environment by unmanaged solutions. You should never make changes to your live production environment directly; you should always create solutions and move them through your life cycle management process. You have the following options:

- **Maintain customizations (recommended)**: Leaves any unmanaged customization untouched.
- **Overwrite customizations (not recommended)**: Overwrites any unmanaged customizations that have been made directly in the target environment.

The best way to manage changes that have been made to unmanaged solutions is to create patches and clone solutions.

Cloning solutions and patches

You have two options when you're updating the solutions that you'll be deploying as managed solutions:

- **Patch:** A patch is a minor change or bug fix for a solution.
- **Clone:** A clone is a new major version of the solution.

Both patches and clones simplify how managed solutions can be developed and deployed.

Creating a solution patch

To create a patch for a solution, select the solution you wish to use and click on the **Clone a patch** button on the toolbar in the Maker portal:

Figure 20.21 – Clone

A new empty solution will be created with the same name, as shown in the following screenshot:

Solutions

Display name		Name ↓	Created	Version
PL-200	⋯	PL200_Patch_95e5ba...	8/17/2020	1.0.1.4
PL-200	⋯	PL200	6/23/2020	1.0.0.4

Figure 20.22 – Patch and parent solution

A patch is always linked to its parent solution. The parent solution is locked. You cannot edit the parent solution; you can only add components to, and create components in, the patch solution.

Here, you can see that the version number for the patch has been automatically updated.

Setting the version number for a solution patch

When creating a patch, you must specify a version number in the format
`major.minor.build.revision`. For a patch, you can only set the final two parts: the
build and revision numbers. The build number is automatically incremented.

The version for a patch must have the same major and minor number, and a higher build or
release number than the parent solution version number.

If a solution has multiple patches, new patches must have a higher build or
release number than any of the other existing patches for that solution.

Cloning solutions

Cloning a solution doesn't create a copy of the solution; it rolls up all the patches in the
solution and creates a new version of the solution. Once you've done this, you are left with
a single new version of the solution.

Importing a cloned solution

Upon importing a cloned solution into the Maker portal, a pane on the right-hand side will
appear that contains details of the cloned solution, as shown in the following screenshot:

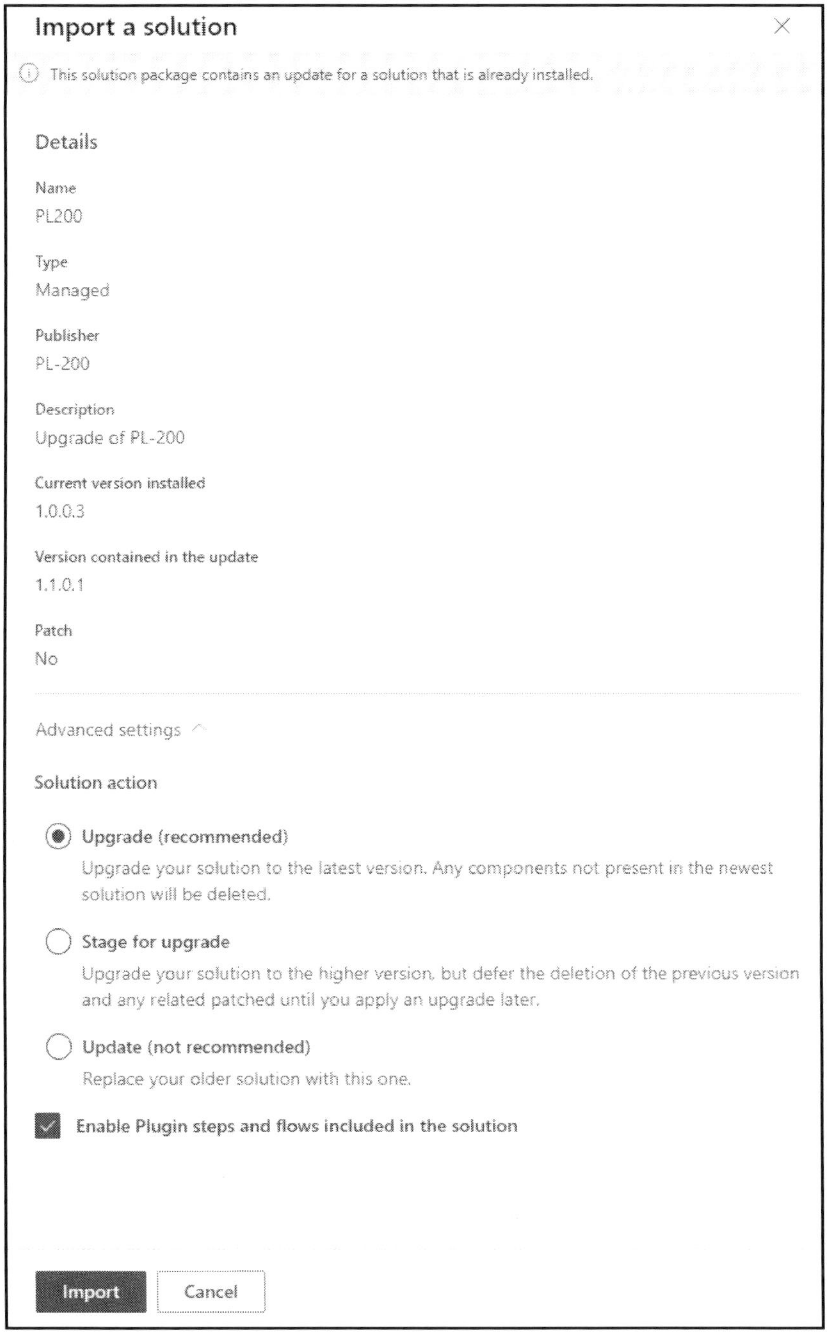

Import a solution   ✕

ⓘ This solution package contains an update for a solution that is already installed.

Details

Name
PL200

Type
Managed

Publisher
PL-200

Description
Upgrade of PL-200

Current version installed
1.0.0.3

Version contained in the update
1.1.0.1

Patch
No

Advanced settings ⌃

Solution action

◉ **Upgrade (recommended)**
Upgrade your solution to the latest version. Any components not present in the newest solution will be deleted.

◯ **Stage for upgrade**
Upgrade your solution to the higher version, but defer the deletion of the previous version and any related patched until you apply an upgrade later.

◯ **Update (not recommended)**
Replace your older solution with this one.

☑ **Enable Plugin steps and flows included in the solution**

[Import]   [Cancel]

Figure 20.23 – Importing an update to a managed solution

Here, you can see that there is a notification at the top of the pane stating that this is an update. Expanding **Advanced settings** will show the same actions shown in *Figure 20.19*.

When you import the cloned solution, any patches are automatically removed.

Setting the version number for a cloned solution

When cloning a solution, you must specify a version number in the format `major.minor.build.revision`. For a cloned solution, you can only set the major and minor numbers.

The version number for a cloned solution must have a higher major or minor number than the parent solution version number.

Summary

In this chapter, we learned about the role of the functional consultant when it comes to deploying solutions.

You should now understand unmanaged and managed solutions, as well as how to create and distribute solutions. You should now be able to create patches for solutions and understand version numbering. You should also be able to build solutions, as well as export, import, and update solutions.

This is the concluding chapter of this book. In the next section, you will find practice tests, as well as tips and tricks for taking the exam.

Questions

Now that you've read this chapter, test your knowledge with these questions. You can find the answers to these questions under `Assessments`, at the end of this book:

1. When you clone a solution, which component number in the version is incremented automatically?

   A) Major
   B) Minor
   C) Build
   D) Revision

2. When you clone a patch, which two components in the version can you change?

   A) Major
   B) Minor
   C) Build
   D) Revision

3. You need to advise the functional consultants on what solution type they should use for their customizations. What should you recommend?

   A) Use the Default solution
   B) Use the Common Data Services Default solution
   C) Clone a solution
   D) Use a new managed solution
   E) Use a new unmanaged solution

4. You import an unmanaged solution into your production system. A week elapses and you need to roll back your changes. What should you do?

   A) Delete the solution
   B) Import the previous version of the solution
   C) Manually edit all the components in the solution
   D) Restore from backup

5. You need to transfer a bug fix from your development environment to your test environment for testing prior to deploying the fix to production. What should you do?

   A) Clone the solution
   B) Clone a patch
   C) Create a new unmanaged solution and export it as unmanaged
   D) Create a new unmanaged solution and export it as managed
   E) Export the existing solution

6. You deploy all your customizations as multiple managed solutions, with each app in its own solution. You need to remove an app from your production system. What should you do?

   A) Delete the solution in the Maker portal
   B) Remove the app from the solution in the Maker portal
   C) Navigate to the list of apps in the Maker portal and delete the app
   D) Clone the solution in the Maker portal

Further reading

For more details on the topics that were covered in this chapter, please refer to the following resources:

- **Solutions overview:** `https://docs.microsoft.com/powerapps/maker/common-data-service/solutions-overview`
- **Using the solution checker to validate your model-driven apps in Power Apps:** `https://docs.microsoft.com/powerapps/maker/common-data-service/use-powerapps-checker`
- **Application life cycle management (ALM) with Microsoft Power Platform:** `https://docs.microsoft.com/power-platform/alm/`
- **Creating and updating solutions:** `https://docs.microsoft.com/power-platform/alm/update-solutions-alm`
- **Solution layers:** `https://docs.microsoft.com/power-platform/alm/solution-layers-alm`
- **Using segmented solutions:** `https://docs.microsoft.com/power-platform/alm/segmented-solutions-alm`

21
Tips and Tricks

Certification exams can be quite scary if you haven't taken one before. There is a lot you can do to help revise for the exam. You can also reduce your stress levels when taking the exam by getting your logistics sorted out well beforehand.

In this chapter, we will go over some tips and tricks for exam preparation, the exam objectives, how questions are phrased, and how to get ready for the exam. This chapter should make the exam day less stressful and more successful.

In this chapter, we will cover the following topics:

- Reviewing the exam objectives
- Understanding how exams are structured
- Preparing for the exam
- Tips when taking the exam

 The tips you read here are what works for me. You may be different as everyone learns in different ways. Some people like to listen, some to read, and some to do. Most learners use a mixture of all three.

Let's start with the exam objectives.

Reviewing the exam objectives

In Chapter 1, *PL-200 exam*, we went through the objectives. There are five objectives in the exam. Each objective has a percentage associated with it that shows how much of the exam relates to that objective.

- Configuring the Common Data Service (25-30%)
- Creating apps by using Power Apps (20-25%)

- Creating and managing Power Automate (15-20%)
- Implementing Power Virtual Agents chatbots (10-15%)
- Integrating Power Apps with other apps and services (15-20%)

Each of these objectives has two or more sub-objectives that explain further what the exam will test. For instance, the Create and Manage Power Automate objective has three sub-objectives:

- Create flows
- Create and manage business process flows
- Build UI flows

Then, for each sub-objective, there are bullet points. These are the tasks and items in the exam that are written from this list of tasks. For example, the Build UI flows sub-objective has four tasks:

- To describe types of UI flows
- To identify use cases for UI flows
- To differentiate between attended and unattended UI flows
- To record business process tasks

Microsoft has a statement on the exam page that you should bear in mind. The statement says that the tasks listed may not be definitive. So there may be items in the exam that are not covered by the tasks. However, as you have read this book, you are well placed to pass the exam.

You should browse the PL-200 exam page at `https://docs.microsoft.com/learn/certifications/exams/pl-200` and click on the **Download exam skills outline** link. This will open a PDF that contains all the objectives, sub-objectives, and tasks.

Revising for an exam

The method I use when taking an exam is to download the objectives and copy the objectives, sub-objectives, and tasks into a spreadsheet.

I evaluate how well I understand each of the tasks. I create my revision plan from the results of the evaluation.

I try and revise for a minimum of 30 minutes per day. I find that making time for regular revision helps me learn.

I also try to #GetHandsOn. By this I mean using the Power Platform, customizing and creating apps in a Power Platform environment.

If you do not have access to a Power Platform environment, you should create a trial. You can sign up for free with the community plan at `https://powerapps.microsoft.com/communityplan` or start a free 30-day trial. You can find my trial instructions at `https://tinyurl.com/trydyn`.

Microsoft exams follow the same structure.

Understanding how exams are structured

Microsoft's role-based exams, such as PL-200, have between 40 and 60 questions. Some questions are worth more than others, but do not worry about that. Just focus on answering the questions.

You will have 180 minutes for the exam plus another 30 minutes to read the instructions and the non-disclosure agreement, complete the surveys, and provide feedback.

Microsoft exam questions are structured with the following four parts:

- Technical environment or scenario: You have a hybrid deployment of ...
- Problem statement/requirements: Users report that ...
- Goal statement: You need to ...
- Question statement: What should you do ...?

The goal is what you are trying to achieve. The first two parts explain the scenario or issue you are trying to answer. Questions will always have a goal and a question statement. You may not have a scenario or problem statement.

The exam will be in several sections. You will get a summary at the end of each section. Once you complete a section, you cannot go back to it.

You can find Microsoft's exam FAQ at `https://docs.microsoft.com/learn/certifications/frequently-asked-questions`. The FAQ covers many of the questions test takers have.

Microsoft exams aim to have about 50% of the questions as single or multiple choice. The other 50% are referred to as innovative questions.

Understanding the question types

There are several different question types in Microsoft exams. Microsoft reviews and changes exams every 60-90 days, adding new questions and removing questions that are no longer relevant or correct.

Before you take the exam, you should become familiar with the different types of questions that you may encounter. You can see a list of the question types with demonstration videos at `https://docs.microsoft.com/learn/certifications/certification-exams#exam-formats-and-question-types`.

You should expect to see another type in the exam. You are presented with a problem and then asked a series of yes/no questions that have possible solutions. You will be asked whether the solution solves the problem.

You should also expect one or more case study questions. Case studies contain a lot of text explaining a business scenario, requirements, issues, and other details. You will then get a series of questions on the case study. Case studies can take a lot of time to read and absorb. Make sure you watch the video for the case study question type at the earlier link.

At the time of writing, there are no **Performance-Based Testing (PBT)** labs on the Power Platform exams. PBT is where the exam opens a browser and asks you to complete a series of tasks. You are not scored in terms of how you achieve the task, just that the task has been completed correctly.

You may experience PBT if you take an Azure exam. Eventually, Microsoft will add PBT to the Power Platform exams. Personally, I enjoy PBT as I find I can more easily do things that involve remembering minutiae. You can read more on PBT at `https://docs.microsoft.com/learn/certifications/posts/performance-testing-is-coming-to-microsoft-exams`.

Now to prepare for and book the exam.

Preparing for the exam

You will need a Microsoft account, and an outlook.com or Hotmail account, to book an exam. You should navigate to the Learning dashboard at `http://aka.ms/learningdashboard` and sign in.

If you have not taken an exam before, you will need to create a Learning profile. It is best to do this ahead of booking your exam in case you have technical difficulties.

In the learning profile, you must enter your name as it is on the ID you will use in the exam. Your ID will be verified against these details.

To book the exam, navigate to `https://docs.microsoft.com/learn/certifications/exams/pl-200`, click on **Schedule exam**, and follow the many steps. You can either take the exam in a test center, or you can take the exam online at home. If you plan to take the exam at home, make sure you read this page carefully and that you can meet the criteria: `https://docs.microsoft.com/learn/certifications/online-exams`.

Right, now for D-day; taking the exam.

Tips when taking the exam

You can normally check in for your exam 30 minutes before your scheduled time. I like to do this in case there are any technical difficulties. If you are taking your exam online, you should be aware the check-in process can take 20 minutes. If you haven't started your exam within 30 minutes of the scheduled start, then you will void your exam.

Key tips for the exam:

- Answer all the questions.
- There is no penalty for guessing.
- Some questions cannot be skipped.
- Mark items for review if you are not sure of your answer.
- Time is not normally a factor in this exam.
- If you find yourself staring at an item for more than a couple of minutes, mark it for review and come back to it later.

This is a tip that I was only told recently, and I wished I had known about it earlier. On case study questions, it is often necessary to find a word from the question goal among the text. The secure browser used in the exam supports this search capability. Press *CTRL+F* and you can search for the word on the page!

One of the best pieces of advice I was ever given is, do not change your answer unless you are 100% convinced you chose the wrong answer. You will start to doubt yourself in an exam. Your gut instinct answer is more likely to be correct than the next answer you think may be correct.

Good luck!

22
Practice Test 1

This appendix contains a complete sample test with instructions. As with the actual certification exam, you are encouraged to follow the time and other restrictions provided in the instructions. Upon completion, review your answers in `Answers to Practice Test 1`. You can retake this test multiple times with study sessions in between.

The following topics will be covered in this appendix:

- Introducing the test
- Instructions for the test
- Practice test 1
- Post-test instructions

By the end of this test, you will have learned various test scenarios and their relevance to an actual certification exam and taken a timed practice test.

Introducing the test

This practice test consists of 22 questions covering the objectives of the PL-200 exam. These questions are not taken from the certification exam but have been created in a similar manner to the exam questions.

In a book, we cannot simulate the interactive question types such as drag and drop or active screen, but we have formulated such questions in text, so you will see some questions that have two or three answers.

The test has three sections. In a certification exam, you cannot go back to a previous section once you have started the next section.

Instructions for the test

Practice tests should be approached in the same way you would approach a certification exam.

You should do the following:

- Take this practice test in one sitting with no breaks.
- Close down all windows and browsers on your computer.
- Have a clean desk with no books or other material.
- Set up a timer to count down the time remaining in the exam.
- Do not look ahead; answer each question in turn.
- Review each section before moving to the next section.

Before you start the test, make sure you have read the `Tips and Tricks` chapter.

When taking the test, write down the answers to each question for scoring and review them after the exam.

Practice test 1

You have 60 minutes and 22 questions.

Section 1

This section contains a series of questions that present the same scenario. Each question in the series contains a unique solution that might meet the stated goals. Some question sets might have more than one correct solution, while others might not have a correct solution.

You cannot go back or review questions of this type in the actual certification exam.

Scenario

You are a Power Platform functional consultant.

You need to create an Excel template that is only available to some users.

Question 1

Solution: In the user's security role, set the privilege for the **Document Template** entity to Read.

Does this solution meet the goal?

    A) Yes
    B) No

Question 2

Solution: Create an organizational template and assign a security role to the template.

Does this solution meet the goal?

    A) Yes
    B) No

Question 3

Solution: Create a personal template and share the template with the team.

Does this solution meet the goal?

    A) Yes
    B) No

Section 2

This section contains questions that are independent of each other.

Question 4

You are a Power platform functional consultant designing the data model for a model-driven app.

The app needs to show data from a table in an Azure SQL database.

You need to specify the properties of the entity for this data.

What should you do?

    A) Create the entity as an activity entity.
    B) Set the ownership of the entity to user or team owned.
    C) Define an alternate key for the entity.
    D) Create the entity as a virtual entity.

Question 5

A model-driven app performs a calculation using server-side plugin code.

Users require that the result of the calculation be displayed immediately whenever the fields involved in the calculation are changed.

You need to replace the plugin and perform the calculation using no-code configuration.

What feature should you use?

    A) Business rule
    B) Calculated field
    C) Power Automate flow
    D) Classic workflow

Question 6

You are a Power Platform functional consultant modeling the data for a model-driven app.

The team members on the project need to be able to understand your data model.

You need to create a visual representation of the data model.

What should you do?

    A) Create an Excel workbook listing all entities, fields, and relationships.
    B) Create an entity relationship diagram.
    C) Create a Word document containing screenshots of the entity relationships.
    D) Create a Word document containing snapshots of the business process flows.

Question 7

You are creating a new model-driven app for a customer where there are already a number of Power Platform apps deployed.

You need to distribute your app and other customizations from your development environment into the production environment.

You need to provide the capability to roll back your changes.

How do you package your changes?

    A) Export the default solution.
    B) Export the Common Data Service default solution.
    C) Export an unmanaged solution.
    D) Export a managed solution.

Question 8

You administer a system based on Common Data Service with a model-driven app provided by a third-party vendor.

The app is in a managed solution supplied by the vendor. Users require a new view for a custom entity in the app.

How can you make the changes?

For each of the following statements, select Yes if the statement is true. Otherwise, select No.

1. Edit the solution provided by the ISV.
2. Create a new managed solution and add the entity to the app.
3. Change the managed properties for the entity.

Question 9

You are a Power Platform functional consultant creating a new model-driven app.

You need to transfer your app from the development environment to the production environment.

You need to add components to the solution.

Which three components can you include with an entity in a segmented solution? Each correct answer presents part of the solution.

A) Email template
B) Form
C) Alternate key
D) Option set
E) Views

Question 10

You have a canvas app, a model-driven app, and a portal app in a Power Platform environment. You create a business rule to validate data.

The business rule does not work either when creating a record using the canvas app, or when creating a record in the portal.

You need to validate the data however it is created.

What should you do?

A) Add the fields used in the business rule to the screen and web page.
B) Change the scope of the business rule to All forms.
C) Change the scope of the business rule to Entity.
D) Take a snapshot of the business rule.

Question 11

You develop a canvas app.

Users report that they are not using the latest version of the app.

What should you do?

    A) Share the app.
    B) Publish the app.
    C) Run the app checker.
    D) Run the solution checker.

Question 12

You create canvas apps for users in your department.

A user requires an app that shows a list of records.

What control do you add?

    A) Form
    B) Media
    C) Combo box
    D) Gallery

Question 13

You create a custom entity, *Entity A*.

A user is assigned three security roles, *Role X*, *Role Y*, and *Role Z*.

The security role *Role X* has Read privilege on *EntityA* set to `Parent-Child Business Unit`, the security role *Role Y* has Read privilege on *EntityA* set to `Business Unit`, and the security role *Role Z* has Read privilege on *Entity A* set to `None`.

What is the effective access level on *Entity A* for this user?

    A) None
    B) User
    C) Business Unit
    D) Parent-Child Business Unit
    E) Organization

Question 14

You are an administrator for a Power Platform environment that employs all features of the security model.

You are adding users to the environment. Users must be restricted to data in their own team.

Before a user can be assigned a security role, what must they be assigned to?

    A) A business unit
    B) An access team
    C) A security group
    D) A field security profile

Question 15

You are a Power Platform functional consultant creating a model-driven app for a multinational organization.

You have users that want to use different languages in the app.

You need to provide translations for your customized fields into a language.

What must you do first?

    A) Select the language in Personal options
    B) Enable the language in Settings
    C) Add the currency for the language
    D) Run the solution checker

Question 16

You are a Power Platform functional consultant.

You create a custom entity in Common Data Service. You use a Power Automate flow to create a channel in a team when a record is created in the entity.

You need to ensure that the flow will trigger when a record is created in the custom entity.

What should you do?

   A) Enable connections in the entity properties.
   B) Add the timeline control to the form.
   C) Enable the business process flow in the entity properties.
   D) Enable change tracking in the entity properties.

Question 17

You create a model-driven app.

The app contains an entity, *Entity T*.

Users are not finding records for *Entity T* when searching when the user selects *EntityT* in the app's left-hand navigation.

What should you configure?

   A) Quick Find view
   B) Quick view form
   C) Associated view
   D) Lookup view

Question 18

You are a Power Platform functional consultant that has joined a project using Common Data Service.

You need to evaluate the use of the custom entities in the Common Data Service solution.

For each of the following statements, select Yes if the statement is true. Otherwise, select No.

   1. Deleting a custom entity deletes all activities related to records for the entity.
   2. You can change the prefix for the custom entities.
   3. You can enable and disable auditing for the custom entities.

Section 3 – Case study

This section contains a series of questions for a case study. Read the case study and answer each question.

Overview

You work for an organization that is adopting the Power Platform.

Existing environment

You have data in the following data stores:

- On-premises Microsoft SQL Server
- Excel spreadsheets in OneDrive for Business

You have the existing applications:

- **Expenses application**: This was developed in Visual Basic and runs on Windows computers and captures details of travel expenses. Data is stored using SQL Server.
- **Authorization application**: This was developed with Microsoft **Active Server Pages** (ASP) and controls the authorization of travel expenses. Data is stored using SQL Server.
- **Analytics application**: This provides analysis of expenses and authorizations. Data is exported to Excel to produce charts and visualizations.

Problem statement

The management of your organization is looking to automate time-consuming manual processes.

They have identified the entry and approval processing for travel expenses as a trial for the Power Platform's capabilities.

Requirements

Users must be able to upload pictures of their receipts to a shared OneDrive for Business folder.

Receipts for expenses must be scanned and data automatically entered into the Expenses application.

The approvals system must be replaced. Analytics applications must be kept.

Issues

The trial will only test expenses for around 20 users. The eventual system will need to support expenses for 500 users.

Question 19

What do you need to configure to automate the Expenses application?

A) SQL Server connector
B) On-premises data gateway
C) Selenium IDE
D) Internet Explorer

Question 20

What should you use to replace the Authorization application?

A) Power Automate UI flows
B) Power Automate business process flows
C) Power Automate approvals
D) Model-driven app

Question 21

Which two components do you need to automate the entry of expenses?

A) Power Automate UI flows
B) AI Builder
C) Model-driven app
D) SQL Server Connector
E) Canvas app

Question 22

What do you need to enable the Analytics application to carry on producing its output?

A) AI Builder.
B) Use the Excel for OneDrive connector.
C) Power BI.
D) Use the SQL Server connector.

Post-test instructions

After you have completed the exam, review your answers against the answers given in `Answers to Practice Test 1`.

If you answered anything incorrectly, find the topic of the question in the book's chapters and revise the content. You should also look at the user interface in the Power Platform for that topic and work through the steps to complete the task.

You should be aiming to score 80% or above.

23
Answers to Practice Test 1

In this appendix, you can check the answers to the questions in `Practice Test 1`.

Answers to practice test 1

Each answer includes an explanation and a link to any related documentation. To prepare for the exam, identify any questions you answered incorrectly and study those topics.

Section 1

1. **No** – Document Templates is the correct entity to set privileges. Having read privileges is necessary but not sufficient. Enabling read makes all Word and Excel templates available to users rather than just a subset. You can only set the access level to None or Organization.
2. **Yes** – If you upload an Excel template into **Settings**, it will be an organizational template. You can then enable security role(s), which will restrict the template to only users who have that security role.
3. **Yes** – A personal Excel template can be shared with users or teams.

Section 2

1. **D** – Virtual entity. This is the only option that will allow data to be read from an external data source.

2. **A** – Business rule. This is the only option that will perform the calculation without saving the record and will display the result the moment any field referenced by the rule is changed.

3. **B** – Entity relationship diagram. This is the only option that shows a visual representation of the entities and their relationships.

4. **D** – Managed solution. This is the only option that will allow the changes to be uninstalled.

5. 1. **No** – The ISV solution is managed. You cannot edit a managed solution.
2. **No** – You cannot add a component from a managed solution into another solution for that you will export as managed.
3. **No** – Only the ISV will be able to change the managed properties of a component of the managed solution.

6. **B, C,** and **E** – Email templates and option sets are their own component in solutions.

7. **C** – Change the scope to the entity. Business rules do not apply in canvas apps or on portal pages, so to perform the validation, the scope must be set to Entity. The data validation in the rule will be performed when the record is saved to Common Data Service either through the canvas app or the portal.

8. **B** – Publish. When you make a change to a Canvas app and save, a new version is created. To make the latest version available, you must publish the app. As the user can see an older version of the app, it has already been shared with them. Note: an app is published when it is first saved.

9. **D** – Gallery. The Gallery control displays a list of items from a data source.

10. **D** – Parent-Child Business Unit. The user has the least restrictive access level of the three security roles.

11. **A** – Business Unit. A user must be assigned to a business unit before being assigned to a security role. Users are added the root business unit by default. If you assign a security role and then move the user to a different business unit, their security role will be removed.

12. **B** – Enable the language in Settings. Before you can export labels for translation, you must enable the language(s) that you want to add translations for.

13. **D** – To invoke a Power Automate trigger, the Common Data Service entity used with the flow must have Change Tracking enabled.

14. **A** – Quick Find view. The Quick Find view defines the fields searched on when searching within a view or from a multi-entity categorized search.

15. 1. **Yes** – All records for the entity will be deleted, along with any notes and activities for those records.
    2. **No** – You cannot change the prefix for an entity after it has been created.
    3. **Yes** – Auditing can be enabled and disabled on custom entities at any time.

Section 3 – case study

1. **B** – On-premises data gateway. You need to install an on-premises data gateway to automate a Windows desktop application.

2. **C** – Power Automate approvals. You can use the approvals functionality to handle the authorization of expenses.

3. **A and B** – Power Automate UI flows and AI Builder. You need AI Builder to process the scanned images of the receipts to extract the data and Power Automate UI flows to automate the entry of the data into the Expenses application.

4. **D** – SQL Server Connector. The Analytics application holds its data in the on-premises SQL Server instance. The Authorization application read and wrote into this database. The Power Automate approvals flow will need to connect to the on-premises SQL Server instance and record the outcomes of approvals.

24
Practice Test 2

This appendix contains a complete sample test with completion instructions. As with the actual certification exam, you are encouraged to follow the time and other restrictions provided in the instructions. Upon completion, review your answers in `Answers to Practice Test 2`. You can retake this test multiple times with study sessions in between.

The following topics will be covered in this appendix:

- Introducing the test
- Instructions for the test
- Practice test 2
- Post-test instructions

At the end of this test, you will have learned various test scenarios and their relevance to an actual certification exam and taken a timed practice test.

Introducing the test

This practice test consists of 30 questions covering the objectives of the PL-200 exam. These questions are not taken from the certification exam but have been created in a similar manner to the exam questions.

In a book, it is not possible to simulate the interactive question types, such as drag and drop or active screen, but we have formulated questions in text, so you will see some questions that have two or three answers.

The test has four sections. In a certification exam, you cannot go back to a previous section once you have started the next section.

Instructions for the test

Practice tests should be approached in the same way as you would a certification exam.

You should do the following:

- Take this practice test in one sitting with no breaks.
- Close down all windows and browsers on your computer.
- Have a clean desk with no books or other material.
- Set up a timer to count down the time remaining in the exam.
- Do not look ahead; answer each question in turn.
- Review each section before moving on to the next section.

Before you start the test, make sure you read the `Tips and Tricks` section.

When taking the test, write down the answers to each question for scoring and review after the exam.

Practice test 2

You have 90 minutes to answer 30 questions.

Section 1

This section contains a series of questions that present the same scenario. Each question in the series contains a unique solution that might meet the stated goals. Some question sets might have more than one correct solution, while others might not have any correct solution.

You cannot go back or review questions of this type during the actual certification exam.

Scenario

You are a Power Platform functional consultant.

You need to allow external users to access their data and submit requests.

Question 1

Solution: Enable Open registration.

Does this solution meet the goal?

    A) Yes
    B) No

Question 2

Solution: Send the user an invitation code.

Does this solution meet the goal?

    A) Yes
    B) No

Question 3

Solution: Add external users as guests to Azure Active Directory.

Does this solution meet the goal?

    A) Yes
    B) No

Section 2

This section contains a series of questions that present the same scenario. Each question in the series contains a unique solution that might meet the stated goals. Some question sets might have more than one correct solution, while others might not have any correct solution.

 You cannot go back or review questions of this type during the actual certification exam.

Scenario

You are a Power Platform functional consultant.

You are building an AI object detection model using AI Builder.

You need to analyze a photo taken on a mobile phone and identify the object within the photo.

Question 4

Solution: Add a control to a canvas app.

Does this solution meet the goal?

    A) Yes
    B) No

Question 5

Solution: Use the Predict action in a Power Automate flow.

Does this solution meet the goal?

    A) Yes
    B) No

Question 6

Solution: Use the formula bar in a canvas app.

Does this solution meet the goal?

    A) Yes
    B) No

Section 3

This section contain questions that are independent of one another.

Question 7

You are a Power Platform functional consultant.

You are creating a portal for external users.

You need to change the layout for the home page.

What should you customize?

    A) Page template
    B) Liquid template
    C) Web page
    D) Web template

Question 8

You build a model-driven app using the Common Data Service.

You create a connection between two records, Record1 and Record2, of *Entity X*. You select the connection role, Role A.

You need to restrict the connection from Record2 to Record1 to be RoleB.

What should you configure?

A) Configure the connection role for RoleA so that it can only be used for the record type of Entity X.
B) Create a workflow that will create a matching connection with RoleB whenever a new connection for RoleA is created.
C) Configure the connection role for Role A, and add a new matching connection role named RoleB that applies to Entity X.
D) Create a Power Automate flow that the user must manually run to create the connection. The flow prompts the user to select both sides of the connection role.

Question 9

You build a model-driven app using the Common Data Service.

You have an entity with 240,000 records.

Users need to extract all records.

What should you use?

A) Export to Excel static
B) Export to Excel dynamic
C) Run the Report Wizard and save to Excel
D) Open in Excel Online

Question 10

You have an app built on the Common Data Service.

Users require printed output of their data.

You need to print output from the Common Data Service.

What should you use?

A) View
B) Report Wizard
C) Chart
D) Dashboard

Question 11

You have an app built on the Common Data Service.

Users want to see their company logo in visualizations.

What should you configure?

    A) View
    B) Report Wizard
    C) Chart
    D) Dashboard

Question 12

You create a model-driven app. You create multiple forms for an entity and assign security roles to the forms. Each form is assigned to a single security role.

You need to make sure that users default to a form if they do not have one of the security roles.

What should you configure?

    A) Form Order set
    B) Fallback form
    C) OnLoad event
    D) Form selector

Question 13

You are a Power Platform functional consultant.

You need to choose the Excel export options for the following scenarios.

For each scenario here, choose from the following options:

  • Dynamic worksheet
  • Excel Online
  • Static worksheet

  1. Quickly edit multiple records to fix the values in an option set.
  2. Users without a Power Platform license must be able to see data.

3. Users must only be able to see data that matches their security role.
4. Refresh to see the latest data.

Question 14

You create visualizations in a model-driven app.

You need to add the following visualization to dashboards.

For each visualization here, choose from the following options:

- Standard dashboard
- Interactive experience dashboard
- Personal dashboard

1. A Power BI tile
2. A tag chart
3. A personal view

Question 15

You are managing a Power Platform environment. Duplicate detection is configured.

You run a duplicate detection job and a duplicate record is found. RecordA has a duplicate record, RecordB.

You need to to remove duplicate RecordB, but use the value of a field from RecordB on RecordA.

What four actions should you perform in order?

A) Deactivate RecordB
B) Select the field
C) Merge
D) Update RecordA with the field
E) Select RecordA
F) Select RecordB
G) Select both records

Question 16

You are creating a model-driven app using the Power Platform.

You want to improve data quality. You create a business rule.

You need to prompt the user with a default value when populating a field on the form.

Which two actions should you perform?

A) Set required
B) Lock field
C) Display an error message
D) Add a condition
E) Set the default value
F) Add a recommendation

Question 17

You are a Power Platform functional consultant. A business rule has been defined to calculate the number of days between a start date and end date fields. The business rule is activated.

The business rule is not calculating the number of days when data is entered into the model-driven app form. There is no error message.

What is causing the issue?

A) The start and end dates are not on the form.
B) The start and end dates are read-only.
C) The requirement for the start date and end date fields is set to optional.
D) The start and end dates are on the form but are hidden.

Question 18

You create a Power Automate button flow for a custom entity. The button sends an invitation to a OneDrive for Business file by email.

You share the button flow with other users.

Which users can view the flow button run history?

A) Flow administrators can see the flow run history in the Power Automate portal.

B) Users can see their own flow run history on the Power Automate mobile app.

C) All users can see the flow run history for every user.

D) You can see the flow run history for every user on the Power Automate mobile app.

Question 19

You are a Power Platform functional consultant.

You create a custom entity in the Common Data Service. The environment uses a business unit hierarchy to control access to data. Users should only see the data relevant to them and their team.

Managers report that they cannot see the records for all of their employees who report to them.

Which security feature should you use?

A) Security roles

B) Position hierarchy

C) Field level security

D) Manager hierarchy

Question 20

You are a Power Platform functional consultant building a model-driven app.

You have a requirement that when a user selects the value **Other** in an option set, the user can add a new value to the form.

What should you configure?

A) Business process flow

B) Power Automate flow

C) Business rule

D) Form properties

Question 21

You create the data model in the exhibit for a Power Platform solution.

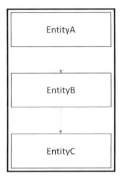

Exhibit for Question 21

EntityA has a one-to-many relationship to EntityB. EntityB has a one-to-many relationship to EntityC.

You need to create the fields on EntityB to meet different business requirements.

For each of the following statements, select Yes if the statement is true, otherwise, select No.

1. A rollup field can aggregate a field on EntityA.
2. The condition in a calculated field can use a field in EntityA.
3. A rollup field that counts the number of records must have the whole number data type.

Question 22

You are creating a model-driven app. You create a custom entity.

You create a self-referential one-to-many relationship on the custom entity.

You want to change the fields displayed when a user uses the hierarchical display.

What form should you customize?

A) Main
B) Quick create
C) Card
D) Quick view

Question 23

You create a model-driven app and configure the sub-grid on a form to be an editable grid.

There is a business rule defined for the entity in the sub-grid.

Users report that they cannot edit a drop-down list on the grid. Other fields can be edited.

What is the cause?

A) The drop-down list is for the status field.
B) The business rule is hiding the field.
C) The field in the business rule condition is not in the view.
D) Field security is applied to the field.

Question 24

You are a Power Platform functional consultant.

You create a canvas app.

You need to store your data when the canvas app loses connection to the internet.

What functions should you use?

A) SaveData and LoadData
B) Location
C) Patch
D) App

Question 25

You are a Power Platform functional consultant using the Common Data Service

You are integrating Power Automate with another system that has a RESTful API. There is no prebuilt connector.

You need to create a two-way integration with this system.

What should you do?

A) Create a service endpoint.
B) Create a custom connector.
C) Create a Power Automate UI flow.
D) Create a data flow with Power Query.

Section 4

This section contains a series of questions for a case study.

Overview

You are a Power Platform functional consultant.

You work for a company looking to improve internal and external communications by implementing chatbots.

Existing environment

The company uses the Common Data Service and has several model-driven and canvas apps in production.

Dynamics 365 Customer Service and Customer Service Insights are used in the support center.

Requirements

- Chatbots need to leverage existing support information.
- Chatbots must not attempt to escalate to a human agent when handling unknown questions unless the bot has asked a series of prompts designed to determine the user's enquiry.
- The chatbot must understand the company's products.
- Chatbots must be able to be edited by members of the project team.
- Internal chatbots must be available in Microsoft Teams.
- External chatbots must be available on the company website.

Issues

- Users without a Power Platform license need to test the chatbot before it is deployed.
- Users are being prompted multiple times during a bot session for the same question when they are switched to different topics.

Question 26

How should you meet the requirement to leverage existing support information?

A) Use Suggest topics.
B) Create a custom entity.
C) Use Q&A Maker.
D) Create topics from Customer Service Insights.

Question 27

How should the bot identify the company's products?

A) Create a topic for each product.
B) Create a custom entity for products and add each product.
C) Create an action and use Power Automate flow to query the product catalog.
D) Add variables.

Question 28

How should you handle the unknown question requirement?

A) Add a fallback topic.
B) Create a custom entity.
C) Delete the Escalate topic.
D) Use Power Automate flow.

Question 29

How should you resolve the testing issue?

A) Deploy the bot to Microsoft Teams.
B) Create a WordPress site and embed the bot.
C) Share the bot with users.
D) Use the demo website.

Question 30

You need to prevent the multiple question issue. What should you do?

A) Merge topics into a single topic.
B) Set variables as bot variables.
C) Use adaptive cards.
D) Add trigger phrases.

Post-test instructions

Once you have competed the exam, review your answers against the answers given in Answers to Practice Test 2.

If you answered incorrectly, find the topic or task of the question in the chapters and review the content. You should also look at the user interface in the Power Platform for that topic and work through the steps to complete the task.

You should be aiming to score 80% or above.

25
Answers to Practice Test 2

In this appendix, you can check the answers to the questions in `Practice Test 2`.

Each answer includes an explanation and a link to any related documentation. To prepare for the exam, highlight any questions you answered incorrectly and then study those topics.

Answers to Practice Test 2

Section 1

1. **Yes**. Open registration is the least restrictive sign-up configuration where the portal allows a user account to be registered by providing a user identity. Refer to `https://docs.microsoft.com/powerapps/maker/portals/configure/configure-portal-authentication`.

2. **Yes**. The user can redeem the invitation code when signing into the portal. Refer to `https://docs.microsoft.com/powerapps/maker/portals/configure/set-authentication-identity`.

3. **No**. Guest users in Activity Directory are not enabled to access the portal.

Section 2

1. Yes. You can add the object detection control to analyze images taken by the camera in a canvas app. Refer
    to `https://docs.microsoft.com/ai-builder/object-detector-component-in-powerapps`.
2. **Yes**. The Predict action in a Power Automate flow is a generic action that be used with any of the AI Builder models. Refer
    to `https://docs.microsoft.com/ai-builder/use-in-flow-overview`.
3. **No**. The object detection model uses a control, not the formula bar.

Section 3

1. **D** – Web template. You edit the HTML in the web template. Web templates are the foundation of a web page. Refer to `https://readyxrm.blog/2019/08/16/overview-of-the-powerapps-portals-management-app`.
2. **C** – Matching connection role. To restrict which connection roles can be combined, you need to define matching connection roles. Refer
    to `https://docs.microsoft.com/powerapps/maker/common-data-service/configure-connection-roles`.
3. **C** – Run the Report Wizard and save to Excel. The limit for exporting to Excel is 100,000 rows. Only a report generated using the Report Wizard will be able to export all the data. Refer
    to `https://docs.microsoft.com/powerapps/user/create-report-with-wizard`.
4. **B** – Views, charts, and dashboards cannot be printed. A Report Wizard report can be printed. Refer
    to `https://docs.microsoft.com/powerapps/user/create-report-with-wizard`.
5. **D** – Dashboard. You cannot add images to views, charts, or the Report Wizard. You can create an image web resource containing the logo and add the web resource to a dashboard.
6. **B** – Fallback form. The fallback form is used when no forms match the security role of a user. Refer
    to `https://docs.microsoft.com/powerapps/maker/model-driven-apps/control-access-forms`.

7. 1. **Excel Online** – Excel Online allows you to quickly edit a list of records, change values, and save back to the Common Data Service.

2. Static worksheet – Exporting to a static worksheet allows you to give the worksheet to users without a license as only the data is exported.

3. **Dynamic worksheet** – Exporting to a dynamic worksheet means that the data is not exported, and that the worksheet has a query. Any user accessing the worksheet will cause the query to execute and they will see the data that matches their security role.

4. **Dynamic worksheet** – The Dynamic worksheet can be refreshed to get the latest data.

8. 1. **Personal dashboard** – A Power BI tile can only be added to a personal dashboard.

2. **Interactive experience dashboard** – Tag and Doughnut charts are used in the visual filter pane of interactive dashboards to filter the streams of data.

3. **Personal dashboard** – Personal views can only be added to personal dashboards.

9. G->C->E-> B. You should select both records, then click on **Merge**, then select the master record, which is **Record A**, and finally select the field.

10. **D** and **F** – Recommendations are used to prompt the user to enter a value into a field. The value they are recommending is shown in a textbox with an accept button. When a user accepts the value, it is entered automatically. You need a condition to tell the rule when to show the recommendation.

11. **A** – Fields referenced in a business rule must be on the form for the business rule to perform the actions in the rule.

12. **D** – As the owner of the button flow, you can see the flow run history for all users.

13. **B** – Position hierarchy. As the manager can see some of their direct reports data, it is likely that the other direct reports are in a different business unit and in a different part of the hierarchy. Using security roles will expose too much data. You should use hierarchical security. The manager hierarchy relies on the business unit hierarchy, so will not find all direct reports. Position hierarchy ignores the business unit structure.

14. **C** – Business rule. Business rules can automatically show another field on the form and make it mandatory when a particular value is selected in an option set.

15. 1. **No** – Rollup fields aggregate the many ends of the relationship. A rollup field on Entity B will aggregate a field on Entity C.
2. **Yes** – Calculated fields can reference fields for many-to-one relationships. A calculated field on Entity B can reference fields on Entity A.
3. **Yes** – Rollup fields that count records must have the whole number data type.

16. **D** – Quick view. The quick view form is used to display the fields in the tile in the hierarchical display of records.

17. **A** – Status and Status reason fields cannot be edited in an editable grid. The show visibility action is not supported in editable grids. Field security cannot be applied to the status and status reason fields. If the field in the condition for the business rule is not in the view, the business rule will not run.

18. **A** – **SaveData** and **LoadData** are used to save and retrieve data from local storage.

19. **B** – Custom connector. As the system you want to integrate with has a RESTful API, you can create a custom connector for this API.

Section 4

1. **D** – Customer Service Insights. You can create topics and trigger phrases for your bot from within Customer Service Insights.

2. **B** – Custom entity. Entities allow a bot to identify objects and terminology in the test phrases entered by users. There is a set of prebuilt entities for common objects. You can create custom entities for your own organization.

3. **A** – Fallback topic. If the chatbot cannot determine which topic to use, the chatbot will use the **Escalate system** topic. You can change this behavior by adding a fallback topic

4. **D** – Demo website. When you publish a bot, a demo website is created. You can share the URL of this website with any user.

5. **B** – Bot variables. Variables are used only within a topic. You can use variables to skip questions based on previous responses. Setting variables as **Bot** variables means the variables can be used by all topics in the bot. Thus, the bot can skip questions already asked in other topics.

Assessments

In this part of the book, you can check the answers to the review questions at the end of each chapter. Each answer includes an explanation and a link to any related documentation. To prepare for the exam, highlight any questions you answered incorrectly and study those topics.

Chapter 1

1. Answer: **False**. The Dynamics 365 Functional Consultant role is more than just customizing Dynamics 365 apps. The role involves customizing Power Platform but also the entire project life cycle before and after customization takes place.

2. Answer: **False**. The Power Platform Functional Consultant role does not involve extending Power Platform. Extending it is covered by the Power Apps Developer role.

3. Answer: **False**. The PL-200 exam has more question types than just multiple choice.

4. Answer: **A and C**. The PL-200 exam is aimed at functional consultants who are brought into a project after the project has been planned and initiated. The solution architect will require the PL-200 exam as an associate-level certification as a pre-requisite.

5. Answer: **C - Applying**. Questions in the PL-200 exam are in the middle of Bloom's taxonomy, above remembering and understanding, but below creating, that is, evaluating, analyzing, and applying.

Chapter 2

1. Answer: **False**. You can only reset a sandbox environment. To reset a production environment, you must first change it to a production environment.
2. Answer: **False**. After the environment has been copied, it is placed in Administration mode and only the system administrator users can access the environment.
3. Answer: **True**. AI Builder requires a Common Data Service database.
4. Answer: **C**. Dynamics 365 Field Service is the application used to manage, schedule, and deliver work on customer sites.
5. Answer: **C, D,** and **F**. You can only create production, sandbox, and trial environments.

Chapter 3

1. Answer: **A**. Each environment can only have one Common Data Service database.
2. Answer: **B**. The Common Data Model is a set of schema definitions that describe common business entities. Using these definitions will aid integration between systems.
3. Answer: **False**. You cannot delete entities provided by Microsoft. You can only delete custom entities you have created.
4. Answer: **False**. A calculated field is updated when a record is saved and retrieved.
5. Answer: **False**. Rollup fields are recalculated on an hourly schedule.
6. Answer: **True**. The display name and plural name can be changed at any time.
7. Answer: **B**. An ERD is used to document the data model.

Chapter 4

1. Answer: **B** and **D**. A business rule will only work on a form when all the fields referenced in the business rule are on the form and the scope is set to be the name of the form, `All forms`, or `Entity`.

2. Answer: **B, C, E**. You need to make sure the field is visible on the form. The field should not be read-only (locked) and you need to set the field to be business required.

3. Answer: **B**. Canvas apps do not use business rules but if the business rule has a scope of `Entity`, any data changes made by the canvas app will cause the business rule to execute on the Common Data Service.

4. Answer: **I then D then E then F**. A condition is always included in a new business rule, but you need to set the rule condition. You need to use the business required action to make the field mandatory. You should then save the business rule. The save will validate automatically. Finally, you activate the business rule.

5. Answer: **B**. Recommendations prompt the user and if the user accepts, the recommendation will set the value of the field.

Chapter 5

1. Answer: **C**. Asynchronous workflow logs are system job records.

2. Answer: **B**. The common error with workflow is to leave the scope as `User`, so it will not run for all users. Setting the scope to `Organization` will solve this issue.

3. Answer: **A**. If the action process is linked to an entity, then you must use the `Bound` action in Power Automate flow.

4. Answer: **C**. You cannot have wait conditions in a real-time workflow.

5. Answer: **D**. A workflow can only be added as a stage entry or exit workflow if the workflow is set to be on-demand.

Chapter 6

1. Answer: **A and C** . Import from Excel supports CSV, Excel, and XML files.

2. Answer: **B**. You should download a data template. The template contains data types set for each column.

3. Answer: **A**. The configuration migration tool can copy reference data from one environment to another.

4. Answer: **D**. Power Query is an extract, transform, and load tool.

Chapter 7

1. Answer: **B**. A duplicate detection rule will check for duplicates when records are created, updated, or imported.
2. Answer: **D, B, C**. Audit must be enabled at the organization, the entity, and the field levels.
3. Answer: **C**. Audit logs are rolled over every 90 days.
4. Answer: **B**. Audit only logs data changes not reads or queries.

Chapter 8

1. Answer: **A** - Share the app. When you share an app, you are asked to select one or more security roles for the app.
2. Answer: **B** - Accounts in their business unit only. As the access level is a business unit, it doesn't matter which business unit the user is in, they will only see records that are in their business unit.
3. Answer: **D** - Parent-Child Business Unit. The user has the least restrictive access level.
4. Answer: **D** - Share the app and select the appropriate security role.
5. Answer: **B** - Reflect the highest level of access.
6. Answer: **B** - Business unit. If you add a security role and then change the business unit, all security roles are removed.
7. Answer: **C** - Azure Active Directory.

Chapter 9

1. Answer: **A and B**. You cannot delete a view created when the entity was created but you can activate it and you can remove it in App Designer.
2. Answer: **A, B, and C** . You can hide tabs, sections, and fields. You cannot hide subgrids or the timer. You would have to hide the section the subgrid or timer was in.
3. Answer: **D**. The card view can optionally be used in the timeline.
4. Answer: **C**. Dashboards are added to subareas in the site map.
5. Answer: **C**. The associated view is used for related records.

Chapter 10

1. Answer: **B** - Publish. When you make a change to a canvas app and save, a new version is created. To make the latest version available, you must publish the app. As the user can see (an older version of) the app, it has already been shared with them. The app checker and solution checker find errors in the app.

2. Answer: **C** - Common Data Service. Dynamics 365 Sales is built on the Common Data Service. The Common Data Service connector should be used. You cannot access the Azure SQL database in Common Data Service directly. The Common Data Model holds the schema definitions for various business applications including Sales. The Dynamics 365 Customer Engagement connector has been deprecated and will therefore be removed at a later date.

3. Answer: **A** - Share. Sharing an app with a user or group makes the app available for a user either on the web or their mobile device.

4. Answer: **D** - Gallery. The **Gallery** control displays a list of data from a data source.

5. Answer: **B** - Azure AD Security Group. Best practice is to share apps with Security Groups rather than users.

Chapter 11

1. Answer: **B**. Authenticated portal users must have a web role to access data.

2. Answer: **D**. The community template contains blogs.

3. Answer: **C**. The email invitation contains an invitation code that the portal user entered when registering on the portal.

4. Answer: **A**. Enabling the entity permissions option on a page means that unauthenticated users and authenticated users without the correct entity permissions cannot access the page.

Chapter 12

1. Answer: **C**. When editing a flow, the flow checker will show any errors.

2. Answer: **D**. Sharing the flow will allow other users to monitor the flow.

3. Answer: **A**. The `Apply to each` action will loop through all the records in the list.

4. Answer: **B**. All of the run history, including the runs initiated by users with whom a button is shared, appears in the button creator's Power Automate mobile app.
5. Answer: **C**. The Common Data Service (current environment) connector is only available within a solution.
6. Answer: **B**. The `For selected record` trigger is only available in the Common Data Service connector.
7. Answer: **C**. The `Recurrence` trigger runs a flow at regular intervals. This is a scheduled flow.

Chapter 13

1. Answer: **B and C**. The business process flow will not be used if it does not belong to the model-driven app and if users do not have privileges on the business process flow entity in their security role.
2. Answer: **D**. Setting the data step to `required` prevents the user from moving to the next stage if the field is empty. Setting the field to `business required` will prevent a record from being created.
3. Answer: **C**. A business process flow can have 30 stages each with 30 steps.
4. Answer: **A**. A field used in a condition must be a data step in the stage before the condition.
5. Answer: **B**. Workflows must be configured to run on demand to be used in a business process flow. They can be either real-time or background.
6. Answer: **C**. Creating a business process flow creates an entity that holds details of which stage each instance of a business process has reached. The entity is named after the business process flow. You should create your chart on this entity.
7. Answer: **B**. When moving from a stage to another stage that has a different entity, you should ensure that the relationship is selected.

Chapter 14

1. Answer: **C**. Variables start and end with a % symbol.
2. Answer: **B**. Instant Power Automate flows can be used to manually start a UI flow.

3. Answer: **B and D**. Windows 10 Professional and Windows Server 2016 support UI flows.

4. Answer: **D**. You should use an unattended UI flow to scale the number of UI flows run.

Chapter 15

1. Answer: **B**. A Power Virtual Agent must be published before it can be added to a channel.

2. Answer: **D**. The billing tab shows how much of your session capacity has been used.

3. Answer: **D**. You should submit your bot for approval. When approved, it will be available for all users.

4. Answer: **B and C**. A new bot must be created in an environment and you must select the language used.

Chapter 16

1. Answer: **B**. Each topic has its own conversation path.

2. Answer: **A**. Entities are used to identify a user's intent.

3. Answer: **A**. Adding a fallback topic allows the bot to ask further questions to determine the user's intent.

4. Answer: **B**. If you don't add a fallback topic, the bot will prompt the user twice if it does not understand, before escalating.

Chapter 17

1. Answer: **C and E**. Power BI Desktop and the Power BI service can both create reports.

2. Answer: **C**. You can trigger a Power Automate flow from a Power BI alert.

3. Answer: **B and C**. You can share a visualization by sharing either a report or a dashboard with other users.

4. Answer: **B**. The user will need access to the Power BI dashboard to view a Power BI tile in a model-driven app.

5. Answer: **A**. You must populate a dataset from the dataflow in order to create a visualization.

6. Answer: **C**. Dataflows use Power Query to transform data.

7. Answer: **C**. You can embed a canvas Power App in a Power BI report. The canvas app can take action from within the report.

Chapter 18

1. Answer: **E**. Forms processing is a model type. The other answers are pre-built models.

2. Answer: **C**. The prediction model type can forecast a numeric value.

3. Answer: **B**. You must share the model for other users to be able to use the model.

4. Answer: **A**. The business card reader model is available in the quick create form for leads.

Chapter 19

1. Answer: **B**. Email templates are solution aware.

2. Answer: **Yes**. You can restrict access to an organizational template with security roles.

3. Answer: **Yes**. You can share a personal template with users and teams.

4. Answer: **No**. Article templates are used for the knowledge base and not document templates.

5. Answer: **C**. Integration with SharePoint is required. You must enable server-based integration.

6. Answer: **C**. To configure a Word template, you must enable the **Developer** tab in Word.

7. Answer: **B**. To add canvas apps to Teams, you need to set the `Global App Setup` policy in the Teams admin center.

8. Answer: **B and C**. You can add a canvas app to a channel or run a canvas app from the Teams app bar.

9. Answer: **D**. Power Automate can perform a series of Teams management actions, including creating a channel.

Chapter 20

1. Answer: **B**. The minor version number is incremented when you clone the solution.
2. Answer: **C and D**. You can change the build and revision numbers when you clone a patch.
3. Answer: **E**. You should create a new unmanaged solution to hold your customizations.
4. Answer: **C**. You have to manually edit components to undo the changes applied by an unmanaged solution.
5. Answer: **B**. Patches are for small fixes.
6. Answer: **A**. Deleting a managed solution, delete the components in the solution.

Other Books You May Enjoy

If you enjoyed this book, you may be interested in these other books by Packt:

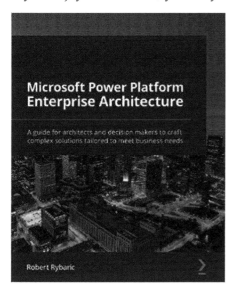

Microsoft Power Platform Enterprise Architecture
Robert Rybaric

ISBN: 978-1-80020-457-7

- Understand various Dynamics 365 CRM, ERP, and AI modules for creating Power Platform solutions
- Enhance Power Platform with Microsoft 365 and Azure
- Find out which regions, staging environments, and user licensing groups need to be employed when creating enterprise solutions
- Implement sophisticated security by using various authentication and authorization techniques
- Extend Power Apps, Power BI, and Power Automate to create custom applications
- Integrate your solution with various in-house Microsoft components or third-party systems using integration patterns

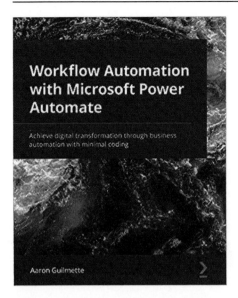

Workflow Automation with Microsoft Power Automate
Aaron Guilmette

ISBN: 978-1-83921-379-3

- Get to grips with the building blocks of Power Automate, its services, and core capabilities
- Explore connectors in Power Automate to automate email workflows
- Discover how to create a flow for copying files between two cloud services
- Understand the business process, connectors, and actions for creating approval flows
- Use flows to save responses submitted to a database through Microsoft Forms
- Find out how to integrate Power Automate with Microsoft Teams

Leave a review - let other readers know what you think

Please share your thoughts on this book with others by leaving a review on the site that you bought it from. If you purchased the book from Amazon, please leave us an honest review on this book's Amazon page. This is vital so that other potential readers can see and use your unbiased opinion to make purchasing decisions, we can understand what our customers think about our products, and our authors can see your feedback on the title that they have worked with Packt to create. It will only take a few minutes of your time, but is valuable to other potential customers, our authors, and Packt. Thank you!

Index